Ryan Ver Berkmoes

Ryan grew up in Santa Cruz, California, which he left at age 17 for college in the Midwest because he was too young and naive to realize what a beautiful place Santa Cruz is. He took five years to complete his four-year degree at the University of Notre Dame because the newfound joys of working at the campus newspaper and at a local TV station made such mundane matters as attending class seem frivolous. His first job in Chicago, in 1983, was at a small muckraking publication where he had the impressive title of Managing Editor: he was second on a two-person editorial staff and the first person was called Editor. After a year of 60-hour workweeks, Ryan took his first trip to Europe, which lasted for seven months and confirmed his long-suspected wanderlust. Since then his byline has appeared in the *Chicago Sun-Times*, *Chicago Tribune*, *Chicago* magazine, *The Official Chicago Bar Guide* and quite a few other publications with the word 'Chicago' in the title. His writings have included international breaking news, serious features, investigative pieces, arts criticism, entertainment writing and satire. He currently resides in Frankfurt, Germany, with his journalist wife, Sara Marley.

From the Author

I would like to thank the following people, without whose contributions – professional, personal or both – this book would have been impossible.

My wife, Sara Marley, an incomparable reader who gave support, love, advice and nutritious food and tactfully notified me when a shower was advisable. Her enthusiasm for and love of Chicago surpasses my own. My parents, Peter and Lucille Ver Berkmoes, whose simple enjoyment and pride in my efforts is love in itself. Cyndi and Russ Lester, my sister and her husband, who showed me how cold Chicago's charms could seduce two thin-blooded Californians.

I also want to thank my coauthor on my first book and dear friend John McGrath, who was with me in Red Hour explorations of the city and whose name I hope will appear next to mine on a future work. Janice Somerville, who once sacrificed her car pool to enjoy Chicago's delights and who now offers her spare futon when I'm in town. Kate Campion and Ted Allen, two major reasons I need to return to the city often and who found the answers to questions I dopily forgot to research myself. John Holden, who to me is the perfect Chicagoan in every good sense and who throws damn good parties for visiting authors. All of my *Gridiron Show* friends deserve special thanks for giving me years of insights and joy at living in Chicago. In Frankfurt, I want to single out Angela Cullen and Dörte Sältz, the two best coworkers I've ever had and whose foul-mouthed banter I missed desperately while writing this book. And because I forgot to mention him in my first book, I thank Mark Rust, who will serve as my defense attorney when the inevitable lawsuits pour in.

Katja Lindy and Heidi Kooi, in the Chicago Office of Tourism, are proof that this department is on the right track. Lois Weisberg, commissioner of the Chicago Department of Cultural Affairs, has a deep affection for the city and its people that impresses me still.

Many editors deserve thanks for their assignments and encouragement through the years, the results of which are found on these pages. Tim Bannon, Darel Jevens and Dick Babcock stand out for many reasons beyond the fact that they always paid promptly. At Lonely Planet, I want to thank Caroline Liou for giving me the chance to write about my favorite city in the world, Kate Hoffman for her supportive emails, one of which came at an especially key moment, and Alex Guilbert, Hayden Foell and Scott Summers for their enthusiasm for the project. And, of course, many thanks to Jacqueline Volin, the editor who made sense out of my produce and who thinks with the right side of her brain.

And finally, I thank 10,000 Maniacs, whose album *Our Time in Eden* became the ritualistic start of each day's writing session.

From the Publisher

In Lonely Planet's US office, Jacqueline Volin edited this 1st edition. Kate Hoffman advised and proofed. Thanks to Jeff Campbell and Caroline Liou for proofing in a pinch, and to Brigitte Barta for advice. Hayden Foell and Scott Summers designed the book. Hayden drew the maps, with guidance from Alex Guilbert and last-minute help from Beca Lafore. Hugh D'Andrade designed the cover. Hayden and Hugh created the illustrations.

Warning & Request

Things change – prices go up, schedules change, good places go bad and bad places go bankrupt – nothing stays the same. So, if you find things better or worse, recently opened or long since closed, please tell us and help make the next edition even more accurate and useful.

We value all of the feedback we receive from travelers. A small team reads and acknowledges every letter, postcard and email, and ensures that every morsel of information finds its way to the appropriate authors, editors and publishers. All readers who write to us will find their names in the next edition of the appropriate guide and will also receive a free subscription to our quarterly newsletter, *Planet Talk*. The very best contributions will be rewarded with a free Lonely Planet guide.

Excerpts from your correspondence may appear in new editions of this guide; in *Planet Talk*; or in the Postcards section of our website – so please let us know if you don't want your letter published or your name acknowledged.

Chicago

Ryan Ver Berkmoes

LONELY PLANET PUBLICATIONS
Melbourne • Oakland • London • Paris

Chicago

1st edition

Published by
Lonely Planet Publications
Head Office: PO Box 617, Hawthorn, Vic 3122, Australia
Branches: 150 Linden St, Oakland, CA 94607, USA
                10A Spring Place, London NW5 3BH, UK
                1 rue du Dahomey, 75011 Paris, France

Printed by
Colorcraft Ltd, Hong Kong
Printed in China

Photographs by
Rick Gerharter, Ray Hillstrom, Robert Holmes, Ryan Ver Berkmoes

Front cover: *Flamingo* at the Federal Center, Chicago, Randy Wells, Tony Stone Images
Title page: detail of *Flamingo*, Randy Wells, Tony Stone Images

Published
May 1998

**Although the author and publisher have tried to make the information as
accurate as possible, they accept no responsibility for any loss, injury or
inconvenience sustained by any person using this book.**

National Library of Australia Cataloguing in Publication Data

Ver Berkmoes, Ryan.
    Chicago.

    Includes index.
    ISBN 0 86442 549 X.

    1. Chicago (Ill.) – Guidebooks. I. Title.

917.731104

text & maps © Lonely Planet 1998
photos © photographers as indicated 1998

Permissions
Chinese, Water ewer (He), bronze inlaid with copper, Eastern Zhou dynasty, Warring States period
(480-221 BC), 4th century BC, ht: 22.4cm; diam: 21cm, Lucy Maud Buckingham Collection, 1930.366
overall. Photograph by Robert Hashimoto.

John Singleton Copley, American, c.1738-1815, Mrs Daniel Hubbard (Mary Greene), oil on canvas,
c.1764, 50¼ x 39¾in, The Art Institute of Chicago Purchase Fund, 1947.28

Archibald John Motley Jr, American, 1891-1981, Nightlife, oil on canvas, 1943, 91.4 x 121.3cm,
Restricted gift of the James W Alsdorf Memorial Fund, Mr and Mrs Marshall Field, Jack and Sandra
Guthman, Ben W Heineman, Ruth Horwich, Lewis and Susan Manilow, Beatrice C Mayer, Charles A
Meyer, John B Nichols, Mr and Mrs EB Smith Jr; Goodman Endowment, 1992.89

Gustave Caillebotte, French, 1848-1894, Paris Street; Rainy Day, oil on canvas, 1876/77,
212.2 x 276.2cm, Charles H and Mary FS Worcester Collection, 1964.336

Contents

Introduction

Chicago should be the first stop on any visitor's itinerary to the US. And any American who hasn't yet been here (changing planes at O'Hare doesn't count) should make tracks immediately.

Why? Simply because it's the most American of cities. Sure, New York is the biggest and most famous, but it's really another country. Washington, DC? An anomaly most taxpayers would rather give back to the British. New Orleans? A carnival. San Francisco? A beautiful freak show. Los Angeles? Well, there's probably some reason for it, but who knows? As for loudmouth self-boosters such as Dallas or Denver, get back to me in 100 years.

But you can't generalize about the place, other than to say that it's flat, it's on the lake and the Cubs suck. The diversity of commentary on Chicago – good and bad – is altogether fitting, because it is such a diverse place.

Chicago combines a wealth of delights in one very visitor-friendly package. Great music? Ya got it! Good food? Order more! Beautiful lakefront? Yeah, but pick up your trash! Great summer festivals? Party on! Brutal winter storms? Well, yeah, but they put hair on ya!

The Magnificent Mile is famous for its shops, the Art Institute has a world-class collection and the Loop is bustling. These are some of the reasons why Chicagoans are proud of their town and why, for the first time in years, the city's population is growing. Crime is down, the schools are looking up, the parks have never been greener, and there's a sense that Chicago is a place that people don't just want to visit but where they also want to live. Significant problems continue with race and poverty, but now there's a sense that even those explosive issues can be successfully confronted.

It has been said that you can go around the world in 80 hours without leaving the city. (You can, and you'll miss only a few countries.) Chicago is a kaleidoscope of neighborhoods encompassing every ethnic, racial and religious background. Itinerant artists ponder their navels in Wicker Park, old Polish women scrub their stoops on Milwaukee Ave, a Vietnamese woman works 18-hour days in her new Argyle St restaurant, yuppies spoil their perfect child in Lincoln Park, an African American mother organizes her block on the West Side, blue-collar guys in Bridgeport badmouth whoever is playing the Bears, an old-as-the-hills musician sings the blues in a South Side tavern. These portraits and a million more – make that 2.7 million more – can be seen at any time.

There is a downside to this diversity: the neighborhoods and their residents can be wary of outsiders, showing a kind of fear grounded in prejudice and ignorance. (But then, Chicago is the most American of cities, right?)

What unites Chicagoans is their no-nonsense attitude. Problems are not meant to be pondered, they are meant to be confronted head-on and tackled. Look at two of the most popular Chicago Bears of all time: Mike Singleterry and Dick Butkus. They were loved not for their on-field finesse but because they took the heads off opposing players.

Add to this attitude a confident self-reliance: when the city's downtown was destroyed by the great fire of 1871, Chicago invented the skyscraper and filled the Loop with remarkable towers a mere 15 years after the disaster; when Prohibition dried up alcohol, Al Capone supplied it; when actors need to create comedy, they don't wait for a script, they improvise.

Underneath this confidence, however, lies a deep insecurity. Chicagoans' once-proud moniker for their home, 'the Second City,' stemmed from their urge to remind people that although their city wasn't number one in population, it still was right up there. Now Los Angeles is number two in population and nobody seems to be in a hurry to adopt 'the Third City' as a motto.

Chicago's cultural institutions benefit from this insecurity. Corporate and individual donors regularly open their wallets when the museums or orchestras come calling. The folks at the top are just as happy to boast about the Art Institute as the regular folks are to brag about the Bulls. And the regular folks take pride in the Art Institute, too, even if they might not know the difference between a Monet and a Miró.

Those who take time to see some of the city will also benefit. They'll find that many Chicagoans are charmed by visitors in a touching, almost shy way. 'Wow, you really like us?' they seem to gush. And whether you're quaffing a beer in a friendly tavern, buying a frock in a designer's boutique, soaking up the blues in a smoky bar or having the best meal of your life in a rollicking restaurant, you'll find out Chicago is a delightful and always fascinating place to visit and explore.

If you miss this town, you'll have missed the heart of America.

Facts about Chicago

HISTORY

Chicago emerged as a world-class city in the late 1800s because of the skills of its population in processing the inherent wealth of America's Midwest. Lumber from the vast virgin forests, grains from the rich soil, livestock, and other natural bounty were bought, sold and processed there. The city's capitalists developed financial means such as the futures markets to make this commerce possible. The railroads grew to accommodate the resulting freight, and soon it was barely possible to cross the nation without changing trains in Chicago.

Constant immigration from abroad and the US itself swelled the population with people who were willing to risk it all to move to Chicago. These adventurers provided a can-do spirit that drove the city to further heights.

After WWII, the national move to the suburbs decreased the size of the city's vital middle class, and in Chicago this move was hastened by racial fears and the death of manufacturing industries. Though Mayor Richard J Daley boasted that Chicago was 'the city that worked,' the social unrest of the 1960s showed just how hollow his words were.

The late 1980s and 1990s have been good for the city. A new generation of professionals is discovering the joys of urban living, among them the Chicago's vibrant cultural and social scene. Billions of dollars in private investment have flowed to neighborhoods, and the city's diversified economic base enabled it to weather the recession of the early 1990s better than others in the US.

A Swamp

No one is sure when Native Americans first lived in the Chicago region, but evidence can be traced back to 1000 AD. By the late 1600s there were many tribes in the region, the dominant one being the Potawatomi.

In 1673 Indians directed French explorer Louis Jolliet and missionary Jacques Marquette to Lake Michigan via the Chicago River. The two, who had been exploring the Mississippi River, learned that the Indians of the region called the area around the mouth of the river 'Checaugou,' after the wild garlic (some say onions) growing there.

RYAN VER BERKMOES
Plaque at Michigan Ave and Wacker Drive

Various explorers and traders traveled through the area over the next 100 years. In 1779 Quebec trader Jean Baptiste Point du Sable established a fur-trading store on the north bank of the river. Of mixed African and Caribbean descent, he was the area's first non-Native American settler and was possibly the first settler period, given that the Indians dismissed the area as a feverish swamp.

After the Revolutionary War, the United States increasingly focused its attention on the vast western frontier. Because of Chicago's position on Lake Michigan, the government wanted a permanent presence in the area and in 1803 built Fort Dearborn on the south bank of the river, on marshy ground under what is today's Michigan Ave Bridge.

Nine years later, the Potawatomi Indians, in cahoots with the British (their

Chicago Firsts

Not every Chicago invention has been as significant as steel-framed skyscrapers (1885) or hospital trauma rooms (1966). Many others have had far-reaching social impact, if only on the palate or wallet.

1893: Cracker Jacks The candy-coated popcorn, peanuts and a prize are still a popular snack.

1893: Zipper People have been groping for them ever since.

1920s: One-Way Ride Gangster Hymie Weiss receives credit for deducing the role cars could play in dispatching rivals. Some historians give this credit to 'Dingbat' Objerta.

1930: Hostess Twinkie Rumors that the very first one is still as fresh as the day it was extruded are thought to be apocryphal.

1930: Pinball Bally is still a large local concern.

1947: Spray Paint Municipalities have been cleaning it off official surfaces ever since. Chicago even banned the sale of spray paint within city limits a few years ago.

1955: McDonald's The first one was actually opened in Des Plaines by Chicagoan Ray Kroc. More than 21,000 branches have opened in 103 countries since, but there's no word on which one coined 'Would you like fries with that?'

1968: 'Police Riot' This term was used in a government report on police behavior at the Democratic Convention.

---

allies in the War of 1812), slaughtered 52 settlers fleeing the fort. During this war such massacres had been a strategy employed throughout the frontier: The British bought the allegiance of various Indian tribes through trade and other deals. In return, the Indians were hostile to the American settlers. The settlers killed in Chicago had simply waited too long to flee the rising tension and thus found themselves caught up in it.

After the war was over, bygones were quickly forgotten as Americans, French, British and Indians turned their energies to profiting from the fur trade. In 1816 Fort Dearborn was rebuilt. Two years later Illinois became a state, although much of its small population lived in the south near the Mississippi River.

During the 1820s Chicago developed as a small town with a population of fewer than 200, most of whom made their living from trade. Records show that the total taxable value of Chicago's land was $8000.

Indian relations took a dramatic turn for the worse in 1832 when Chief Black Hawk of the Sauk Indians led a band of Sauk, Fox and Kickapoo from what is now Iowa to reclaim land swiped by settlers in western Illinois. The US reacted strongly, sending in hundreds of troops who traveled through Chicago, fueling its nascent economy. The army routed the Indians, and the US government requisitioned the rest of the Indian lands throughout Illinois, including those of the Potawatomi in Chicago. The Indians were forced to sign treaties by which they relinquished their land at a fraction of their worth, and all were moved west, ending any significant Native American presence in the city or region.

Chicago was incorporated as a town in 1833, with a population of 340. Within three years land speculation had rocked the local real estate market; lots that had sold for $33 in 1829 went for $100,000. The boom was fueled by the start of construction on the Illinois & Michigan Canal, a state project to create an inland waterway linking the Great Lakes to the Illinois River and thus to the Mississippi River and New Orleans.

The swarms of laborers drawn by the canal construction swelled the population to more than 4100 by 1837, when Chicago incorporated as a city. But the bullish city boosters quickly turned bearish that same year when a national economic depression brought the unstable real estate market crashing down. On paper, Illinois was bankrupt; canal construction stopped for four years.

By 1847 the economy had recovered and the canal was being pushed forward at full pace. More than 20,000 people lived in what had become the region's dominant city. The rich Illinois soil supported thousands of farmers, and industrialist Cyrus Hall McCormick moved his reaper factory to the city to serve them. He would soon control one of the Midwest's major fortunes.

In 1848 the canal opened, and shipping began flowing through the Chicago River from the Caribbean to New York via the Great Lakes and the Saint Lawrence Seaway. It had a marked economic effect on the city. One of its great financial institutions, the Chicago Board of Trade, opened to handle the sale of grain by Illinois farmers, who had greatly improved access to Eastern markets thanks to the canal.

Railroad construction absorbed workers freed from canal construction. By 1850 a line had been completed to serve grain farmers between Chicago and Galena, in western Illinois. A year later the city gave the Illinois Central Railroad land for its tracks south of the city. It was the first land-grant railroad and was joined by many others, whose tracks eventually would radiate out from Chicago. The city quickly became the hub of America's freight and passenger

trains, a status it would hold for the next hundred years.

Rapid Growth

In the 1850s Chicago grew quickly. State St south of the river became the commercial center, as banks and other institutions flourished with the growing economy. The city's first steel mill opened in 1857, the forerunner of the city's economic and industrial diversification. By the end of the decade Chicago had at least seven daily newspapers. Immigrants poured in, drawn by jobs at the railroads that served the expanding agricultural trade. Twenty million bushels of produce were shipped through the city that year. The population topped 100,000.

By then Chicago was no longer a frontier town. Its central position in the US made it a favorite meeting spot, a legacy that continues to this day. In 1860 the Republican Party held its national political convention

RAY HILLSTROM

The 1860 Republican candidate

Pig Problems

In *The Jungle*, Upton Sinclair described the Chicago stockyards this way: 'One could not stand and watch very long without becoming philosophical, without beginning to deal in symbols and similes, and to hear the hog-squeal of the universe.'

They were slaughterhouses beyond compare. By the early 1870s they processed more than one million hogs a year and almost as many steers, plus scores of unlucky sheep, horses and other critters. It was a coldly efficient operation. The pigs themselves were seen as a way to turn corn into a denser, more easily transportable substance that was thus more valuable.

The old saw – that once the animals were in the packing houses, everything was used but the squeal – was almost true. Some bits of pig debris for which no other use could be found were fed to scavenger pigs, who turned the waste into valuable meat. But vast amounts of waste were simply flushed into the south branch of the Chicago River, and it then flowed into the lake. Beyond the aesthetic and health problems that caused, the packers had to contend with other consequences of their pollution.

Meat processed in Chicago was shipped in ice-packed railroad cars to the huge markets in the East. The ice was harvested from lakes and rivers each winter and then stored for use all year long. But ice that was taken from the Chicago River returned to its stinky liquid state as it thawed over the meat on the journey east, thus rendering the carcasses unpalatable. The packers finally had to resort to harvesting their ice in huge operations in unpolluted Wisconsin.

For a look at the packing houses' squalid legacy, see the Bridgeport section of the Things to See & Do chapter. ∎

in Chicago and selected Abraham Lincoln, a lawyer from Springfield, Illinois, as its presidential candidate.

Like other northern cities, Chicago profited from the Civil War, which boosted business in its burgeoning steel and tool-making industries and provided plenty of freight for the railroads and canal. In 1865, the year the war ended, an event took place that would profoundly affect the city for the next hundred years: the Union Stockyards opened on the South Side, unifying disparate meat operations scattered about the city. Chicago's rail network and the development of the iced refrigerator car meant that meat could be shipped east to New York, spurring the industry's consolidation.

The stockyards become the major supplier of meat to the entire nation. But besides bringing great wealth to a few and jobs to many, the yards were also a source of many problems, including water pollution (see Pig Problems).

The stockyard effluvia polluted not only the Chicago River, but also Lake Michigan. Flowing into the lake, the fouled waters spoiled the city's source of fresh water and caused cholera and other epidemics that killed thousands. In 1869 the Water Tower and Pumping Station opened to bring water in from a two-mile tunnel that had been constructed out into Lake Michigan in an attempt to draw drinking water unpolluted by the Chicago River. But this solution proved resoundingly inadequate, and outbreaks of illness continued.

Two years later, the Illinois & Michigan Canal was deepened so that the Chicago River would reverse its course and start flowing south, away from the city. Sending waste and sewage down the reversed river provided relief for Chicago residents and helped ease lake pollution, but it was not a welcome change for those living near what had become the city's drainpipe. A resident of Morris, 60 miles downstream from Chicago, wrote, 'What right has Chicago to pour its filth down into what was before a sweet and clean river, pollute its waters, and materially reduce the value of property on both sides of the river and canal, and bring sickness and death to the citizens?'

The river still occasionally flowed into the lake after heavy rains; it wasn't permanently reversed until 1900, when the huge Chicago Sanitary Canal opened.

The Chicago Fire

On October 8, 1871, the Chicago fire started just southwest of downtown. Although the cause is now debated (see Don't Look at Me – It Was the Cow), the results were devastating. The fire burned for three days, killing 300 people, destroying 18,000 buildings and leaving 90,000 people homeless.

'By morning 100,000 people will be without food and shelter. Can you help us?' is the message sent east by Mayor Roswell B Mason as Chicago and City Hall literally burned down around him. The dry conditions and primitive horse-drawn firefighting equipment allowed flaming embers, carried upward by the heat, to land and start new fires in unburned areas. Almost every structure was destroyed or gutted in the area bounded by the river on the west, what's now Roosevelt Rd to the south and Fullerton to the north.

Mayor Mason earned kudos for his skillful handling of Chicago's recovery. His best move was to prevent the aldermen on the city council from having access to the millions of dollars in relief funds whose donation his fireside message had sparked, thus insuring that the money actually reached the rabble living in the rubble.

The Chicago Historical Society later collected quotes from survivors of the inferno. Bessie Bradwell, then 13, described her mother's quick evacuation from their home: 'With her birdcage tightly clasped in her arms and the poor little bird gasping for breath in the smoke, she went down to the lake . . . '

A young Clarence Augustus Burley, later the president of the historical society, tried exploring his evacuated neighborhood. 'At the corner of Randolph Street was a fire engine standing idly without hose or any appliances for firefighting, and as I passed, a huge plank about six feet long, all on fire, whirled over and dropped beside it. Huge cinders of like kind were dropping all about, and I did not consider it wise to wait.'

Chicago Tribune writers James T Sheahan and George T Upton explored the city as the ashes cooled and later published a detailed and highly imaginative account of what they found. An excerpt: 'Yonder, burnt and bruised and blackened, stands the church, its pealing organ stilled forever. Through its gaping portals no more wedding parties shall pass. . . . The young men who, in the intoxication of first love, followed their sweethearts there, and who endured the sermon for the sake of being near the beloved, have outlived the

Don't Look at Me – It Was the Cow

For more than 125 years, legend has had it that a cow owned by a certain Mrs O'Leary kicked over a lantern, which ignited some hay, which ignited some lumber, which ignited the whole town. The image of the hapless heifer has endured despite official skepticism from the start. Now that story may have been milked for the last time.

Richard Bales, a lawyer and amateur historian, has spent years examining the case from every angle. His conclusion is that Bessie was a victim of circumstances. It seems that Mrs O'Leary's barn was shared by a neighboring family. Each day Daniel 'Peg Leg' Sullivan dropped by to feed his mom's cow. Bales' evidence, gathered from thousands of pages of postinferno investigations, indicates that 'Peg Leg' accidentally started the fire himself and then tried to blame it on the bovine. After all, if you had just burned down what was then the fourth-largest city in the US, who would *you* blame?

The Chicago City Council has accepted Bales' version of the story; in 1997 the cream of Chicago politics passed a resolution officially absolving the O'Leary family of blame. Of course, for proponents of the cow story, this revision is udder nonsense. ∎

Loop skyscrapers

passionate ardor of them, and will not regret the ruined sanctuary, which, to them, was the temple of Cupid, and not Jehovah.'

Chicago Reborn

Despite the human tragedy, the fire's effect on Chicago was much the same as that of a forest fire: within a few years there was rapid new growth, a wealth of new life. The best architects in the world poured in to snare the thousands of rebuilding contracts, giving Chicago an architectural legacy of innovation that endures today. (See Chicago Architecture: A Study in Innovation for details.) Rebuilding efforts added to the city's economy, which had been scarcely slowed by the conflagration, and by 10 years after the fire, the population of Chicago had tripled.

The later decades of the 19th century saw Chicago on a boom-and-bust economic cycle. While in general the economy grew, it often fell prey to short-lived recessions. During one of these in 1873, thousands of men thrown out of work marched on City Hall, demanding food. The police,

who were always on call for governmental and economic interests, beat the protesters, who had dispersed after they were promised free bread. It was the beginning of a history of clashes between labor and police that would stretch over the next 50 years.

In 1876 strikes began in the railroad yards as workers demanded an eight-hour workday. Traffic was paralyzed, and the unrest spread to the McCormick Reaper Works, which was then Chicago's largest factory. The police and federal troops were called in and broke up the strikes, killing 18 civilians and injuring hundreds more.

By then May 1 had become the official day of protest for Chicago labor groups. On that day in 1886, 60,000 workers in the city went on strike, demanding an eight-hour workday. As was usual, police attacked the strikers at locations throughout the city. Three days later, self-described 'anarchists' staged a protest in Haymarket Square during which a bomb exploded, killing seven police officers. The government reacted strongly to what became known as 'the Haymarket Riot.' Eight anarchists were convicted of 'general conspiracy to murder' and four were hanged, although only two had been present at the incident and the actual bomber was never identified.

While the city's workers agitated for better working conditions, other progressive social movements were also at play in Chicago. Immigrants were pouring into the city at a rate of 10,000 a week, and they lived in squalid conditions, enjoying few if any government services. In 1889 two young women from middle-class families, Jane Addams and Ellen Gates Starr, founded Hull House on the city's West Side. The two women opened soup kitchens, set up schools for immigrant children, established English classes for adults and offered other services, such as medical care, to ease the immigrants' hardships.

Meanwhile the city went on a big annexation campaign, nabbing the independent townships of Lake View, Hyde Park and others to gain their tax revenues. Part of this growth was motivated by civic leaders' desire for Chicago to have a large population that would give it prominence on the world stage.

In 1892 society legend Bertha Palmer followed the lead of other Chicago elite by touring Paris. A prescient art collector, she nabbed a score of Monets, Renoirs and other Impressionist works before they had achieved universal acclaim. Her collection would later form the core of the Art Institute.

The 1893 World's Columbian Exposition marked Chicago's showy debut on the international stage. Centered on a grand complex of specially built structures on the lakeshore south of Hyde Park, the exposition became known as 'the White City' for its magnificent white-painted buildings, which were brilliantly lit by electric searchlights. Designed by architectural luminaries such as Daniel Burnham, Louis Sullivan and Frederick Law Olmstead, the fair was meant to show how parks, streets and buildings could be designed in a harmonious manner that would enrich the chaotic urban environment.

Open only five months, the exposition attracted 27 million visitors, many of whom rode the newly built El to and from the Loop. The fair was divided between the high-minded and the lowbrow. In the former category, the Electricity Building, the Women's Building, and other structures offered exhibits showing the beauties possible with the modern age. Catering to more popular tastes, the world's first Ferris wheel spun on the midway and the 'Street of Cairo' exhibit proved itself little more than a thinly veiled excuse to show thinly veiled women dancing the 'hootchy-kootchy,' an erotic belly dance.

The spectacular buildings surrounded ponds plied by Venetian gondolas. The entire assemblage would have huge influence not just in Chicago but around the world, as the fair's architects were deluged with huge commissions to redesign cities. The buildings themselves, despite their grandeur, were short lived, having been built out of a rough equivalent of plaster of

RAY HILLSTROM

Old Town door

Raise a hand in solidarity.

Paris that barely lasted through the fair. The only survivor was the Fine Arts Building, which was really rebuilt from scratch to become the Museum of Science and Industry.

Chicago's labor troubles reached another critical point in 1894, when a recession caused the Pullman Palace Car Company to cut wages. From the huge South Side factory complex, which built railroad cars, worker unrest spread to the railroads themselves, and more than 50,000 workers walked off their jobs, paralyzing interstate commerce. Federal troops were called in to Chicago and gradually broke the strike through a series of battles that left scores of workers injured.

At the turn of the century, Chicago, with a population of 1.7 million, was a far bigger place than anyone could have imagined just seven decades before. Although the city had grown, it still had its original wild and woolly traits, many of which could be found in the notorious Levee District, a one-stop Sodom and Gomorrah south of the Loop run not by gangsters but by the top cops and politicians.

Meanwhile, Chicago's industries continued to prosper at the expense of the environment and worker health. In 1906 Upton Sinclair's fictional account of the stockyards, *The Jungle*, was published. Although Sinclair hoped it would arose sympathy for exploited workers living in squalid conditions, it ignited public fury with its lurid portrayal of conditions in the factories where the public's food was prepared.

Though working conditions were bad, they didn't stop the continual flow of immigrants to Chicago. People from Midwestern farms and impoverished nations in Europe continued to pour in, joined, in the early 20th century, by poor blacks from the South.

The Great Migration

In 1910 eight out of 10 blacks still lived in the southern states of the old Confederacy. Over the next decade a variety of factors combined to change that, as more than two million moved north in what came to be known as the Great Migration.

Chicago played a pivotal role in this massive shift of population, both as an impetus and as a destination. Articles in the black-owned and nationally circulated *Chicago Defender* proclaimed the city a worker's paradise and a place where blacks were free from the horrors and repression of the South. Ads from Chicago employers promised jobs to anyone willing to work.

These lures, coupled with glitzy images of thriving neighborhoods like Bronzeville, inspired thousands to take the bait. From 44,103 in 1910, Chicago's black population zoomed to 109,458 in a decade and continued growing. The migrants, often poorly educated sharecroppers with big dreams, found a reality not as rosy as promised. Chicago did not welcome blacks with open arms. In 1919 white gangs from Bridgeport led days of rioting that killed dozens. Employers were ready with the promised jobs, but many hoped to rid their factories of white unionized workers by replacing them with blacks, which further exacerbated racial tensions. Blacks also found that they were promoted and advanced only so far before reaching an unofficial ceiling on their progress.

Blacks were also restricted to living in South Side ghettos by openly prejudicial real estate practices that kept them from buying or renting homes elsewhere in the city.

Prohibition

Efforts to make the United States 'dry' had never found favor in Chicago; the city's vast numbers of German and Irish immigrants were not about to forsake their favored libations. During the first two decades of the 20th century, the political party that could portray itself as the 'wettest' would win the local elections. Thus the nationwide enactment in 1920 of Prohibition, the federal constitutional amendment making alcohol consumption illegal, was destined to be poorly adhered to in Chicago, where voters had gone 6 to 1 against the law in an advisory referendum. However, few could have predicted how the efforts to flout Prohibition would forever mark Chicago's image worldwide (see Capone's Chicago).

An important year for the city, 1933 saw Prohibition repealed and a thirsty populace return openly to the bars in droves. Another world's fair, this time called the Century of Progress, opened on the lakefront south of Grant Park and promised a bright future filled with modern conveniences, despite the Great Depression. And in 1933 Ed Kelly became mayor. With the help of party boss Pat Nash, he strengthened the Democratic Party in the city, creating the legendary 'machine' that would control local politics for the next 50 years. Politicians doled out thousands of city jobs to people who worked hard to make sure their patrons were reelected. The same was true for city vendors and contractors, whose continued prosperity was tied to their donations and other efforts to preserve the status quo.

RAY HILLSTROM

Capone's Chicago

Chicagoans traveling the world often experience a distinctive phenomenon when asked where they're from. When they answer 'Chicago,' the local drops into a crouch and yells something along the lines of 'Rat-a-tat-a-tat, Al Capone!' Although civic boosters bemoan Chicago's association with a scar-faced hoodlum, it's an image that has been burned into the public consciousness by television shows such as *The Untouchables*, movies and other aspects of pop culture.

Capone was the mob boss in Chicago from 1924 to 1931, when he was brought down on tax evasion charges by Elliot Ness, the federal agent whose task force was given the name 'The Untouchables' because its members were supposedly impervious to bribes. (This wasn't a small claim, given that thousands of Chicago police and other officials were on the take, some of them taking in more than $1000 a week.

Capone came to Chicago from New York in 1919. He quickly moved up the ranks to take control of the city's South Side in 1924. He expanded his empire by making 'hits' on his rivals. These acts, which usually involved thousands of bullets shot out of submachine guns – or, 'Tommy guns' – were carried out by Capone's lieutenants. Capone earned the nickname 'Scarface' because of the large scar on his left cheek, the legacy of a dance hall fight.

The success of the Chicago mob was fueled by Prohibition. Not surprisingly, the citizens' thirst for booze wasn't eliminated by government mandate, and gangs made fortunes dealing in illegal beer, gin and other intoxicants. Clubs called 'speakeasies' were highly popular and were only marginally hidden from the law, an unnecessary precaution, given that crooked cops usually were the ones working the doors. Commenting on the hypocrisy of a society that would ban booze and then pay him a fortune to sell it, Capone said: 'When I sell liquor, they call it bootlegging. When my patrons serve it on silver trays on Lake Shore Drive, they call it hospitality.'

It can be hard to find traces of the Capone era in Chicago. The city and the Chicago Historical Society take dim views of Chicago's gangland past, with nary a brochure or exhibit on Capone or his cronies (though the CHS bookstore does have a good selection of books). Many of the actual sites have been torn down; what follows are some of the more notable survivors.

Capone's Chicago Home At 7244 S Prairie Ave, this home was built by Capone and mostly used by his wife, Mae, son 'Sonny' and other relatives. Al preferred to stay where his vices were. The house looks almost the same today.

Maxwell St Police Station Doings at this station, at 943 W Maxwell, two blocks west of Halsted (Map 10), were typical of the corruption rife in the Chicago Police Department in the 1920s. At one time, five captains and about 400 uniformed police were on the take here.

City Hall This building, at 121 N La Salle St (Map 3), was the workplace of some of Capone's best pals. During William 'Big Bill' Thompson's successful campaign for mayor in 1927, Al donated well over $100,000.

Holy Name Cathedral At 735 N State St (Map 3), this was the scene of two gangland murders. North Side boss Dion O'Banion was gunned down in his floral shop at 738 N State in 1924 after he crossed Capone. In 1926 his successor, Hymie Weiss, died en route to church in a hail of Capone-ordered bullets emanating from a window at 740 N State. These bullets also damaged the cathedral's facade; look for the pock marks.

St Valentine's Day Massacre Site In perhaps the most infamous event of the Capone era, seven members of the Bugs Moran gang were lined up against a wall in a garage by mobsters dressed as cops and gunned down. After that, Moran cut his losses and Capone gained control of Chicago's North Side vice. The garage at 2122 N Clark St was torn down in 1967 to make way for a retirement home. The building just south remains. A house used as a lookout by the killers stands across the street at 2119 N Clark St.

The Green Mill This tavern was one of Capone's favorite nightspots (4802 N Broadway, ☎ 773-878-5552; Map 8). During the mid-1920s the cover for the speakeasy in the basement was $10. You can still listen to jazz in its swank setting today.

Mt Carmel Cemetery Capone is now buried in this cemetery, on Roosevelt Rd at Wolf Rd in Hillside, west of Chicago. He and his relatives were moved here in 1950. Al's simple gray gravestone is concealed by a hedge; it reads 'Alphonse Capone, 1899-1947, My Jesus Mercy.' It has been stolen and replaced twice. Capone's neighbors include old rivals Dion O'Banion and Hymie Weiss. Both tried to rub out Capone, who returned the favor in a far more effective manner.

The American Police Center This no-nonsense museum (☎ 312-431-0005), 1717 S State (Map 4), is dedicated to cops. Among the myriad displays is one focusing on 1920s Chicago. There are plenty of examples of the era's weapons, as well as some grisly photos of gangsters on the receiving end of lawmen's bullets. Not surprisingly, the strictly partisan displays here make no mention of police corruption during the Capone era – or any other era, for that matter.

For a guided tour of many of these sights, along with enthusiastic amateur theatrics, try **Untouchable Gangster Tours** (☎ 773-881-1195). Using an old school bus, two actors lead the tour, taking people for a $20 ride that's part show, part history. Finally, as you think of the romance that has come to be associated with the Capone era, remember that gangs continue to peddle vice throughout the city today. But their toll on society is much worse: whole neighborhoods have been devastated by the drug trade and its inherent criminality. The murder rate in Chicago for contemporary gang members is often more than 10 times that of 1926, when 75 mobsters were killed. ■

Mayor Richard J Daley

The zenith of the machine's power began with the election of Richard J Daley in 1955. Initially thought to be a mere party functionary, Daley was reelected mayor five times before dying in office in 1976. With an uncanny understanding of machine politics and how to use it to squelch dissent, he dominated the city in a way no mayor had before or has since. His word was law, and a docile city council routinely approved all his actions, lest a dissenter find his or her ward deprived of vital city services.

But Daley and those in the entrenched political structure were oblivious – both by intent and accident – to many of the changes and challenges that Chicago faced in the 1950s and later. After suffering through the depression, the city experienced sudden affluence during WWII. Factories ran at full tilt, and once again people flocked to Chicago for jobs during the war years. In 1950 the population peaked at 3.6 million. But the postwar economic boom also made it possible for many Chicagoans to realize the dream, then new, of buying their own home. Farms and wetlands surrounding the city were quickly turned into suburbs that became home to scores of middle-class people fleeing the crowded city.

The tax base diminished and racial tensions grew. Blacks moved from the ghettos on the South Side to other areas of the city, while whites, succumbing to racism fueled by fears of crime, grew terrified at the prospect of ethnically integrated neighborhoods (see White Flight).

In 1957 *Life* magazine reported that Chicago police were the most corrupt in the nation. Although Daley and the machine howled with indignation, further exposés by the press revealed that some cops and politicians were in cahoots with various crime rings. None of this was news to the average Chicagoan.

Chicago's voting practices were also highly suspect, never more so than in 1960, when John F Kennedy ran for president of the US against Richard Nixon, then vice president. The night of the election, the results were so close nationwide that the outcome hinged on the vote in Illinois.

Mayor Daley called Kennedy and assured him, 'With a little bit of luck and the help of a few close friends, you're going to carry Illinois.' Kennedy did win Illinois, by 10,000 votes, which gave him the presidency. For many, that was the perfect embodiment of electoral politics in Chicago, a city where the slogan has long been 'Vote early and vote often' and voters have been known to rise from the grave and cast ballots.

In 1964 the Civil Rights movement came to Chicago. Martin Luther King Jr spoke at rallies, demanding better conditions for blacks and an end to segregation. He led marches through all-white neighborhoods where racist residents attacked the marchers with rocks and bottles. In one,

Mayor Daley I

White Flight

From the late '50s through the '70s, Chicago's ethnic neighborhoods on the South, West and southwest sides underwent rapid change. Whole neighborhoods of bungalows filled with Irish, Lithuanian and other immigrant residents became populated entirely by black residents in a matter of months.

The causes were both simple and complex. White ethnics, conditioned by racism and fear to avoid having blacks as neighbors, engaged in panic selling at the appearance of an African American on the block. 'For Sale' signs sprouted like weeds throughout the neighborhoods. People who had worked two or more jobs to afford their dream home sold at below-market prices and fled with their families to the suburbs.

The blacks who could afford to do so fled the slums and snapped up the homes but soon found they had a new set of problems: insurance companies and mortgage lenders engaged in 'redlining,' the practice of refusing to write policies and grant loans in areas that had 'gone black.' The new homeowners were often forced to get their mortgages and insurance from unscrupulous businesses – many of them owned by African Americans – that charged far above market rates. Soon some families were forced to default on their loans, and their once-tidy homes became derelict, blighting otherwise healthy blocks.

Discrimination also took the form of 'housing covenants,' unwritten agreements in the real estate industry whereby houses in certain neighborhoods were not sold to people deemed 'unsuitable.'

Government agencies attempted to alleviate these problems by outlawing 'For Sale' signs, punishing firms that engaged in redlining, and requiring banks to open branches in African American communities and grant mortgages there under the same conditions applied to white communities. That slowed the destabilizing turnover of neighborhoods, and in the few places where true integration has occurred, neighboring black and white homeowners find that they share many of the same concerns: good schools, low crime rates, affordable taxes, timely trash removal, instant eradication of snow and the necessity of another championship title for the Bulls. ■

King was hit in the head by a brick, foreshadowing events for which Daley and the machine would be ill prepared.

The year 1968 proved an explosive one for Chicago. When King was assassinated in Memphis, Tennessee, the West Side exploded in riots and went up in smoke. Whole stretches of the city were laid to waste, and Daley and the many black politicians in the machine were helpless to stop the violence. Worse yet, the city's August hosting of the Democratic National Convention was a fiasco of such proportions that its legacy dogged Chicago for decades (see When Cops Riot).

Meanwhile, the city's economic structure was changing. In 1971 the last of the Chicago stockyards closed. Elsewhere in the city, factories and steel mills closed as companies moved to the suburbs or the southern US, where taxes and wages were lower. A decade of economic upheaval saw much of Chicago's industrial base erode. Many companies simply went of business during the late-1970s recession. Chicago and much of the Midwest earned the moniker 'Rust Belt,' describing their shrunken economies and closed and rusting factories. The human costs in the city were high; thousands of blue-collar workers lost their high-paying union jobs with virtually no hope of finding replacement work.

But two events happened in the 1970s that were harbingers of the city's future. The world's tallest building (at the time), the Sears Tower, opened in the Loop in 1974, beginning a development trend that would spur the creation of thousands of high-paying jobs in finance, law and other areas be created in the Loop. And in 1975

When Cops Riot

With the war in Vietnam rapidly escalating and general unrest spreading through the US, the 1968 Democratic National Convention became a focal point for protest groups of all stripes. Even though then-president Lyndon Johnson announced he was washing his hands of the mess and not running for reelection, the convention of the political party in charge of the US government was an irresistible draw for anyone with a beef – which in the late 1960s seemed like just about everybody.

Regardless, conservative old Mayor Daley – the personification of a 'square' if there ever was one – was planning for a grand convention. Word that protesters would converge on Chicago sparked plans to crack the head of anybody who got in the way of Daley's show. Calls in the press and from other politicians for the protesters to be granted parade permits were shot down.

Enter Abbie Hoffman, Jerry Rubin, Rennie Davis, Tom Hayden, Bobby Seale and David Dellinger. They called for a mobilization of 500,000 protesters to converge on Chicago, and their plans steadily escalated in the face of city intransigence. As the odds of confrontation became high, many moderate protesters decided not to attend.

When the convention opened there were just a few thousand young protesters in the city. But Daley and his cronies spread rumors to the media to bolster the case for their warlike preparations. Some of these whoppers included claims that hippie girls would pose as prostitutes to give the delegates venereal disease and that LSD will be dumped into the city's water supply. What these tales unwittingly implied about the morals of the delegates and exactly how much LSD would be required to have an appreciable effect on Lake Michigan, the city's water supply, went unaddressed.

The first few nights of the August 25-30 convention saw police staging midnight raids on hippies and protesters attempting to camp in Lincoln Park. The cops went on massive beating sprees, singling some out for savage attacks. Teenage girls were assaulted by cops with clubs who shouted, 'You want free love? Try this!' Journalists, ministers and federal Justice Department officials were appalled.

The action then shifted to Grant Park, across from the Conrad Hilton (now the Chicago Hilton & Towers), where the main presidential candidates were staying. A few thousand

the Water Tower Place shopping mall opened on N Michigan Ave. It proved a surprising lure for suburbanites, despite the presence of the very same stores in their own malls. Developers began to realize that the urban environment was an attraction in itself.

Daley's death from a heart attack in 1976 began a process of political upheaval and reform that continued through the 1980s. Chicago's normally docile voters were enraged in 1978, when the city council cheerfully voted itself a 60% pay hike at the height of a recession and record unemployment. Then, in January 1979, four feet of snow hit Chicago. Daley's 'city that works' didn't, and voters gave Mayor Michael Bilandic a permanent Florida vacation (see the sidebar White Blight), electing outsider Jane Byrne.

The colorful Byrne opened up Chicago to filmmakers, allowing the producers of *The Blues Brothers* to demolish part of Daley Center. She appointed her husband, a gregarious old journalist, as her press secretary, and he soon was answering questions at press conferences with lines such as, 'The mayor told me in bed this morning . . .' Byrne made the symbolic gesture of moving into the Cabrini-Green, the deeply troubled Near North housing project, but she also showed deep insensitivity to blacks on several issues, stoking deep-seated anger.

The People's Mayor

In the fall of 1982, a Who's Who of black Chicago gathered in activist Lu Palmer's basement on the South Side. The mood was tense. Newspaper columnist Vernon Jarrett protesters held a rally, which was met by an overwhelming force of 16,000 Chicago police officers, 4000 state police officers, and 4000 members of the National Guard armed with tear-gas grenades, nightsticks and machine guns.

When some protesters attacked a few officers, the assembled law enforcers staged what investigators later termed a police riot. Among the low-lights: cops shoved bystanders through plate-glass windows and then beat them as they lay bleeding amid the shards; police on motorcycles ran over protesters; police chanting 'Kill, kill, kill!' swarmed journalists and attempted to do just that; and when wounded conventioneers were taken to the hotel suite of presidential candidate Gene McCarthy, cops burst through the door and beat everybody in sight.

The next night Daley went on national TV and attempted to defend the mayhem with an outright lie: he said he knew of plans to assassinate all the presidential candidates. In reality, what Daley and the police did was play right into the hands of the most extreme of the protesters, who had hoped to provoke just such a sorry spectacle.

The long-term effects of the riots were far greater that anyone could have guessed. The Democratic candidate for president, Hubert Humphrey, was left without liberal backing after his tacit support of Daley's tactics, with the result that Republican Richard Nixon was elected president. Chicago was left with a huge black eye for decades. Once the most popular home to the hugely lucrative political conventions, it saw none return for almost 30 years, until 1996. The stories of police brutality, coupled with reports of rampant corruption in the department, led to decade-long changes that made the Chicago police force more racially balanced than it had ever been and one of the most professional in the country.

Lyndon Johnson's attorney general refused to prosecute any of the protesters for conspiring to riot in Chicago. But in 1969 President Nixon ordered just such prosecutions, even though the actions of those charged may well have helped elect him. The 'Chicago Seven' trial became a total farce; the accused used it as a platform for protest, and aging judge Julius Hoffman showed a Daley-like tolerance for their antics by sentencing them to prison for contempt of court. However, on the central charges of inciting riots, all seven were acquitted. ■

was so angry he was ready to punch Harold Washington. So were a lot of other people who had spent months working their butts off to build the incredible movement that was ready to propel Chicago's first African American mayor – and a reformist to boot – into office. His election would present an obvious change in terms of race, but it was a far bigger challenge to the entrenched interests that had dominated city politics for decades. And now the candidate was dithering about whether he wanted to make the huge commitment to run.

Then-congressman Washington was making it clear that he didn't want to be the sacrificial lamb to a reelection juggernaut by Mayor Byrne. But months earlier, in another meeting in Palmer's basement, he had told Jarrett and the rest that he would consider running if they registered 50,000

new voters. They registered 150,000. The movement to elect Washington was bigger than anybody could have imagined or hoped.

Eventually, an irate Washington stormed out of the meeting at midnight, but he couldn't stop the phenomenon he'd tacitly allowed to take root. He did run, and he won the Democratic primary when Byrne and Richard M Daley split the white vote, and he went on to win the general election.

Washington's first term was best described by the *Wall Street Journal*, which called Chicago 'Beirut on the Lake': the entrenched political machine reacted to him with all the hostility you'd expect from people who saw their cozy system under full attack. Much of the political and social chaos that marked the years from 1983 to 1987 had ugly racial overtones, but at the

The People's Mayor

heart of the conflict was the old guard refusing to cede any power or patronage to the reform-minded mayor. In retrospect, the chaos was good for the city, because it opened up the political process.

The irony is that when Washington died seven months after he was reelected in 1987, he and his allies were just beginning to enjoy the same spoils of the machine they had once battled. Washington had a solid majority of allies on the city council and was poised to begin pushing his own ambitious programs.

A lasting legacy of the Washington years has been the political success of the African American politicians who followed him. Democrat US Senator Carol Moseley-Braun's election in 1992 can be credited in part to Washington's political trailblazing. And John Stroger, the first black president of the Cook County Board of Commissioners, was elected in 1994.

Overall, the 1980s were a good decade for the city. The mid-decade economic boom in the US was especially strong in Chicago. Scores of young urban professionals – the oft-reviled 'yuppies' – found jobs in the fast-growing service and professional sectors and helped spark a real estate boom that saw large portions of the aging North Side renovated and made upscale.

As they aged and started families, many of the first yuppies stayed in the city rather than following their parents to the suburbs. The result has been a continuous two-decade-long boom of gentrification. As values in some neighborhoods soar, adjoining areas begin to benefit; the comparatively low prices attract new residents and investors. Development has now spread to portions of the city west and south of the Loop.

Daley Redux

In 1989 Chicago elected as mayor Richard M Daley, the son of Richard J Daley. Like his father, Daley has an uncanny instinct for city politics. Unlike his father, he has shown much more political savvy in uniting disparate political forces. He has shrewdly kept African Americans within his political power structure, thus forestalling the kind of movement that propelled Washington to the mayor's office.

After Daley's election the city enjoyed two years of cooperation between City Hall and then-governor Jim Thompson, who lived in and loved Chicago. Until then, the squabbles in city government had prevented the city from working effectively with the state. Hundreds of millions of public dollars that had languished during the 1980s were released. Among the projects that have now borne fruit are an O'Hare expansion, the new South Building and hotel at McCormick Place, and the complete reconstruction of Navy Pier, which turned the pier into a meeting and tourist site.

Daley has moved to solidify his control of the city in a way his father would have applauded, but in a much more enlightened manner. Old semi-independent bureaucracies such as the Park District and Department of Education have been restructured under Daley protégés. The parks are much improved, and the schools – recently the very worst in the nation – are showing signs of marked improvement.

But many challenges remain. The Chicago Transit Authority is underfunded and has been cutting service, the Chicago

Housing Authority needs to find scarce funds to transform its horrific and violent projects, and many parts of the South and West sides of the city are still suffering and in serious disrepair.

To the delight of residents and commentators, Daley is prone to frequent and amusing verbal blabber, such as this classic, which he used to explain why city health inspectors had gone on a binge of restaurant closures: 'Whadda ya want? A rat in yer sandwich or a mouse in yer salad?'

Chicagoans' general confidence in their city allowed a potentially traumatic 1990 event to pass almost unnoticed. Long called the 'Second City' because of its number-two spot on the population roster of US cities (New York is first), Chicago fell to third place when the 1990 census showed a population of 2.78 million, placing it third, behind Los Angeles (3.49 million) and New York (7.32 million). Any lingering sadness was dispelled a year later, when the Chicago Bulls won the first of five national basketball championships. And the 1994 World Cup opening ceremony focused international attention on the city.

In 1996 a 28-year-old demon was exorcised when the Democratic National Convention returned to Chicago. Millions of dollars were spent spiffing up the city, and thousands of cops underwent sensitivity training on how to deal with protests. The convention went off like a dream and the city felt collectively on a roll.

GEOGRAPHY
Once flat and swampy, Chicago now is merely flat. The Chicago River was once a slow, limpid stream, barely providing drainage for its twin branches, whose Y-shape adorns the city's official symbol. But extensive canal and channel digging over the years has transformed the river into a major waterway.

The city, in the northeastern part of Illinois, covers 228 sq miles. It's 25 miles long and 15 miles wide at its widest point on the far North Side. The lakefront within the city limits is 29 miles long.

CLIMATE
The nickname 'Windy City' actually has nonmeteorological origins: it was coined by newspaper reporters in the late 1800s in reaction to the blustery boastfulness of Chicago's politicians. Nevertheless, Chicago *is* windy, with everything from cool, God-sent lake breezes at the height of summer to skirt-raising gusts in the spring to spine-chilling, nose-chiseling blasts of icy air in the winter.

All four seasons are fully observed, with late spring and early fall being generally warm, clear and dry. Winter and summer behave as expected (see climate chart), but early spring and late fall can freely mix nice days with wretched ones.

Chicago has no true rainy season; its 34 inches of average annual precipitation are spread throughout the year. In the winter it can be wadded into snowballs if some city worker doesn't clear it away first. In spring and fall the storms tend to last for several hours, but they come with plenty of warning from the sky and from forecasters. In the summer, as in much of the central US, thunderstorms build in the afternoons and can appear with sudden violence for 10 minutes, then disappear. This happens on the clearest of days and often catches people unawares. Lightning usually accompanies the thunderstorms but rarely strikes people in the city.

Unlike stormy days, cloudy ones are not spread so evenly throughout the year.

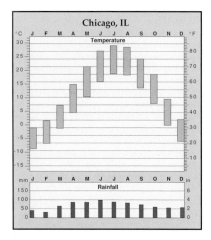

Although the number of annual gray days averages a not-so-sunny 46%, they are grouped heavily from November to March. (You may not realize just how heavily they're grouped until the sun breaks through one day and you can't remember when it last appeared.)

On the score card of summer enjoyment, Chicago gets high marks on one (mosquitoes) and not-so-high marks on another (humidity). All that pavement and development means that mosquito counts are very low, and many people never suffer a bite all season; but in July and August the humidity can be uncomfortably high.

ECOLOGY & ENVIRONMENT

Few square inches of Chicago have not been subject to massive development and change in the past 150 years.

The years when Chicago was a blighted industrial landscape are gone, but their lingering effects remain. Much of the lake bottom is covered by mud laced with heavy metals and other toxic substances from the stockyards and steel mills. Although the water itself is clean and good enough if you want to go swimming, large, bottom-feeding lake fish such as trout and coho salmon are considered unsafe to eat if they are caught from the southern end of Lake Michigan.

The water quality of the Chicago River, which was reversed to send pollution out of town, is gradually improving. It too has problems with toxic sediment, and during heavy storms the sewers still pour polluted overflow into it. But the dream of Loop workers being able to fish in the river at lunchtime is no longer unthinkable. Still, the water is not safe for swimming.

Air quality is like that in other urban areas: not very good due to heavy traffic.

FLORA & FAUNA

Chicago was once a huge swamp and wetland, the areas on the lake north and south of the river primarily dunes. No trace of this past remains, except for a slight rise in Lincoln Park, which was built on a sand dune. Native vegetation such as the delicate wild onion that gave the city its name is long gone. To see some of the wildflowers that used to cover much of the inland area, visit the Wildflower Works at the north end of Grant Park (see Things to See & Do).

The trees lining the streets are mostly hardy varieties such as locust and ash, which can weather the road salt and other forms of urban abuse. The city is becoming increasingly green thanks to Mayor Richard M Daley's love of trees. Even as other city programs have been slashed, the tree-planting program gets more money each year for tens of thousands of new trees on the streets and in the parks.

After decades during which the only wildlife in the city consisted of unruly residents and rats, various native species are beginning to return in numbers that are sparking scientific study. Such woodsy creatures as skunks and opossums have found that temperate garages off alleys make wonderful winter homes. Deer have been found in Lincoln Park, which is remarkable because the nearest woods they could have come from are more than five tough urban miles away.

One of the most amazing occurrences is the increasing number of coyotes moving into the city. After generations of shunning people, this extremely shy species seems to be evolving into an urban predator. One

RAY HILLSTROM

The Chicago Board of Trade peers down the canyon of LaSalle St.

notable coyote gained fame on the Gold Coast for several months for prowling the alleys at night, feasting on rats and other vermin. Its welcome only came to an end after it took out a poodle. (Privately, many neighbors preferred the coyote.)

GOVERNMENT & POLITICS

Chicago politics is a popular spectator sport. The prevalence of elections – city elections fall every four years, the next one being in 1999 – keeps interest high. These are bruising and colorful affairs, with no restraint shown by the candidates when it comes to accusing opponents of every possible misdeed.

State elections are held every four years, two years off the federal cycle; the next Illinois elections are in 1998. These affairs often feature 'downstate-friendly' candidates, who represent the legions of Illinois farmers resentful of Chicago for gobbling up their taxes.

State Politics

For most of the history of Illinois, Chicago dominated state politics. Even when a Republican slipped in as governor on the strength of votes from the state's farmers – which has happened frequently – the city held sway in the Senate and House. But the shrinkage of Chicago's population in the 1970s, coupled with the resulting growth of the suburbs, has altered the balance. The suburbs are heavily Republican, and when they vote in combination with the farmers, Chicago's hegemony is no longer assured.

As this was being written, prior to the 1998 state elections, the outgoing governor, Jim Edgar, was planning to retire after an unspectacular career, leaving the office up for grabs. The Senate was controlled by Republicans and their leader, Pate Philip, who is known for his racist and sexist outbursts. The House was in the control of Democrats with ties to the city, but their hold was tenuous.

County Politics

It's easy to forget that Chicago is part of Cook County, which is why the 'County' half of the County-City Building is frequently forgotten. Cook County is a diverse place, consisting of the city and the affluent and impoverished suburbs surrounding it.

County government does little that affects the city – and is usually quite compliant with whoever is mayor when it does. The present county president is John Stroger, a long-time politician who is the first African American to hold the job.

City Politics

Here's where the action is. Chicago's city government has a mayor, elected every four years, who runs the executive branch and appoints managers in the various city departments, such as Planning, Aviation, Streets and Sanitation, etc. The city council consists of 50 aldermen who are elected every four years and represent small geographic districts.

Maintaining so many politicians and their related offices and staffs is expensive, but proposals to shrink the city council always run aground for the simple reason that the voters like things as they are. Certainly, this amount of bureaucracy is ripe for abuse and corruption (more on that later), but for the average Chicagoan it works well: You got a pothole in front of your house? Somebody stole your trash can? The neighbor's leaving banana peels all over your stoop? Mundane as they are, those are the kinds of matters that directly affect people's lives, and they can be taken care of with a call to the alderman.

With the districts so small in size, the politicians and their staffs can't afford to anger any voters, because angry voters start voting for somebody else. At the heart of this system is a phrase the late *Chicago Tribune* columnist Mike Royko used to say should be the motto for the city: 'Where's mine?' The entire system of city politics is based on a simple structure: The voter wants her alley cleaned, and the alderman wants her vote. If the alderman wants a lot of votes, he or she gets a bunch of plums for the district in the form of city jobs or big spending projects from the mayor. If the mayor wants votes for his or her programs from the city council, he or she doles out money in programs to the aldermen.

The Machine Chicago's vaunted machine is not even a shell of its former self. There was a time when the politicians approved the hiring in all departments, which ensured armies of loyal workers at election time, but that era came to a crashing end in 1979, when political hiring was prohibited for all but top-echelon jobs.

Without all those jobs to give out, the power of the politicians – especially the aldermen – was sharply reduced. That helped Harold Washington get elected mayor in 1983 and is the reason the current Mayor Daley must appeal to a broad range of voters if he hopes to get reelected.

The machine reared its old head in 1996, when Democrats from all over the city united in an effort to defeat the Republican Michael Flanagan, who had won jailed Democrat Dan Rostenkowski's seat in the US House of Representatives in 1994. A gigantic thorn in the Democratic side, Flanagan was crushed.

RAY HILLSTROM
White blight on S Michigan Ave

White Blight

Any Chicago politician can tell you that snow is a substance sent by God to ruin political careers, and because of that, each and every delicate little flake that falls on the city is seen as an invader to be eradicated, whatever the cost.

At the first sign of flurries, official Chicago mounts a counterattack that rivals the Normandy invasion in its fury and single-minded sense of purpose. After all, everybody in city government remembers what happened to Mayor Michael Bilandic, who was sunning himself in Florida in January 1979 when the city was smothered by one of the worst blizzards of the century. Never mind that experts say the volume of snow precluded any response that would have saved the city from being buried for weeks. Images of the tanned Bilandic tut-tutting about the white stuff while people had heart attacks trying to dig out their cars were what stuck with the voters when they went to the polls two months later and sent a message that rocked Chicago's political machine.

Since then every mayor has gone to battle at the fall of the first flake. If you are in Chicago for a snowfall, you will be treated to quite a show. First, more than 400 salt trucks with plows hit the streets with bright flashing yellow lights. Next come waves of hundreds of garbage trucks hurriedly fitted with plows. They are followed by bulldozers, graders, dump trucks and other heavy equipment. Snow-parking rules go into effect, and any mope who leaves his or her car parked on an arterial street will find it towed.

At 10 pm, watch the local newscasts. Each will have breathless reporters live at the command center of the Department of Streets and Sanitation. In a milieu much like NASA's mission control, reports of snow incursions are immediately dispatched.

Tiny snowdrift forming at Clark and Diversey? Send in a platoon of plows! Patches of ice on the Randolph Bridge? Get a battalion of salt trucks over there! Homeless man refusing to leave box on Lower Wacker Drive? Send in a squad of cops to arrest him and toss him into a toasty cell. (Less stubborn sorts can avail themselves of the scores of 'warming centers' the city opens around the city.)

Outsiders might consider this response overkill, but Chicagoans take pride in its exemplification of can-do attitude. No matter that the thousands of tons of salt dumped every year dissolve concrete, bridges, cars, trees, boots and everything else; nobody complains. In 1992 a deep cold snap hit the Midwest and several cities ran out of salt. 'What's the situation locally?' reporters asked. While cars skated on other cities' streets, it was cheerfully revealed that Chicago still had enough salt for several years, because each year the city buys at least three times what it needs. You can see some of these huge bluish-white mountains on vacant land around town.

Of course, anybody who has been to places such as Washington, DC, Atlanta or Dallas, where just a few flakes can cause pandemonium, might appreciate Chicago's war on the stuff. And they might enjoy the show as well. ∎

Ethics For a good laugh, stop by the information desk in front of the elevators at City Hall, 121 N LaSalle St, and pick up the brochure from the Chicago Board of Ethics. It's a high-minded bunch of pap expressing the commitment of the city government to thwart theft from the city, acceptance of bribes and operation of a private business on city time, as well as a bunch of other malarkey about honest government.

What makes this little brochure no better than twaddle are the antics of city officials and employees, most entertainingly covered in the local press. Examples follow.

In a sting dubbed Operation Greylord, the federal government sent scores of county judges to the pokey in the 1980s after catching them literally stuffing cash in their pockets to fix cases.

Representative Dan Rostenkowski, the third most powerful man in the United States Congress and a Bucktown resident, was caught masterminding scams for rewards worth little more than peanuts and was sent to jail in 1994.

In 1995 Representative Mel Reynolds was sent to prison for having sex with a minor. Among the evidence against him were tapes of a chat he had on the phone with a young girl about the color of her panties.

In a 1997 scandal referred to as Operation Silver Shovel, three alderman were indicted for refusing no bribe, no matter how small. This is an ongoing operation mounted by the US Attorney's Office in Chicago, which stays busy prosecuting local politicians.

During your visit to Chicago, you are bound to enjoy press coverage of the latest scandals. Odds are good that you may even enjoy an aldermanic indictment or two.

ECONOMY

The value of Chicago's annual goods and services tops $150 billion. The service industries employ close to three-quarters of the workers in Chicago, some of the major areas being insurance, banking, accounting, commodities and options trading, retail, health care, advertising, entertainment, communications, hosting meetings and conventions, hospitality, law and education.

Visitors, whether in Chicago for business, fun or both, were responsible for an estimated $15 billion in expenditures in 1997 and represent a vital part of the city's economy.

Fifteen *Fortune* 500 firms are based in Chicago, with another 20 in the surrounding suburbs. Among them are the following major players.

Amoco, the global oil giant, made $2.8 billion in profits in 1996.

Although the huge Leo Burnett Advertising agency's output is often banal, there's no doubt that Tony the Tiger, Mr Whipple, the Pillsbury Doughboy and a menagerie of other ad campaigns have found a place in the American psyche. On a darker side, the Burnett-hatched Marlboro Man has popularized and glamorized cigarette smoking worldwide. Recently the agency has gone through a tough stretch, as blue chip clients McDonald's and United Airlines left Burnett after long relationships.

Chicagoan Ray Kroc bought a successful hamburger stand from two brothers in California in 1955. He studied the concept and reduced it to its simple core of cheap assembly-line burgers of dependable, if not spectacular, quality served in squeaky clean surroundings. Since he opened his first McDonald's outlet, just beyond the city limits in Des Plaines, the world has not been able to get enough.

The Sears merchandise group decamped for the suburbs in 1992, leaving their landmark building one-third empty. But the executive offices stayed on the high floors downtown.

United, the world's largest airline, has always been based at the world's busiest airport: first Midway and then O'Hare.

RICK GERHARTER

Humble beginnings

POPULATION & PEOPLE

Some 2.7 million people live in the city, a figure that has stabilized after falling from the high of 3.6 million in 1950. The decline is due to the economic and social devastation of some neighborhoods and, oddly, the economic success of others: yuppies live singly or in pairs in apartments that once housed whole families.

Almost 40% of Chicagoans are African Americans, but the percentage is slowly diminishing as the Hispanic community expands and blacks move to surrounding suburbs.

RICK GERHARTER

Kids at Oak St Beach

Immigrants continue to arrive in droves. Many have long-established support groups that quickly find work for the new arrivals, which is why many newsstands are run by Pakistanis, many dry cleaners are run by Koreans and many of the office buildings are cleaned by Polish women.

The Hispanic community is the fastest growing in Chicago, constituting more than 20% of the total population. Chicago's diverse Hispanic population embraces sizable communities of Mexicans, Central Americans, Puerto Ricans and Cubans. Major Hispanic neighborhoods are on the Northwest Side, in Pilsen and farther south through Canaryville.

Chinese American residents don't just live in Chinatown – they are also centered on Argyle St on the North Side, where they are part of a large community comprising Vietnamese and Cambodians as well. Koreans are centered on Lawrence Ave, and many Indians and Pakistanis live near Devon Ave and throughout the far north neighborhoods. At 4% of the total population, Chicago's Asian communities are growing fast.

Sometimes it seems there are more Irish in Chicago than Dublin. And that refers to those who were born in Ireland, not the millions of descendants of the first major group of Irish to inhabit the city. Many of the Irish-born people in Chicago work as nurses and construction workers for a few year and then return home.

Chicago has long welcomed Poles with open arms, and it was an early supporter of the Solidarity movement in Poland. Along stretches of Milwaukee Ave you will hear only Polish spoken.

ARTS

The arts community in Chicago is diverse thanks to its population, its long tradition of monetary support for the arts and its regional pull on young artists from the Rockies to Appalachia.

Businesses have come to see the economic potential of the arts that draw people to the city as tourists and as prospective employees. The challenge in the early 1990s by the Chicago Symphony and the Lyric Opera to the corporate community for new money to renovate their homes resulted in $100 million in short order. Of the 25.2 million visitors to Chicago in 1995, 26% cited the city's cultural attractions as their primary reason for visiting.

Of course, the big money doesn't always make it to the pockets of the artists themselves. Chicago actors who belong to Actors' Equity – the rough equivalent of a union – average only $5000 a year in pay. Non-Equity members often work free. The difficult existence of many artists bouncing from show to show, commission to commission or sale to sale has a hidden benefit for the city at large: to make ends meet, these smart and creative people often work in restaurants and bars, which often makes for a lively evening out in almost any place you choose.

Music

Though most kinds of music are performed in the city, Chicago has had a special influence on a few genres. Jazz, blues and gospel – and by extension, rock – have enjoyed remarkable innovations thanks in some part to Chicago.

Blues The same Illinois Central trains that brought a generation of blacks to Chicago in the Great Migration brought the blues as well.

Early on, blues in the city closely resembled the variety played in the bayous of Mississippi and Louisiana. But the demands of noisy clubs and the perhaps less tangible pressures of urban life soon resulted in a more aggressive, amplified sound that is the basis of Chicago blues.

Muddy Waters

Muddy Waters arrived on the scene in 1943 and is widely regarded as the most important blues musician to work in Chicago. His influence runs deep, extending to early rock groups such as the Rolling Stones and the Paul Butterfield Band. His sideman in later years was Buddy Guy, whose electric-guitar work influenced musicians such as Eric Clapton, Stevie Ray Vaughan and Jimi Hendrix. Guy continues to operate the club bearing his name in the South Loop (see the Jazz & Blues section in the Entertainment chapter).

Jazz In 1922 Louis Armstrong came to Chicago from New Orleans to join King Oliver's Creole Jazz Band, which cut some of the most influential recordings in jazz history the next year. His solo style soon flourished in the city, as he wowed crowds in Bronzeville and other venues, giving his trumpet a workout only the toughest brass could withstand.

Jelly Roll Morton was another immigrant from New Orleans. He, Armstrong and many others gave Chicago jazz a freewheeling, powerful expression that defied the efforts of snobs to reduce jazz to static parlor listening.

Others who defined Chicago jazz were Benny Goodman, Bix Beiderbecke, Eddie Condon and Bud Freeman. In the 1960s a group of musicians formed the Association for the Advancement of Creative Musicians (more commonly known by its acronym, AACM), which continues to push the envelope of jazz, redefining the genre even as new definitions are articulated.

Gospel Blues and jazz were the seeds of this soulful singing, which emanates from churches all over the South Side every Sunday. Huge choruses clap their hands, chant, shout, wail and create music that both inspires and speaks for the huge congregations of the primarily Baptist churches. Much of the credit for creating the gospel sound, at once mournful and joyous, goes to Thomas A Dorsey, music director at the Pilgrim Baptist Church in Bronzeville, who died in 1993 at age 93. Mahalia Jackson is just one of the great Chicago gospel singers who have launched careers in South Side churches. Popular singers Ruth Brown and Faye Adams did as well, and so did Little Richard and Chuck Berry.

RYAN VER BERKMOES
Navy Pier wildlife

Fine Arts

Chicago is a great place for art lovers – it has several museums with a wide range of collections, and plenty of galleries to suit any taste. The Things to See & Do chapter has sections on Chicago's art museums. The Shopping chapter has listings of galleries and neighborhoods where art may be both seen and purchased.

Public Art In the late 1960s Chicago began to require that developers include provisions for public art in their projects. The decidedly mixed results can be seen throughout downtown. See the Things to See & Do chapter for walking tours of the varied sculptures in the Loop and Grant Park.

Architecture

See the special Architecture section for a full discussion of Chicago's place on the world stage of architecture and a walking tour of its rich architectural milieu.

Film

Few know that Chicago until 1920 was a center of the American film industry. Charlie Chaplin was the star of Essanay Film Studios on Argyle St from 1907 to 1917, when they heard that land could be bought for cheap out west in some new place called Hollywood.

    Among his many quirks was Mayor Richard J Daley's hatred of filmmakers; he did his best to bar them from the city. His

The great Satchmo

Chicago in the Movies
Here are some notable films shot in Chicago:

Call Northside 777 (1948) – This often ignored Jimmy Stewart vehicle about a cynical reporter was filmed on location throughout the West Side. It has excellent shots of gritty city blocks later demolished for expressways.

North by Northwest (1959) – The middle part of this Hitchcock classic has scenes filmed on location with Cary Grant at the Omni Ambassador East, on North Michigan Ave, at the now demolished Dearborn Station train shed and at Midway Airport.

Nightmare in Chicago (1964) – This forgotten early thriller by director Robert Altman was shot entirely in the city. The gripping story follows a psychopath who terrorizes the town.

The Blues Brothers (1980) – In possibly the best-known Chicago movie, Second City alums John Belushi and Dan Aykroyd tear up the city, including City Hall. The scenes with the hapless Nazis in the Pinto were filmed in Milwaukee.

Ordinary People (1980) – Robert Redford's Oscar-winning directorial debut, about a really screwed-up rich family, is an intelligent and engrossing drama.

The Hunter (1980) – Steve McQueen's last film is a big dud, but a car has a great role swan-diving into the river from Marina City.

Risky Business (1983) – In this darkly satiric parable about all the things not to do when the folks leave home, Tom Cruise and Rebecca De Mornay have the most pleasurable El ride of all time.

Code of Silence (1985) – Chuck Norris single-handedly cleans up Chicago in this one. There's an excellent chase on top of the El.

About Last Night (1986) – The David Mamet play on which this was based is titled *Sexual Perversity in Chicago*. It was light-years better than this watered-down snoozer, made by a Hollywood terrified by the original name. It features some of the worst bars in town.

The Color of Money (1986) – Martin Scorsese's sequel to *The Hustler* has Paul Newman and Tom Cruise cruising the West Side.

Ferris Bueller's Day Off (1986) – John Hughes' cinematic postcard for the city has a rich North Shore teen discovering the joys of the city.

Native Son (1986) – Based on the 1940 novel of the same name by Richard Wright, this tense drama, directed by Jerrold Freedman, plays out the disturbing repercussions of a young white woman's accidental murder by Bigger Thomas, a poor young black man. Much of the film was shot in Hyde Park and the South Side.

Running Scared (1986) – Gregory Hines and Billy Crystal star in this buddy movie about wise-cracking Chicago cops. There's a splendid car chase *on* the El.

death in 1976 coincided with Hollywood's desire to find fresh locations. Chicago fit the bill perfectly, and for the past 20 years the city has starred in hundreds of films and TV shows. Sappy comedy director and producer John Hughes can't stay away.

The industry Daley shunned now pumps millions a year into the city economy and employs hundreds. Chicagoans acted like a bunch of star-struck rubes when the first wave of productions hit town, but they now hardly break their fast strides to give a location set a second glance.

Literature
In 1900 Theodore Dreiser wrote *Sister Carrie*. In many ways, it is the perfect Chicago book: the mean streets of the

The Untouchables (1987) – Kevin Costner saves Chicago from Al Capone. The infamous baby carriage scene on the steps was filmed in Union Station, the exploding grocery store is at Clark and Roscoe, the ball-bat banquet was in the Blackstone Hotel and the trial was in the Cultural Center.

The Package (1989) – Gene Hackman stars in this political thriller, which uses Chicago's dismal gray winters to dramatic advantage.

Uncle Buck (1990) – John Candy and John Hughes just couldn't leave the city. This is one of several of their films that had portions shot in Chicago; another is *Planes, Trains and Automobiles* (1987).

Backdraft (1991) – For director Ron Howard's ode to those regular-guy Chicago firefighters, lots of abandoned buildings went up in flames.

Only the Lonely (1991) – This film features John Candy in his least-stupid role as a cop who has to choose between mom and girlfriend. The Music Box Theater stars.

Blink (1993) – Madeleine Stowe stars in this thriller, which was filmed all over town.

The Fugitive (1993) – Harrison Ford stars as the falsely accused main character in this action film, with great scenes in City Hall and the Chicago Hilton & Towers and on the El. The author of this guide found himself standing next to Ford during the filming of the chase through the actual St Patrick's Day Parade.

Go Fish (1994) – Director Rose Troche's somewhat experimental film shows what it takes for one Chicago lesbian to get a date.

Hoop Dreams (1994) – This stirring documentary follows the high school bastketball careers of two African American teenagers from the South Side. Filmmakers Frederick Marx, Peter Gilbert and Steve James interview the young men and their families, coaches, teachers and friends over several years, showing how the dream of playing collge and pro ball – and escaping the ghetto – influences their life choices.

While You Were Sleeping (1995) – Sandra Bullock stars as the kind of CTA ticket vendor who could only exist in the movies.

In addition, although it was filmed entirely in Hollywood, *His Girl Friday* (1940), is a marvelous remake of Ben Hecht's *The Front Page* (1931). Hecht, who scripted both, worked as a Chicago reporter during the peak of the newspaper circulation wars in the 1920s. The movies are based on his experiences covering trials at the old Criminal Courts Building that still stands at Kinzie and Dearborn, although it's now used as an office building.

The TV series *ER* has exterior scenes filmed in Chicago in every episode. These tend to be postcard stuff and are fun for Chicagoans to watch because of their ludicrous continuity: characters manage to jump miles around town during one short stroll. ∎

gritty city rob our heroine of her virtue, but in the best 'Where's mine?' tradition, she turns this seeming setback into profitable gain. Much of Chicago's best literature has this same gritty reality pervading its pages.

Carl Sandburg's 1916 poem 'Chicago,' merely one in his exceptional collection titled simply *Chicago Poems*, captures a spirit of the city that endures even as the details have changed: 'Hog Butcher for the World, / Tool Maker, Stacker of Wheat, / Player with Railroads and the Nation's Freight Handler; / . . . City of the Big Shoulders.'

The elusive Saul Bellow turns out high-profile works, which in 1976 garnered the Nobel Prize for Literature. His novels

Nelson Algren

A product of the mean streets of the city, Nelson Algren (1909-81) was the quintessential Chicago fiction writer. His realist writing is as no-nonsense as the culture from which it is derived. He lived for many years at 1958 W Evergreen in the then-sordid Wicker Park neighborhood, and he found his characters and places on the surrounding streets.

In 1950 Algren won the first National Book Award, bestowed by American publishers, for *The Man with the Golden Arm*, a novel set on Division St near Milwaukee Ave. Chronicling the lives of people struggling to survive within the confines of their neighborhood, this tale is shaped by varying degrees of desire, hope and loyalty, themes that have defined the lives of generations of Chicagoans. Algren's years spent living on the streets of Chicago come through in his characters. In the following excerpt, Algren explores the relationship between the deeply troubled central character, Frankie, and his sometime friend Sparrow:

Sparrow himself had only the faintest sort of inkling that Frankie had brought home a duffel bag of trouble. The little petit-larceny punk from Damen and Division and the dealer still got along like a couple of playful pups. 'He's like me,' Frankie explained, 'never drinks. Unless he's alone or with somebody.'

Algren's other works include *The Neon Wilderness* (1947), *A Walk on the Wild Side* (1956) and *The Last Carousel* (1973). ■

focus on the strengths and weaknesses of humanity through studies of flawed figures. These works include *Herzog*, *Humbolt's Gift* and *The Dean's December*.

Gwendolyn Brooks became the first African American to win the Pulitzer Prize for her 1949 book of poetry *Annie Allen*. Her works, which focus on African Americans in Chicago, include *A Street in Bronzeville*.

The classic Studs Lonigan trilogy, by James T Farrell, conveys the aspirations of Irish American immigrants and the nightmarish realities of their lives.

Leaving his CTA bus far behind, former driver Larry Heinemann based his first works on his experiences as a grunt in Vietnam. *Paco's Story* won the National Book Award for Fiction in 1987. His more recent novels have focused on the oddities of contemporary life in the city.

Before he was found hanging outside his Loop office window in 1996, Eugene Izzi made a name for himself by writing hard-edged mysteries set in the city. His last book was *A Matter of Honor*.

Cris Mazza, a University of Chicago creative writing professor, turns out books with such unusual plots that one right-wing Republican called her writing 'an offense to the senses.' Her recent novel *Dog People* features razor-sharp writing and a cast of colorful characters, among others a fascist dog trainer, a lesbian dancer and a loveless caterer.

Sara Paretsky's VI Warshawski detective novels at first seem like so much genre fiction, but within the gritty narratives about a woman private investigator, she weaves her own deep commitment to social justice.

Commonly known as 'an old man with a tape recorder,' the ageless Studs Terkel is much more; he's a compassionate chronicler of the lives of everyday people, making the seemingly mundane deeply moving. Among his works are *Division Street: America*, *The Good War: An Oral History of World War II* and *Working*.

A seemingly unstoppable producer of screenplays disguised as books, Scott Turow is actually more interesting than his plots, which always seem to feature a heroine destined to be played by Julia Roberts being pursued by Gene Hackman-like baddies; he still works as a Loop lawyer and writes his books during his commute on the Metra train.

Theater
Moviegoers familiar with the carpet-chewing performances of John Malkovich and Gary Sinise will be familiar with the tenets of the Chicago style of acting, for which the two Steppenwolf Theater principals receive much credit: a fiery intensity marked by loud, physical acting.

In many ways the pair built on a tradition that had begun in the 1960s, when modern improvisational comedy, a Chicago invention, began leaving its mark on the actors who graced the stages. To succeed, improv called for deep commitment from the ensemble casts, in which everyone depended on everyone else for a performance to succeed.

Beginning in the 1970s the tough, machine-gun-fire bursts of dialogue in David Mamet's plays only added to Chicago theater's reputation for hard-edged, raw emotion. And legions of young actors and directors continue to fuel the theatrical fire with their burning desires to make their marks.

RELIGION
Chicago has the largest Catholic archdiocese in the country. Immigration from Catholic countries such as Mexico and Poland ensures that will continue. Baptist churches are prevalent throughout the South Side. A large Jewish community is long established.

The Yellow Pages lists thousands of churches, representing any of 119 denominations. The number and variety reflects the large and varied population. Some of the choices: Russian Orthodox, Mennonite, Christian Chinese, Islamic and Armenian Apostolic.

LANGUAGE
English is the major spoken language. In the heart of some of the ethnic enclaves you'll hear languages such as Spanish, Polish, Korean or Russian, but almost all business is conducted in English.

Chicago Architecture

Chicago Architecture: A Study in Innovation

Two great explosions of creative energy and innovation mark Chicago architecture. The first came after the 1871 fire, when architects from around the world flocked to the city for commissions. Most were young – the average age was under 30 – and had something to prove. They found a city happy to give them the scorched Loop as a stage, and within three decades they invented the modern skyscraper, with its steel frame, high-speed elevators and curtain walls of glass. More aesthetically, they defined a new form of architecture that came to be called 'the Chicago School.' Tossed aside were the classical forms of Greece and Rome that architects the world over continued to apply to major works. The Chicago School stressed economy, simplicity and function.

These architects closely adhered to Chicago School architect Louis Sullivan's mandate that 'form follows function.' Though the basic tenet held true – the buildings did draw their facades from the underlying logic of the regular steel bracing beneath – that didn't result in a lack of adornment. The architects used a powerful language of simple geometric shapes, primarily strong vertical lines crossed by horizontal bands. Relief came from bay windows, curved corners, sweeping entrances and other details, which gave the buildings a pragmatic glory that reflected the city around them.

RICK GERHARTER

Loop skyline

Chicago contributed again to world architecture after WWII. Led by Ludwig Mies van der Rohe, the new 'International Style' swept architecture. This style truly was the pared-down embodiment of Sullivan's mandate: the very structure of buildings – the steel frame – was no longer the inspiration for a building's look, it was the look. The oft-copied steel-and-glass towers, similar to the Federal Center, at Dearborn and Adams, were built in every country around the world, unfortunately often without Mies' careful eye for details.

From 1950 through 1980, the Chicago architectural firm of Skidmore, Owings & Merrill became the IBM of their day. No corporate manager was ever fired for hiring SOM and their bands of Mies disciples to design a building.

During the go-go era of the 1980s, commercial space in the Loop almost doubled, and high-rise offices spread to the Near North. Many of these buildings were influenced by Postmodernism, the movement emphasizing eclectic designs drawn from older styles and other art forms. New construction was stalled by the real estate crash at the end of the decade, but today occupancy in the Loop and surroundings is healthy, and another wave of construction seems in the offing. It remains to be seen what architectural movement Chicago will next produce or embrace.

RICK GERHARTER

Staircase inside the Rookery

Architects
Here are some of the most important people associated with Chicago's architecture whose work can be found throughout the city.

RICK GERHARTER
Sears Tower

Daniel Burnham A principal in the development of the Chicago School of architecture (see the sidebar 'Make No Little Plans . . . ').

Bertrand Goldberg Uses concrete to create fluid structures such as Marina City (1959 to 1967) and River City (1986).

Bruce Graham A leading partner at Skidmore, Owings & Merrill who designed massive structures such as the John Hancock Center (1969) and the Sears Tower (1974), which continued Chicago's burly and aggressive style of architecture.

William Holabird & Martin Roche Partners who took the Chicago School to commercial success, applying its tenets to more than 80 buildings in the Loop. Notable survivors: the Pontiac Building (1891) and the Marquette Building (1894).

Helmut Jahn A controversial architect who reversed the Sullivan tenet and designed buildings in which function follows form. His early work, such as the modernist Xerox Centre, is overshadowed by his later showy works, such as the notorious James R Thompson Center (1985, see Part Four) and the masterful United Airlines Terminal One at O'Hare (1988).

'Make No Little Plans . . . '

Daniel Burnham was the lead planner of the 1893 World's Columbian Exposition. His concept 'City Beautiful' called for cities to be designed along a grand scheme that extended beyond buildings to streets, parks and the entire urban landscape. His 1909 plan for Chicago guided development for the next 30 years. Burnham's ideas influenced city design around the world.

Proving as good at quotes as he was at design, Burnham made the following exhortation to his colleagues:

Make no little plans; they have no magic to stir men's blood and probably themselves will not be realized. Make big plans; aim high in hope and work, remembering that a noble and logical diagram once recorded will never die, but long after we are gone will be a living thing, asserting itself with growing intensity. Remember that our sons and grandsons are going to do things that would stagger us. Let your watchword be 'order' and your beacon 'beauty.'

Fazlur Khan The structural engineer who made the Hancock Center and Sears Tower not only possible, but economically feasible. His prominent exterior cross-bracing on the former was so efficient that material costs for the 100-story building were no more than those for a conventional 45-story affair.

Ludwig Mies van der Rohe Brought his Bauhaus School ideas to Chicago when he fled the Nazis and Germany in the 1930s. His 860 and 880 N Lake Shore Drive apartments (1951) set the style for three decades of international architecture (see the Gold Coast section of Things to See & Do).

John Wellborn Root Burnham's partner, who designed the Monadnock Building (1891) and the Rookery (1888), among many other Chicago School classics, before his untimely death at age 41.

Louis Sullivan A master of ornamentation whose skill is evident in the entrance to Carson Pirie Scott (1903) and in the preserved bits of the destroyed Chicago Stock Exchange at the Art Institute. He usually created his work in partnership with engineer Dankmar Adler.

Frank Lloyd Wright Visionary behind the revolutionary Prairie School style of architecture, which derived its form from its surroundings: buildings were low, heavily emphasizing the horizontal lines of the Midwestern landscape. In contrast to the simple lines of the architecture, Wright added myriad precise details, appreciable on closer inspection. See the Oak Park section in Things to See & Do, and the Robie House section under Hyde Park in the same chapter, for more on Wright.

RICK GERHARTER

Detail, Carson Pirie Scott

RYAN VER BERKMOES

Robie House, Hyde Park

46

Residential Styles
As you explore Chicago's neighborhoods, you will see several types of housing repeated over and over. The following styles are listed roughly in their order of appearance in Chicago.

RICK GERHARTER
Old Town cottage

Cottages & Frame Houses Chicago's great contribution to residential construction was the two-by-four. Until the system of knocking houses together from precut boards and mass-produced nails was developed in the city in 1833, building a house was a long and costly process of sawing timber and stacking rocks. Thousands of cottages and frame houses burned like matchsticks in the 1871 fire, but many more were built later in areas of the city where they weren't outlawed by the city's fire code. Look for them in Wicker Park and Old Town.

Queen Anne Houses Commonly called Victorian houses, these residences proliferated in the late 19th century and are notable for their wealth of detail and ornaments, which the masses could afford thanks to assembly-line production techniques developed in lumber factories southwest of the Loop. The houses can be found throughout the north and northwest sides of the city.

RICK GERHARTER
Old Town's Crilly Court: Variations on the Queen Anne theme

Graystones Two and three stories tall, these dignified residences met the city's tough fire code and were popular from 1890 to 1920. The expensive limestone was used only in front; the rest of the structures are composed of ordinary brick. Some were built as single-family homes, others as apartments. Graystones are found throughout the city; a huge concentration of them is in the Wrigleyville neighborhood.

Apartment Buildings These come in all shapes and sizes, from three-story multi-unit affairs from the late 1800s to the airy courtyard buildings of the 1920s to some really awful concrete high-rises that appeared after WWII. In the early 20th century Chicago's population density rose so much that by 1920 two-thirds of the city's residents lived in apartments.

Three-Flats Joined by their less ambitious cousins, the two-flats, these buildings filled many of the city's neighborhoods from the 1910s through today. Set on the usual narrow Chicago lot, the buildings feature apartments with light front rooms and airy back kitchens with wooden porches (many of which are now enclosed to increase living space). Dark bedrooms open off a long hall that runs the length of the apartment. Since the 1970s, thousands of these buildings have been renovated throughout the North Side for a new generation of apartment dwellers and condo buyers.

Storefronts with Apartments Throughout the 20th century, storeowners and developers have placed living spaces above small retail shops. Examples of this practice can be found along any of Chicago's retail streets, especially in the neighborhoods. A contemporary equivalent of this practice can be found in the condos high above the Michigan Ave vertical malls, such as Water Tower Place and 900 N Michigan.

Bungalows

Built by the tens of thousands along Chicago's outlying streets from the 1920s through the 1950s, bungalows filled the subdivisions of their day. Aimed squarely at factory workers, their common terms of $1000 down, as well as the easy payments on their builder-financed $5000 mortgages, brought single-family home-ownership to a generation. Stolid and compact on lots 25 feet wide, the homes introduced the booming middle class to features their parents had considered luxuries: central halls, which gave privacy to bedrooms; ceramic-tiled bathrooms, which had hot and cold water; and kitchens with built-in cabinets and counters. Provisions were made for gas ranges, refrigerators and ever growing collections of electrical appliances. Architectural details inspired by Frank Lloyd Wright's Prairie School brought character to the 'bungalow belts' that soon circled the city. These sturdy homes – most are still standing – have proven endlessly adaptable through the years. Roofs have been popped up to create full second floors; basements have been finished for rumpus rooms; kitchens and bathrooms have been remodeled to reflect the latest whims of design and convenience. Today a bungalow in good shape easily costs $150,000 or more.

Loop Architecture – A Walking Tour

The Loop is a festival of important, beautiful and interesting architecture. Just by walking its streets for about half a day, you can trace the development of modern architecture in Chicago, the US and worldwide. This walking tour is arranged in five parts, which you can explore all at once or in stages – simply follow the maps for each. You can explore the public spaces of most buildings during office hours on weekdays. Weekend entrance is much more problematic. Note that the proper name for some buildings is actually their address.

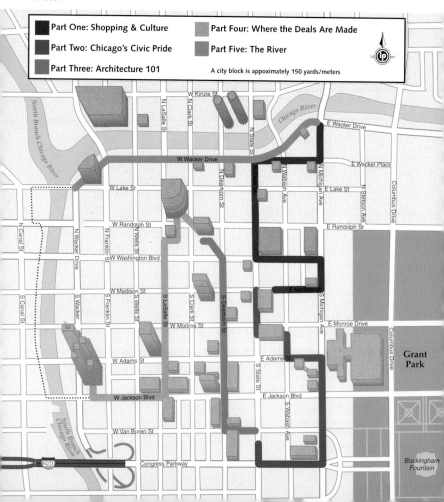

Bird's-eye view of the Michigan Ave Bridge with 360 N Michigan in the foreground, the Wrigley Building at the far left and the Tribune Tower at the back left

Part One: Shopping & Culture

This walk takes you past structures that date from early in the 20th century when the North Loop was the entertainment center of Chicago. Begin at the south end of the Michigan Ave bridge and walk south.

❶ Carbide & Carbon Building, 230 N Michigan

Although it seems black, the exterior of this 1929 Burnham Brothers building is actually made of very dark green terra cotta; it just could use a good cleaning. The tower, with its setback, is detailed in gold leaf.

❷ 35 E Wacker

Built as 'the Jeweler's Building' by Thielbar & Fugard in 1926, this structure once had an interior elevator system that allowed tenants to park their cars securely near their offices. The four corner towers at the setback above the 24th floor hide water tanks. The domed pinnacle is occupied by the offices of noted architect Helmut Jahn.

❸ Chicago Theater, 175 N State

Restored by the city in 1986, this 3800-seat theater is a grand example of the movie palaces of the 1920s. Its architects, Rapp & Rapp, cut their teeth on the 1921 commission and went on to design scores of theaters that increasingly came to resemble fantastic wedding cakes. The theater surrounds the Page Brothers Building, which was built in 1872 right after the fire. The Lake St facade is formed of cast iron, one of two such structures left in the city.

❹ Marshall Field & Co, 111 N State

Covering an entire block, Marshall Field's was built in five stages by and his firm between 1892 and 1914. The southeastern corner (at Washington and Wabash) was the earliest stage and has massive load-bearing walls. On the State St side, the soaring ground-floor retail spaces are topped by Tiffany skylights. The whole store was given a costly reconstruction in 1992, when a central escalator atrium was added.

❺ Reliance Building, 32 N State

Built in the early 1890s by Burnham & Root, the Reliance Building, with its 16 stories of shimmering glass framed by brilliant white terra-cotta details, is like a breath of fresh air. Its lightweight internal metal frame – much of which was erected in only 15 days – supports a glass facade that gives the building a feeling of lightness, a style that didn't become universal until after WWII. Narrowly avoiding demolition – a common fate for Chicago's architectural gems in this town where preservation often takes a back seat to commercial interests – the Reliance had its exterior restored 1995, and it is now slated to be converted from offices into a hotel, a use more befitting its small floors.

❻ Chicago Cultural Center, 78 E Washington

Thank the British for this beautiful 1897 public building. After the 1871 fire, the Brits sent over 8000 books to be used to establish a free library for the people of Chicago. Many were autographed by the donors, such as Thomas Carlyle, Lord Tennyson and Benjamin Disraeli. The Chicago Public Library was established on the basis of that donation, and this building was

RICK GERHARTER

Reliance Building

RICK GERHARTER

Interior, Chicago Cultural Center

RICK GERHARTER

35 E Wacker

created by Shepley, Rutan & Coolidge to house it. In 1977 the building was renovated for use as a cultural center. Today the books are in the Harold Washington Library Center (see Part Two), but the magnificent public spaces remain. See the Loop section of the Things to See & Do chapter for details.

❼ 6 N Michigan

From his corner office in this building, Montgomery Ward fumed as he saw developers encroaching on Grant Park (see The Man Who Saved the Lakefront, a sidebar in Things to See & Do). The 1899 structure designed by Hugh MG Garden and Richard E Schmidt is much altered from the way it looked when it was the center of Ward's operations, but many charming terra-cotta details, such as reliefs of plants and animals, still exist – albeit under layers of grime.

❽ Carson Pirie Scott & Co, 1 S State

When the major part of this building was completed in 1906, critics said it was too ornamental to serve as a retail building. You be the judge, as you admire Louis Sullivan's superb metalwork around the main entrance, at State and Madison. Though it is Sullivan who insisted 'form follows function,' it's hard to see that theory at work in this lavishly flowing cast iron. Amid the flowing botanical and geometric forms, look for Sullivan's initials, LHS. The rest of the building is clad simply in white terra cotta. This was the first department store to have an all-steel frame.

Part Two: Chicago's Civic Pride

This segment of the tour crosses Chicago's cultural ground zero, along Michigan Ave. The sweep of buildings fronting Grant Park has received landmark status. The facades seen from Grant Park are a study in skyscraper development up to WWII. Only the Borg-Warner building, across from the Art Institute on the southwest corner of Adams and Michigan, rings a sour note, as welcome here as the Borg are on *Star Trek*.

Begin at the southwest corner of State and Madison, across from Carson Pirie Scott.

❶ Chicago Building, 7 W Madison

This 15-story 1904 building is typical of many designed by the firm Holabird & Roche throughout the Loop during the late 19th and early 20th centuries. The windows fronting State St are classic Chicago style: two narrow sash windows on either side of a larger fixed pane. After a modest career, the building reopened in 1997 as a dorm for the School of the Art Institute – another innovative use of older Loop office buildings. The preserved cornice is unusual, since most older buildings have had theirs removed for maintenance reasons.

RICK GERHARTER

Classic Chicago style windows on the Gage Building

❷ Palmer House Hilton, 17 E Monroe

Completed in 1927, this luxury hotel, designed by Holabird & Roche, is the fourth to bear the name of former owner Potter Palmer. His Francophile wife Bertha's tastes were responsible for the ornate French lobby, with its ceiling of delicate mosaics. Enter on State St, pass through the shopping arcade and take the escalators up to the lobby before exiting onto Wabash.

❸ Symphony Center, 63 E Adams & 220 S Michigan

This complex consists of the original Orchestra Hall (1905, DH Burnham & Co), on Michigan Ave, and a remodeled former liquor warehouse on Adams St (1904, Richard Schmidt and Hugh MG Garden). The two were joined by a soaring glass atrium in 1997, when the Chicago Symphony Orchestra completed the $110 million reconstruction of its headquarters and performance hall.

The Art Institute

❹ Art Institute of Chicago, Michigan Ave at Adams St

The classic approach to Chicago's premier cultural institution is to walk eastward on Adams in the afternoon and watch the sunlit facade slowly reveal itself. The original building, designed by Shepley, Rutan & Coolidge, dates from 1893 and has been expanded several times. Across the train tracks is the large Columbus Drive wing, designed by Skidmore, Owings & Merrill and added in 1977; the large Rice Building, designed by Hammond, Beeby & Babka, came along in 1988. The bronze lions fronting the main entrance have been beloved mascots since 1894.

Lobby, Palmer House Hilton

❺ Santa Fe Center, 224 S Michigan

Architect Daniel Burnham kept his offices in this sparkling white terra-cotta building, which he designed in 1904. The unusual top-floor porthole windows make the structure stand out even more from its neighbors. Enter the lobby and look upward at the vast light well Burnham placed in the center. This was a feature he also gave the Rookery (see Part Four). A 1985 renovation raised the glass canopy from the second floor to the building's top.

❻ Fine Arts Building, 410 S Michigan

Built by Solon Beman in 1885, this building was once home to the Studebaker carriage and automobile showrooms. In 1917 it was reconstructed by Andrew Rebori as a home for the arts. Small music and literary companies still dominate its floors. Check out the murals on the 10th floor and the inner light well, overlooked by interior balconies. The rough stone exterior base was widely copied by neighboring buildings.

❼ Auditorium Building, 430 S Michigan

This 1889 building, designed by Louis Sullivan with Dankmar Adler, is one of the city's greatest. Behind its granite and limestone facade hides a magnificent 4300-seat theater with some of the best acoustics and sight lines in the city. Originally a hotel and office space, it is now largely occupied by Roosevelt University. The 10th-floor library was once an ornate restaurant. Inquire about viewing the theater, which still hosts performances. The arcade on Congress Parkway was created when the sidewalk was sacrificed for the widening of the road in the 1950s.

❽ Harold Washington Library Center, 400 S State

The building named after the man dubbed 'the people's mayor' (see the sidebar of that name in Facts about Chicago) is appropriately enough 'the people's library': The city invited several architectural firms to submit designs, which were displayed in the Chicago Cultural Center (see Part One) for several months in 1989. Thousands of citizens inspected the competing proposals and voted for their choice. Robustly traditional, with details derived from many classic Chicago forms, this 1991 Hammond Beeby & Babka building was the winner. Note the whimsical copper roof details, including studious-looking owls.

RAY HILLSTROM
Detail on the Harold Washington Library Center

Part Three: Architecture 101

Think of this march north on Dearborn St as an introductory course in architecture: in six blocks you'll find major works representing more than 100 years of architecture. The route passes several public sculptures (see the Chicago's Front Yard sidebar in the Things to See & Do chapter).

From the library, walk one block west under the El on Van Buren St to Dearborn.

❶ Old Colony Building, 407 S Dearborn

The rounded corner bays on this 1894 tower, designed by Holabird & Roche, were once a common architectural feature. This building is the sole survivor of that era.

❷ Fisher Building, 343 S Dearborn

The main structure of this yellowish terra cotta-clad building was completed in 1896; the simpler northern addition was added in 1907. Inspired by the name of the developer, Lucius G Fisher, architect Daniel Burnham gave the exterior a playful menagerie of fish, crabs, shells and other sea creatures.

RICK GERHARTER
Monadnock Building

❸ Monadnock Building, 53 W Jackson

Really two structures, an 1891 northern portion and an 1893 southern addition, this building can be considered the Loop Lourdes for architecture buffs on a pilgrimage: together the two parts compose the nonmissing link in American skyscraper development. The original portion of the building was constructed entirely with load-bearing walls that are six feet wide at the base. Working with brick, architects Burnham & Root fashioned a free-flowing facade from base to cornice that becomes almost sensuous around the bottoms of the window bays. Having reached the realistic limits for that type of construction, the addition was built with a then-revolutionary metal frame.

④ Chicago Federal Center, Dearborn between Jackson & Adams

Ludwig Mies van der Rohe gave this complex his signature austere look in his original 1959 design. In 1964 the 30-story Dirksen Building was the first completed, and it holds the federal courts. The 42-story Kluczynski Building came along in 1974 and is home to various federal agencies. The post office, finished the same year, completes the troika and was designed to be as tall as the lobbies in its two neighbors. *Flamingo*, a bright red sculpture by Alexander Calder, provides a counterpunch to Mies' ebony palette.

⑤ Marquette Building, 140 S Dearborn

Above its massive base, the Marquette is really an E-shaped building facing north. When it was designed by Holabird & Roche in 1893, natural light and ventilation were vital considerations, owing to the skimpy light bulbs and nonexistent mechanical ventilation of the time. The same firm was hired for the building's 1980 renovation. Sculptured panels above the entrance and in the lobby by Tiffany and others recall the exploits of French explorer and missionary Jacques Marquette.

RICK GERHARTER

Kluczynski Building, Chicago Federal Center

RICK GERHARTER

Marquette Building

RICK GERHARTER
First National Bank of Chicago

⑥ Inland Steel Building, 30 W Monroe

Completed in 1958, this Skidmore, Owings & Merrill design was the first Loop high-rise with full central air-conditioning. Its innovations didn't stop there; the tower visible on Monroe St houses the elevators and mechanical services that allow the floors in the main portion of the stainless steel-clad structure to remain unbroken by columns.

⑦ First National Bank of Chicago, Dearborn between Monroe & Madison

The gracefully curving shape of this 60-story tower, designed by Perkins & Will and finished in 1969, gives the Midwest's largest bank a distinctive profile on the skyline. The multilevel plaza on Monroe is popular at lunchtime. Marc Chagall's mosaic *The Four Seasons* recently gained an architecturally sensitive weather cover.

⑧ Richard J Daley Center, Dearborn between Washington & Randolph

Another classic Chicago Miesian building, the 31-story Daley Center was called the Chicago Civic Center when it was completed by CF Murphy Associates in 1965. The building is clad in Cor-Ten steel, a type developed to never need paint: a layer of oxidation forms on the steel's surface, which protects it and gives the metal its distinctive bronze color. Inside, the scores of county courtrooms have ceilings two floors high. Besides hosting what Chicagoans refer to simply as 'the Picasso,' an untitled sculpture by the great 20th-century artist, the plaza is the scene of regular performances and protests.

RICK GERHARTER
The Picasso at the Richard J Daley Center

Part Four: Where the Deals Are Made

Government and finance coexist on LaSalle Street. Chicago's corporate heart extends west past Wacker Drive to the canyon of high-rises surrounding the south branch of the Chicago River.

At the northwest corner of the Daley Center, cross Clark and Randolph streets.

❶ James R Thompson Center, 100 W Randolph

This bulbous building was completed as the State of Illinois Center in 1986 and has a shape reminiscent of its namesake governor, who commissioned it. It has been controversial from the start, not just for its shape but for its all-glass design that extended deep inside. Architect Helmut Jahn thought the structure should be a metaphor for open government and left off doors, ceilings and walls from interior offices. The effect was to produce a vast greenhouse filled with overheated bureaucrats, who held up thermometers showing temperatures of 110°F and higher for a gleeful media. When the imperious Jahn took a tour of what he had wrought, he was confronted by a secretary who complained about her heat stroke. Jahn suggested she get a new job. Vastly improved air-conditioning has lowered temperatures, and everybody loves the soaring atrium lobby.

RICK GERHARTER

James R Thompson Center

❷ County Building & Chicago City Hall, 121 N LaSalle

Serving two government bodies, this 1911 Holabird & Roche building is adorned with 75-foot columns that were a challenge to construct and support. Chicago proclaims its political dominance over Cook

Interior, James R Thompson Center

County by giving its half of the building (the west) much richer fixtures. Enter through Randolph St and exit at LaSalle St.

⑤ 190 S LaSalle
New York architect Philip Johnson's sole contribution to Chicago (1987) bows heavily to long-gone Chicago architectural gems. The gabled roof is inspired by surrounding buildings and is best viewed from the Sears Tower Skydeck. The lobby, with its vaulted ceiling covered in gold leaf, is designed to impress the building's lawyer tenants and overwhelm their clients.

⑥ The Rookery, 209 S LaSalle
Named after the pigeons who used to nest here, the 1885-88 Rookery is one of Chicago's most beloved buildings. The original design by Burnham & Root, with its load-bearing granite and brick walls, sur-

Lobby, 190 S LaSalle

rounds a spectacular atrium space that was remodeled in 1907 by Frank Lloyd Wright. A lavish restoration in 1992 has returned the building to its peak grandeur.

RICK GERHARTER
Chicago Board of Trade

❺ Federal Reserve Bank, 230 S LaSalle; Bank of America, 231 S LaSalle

These buildings were constructed in 1922 and 1924, respectively, by Graham, Anderson, Probst & White. Their major exterior difference is that the federal building has Corinthian columns, while its sibling's are Ionic. Formerly the Illinois Merchants Bank and later Continental Illinois Bank, the Bank of America has a second-floor public banking area that would do any Roman god proud. In fact, when he saw the finished work, Louis Sullivan suggested that the bankers wear togas.

❻ Chicago Board of Trade, 141 W Jackson

The original 1930 Holabird & Root tower, fronting LaSalle St, is a classic 45-story Art Deco skyscraper topped with a statue of Ceres, the Roman goddess of agriculture. To the rear, a 1980 addition by Helmut Jahn nicely complements the original. Inside, the earlier building has

Inside the Rookery

RICK GERHARTER

a sumptuous lobby; the addition has a 12th-floor atrium featuring a classic mural of Ceres that once adorned the original's main trading floor.

⑦ Sears Tower, 233 S Wacker

The best view you'll have of this giant is from some other part of town. Up close all you can do is crane your neck and stare up at the dizzying height. By some factors still the world's tallest building (see the Tower Envy sidebar in Things to See & Do), this 110-story tower, completed in 1974, was executed by Skidmore, Owings & Merrill architect Bruce Graham and structural engineer Fazlur Khan. It consists of nine structural square 'tubes' that rise from the building's base, two stopping at the 50th floor, two more ending at the 66th floor, three more calling it quits at 90 stories and two stretching to the full height. Nobody ever liked the arrangement of the base, which mixed tourists with frazzled office

workers. A 1985 remodeling helped, adding the odd Wacker entrance, but it took a major 1992 reworking sparked by Sears' move to the suburbs to really fix things. The building is now owned by an investment trust; Sears' corporate headquarters will remain on Wacker until 2000 but may move after that.

RICK GERHARTER
Sears Tower

Part Five: The River

Walking toward Lake Michigan along the Chicago River is a quintessential Chicago experience. The rumble of the El trains crossing the river, the utilitarian charm of the drawbridges and the proliferation of proud buildings on both banks make it at once gritty and refined.

From the Sears Tower, cross the south branch of the Chicago River and walk north on the Riverwalk along the west bank. At Randolph, jog slightly west and continue one block to Lake St. Walk back across the river on the north side of the bridge and continue walking east along the south bank of the river.

❶ 333 Wacker Drive

Completed in 1983, this curving green structure is the most popular Loop tower to emerge from the 1980s building boom. It is a masterful utilization of the odd triangular site on the curve in the river. Water and sky play across the mirrored glass in an ever changing kaleidoscope of shapes and colors. Architect William E Pedersen's neighboring 1989 encore, at 225 W Wacker, is much more conventional.

ROBERT HOLMES

333 Wacker Drive

RICK GERHARTER

Merchandise Mart

2 Merchandise Mart, north bank of the river between Franklin & Wells

Completed in 1930 by Graham, Anderson, Probst & White as a wholesale store for Marshall Field & Co, the Merchandise Mart was converted into commercial space by the Kennedy family, who purchased it in 1945. Its 4.1 million sq feet are encased in the massive limestone exterior, which received a much needed cleaning in 1992. The less said about the 1977 Apparel Center immediately to the west, the better.

3 Helene Curtis Building, 325 N Wells

This 1914 warehouse was given a gaudy makeover by Booth/Hansen & Associates for the cosmetics giant in 1984. The green glass seems as out-of-place today as green eye shadow.

4 RR Donnelley Building, 77 W Wacker

Spanish architect Ricardo Bofill drew inspiration from Greek and Roman temples for this 50-story tower. Completed in 1992 as a last gasp of the '80s building boom, it has a lobby of white marble quarried in Greece, with works by artists from Bofill's native Catalonia, Spain.

5 Leo Burnett Building, 35 W Wacker

Chicago's largest ad agency commissioned Kevin Roche-John Dinkeloo & Associates for this 1989 building. The incongruous metal pillars don't really mesh with the building's other details, which suggest a squarish Prairie School column. As is increasingly common, the structure has not four corner offices per floor, but many, to accommodate the demands of legions of corporate vice presidents.

RICK GERHARTER

Looking west from the Michigan Ave Bridge: Marina City (left) and the IBM Building (center)

⑥ Marina City, north bank of the river between Dearborn & State

Dominated by its twin 'corncob' towers, this mixed-use complex designed by Bertrand Goldberg has had a mixed history since its completion in 1967. The condos that top the spiraling parking garages are quite popular and especially picturesque at Christmastime, when owners decorate the scalloped balconies with a profusion of lights. The marina at the foot of the complex does all right in the summer, but much of the rest of the space, intended for stores, restaurants, a bowling alley and other recreational·services, was mired in bankruptcy court until the House of Blues opened in the long-dead theater (see the Entertainment chapter). The moribund office building is slated to reopen as a blues-themed hotel.

⑦ IBM Building, 330 N Wabash

For many the signature office building by Mies van der Rohe, this 1971 tower was Mies' last American commission. His basic black gives way here to an almost radical combination of rich browns. The building and its breezy plaza are fastidiously maintained by its persnickety owner.

⑧ 75 E Wacker

Neighborless when completed by Herbert Hugh Riddle in 1928, this pencil of a building was even more dramatic when it stood alone. The 42 terra-cotta-clad floors reverse telescope right up to the pointy top.

RICK GERHARTER

75 E Wacker

Other Buildings of Note

Not everything grand about Chicago architecture is in the Loop or Near North. Areas and buildings of architectural significance can be found in Wrigleyville, Wicker Park, the Prairie Avenue District, the University of Chicago, and Oak Park. See those sections, and the Near North section, in Things to See & Do.

Amoco Building, 200 E Randolph, three blocks east of Michigan Ave

If it weren't in the aesthetic desert of Illinois Center (see the sidebar Five Ugly Buildings), the 80-story Amoco Building – Chicago's second tallest in overall height – might get some respect. Then again, it might not, owing to the comedy of errors that produced it. It is one of architecture's biggest technical miscues. When built in 1973 by Perkins & Will, the building was clad in marble from the same quarry Michelangelo used, at the insistence of Amoco's then chairman, John Swearingen, and his wife, Bonnie. To save money, the marble was cut more thinly than ever before, despite warnings from experts that, structurally, it was too weak to withstand the harsh Chicago climate. Within 15 years Amoco knew it had a problem when the marble began falling off the building's 1136-ft facade. The 43,000 panels covering the entire exterior had to be replaced with light-colored granite at a cost equal to the original construction.

RICK GERHARTER

The Tribune Tower (right) and its neighbor to the north, the Hotel Inter-Continental

Wrigley Building, 400 N Michigan at the river

The most photographed building in town was designed by Graham, Anderson, Probst & White with a Hollywood flair: the white terra cotta actually was cast in six shades, which brighten the closer they move to the top, insuring that the building pops out of the sky whether it's high noon or midnight. Lights from neighboring buildings and across the river provide the nocturnal glow. The 'main building' actually occupies almost half the space of the much-larger northern addition.

Both were designed and built between 1919 and 1924. The design combines European classicism with straightforward Chicago roots and makes for a grand entrance to the Magnificent Mile.

Tribune Tower, 435 N Michigan, across from the Wrigley Building

The self-proclaimed World's Greatest Newspaper was never one to let modesty get in the way of bombast. When it announced an architectural competition in 1922 for a new headquarters, the requirement was for 'the most beautiful office building in the world.' The winning entry, by Howells & Hood, was chosen from 264 submissions and borrowed elements of Gothic cathedrals such as flying buttresses and applied them to a skyscraper. That is especially apparent at the top of the building, where the purely decorative buttresses surround a small tower. As on cathedrals, carved figures surround the building's three-story entrance, although here they are from Aesop's fables rather than from the Scriptures. Completed in 1925, the tower gained its less-interesting addition to the north in 1934.

John Hancock Center, 875 N Michigan at Chestnut

Perhaps the most recognizable Chicago high-rise, the 100-story, 1127-foot Hancock Center combines, from bottom to top, shopping, parking, offices, condos, tourist attractions and broadcast transmitters. The first major collaboration of Skidmore, Owings & Merrill architect Bruce Graham and engineer Fazlur Khan, this 1969 building muscles its way into the sky atop a series of cross-braces. Looking at the exterior, you can see where the shorter residential floors begin at the 44th floor. Some apartments even have balconies recessed behind screens.

RICK GERHARTER

John Hancock Center

Architectural Tours

If the walking tours here have whetted your appetite for more in-depth explorations of Chicago architecture, you might want to look into taking a guided tour.

The Chicago Architecture Foundation (CAF; ☎ 312-922-3432) provides a veritable supermarket of Chicago architecture tours. It's worth checking with them to see what tours have been added to their ever-growing roster, which includes Bridgeport, Jackson Park and LaSalle St in the Loop. They have two offices ready to answer questions and sell you something neat: one is on the lower level of the John Hancock Center, 875 N Michigan, the other on the ground floor of the Santa Fe Center, 224 S Michigan.

CAF leads more than 65 **walking tours** of the city and suburbs. Two are offered daily from the Santa Fe Center and cost $10: Early Loop skyscrapers departing at 10 am, and Modern Buildings and Beyond, at 1:30 pm. The Hancock Center office dispatches a tour of N Michigan Ave daily at 10:30 am for $8. The tours last about two hours.

Ninety-minute **boat tours** led by CAF volunteers depart daily from early May through October from the southwest corner of the Michigan Ave Bridge and the Chicago River; they cost $18 (for reservations, call ☎ 312-902-1500). On a tour boat with a wide, open upper deck, the cruise explores both branches of the Chicago River. Besides the informed commentary, the best feature of the tour is the unusual view of the skyline you get from the south branch of the river near River City.

CAF also operates **bus tours** of Chicago, Prairie Ave, Hyde Park, Oak Park and other areas. During the summer they run architectural **bike tours**. Call for schedules.

The Chicago Office of Tourism (☎ 312-744-2400) rents an **audio tour** of the Loop that takes about 90 minutes to complete. For $5 plus a $50 deposit, you rent the tape and player and receive a map and booklet. To take the tour, go to the shop in the Chicago Cultural Center, 77 E Randolph. Tapes may be picked up and dropped off weekdays 10 am to 6 pm, Saturday 10 am to 5 pm, Sunday noon to 5 pm.

RICK GERHARTER

View of the Loop from Grant Park

Five Ugly Buildings

Along with world-class architectural triumphs, Chicago has some world-class duds. The following buildings may mess up the landscape, but at least they make their neighbors look good.

Illinois Center,
south of the Chicago River,
west of Michigan Ave

Not just one ugly building but a whole vast collection of them. This mixed-use development of offices, stores, apartments and hotels has triple-decker roads and other atrocities that completely spoil the view from the north bank of the Chicago River.

Marriott Hotel,
540 N Michigan at Ohio

Even John Buck, the big-time local developer who built this monolith, admits it's ugly. He's been negotiating to have it partially torn down.

Apparel Mart,
350 N Orleans, just west of the
Merchandise Mart

Check out the grime-streaked, windowless south side. This was commissioned by the same folks (the Kennedy clan of political fame) who own the regal Merchandise Mart next door.

1550 Lake Shore Drive

Who thought it would be smart to make the top of this high-priced condo look like a wicker basket?

Asbury Plaza, 750 N Dearborn

This structure breaks with high-rise apartment tradition by providing more walls than windows – the high-rise for people afraid of heights. It's a putrid green color too.

RICK GERHARTER
Illinois Center

RICK GERHARTER
Marriott Hotel

RICK GERHARTER
Apparel Mart

Facts for the Visitor

WHEN TO GO

Depending on what you want to do, it may be wise to plan your visit to Chicago around the seasons. Summer is often hot and humid, and winter is usually shockingly cold, especially when wind chill is factored in. Visitors should note two phrases endlessly repeated by local meteorologists: in summer, 'Cooler near the lake'; in winter, 'Warmer near the lake.'

January through March is the least busy time, when hotels and airfares are usually at their cheapest. Weather-wise it can be damp and cold or snowy for days on end. Temperatures in the teens are not uncommon, and combined with brisk winds they will guarantee that you spend a lot of time indoors.

RICK GERHARTER
An El train in the Loop

Spring can be mild and sunny or it can be an extension of winter. There will be a stretch of beautiful days in April and, conversely, some ugly gray days in June.

July is usually quite warm, but not as warm as August, when it can get really hot. This is the peak of the festival season, with major events taking place in the parks and neighborhoods every weekend. September can be the nicest month of the year, with reliably warm days. The start of the school year means crowds decline.

Fall can be quite nice, with trees in the parks changing color about the second week of October. Days will be mild, with nights increasingly frosty. From Thanksgiving until Christmas the city bustles with shoppers. The weather tends to be gray, and the temperature hovers around freezing.

See the Special Events section later in this chapter for a list of the major festivals you may wish to catch.

Besides the weather, another major consideration in your plans should be whether or not there will be a big convention or trade show in town during your visit. This is important to keep in mind if you will be staying at a hotel, because for major events there will simply be no room at the inn, anywhere. Even the dumps. However, if you don't need a hotel, don't worry. The city is so big, it easily accommodates even the largest influx of visitors.

WHAT TO BRING

Pack light, pack light, pack light. After doing that, take out half the stuff, shove it under the bed and depart for your trip. The first time you have to carry your stuff more than 20 feet, you'll thank me.

Chicago is a casual place. All but the most expensive restaurants will welcome you in anything better than rotten jeans and mangy shoes. Some sort of comfortable nonsneaker walking shoes, dark pants or skirt, and a casual shirt and sweater will cover you for 98% of what you might want to do. Though given the swings in temperature, plan for a few extremes; a pair of shorts and sandals could see comfy service from May through September. Winter wear should include warm and water-resistant shoes, a warm jacket, gloves, a scarf and as your mother may have nagged endlessly, 'Something for your head.'

Obviously, if hitting Charlie Trotter's, meeting clients, trying to impress skeptical in-laws or some other sartorially sensitive event is on your agenda, you'll want to bring something that involves a tie or black

Bad Dates

Following are dates of trade shows and expositions at McCormick Place that will soak up Chicago hotel rooms in much the same omnivorous manner an alderman soaks up graft. Note that just as payola can show up when you least expect it, so too can large events suddenly nab all available rooms.

1998

May 3 to 5 – Supermarket Convention
May 16 to 20 – National Restaurant Show
August 16 to 19 – National Hardware Show
November 8 to 12 – Pack Expo
November 29 to December 4 – Radiological Society Meeting

1999

April 19 to 22 – Comdex Software Show
May 2 to 4 – Supermarket Convention
May 22 to 26 – National Restaurant Show
June 14 to 16 – National Cable Television Association Convention
August 15 to 18 – National Hardware Show
October 28 to 31 – Worldwide Food Expos
November 28 to December 3 – Radiological Society Meeting

2000

April 17 to 20 – Comdex Software Show
May 20 to 24 – National Restaurant Show
June 19 to 23 – Plastics Exposition
August 13 to 16 – National Hardware Show
October 14 to 17 – American Dental Association
November 5 to 9 – Pack Expo
November 26 to December 1 – Radiological Society Meeting

To find out if your intended visit coincides with a major show, you can try to call the Chicago Convention and Tourism Bureau (☎ 312-567-8000), but these folks – the ones who market McCormick Place – may not give you complete information on upcoming shows because of contractual agreements. The best sources are probably the major convention hotels, such as the Hyatt, Sheraton and the Hiltons. If they have rooms for the dates of your visit, then most other places will as well. ■

dress. And of course, there's casual and then there's casual. Wandering around shopping or doing most anything else in nylon sweats that look like they were salvaged from a crashed helium balloon will convince everyone that you really are a rube.

Sunglasses are good to carry throughout the year, especially in the winter: when it gets sunny after a snowstorm, you'll want to avoid going blind. In the toiletry and personal-items department, be most concerned about things special to you, such as prescriptions that might be difficult to fill away from home. One bit of advice I've been giving people for years is to carry the prescription for their eyeglasses or contact lenses with them. If in a jet-lagged stupor you step on your glasses or send your contacts swirling down the drain, you can get them replaced in about an hour at Lenscrafters (☎ 312-819-0205), 205 N Michigan (Map 3), a somewhat pricey but very quick store with its own lab.

One consolation should you forget something or find yourself unprepared for a drastic climatic swing is that you can buy anything you want quite easily, and visitors from abroad will likely pay less than at home. See the Shopping chapter for plenty of details.

Finally, if your hotel has a pool or Jacuzzi, bring a bathing suit. The lake is always open for swimmers, although those who aren't members of the Polar Bear Club (and don't want to hack a hole in the ice in January) will find it most accommodating from late June through mid-September. See the Lakefront section in Things to See & Do for details on beaches.

ORIENTATION

Chicago will be the easiest city you've ever navigated outside of your hometown. Thanks to Edward P Brennan (see Why You Can't Get Lost), the streets follow a logic that is incongruous with the town's turbulent and colorful history.

RICK GERHARTER

Ground zero

The intersection of Madison and State Sts is ground zero in a numbering system that lets you navigate without knowing any street names. From that point, all street numbers are predicated on north, south, east or west, depending on which way they radiate. If you tell me to meet you at 800 West and 3200 North, I will show up at Halsted St and Belmont Ave.

The numbers follow a system that remains constant through the city. 1600 W Madison is the same distance west as 1600 W Chicago. Each increase of 800 in numbers corresponds to a mile. For every increase of 400, there is a major arterial street. For instance, Division (1200 N) is

followed by North (1600 N) and Armitage (2000 N) and so on. Most arterial streets have their own CTA bus line.

Most of the streets are arranged true to the compass: north-south streets run due north and due south. A few major streets, such as Clark, Lincoln and Milwaukee, are arranged on diagonals.

Chicago is known as a 'city of neighborhoods.' You will soon discover there is not a square meter of the city that doesn't have some moniker, such as the Gold Coast, Lake View, Wrigleyville and many, many others. Neighborhood boundaries are sometimes defined by residents down to the inch, while others, such as that between Wicker Park and Bucktown, are open for broad interpretation. Neighborhood names are shown on the maps, and I have used them where appropriate to organize chapters.

MAPS

Maps are widely sold at hotels, drug stores, and newsstands. Rand McNally's 'Chicago' is the most popular, but it doesn't show El lines or stations and is better for driving than walking or touring. It also hasn't kept up to date with roadway developments in the River North and lakefront areas. And it calls Walton St 'Walnut.'

Why You Can't Get Lost

As you make your way through Chicago's orderly system of streets and numbers, radiating from ground zero at State and Madison Sts, you can thank the persistence and zeal of a frustrated bill collector for your ease of navigation. Scouring the city in search of deadbeats, Edward P Brennan got fed up trying to decide which of the city's ten Oak Streets or thirteen Washington Streets or eight 42nds might contain the address he was looking for. And those were just a few of his problems. Some streets changed their names every few blocks, and house numbers followed no set pattern.

In 1901, Brennan proposed a new system based on a regular grid and numbering system. Exhibiting a timeless skepticism of the Chicago City Council's ability to discern the wisdom of the plan, Brennan said of his proposal, [It] may be another job for the undertaker, as its fate is likely to be early death and burial.'

To his surprise, however, the plan was adopted and implemented beginning in 1909. During the next 30 years, Brennan attended more than 600 council meetings to see his plan to maturity, and after researching figures in the city's short history he renamed 300 duplicate street names. The only memorial to this toil – for which he refused payment – is a short street named Brennan Ave in Beverly at 2300 East, from 9600 South to 9772 South. ■

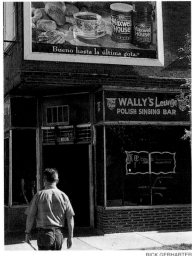
RICK GERHARTER
¿Kielbasa o café?

Some other laminated maps cover only the Loop and Near North, but there's no reason you should restrict yourself to those neighborhoods. Many of the free maps found at the tourist information office, on brochure racks, in visitor magazines and such suffer the same short-sighted restrictions on territory.

The maps in this book are quite comprehensive. You'll really need to supplant them only if you have serious exploration in mind; if that's the case, look for a map that includes the whole city and also shows the El. I couldn't find one, but you might.

TOURIST OFFICES
In the City
The main Visitor Information Center is in the Chicago Cultural Center (☎ 312-744-2400, TTY 312-744-2947), just to the left as you enter at 77 E Randolph at Michigan (Map 3). They have hundreds of brochures and booklets, and maps of varying quality. The staff will endeavor to answer your questions as well. The center also has a rotating display of works by local artists, and it has tables and chairs so you can sit down with your piles of information and figure things out.

The city has two more Visitor Information Centers: in the historic Water Tower at 806 N Michigan (Map 5) (this is the pretty old Water Tower, *not* the mammoth shopping center) and near the main entrance to Navy Pier (Map 3).

You may see other signs proclaiming 'Visitor Information,' but they indicate booths run by tour companies, and the information they provide comes after you've purchased tickets.

Hotel rooms usually come with free visitor magazines such as *Where*. Note the correlation between advertising and editorial before you rely solely on them for advice.

In Advance
For information about events such as festivals and exhibitions, contact the Chicago Office of Tourism office at the Chicago Cultural Center (☎ 312-744-2400, or from anywhere in North America 800-487-2446), 78 E Washington, Chicago, IL 60602 USA. Also check out the Internet Resources appendix at the back of the book for scores of sites filled with information about the city.

For the dates of the most obscure events check with the Mayor's Office of Special Events (☎ 312-744-3315), 121 N LaSalle, Room 703, Chicago, IL 60602 USA.

For information geared toward meetings and conventions, try the Chicago Convention and Tourism Bureau (☎ 312-567-8528, or 312-567-8500 for an automated system that will fax you information you request), 2301 S Lake Shore Drive, Chicago, IL 60616 USA.

There is also the Illinois Bureau of Tourism (☎ 312-814-4732, in North America 800-226-6632), 100 W Randolph, Suite 3-400, Chicago, IL 60601 USA, a well-funded operation that can provide information for both the city and surrounding region.

DOCUMENTS
Passports
With the exception of Canadians, who need only proof of Canadian citizenship with photo ID, all visitors to the US must have a

Winter scene on the river

Although most visitors to the US have no problem entering the country, you should tread carefully from the time you exit your international flight until you have passed through all the formalities and are in the actual arrivals area of the terminal. In addition to the INS people, who will inspect your passport and 'papers,' you will encounter customs officials, who may search your bags, and a Drug Enforcement Agency dog that may sniff your leg and luggage.

The vast majority of these personnel are polite, and in the case of the animals, well behaved. However, if you have problems with any of them, the last thing you should do is argue or otherwise cause them further irritation. The simple truth is that until you have passed through the last formality, you have few if any rights. If various government officers so desire, they can find an excuse to detain you and make your life miserable. It is not uncommon for foreign nationals to be detained for hours over minor procedural questions. If that happens, try to get word to an airline official or even another traveler, who can then notify the people waiting for you outside.

If you are a person of color, the ugly truth is that the odds of being questioned, searched or having your luggage inspected are greater. All the agencies involved will vigorously deny that, but I spent a lot of time with these inspectors and agents for a news story once, and they all confirmed, far off the record, that this is exactly what happens. If it does, endure the procedure without complaint. If you feel especially aggrieved, contact one of the news agencies listed in the Media section (you'll find their phone numbers and addresses in the Chicago phone book) and tell them your story. They're always looking for juicy examples of government malfeasance.

The drinking age of 21 is universally enforced. If reality or nature allows you to pass for younger than 35, bring some form of age identification with you when you go out (such as a passport) so as to assuage the concerns of any bouncers you might encounter.

valid passport and may also require a US visa (see the next section). Check these regulations carefully with the US embassy in your country before you depart. Conservatives in the US government have enacted legislation that allows Immigration and Naturalization Service (INS) officials at airports to toss you in jail overnight and then ship you home on the first flight out without a chance for appeal.

Your passport should be valid for at least six months longer than your intended stay in the US, and you'll need to submit a recent photo with your visa application. Documents of financial stability or guarantees from a US resident (in special cases, the INS can demand that someone entering the country be 'sponsored' by a citizen who promises to provide them with financial support) are sometimes required, particularly for people from Third World nations.

Visas

A reciprocal visa-waiver program applies to citizens of certain countries, who may enter the US for stays of 90 days or fewer without having to obtain a visa. Currently these countries are Andorra, Austria, Belgium, Brunei, Denmark, Finland, France, Germany, Iceland, Italy, Japan, Liechtenstein, Luxembourg, Monaco, the Netherlands, New Zealand, Norway, San Marino, Spain, Sweden, Switzerland, and the UK. Under the visa-waiver program, you must have a round-trip ticket on an airline that participates in the program; you need proof of financial solvency, such as credit cards, a bank account with evidence of a balance beyond two figures or employment in your home country; you must sign a form waiving the right to a hearing over deportation (!); and you will not be allowed to extend your stay beyond 90 days. Consult with your airline or the closest US consulate or embassy for more information.

Other travelers (except those from Canada) will need to obtain a visa from a US consulate or embassy. In most countries the process can be done by mail, but in some, notably Turkey, Poland and Russia, you'll need to go to a US consulate or embassy in person. Visa applicants may be required to 'demonstrate binding obligations' that will ensure their return back home. Because of this requirement, those planning to travel through other countries before arriving in the US are generally better off applying for their US visa while still in their home country, rather than while on the road.

The validity period for US visitor visas depends on what country you're from. The length of time you'll be allowed to stay in the US is ultimately determined by the INS officers at the port of entry, such as an airport.

Visa Extensions Tourists using visas are usually granted a six-month stay on first arrival. If you try to extend that time, the first assumption will be that you are working illegally (an assumption often right on the mark), so come prepared with concrete evidence that you've been behaving like a model tourist: receipts to demonstrate you've been spending lots of your money from home in the US, or ticket stubs that show you've been traveling extensively. Visa extensions in Chicago are pondered at the INS office (☎ 312-353-7335, 800-755-0777), in the Kluczynski Building in the Federal Center at 10 W Jackson (Map 3).

HIV & Entering the US

Anyone entering the US who is not a US citizen is subject to the authority of the INS, which has the final say about whether you enter or not and has full power to send you back to where you came from. Being HIV-positive is not grounds for deportation, but it is grounds for exclusion. What this means is that once in the US, you cannot be deported for being HIV-positive, but you can be prevented from *entering* the US.

The INS does not test people for HIV when they try to enter the US, but the form for nonimmigrant visas asks, 'Have you ever been afflicted with a communicable disease of public health significance?' If you answer yes to this question, the INS may try to exclude you when you reach the US.

If you are HIV-positive but can prove to the consular officials to whom you have applied for a visa that you are the spouse, parent or child of a US citizen or legal resident (green-card holder), you are exempt from the exclusionary rule.

For legal information and referrals to immigrant advocates, potential visitors should contact the National Immigration Project of the National Lawyers Guild (☎ 617-227-9727), 14 Beacon St Suite 506, Boston, MA 02108, and the Immigrant HIV Assistance Project, Bar Association of San Francisco (☎ 415-267-0795), 685 Market St Suite 700, San Francisco, CA 94105. ■

Photocopies

Whatever documents you're required to bring, carry photocopies of them separately from the originals. This will speed replacement in case the originals are lost or stolen. It's also a good idea to leave photocopies of each of your travel documents with someone at home.

Other Documents

Travel Insurance No matter how you're traveling, make sure you take out travel insurance. This should cover you not only for medical expenses and luggage theft or loss, but also for cancellations or delays in your travel arrangements, and everyone should be covered for the worst possible case, such as an accident that requires hospital treatment and a flight home. Coverage depends on your insurance and type of ticket, so ask both your insurer and your ticket-issuing agency to explain the finer points. STA Travel and Council Travel offer travel insurance options at reasonable prices. Ticket loss is also covered by travel insurance. Make sure you have a separate record of all your ticket details – or better still, a photocopy of it. Also make a copy of your policy, in case the original is lost.

Buy travel insurance as early as possible. If you buy it the week before you fly, you may find, for instance, that you're not covered for delays to your flight caused by strikes or other industrial action that may have been in force before you took out the insurance.

Driver's License & Permits Planning to drive? Bring your driver's license and check with your country's national auto club to see if they recommend obtaining an International Driver's License. Note that this document alone won't let you drive; you will need a valid license from your home country as well.

Student Cards If you are a student, by all means obtain and carry an International Student Identification Card (ISIC), which can get you substantial discounts at museums, tourist attractions and on some train and plane fares.

EMBASSIES & CONSULATES
US Embassies Abroad
US diplomatic offices abroad include the following:

Australia
21 Moonah Place
Yarralumla ACT 2600
(☎ 6-270-5900)
There are consulates in Melbourne, Perth and Sydney.

Canada
100 Wellington St,
Ottawa, K1P 5T1
(☎ 613-238-5335)
There are consulates in Calgary, Halifax, Montreal, Toronto and Vancouver.

France
2 rue Saint Florentin
75001 Paris
(☎ 01-42-96-12-02)
There is a consulate in Marseilles.

Germany
Deichmanns Aue 29
53179 Bonn
(☎ 228-3391)
There are consulates in Berlin, Frankfurt, Hamburg and Munich.

Ireland
42 Elgin Rd, Ballsbridge
Dublin
(☎ 1-687-122)

Japan
1-10-5 Akasaka chome
Minato-Ku, Tokyo
(☎ 3-3224-5000)
There are consulates in Fukuoka, Osaka-Kobe and Sapporo.

Mexico
Paseo de la Reforma 305
06500 Mexico City
(☎ 5-211-0042)
There are consulates in Ciudad Juárez, Guadalajara, Hermosillo, Matamoros, Mérida, Monterrey and Tijuana.

New Zealand
29 Fitzherbert Terrace
Thorndon, Wellington
(☎ 4-722-068)
There is a consulate in Auckland.

UK
5 Upper Grosvenor St
London W1
(☎ 0171-499-9000)
There are consulates in Belfast, Northern Ireland, and Edinburgh, Scotland.

CUSTOMS

International travelers will be familiar with the red and green line system at O'Hare. Those with nothing to declare can opt for the green line and hope they are not singled out for a spot check.

Those with something to declare should definitely do so, because if you try to smuggle something in – especially drugs – and are caught, your day will immediately go downhill. Remember, until you clear all the formalities, you have no rights.

Non-United States citizens over the age of 21 are allowed to import one liter of liquor and 200 cigarettes duty free. Gifts may amount to no more than $100 in value.

You may bring any amount of money less than $10,000 into or out of the US without declaration. Amounts greater than $10,000 must be declared. There is no legal limit to the amount of US and foreign cash and traveler's checks you can bring in, but undeclared amounts of more than $10,000 can be confiscated.

MONEY

Nothing works like cash, but in the US you will find that most forms of payment are welcomed. How to get cash is another matter. Read below to consider your options.

Currency

US currency is the only one accepted in Chicago. The dollar ($) is divided into 100 cents (¢). Coins come in the following denominations, with these names and descriptions:

1¢ – penny, copper colored
5¢ – nickel, fat and silver colored
10¢ – dime, the smallest coin, thin and silver colored
25¢ – quarter, silver colored with rough edges
50¢ – half-dollar, larger than a quarter and silver colored, with a profile of John F Kennedy
$1 – dollar, comes in one of two coins, neither as common as the dollar bill: a large, silver-colored coin with a profile of Dwight D Eisenhower (often called a silver dollar), or almost quarter-size, with a profile of Susan B Anthony (called the Susan B Anthony Dollar)

Consulates in Chicago

Chicago is well-served with foreign consulates – check the Yellow Pages under Consulates. Australia closed its Chicago consulate in a budgetary cutback in the early 1990s. The closest representation is the embassy in Washington, DC, at 501 Pennsylvania Ave NW, Washington, DC 20001 (☎ 202-682-1740).

Canada
180 N Stetson Ave,
Suite 2400
(☎ 312-616-1860)

France
737 N Michigan Ave,
Suite 2020
(☎ 312-787-5359)

Germany
676 N Michigan Ave,
Suite 3200
(☎ 312-580-1199)

Ireland
400 N Michigan Ave,
Suite 911 (☎ 312-337-1868)

Japan
737 N Michigan Ave,
Suite 1100
(☎ 312-280-0400)

Mexico
300 N Michigan Ave,
Suite 200
(☎ 312-855-1380)

Poland
1530 N Lake Shore Drive
(☎ 312-337-8166)

South Africa
200 S Michigan Ave,
Suite 600
(☎ 312-939-7929)

Sweden
150 N Michigan Ave, Suite 1250
(☎ 312-781-6262)

UK
33 N Dearborn St, Suite 900
(☎ 312-346-1810)

You are unlikely to see either the half-dollar or dollar coins, unless you go gambling and play the slots.

Bills – paper currency – are confusing to many foreign visitors. They are all the same size and color, regardless of denomination. Be careful to check the denomination in the corners of the bills so you don't pay the wrong amount or receive the wrong amount in change. Bills come in denominations of $1, $2 (rare), $5, $10, $20, $50 and $100. Many places won't accept bills larger than $20, so if you are going out, break large bills at your hotel or a bank.

In 1996, the US Treasury began redesigning the bills to thwart counterfeiters, starting with the $100 bill and proceeding down through the valuations, one bill each year. Old-design currency remains valid during the process. If you receive one of the new $100 bills, which have large, off-center portraits, unlike the other US bills, see if you agree with many who insist that Ben Franklin looks flatulent.

As for carrying money, you should do so as you would at home. If you have more than a few hundred dollars in cash, it would be prudent to place it in a hotel safe. But you can avoid that whole problem by using an ATM card to withdraw only a few days' worth of cash at a time (see ATMs).

Traveler's Checks
Traveler's checks are usually just as good as cash in the US, provided they are in US dollars. Most places will accept them as long as you sign them in front of the cashier, waiter, etc. However, if your traveler's checks are in a foreign currency, you will have to get them exchanged, which is a major hassle (see the Currency Exchange section below).

The advantage of traveler's checks is that they can be replaced if they are lost or stolen. Get them in denominations of $100, so you don't have to carry a fat wad, but be aware that the rules about large bills, mentioned in the previous section, also apply to traveler's checks. Be sure to keep a record of the numbers on your traveler's checks separate from the checks themselves, so if you lose them you can get them replaced.

Finally, even if you plan to get cash using your ATM card or to charge everything on your credit card, it is a good idea to have some backup funds in the form of traveler's checks, in case your card stops working, is eaten by an ATM or falls victim to some other calamity.

ATMs
The vast majority of ATMs in Chicago operate under the 'Cash Station' moniker. You will find them almost everywhere – in convenience stores, gas stations, shopping malls, bars and even banks. In the central part of the city, there's always one within a block or two. If in doubt of where to look, remember that the ubiquitous Jewel grocery stores, White Hen Pantry convenience stores, and First Chicago bank branches are all equipped with Cash Stations.

The Cash Station network is linked up with Cirrus and Plus, the two largest ATM networks worldwide. In addition, they'll cheerfully accept your MasterCard or Visa for cash advances. Some will also take your American Express card, and still others will take Discover as well. Because banks can now dock your account up to $3 for using a nonlocal card, they are all too happy to have these little devices to accept any card you might offer; ATMs have become profit centers. Foreign visitors should note that the exchange rate with an ATM is usually the very best available, much better than what you'll get with traveler's checks. However, fees for using your card may nullify that advantage.

Wherever you're from, be sure to check with your card issuer to confirm that it will work. At the very least you need to have a four-digit password. Finally, there have been some well-publicized robberies of people using ATMs, so exercise your usual amount of caution when taking money out.

Credit Cards
Major credit cards are widely accepted by car rental firms, hotels, restaurants, gas stations, shops, large grocery stores, movie theaters, ticket vendors and other places. In fact you'll find certain transactions impos-

sible to perform without a credit card: you can't reserve theater or other event tickets by phone without one, nor can you guarantee room reservations by phone or rent a car. Even if you want to avoid running up a huge balance that takes the balance of your life to pay off, it is good to have a major credit card in case of an emergency. In bars and nightclubs, cash is still the best bet.

The most commonly accepted cards are Visa and MasterCard. American Express is widely accepted, but not as universally as the first two. Discover and Diners Club cards are usually good for travel tickets, hotels and rental cars, but are less commonly accepted in other situations.

Currency Exchange

Shortly after arriving in Chicago, you will begin noticing there are garishly lit 'currency exchanges' on many street corners. They are not what you might think. They are primarily for people without bank accounts who 'exchange' their 'currency' in return for services such as money orders or check-cashing. If you slip your German marks, French francs or other currency under the bulletproof divider at a currency exchange, they will come sliding right back, possibly with an ill-tempered tirade from the clerk.

To convert currency from other nations into dollars, you need a foreign exchange broker. These are not common, so when you find one (see the next section), exchange enough cash to take care of your needs for a while. And if you plan to travel to smaller towns beyond Chicago, exchange a lot of money before leaving. (This is the one case where it would be advisable to change a lot of money.)

Finally, don't worry about shopping around for exchange rates; they're not very good anywhere, because of the lack of competition. That is another reason to consider using your ATM card to obtain funds. You might also consider changing money into dollars before you leave home; since exchange rates in the US are so bad, this usually ill-advised practice is not so fiscally ruinous.

Foreign Exchange Brokers The arrivals area of Terminal 5, the international terminal at O'Hare, has a foreign exchange service that is generally open for incoming flights.

In the city itself there are a few choices; call to check hours before setting out: American Express has exchange services that favor its cardholders or people carrying its brand of traveler's checks. Look for them at 122 S Michigan (☎ 312-435-2595; Map 3), 625 N Michigan (☎ 312-435-2570; Map 3) and 2338 N Clark, in Lincoln Park (☎ 773-477-4000; Map 6).

Thomas Cook Currency Services has two locations: 111 W Washington, in the Loop (☎ 312-236-0042; Map 3), and 100 E Walton, in the Gold Coast (☎ 312-649-0288; Map 5).

World's Money Exchange (☎ 312-641-2151), above Walgreens at 6 E Randolph (Map 3), has the largest selection of foreign currency, accepting bills from 120 countries.

Chicago's largest bank, First Chicago, will chase you off if you proffer them foreign currency. Try bringing it to American National Bank & Trust (☎ 312-661-5000), 1 N LaSalle at Madison (Map 3), and Northern Trust Bank (☎ 312-630-6000), 50 S LaSalle (Map 3).

Don't expect good rates from these places, but do expect high fees.

At press time, exchange rates were:

Australia	A$1	=	$0.64
Canada	C$1	=	$0.70
France	FF1	=	$0.16
Germany	DM1	=	$0.55
Hong Kong	HK$10	=	$0.13
Japan	¥75	=	$1
New Zealand	NZ$1	=	$0.56
United Kingdom	UK£1	=	$1.63

Costs

People moving to Chicago from New York get down on their knees and kiss the ground the first time they find out how little the apartments cost. Such budgetary enthusiasm extends to other expenses as well, for Chicago is moderate in cost compared to other US urban areas. You can eat very well for $20 a day. Pints of beer average $3, and since you can walk most places, transportation costs are low. (The multitudes of reasons not to have a car in the city are thoroughly documented in the Getting Around chapter.)

Unless you visit at a nonpeak time, you will have a hard time finding bargains on accommodations. But if money is no object, you will find no shortage of world-class hotels, restaurants, shops and more. Enjoy!

Tipping

Tipping is a US institution that can be confusing to foreign visitors (just as the tipping habits in their countries confound American visitors). Wait staff in restaurants, hotel maids, valet car parkers, bartenders, bellhops and others are paid a mere pittance and expect to make it up through tips. So customers are expected to tip them, and indeed, their taxes are based on the assumption that they will be tipped. There's no reason to feel sorry for people working for tips; I know many waiters who make a small fortune because they are good at what they do. And of course, working for tips does contribute to a service worker's desire to deliver good service.

So you have to tip, unless the service is really *appalling*. I have been tempted not to leave a tip just a couple of times. But whom to tip? And how much?

Bartenders – 15%, left in change as you pay for your drinks.

Bellhops – From $2 total to $1 a bag or more, depending on the distance covered.

Cocktail servers – At least 10% to 15%, when you pay for the drinks.

Concierges – Nothing for answering a simple question, to $5 or more for securing tickets to a sold-out show.

Doormen – $1 to $2 for summoning you a cab, depending on the weather.

Hotel maids – $1 to $2 a day, left on the pillow each day.

Restaurant wait staff – 15% is standard, 20% if you're really pleased with the service. An easy rule is to double the tax.

Skycaps – At least $1 per bag.

Taxi drivers – 10% to 15%, even if the individual needs immediate psychiatric attention.

Valet car parkers – $2 when the keys to the car are handed to you.

Whom not to tip: cashiers, ticket vendors working in booths, hotel front desk employees.

Taxes

You will encounter a thicket of taxes as you spend money in Chicago. Sadly for the visitor, many of the taxes are aimed right at you, since you can't vote for (or against) the local politicians who impose them. Calculate the taxes into your budget estimates, because along with tips, they can greatly increase your costs.

The basic sales tax is 8.75%. Some grocery items are taxed at only 2%. Newspapers and magazines, but not books, are tax free. The hotel tax is 14.9%; the car-rental tax is 18%.

POST & COMMUNICATIONS
Mail

The good news is that compared to other countries, sending mail in the US is cheap. The bad news is that Chicago regularly finishes dead last in the US Postal Service's own rankings of service quality. If you're lucky you won't have to wait for any mail to be delivered to you while you are in Chicago; otherwise, you might never leave. Mail carriers are regularly arrested for throwing away mail they didn't feel like delivering.

Letters mailed within the city are often delivered the next day; within the Midwest, two to three days; to the coasts, four to five days; and overseas starts at seven and climbs from there.

Postal Rates Rates rise frequently. In 1997 it cost 32¢ to mail a one-ounce first-class letter within the US. Each additional ounce cost 20¢. Post cards cost 20¢.

International rates (except for those to Canada and Mexico, which are slightly cheaper) were 60¢ for a half-ounce letter, 95¢ for the full ounce and 39¢ for each additional half-ounce. Post cards cost 40¢, aerogrammes 50¢.

Parcels mailed to foreign destinations from the US are subject to a variety of rates. First class can be very expensive. If you're not in a hurry and have stuff you

RAY HILLSTROM

Sunset city

don't want to lug around, consider fourth class, which goes by boat. Those rates can be very low, but delivery to Europe, for instance, takes six to eight weeks. If all you are sending is printed matter such as books, you qualify for an extra-cheap rate.

Receiving Mail You can have mail sent to you care of 'General Delivery' at any post office that has its own ZIP (postal) code. It helps to have your intended date of pickup marked on the envelope ('hold until June 3'), although items are usually held for 30 days before being returned to the sender. See the next section for post office addresses.

Clients of American Express and Thomas Cook can avail themselves of those companies' mail services. Before your trip, check with them for the address you should have people use to reach you at their Chicago offices.

Post Offices The following three post offices have a full range of services and accept general delivery mail. Try to avoid them at lunchtime on weekdays, when they are swamped.

Main Post Office, 433 W Harrison, Chicago, IL 60607 (☎ 312-654-3895; Map 3)
Loop Station, 211 S Clark, Chicago, IL 60604 (☎ 312-427-4225; Map 3)
Fort Dearborn, 540 N Dearborn, Chicago, IL 60610 (☎ 312-644-7603; Map 3)

Telephone
Area Codes The city has two area codes, with more soon to come as the proliferation of pagers, faxes and Internet connections sops up the available supply of numbers. The area code 312 serves the Loop and an area bounded roughly by 1600 North, 1600 West and 1600 South. The rest of the city is

area code 773. The northern suburbs are area code 847, those close to the west and the south 708, and the far west suburbs 630.

Dialing All phone numbers within the US and Canada consist of the three-digit area code followed by a seven-digit local number. If you are calling locally, just dial the seven-digit number. If you are calling to another area code, dial 1 + the three-digit area code + the seven-digit local number. In the city, if you don't use the area code when you should or you do use it when you shouldn't – both of which are common mistakes – you'll get an ear-shattering screech, followed by advice on what to dial.

The country code for the US is 1. The international access code is 011 for calls you dial directly, 01 for calls made collect or on a calling card; dial it first, before you dial the country code.

Calls that are free have area codes of 800 or 888. Numbers that begin with 900 are charged at a premium rate. You most often will see them advertised late at night on TV in ads asking, 'Lonely? Want to have some hot talk?'

Local directory assistance can be reached by calling ☎ 411 or ☎ 555-1212. If you are looking for a number out of your local area code and are sure of the code it's in, dial ☎ 1 + the area code + 555-1212. These calls are no longer free, even from pay phones, which no longer have phone books.

To obtain a toll-free number, dial ☎ 800-555-1212.

Pay Phones Coin phones have been deregulated and charge what the market will bear. A variety of companies operate them. Those from Ameritech are by far the most reliable and cost 35¢. Some pay phones are operated by companies just this side of crooks. If you try to make a long-distance call using their phones and punch in your credit card or calling card number, you will later be horrified that the operator charged you $5 a minute, or some extortionist rate.

American pay phones have not yet adopted the convenient card technology found elsewhere. Have plenty of quarters, dimes and nickels ready (but see the Prepaid Calling Cards section).

Hotel Phones The paradox about calling from your hotel room is that the cheaper the hotel, the more likely phone calls from your room are to be free. On the dubious theory that if you're paying $300 a night for your room then you won't mind being gouged for a call, some of the very best hotels nick you for $1.50 every time you pick up the receiver, even for local or toll-free calls.

Long Distance Hundreds of companies compete for your long-distance business. If you are using a pay phone, check to see which carrier is the default long-distance provider (the company's name is listed in very small type on the rate card, displayed on every phone). Sprint, MCI and AT&T are not the very cheapest, but they refrain from scams. You should do the same thing from your hotel room to make certain that the default long-distance carrier won't charge you a price equivalent to the one you paid for the room.

Prepaid Calling Cards Convenience stores and other places sell cards with a prepaid amount of long-distance phone time on them. To use one, you dial an 800 number and then enter the code number on your card. The company's computer keeps track of how much value you have left. At a prompt, you enter the number you are calling. These cards are often a good deal and a good way to circumnavigate the swamp of phone-call-making minutiae.

International Calls Americans can contract with long-distance companies for some very cheap international rates. If you are staying with someone, find out what they pay and reimburse them. Every other method will cost much more. To get an international line, dial ☎ 011 + the country code + the city or area code (you don't need to dial 0) + the number. From a pay phone, first dial your number, than wait to hear how much it will be. After depositing your first $1.50 to $3 for the first three minutes, be prepared to keep feeding the slot at a rate of $1 to $2 a minute. If the pay phone has a sign saying it accepts credit cards for long-distance or international calls, check the rates very carefully before you punch your credit card number in.

Collect & Country Direct You can call collect (reverse the charges) from any phone. The main service providers are AT&T (☎ 800-225-5288) and MCI (☎ 800-365-5328). These generally have rates less stressful to the lucky recipient of your call than local phone companies or the dreaded third-party firms.

Fax
Pay fax machines are located at shipping outlets such as Mail Boxes Etc, copy places such as Kinko's and hotel business centers. Prices can be high, as much as $1 an outgoing page to a US number or $4 a page to Europe. Receiving faxes costs about half that.

Email & Internet Access
If you set up an email account with a free Internet access service such as hotmail (www.hotmail.com), you can access your email from any computer with a Web connection. Otherwise check with the provider of your account to see how, if possible, you can access it from Chicago.

A section on Internet cafés, where you can get access to the Web, is in the Entertainment chapter. Other places for access are public libraries and the office computers of your friends.

BOOKS
For literature, see the section of that name in the Facts about Chicago chapter.

Most of the books listed here are available in the US, although some may need to be special ordered. Elsewhere your choices are more limited. See the Internet Resources appendix for the addresses of Internet book dealers who can ship books anywhere in the world.

Guidebooks
Lonely Planet's *Travel with Children*, by Maureen Wheeler, will tell you what to do with the little ones while you're on the road.

The Chicago Arts Guide, by June Sawyers and Sue Telingator, is a remarkably comprehensive guide to everything from theater to music to literature in the city. *Illinois Hiking & Backpacking Trails*, by Walter G Zyznieuski and George S Zyznieuski has excellent nature hikes mapped and detailed throughout the state, including 29 around Chicago.

For watering holes, there's *The Official Chicago Bar Guide*, by John McGrath and Ryan Ver Berkmoes. Ahem. Being the latter author of that combo, all I can say is that it's got more bars rated and reviewed than any other source. But fear not, all the best ones are included in the book you're holding.

History
Real estate mogul Dempsey J Travis has a productive sideline gig writing well-regarded books about African Americans in Chicago. His book *Harold: The People's Mayor* is the authorized biography of Chicago's first black mayor, Harold Washington. Travis has also known and heard every jazz great for more than half a century. His 1983 bestseller *An Autobiography of Black Jazz* is a rich chronicle of Chicago jazz and the society that spawned it.

David D Perata's book *Those Pullman Blues: An Oral History of the African American Railroad Attendant* traces the life of a Pullman employee during the time when they played a vital role in the civil rights movement. *Chicago '68*, by David Farber, tells the story from all sides of the disastrous Democratic convention that ended in a police riot. James R Grossman's *Land of Hope* tells the story of the huge migration of blacks from the South to Chicago. *Boss*, by the late, legendary Chicago journalist Mike Royko, is one of the best political books ever written and tells the story of Richard J Daley, the mayor who ruled Chicago from 1955 to 1976.

For a completely different history of Chicago, check out *Nature's Metropolis*, by William Cronon, which discusses the city's development from an environmental perspective. Cronon shows how exploiting the land drove the development of the city and the region.

The definitive work on the famous gangster, *Mr Capone*, by Robert J Schoenberg, shows that when the romanticizing is over, Capone was an amoral violent thug. *Forever Open, Clear, and Free*, by Lois Wille, is a textbook study of how the dedicated efforts of a few can thwart the ambitions of the venal many. In this case it's the heroes who have spent a century preventing developers and crooked politicians from turning the lakefront into a high-rise hell.

General

AIA Guide to Chicago, by the American Institute of Architects Chicago and other groups, is an excellent one-volume source of informed commentary and information about Chicago architecture.

Lois Wille's 1997 book *At Home in the Loop: How Clout and Community Built Chicago's Dearborn Park* shows the forces behind the conversion of the blighted rail yards south of the Loop into a booming community.

The fans' profitable fascination with the losing Cubs is at the center of *Wrigleyville*, by Peter Golenbock. The chapters on the era of owner Philip K Wrigley are a fascinating read about the oddest man to ever own a baseball team.

MEDIA
Newspapers & Magazines

Chicago has a diverse range of publications serving every segment of the population. The city has a long tradition of newspapers and is one of the few American cities to still have separately owned and competing major dailies. Author and playwright Ben Hecht worked in Chicago for many years early in the century, immortalizing the rough-and-tumble world of newspapering in his play *The Front Page*. Reading one, if not both, of the two major dailies is a great way to start the day. On Fridays both papers publish excellent guides to current entertainment and events.

Chicago Tribune The largest newspaper in the Midwest, the *Chicago Tribune* has come far from its quirky days under publisher Robert R McCormick (see The Man Behind the 'World's Greatest Newspaper'). The *Tribune* is known for having good writers who are experts in their areas of coverage, and it has a fair amount of foreign and national news from its bureaus worldwide. Its coverage of the city is often overshadowed by its aggressive coverage of the surrounding suburbs and their affluent readers, whom the paper covets.

The *Tribune* excels at highbrow arts and culture coverage. At the other end of the extreme, it also has the best comics section in town. The Sunday *Trib* weighs in at several pounds and has more than 1,000,000 readers.

Chicago Sun-Times The tabloid competitor to the *Tribune*, the *Chicago Sun-Times* concentrates most of its much smaller resources on comprehensive coverage of the city. The paper has spent years recovering from a disastrous period in the mid-1980s, when it was owned by Rupert Murdoch, whose efforts to turn it into a trashy tabloid drove away hundreds of thousands of readers.

The *Sun-Times* is known for its columnists. Robert Feder is the premier media columnist in the country. Gossip columnist Bill Zwecker has scores of salacious scoops on the notable, and Irv Kupcinet is a legendary veteran who has been churning out prose for more than 50 years. Famous movie critic Roger Ebert is a workhorse, reviewing up to six movies a week (the other half of the TV duo, Gene Siskel, has a somewhat diminished role at the *Trib*). On the editorial pages, Pulitzer Prize-winning cartoonist Jack Higgins skewers the high and mighty with a daily bit of hilarity.

The Man Behind the 'World's Greatest Newspaper'

Colonel Robert R McCormick was one of America's best screwball millionaires. A newspaper publisher along the lines of William Randolph Hearst, he was editor of the *Chicago Tribune* from 1914 until he died, in 1955. Under his leadership, the *Tribune* became a powerful and idiosyncratic newspaper, the apex of an empire that included radio stations (WGN, the call letters for McCormick's station in Chicago, stood for World's Greatest Newspaper), ships, real estate and more. In 1922 McCormick held a worldwide architecture contest that produced the Tribune Tower, at 435 N Michigan (see the Architecture section).

A staunch conservative, McCormick used his newspaper to trumpet his political beliefs. He vilified President Franklin Delano Roosevelt during the 1930s and apologized for Adolph Hitler right up until the Nazi dictator declared war on the US. The front page of the *Trib* under his reign was crammed with editorials and political cartoons. In addition to ideology, however, McCormick also filled the paper with sports coverage, neighborhood news, cartoon strips such as Dick Tracy, and other features popular with readers.

During the cold war McCormick proposed that Chicago's many Eastern European immigrants burn their babushkas as a sign of patriotism. He also initiated the tireless promotion of his idea for a huge convention center on the city's unspoiled lakefront. The paper continued the campaign after McCormick's death and steamrolled politicians into supporting the project by threatening to publish unfavorable articles about them. The resulting McCormick Place has been dubbed 'The Mistake on the Lake,' since there were vast tracts of city land elsewhere that could have been used for the center. It is perhaps the perfect legacy of this eccentric mogul.

For insights into the colonel, you can't miss with a visit to Cantigny, his mansion and estate 30 miles west of Chicago, in Lisle. The collection includes a large herb garden; the colonel's mansion, filled with artwork provided by his two wives; and a rather large and complex museum devoted to the exploits of the US Army's First Division, the force that gave McCormick his title. The estate is open daily 9 am to 6 pm, the mansion Tuesday to Sunday 10 am to 3:15 pm, the museum Tuesday to Sunday 10 am to 4 pm. Admission is free, but they stick you for $5 to park, an unavoidable charge in the suburbs. ∎

Many Chicagoans read the *Sun-Times* for local news and the Midwest edition of the *New York Times* for news from farther afield.

Other Newspapers Besides the *New York Times*, *USA Today* and the *Wall Street Journal* are national newspapers readily available.

With daily circulation down to 20,000, the *Chicago Defender* gives little hint about the pivotal role it once played in the black community, not just in Chicago but across the nation (see The Great Defender).

Many of Chicago's ethnic communities support newspapers such as the Spanish-language *El Heraldo*, the *Polish Daily News* and the *Korean News*. These are available on newsstands or in stores serving those communities.

Each Thursday two free weeklies hit the streets. Be careful that you don't get hit by The *Reader*. This mammoth four-section tabloid lists virtually everything going on in town, from theater to live music to offbeat films to performance art. Navigating your way through this behemoth, which brims with ads for futon stores and coffeehouses, can take hours. Reading the personal ads is a great way to pass time in a bar while waiting to meet someone. The other weekly, *New City*, is a nimbler and hipper publication. By no means complete, it lists major goings-on of interest to younger, more 'alternative' readers. And it has a sly wit that pervades its pages.

The *Windy City Times* is the city's best gay and lesbian weekly, with local, national and entertainment news. *Streetwise* is a bimonthly sold by the homeless and others down on their luck. It's a worthy enterprise aimed at getting people back on their feet through work.

Magazines *Chicago* is a monthly magazine filled with excellent articles and culture coverage. Ted Allen's 'Frontlines' is a witty and irreverent look at the latest trends and events in town. But for visitors, the magazine's greatest value lies in its massive restaurant listings. The hundreds of expert reviews are up to date and indexed by food type, location, cost and more. It's worth picking up to find the latest and greatest places in Chicago's vibrant dining scene.

Moguls and would-be moguls read *Crain's Chicago Business*, a business tabloid that regularly scoops the dailies despite being a weekly. *Windy City Sports* is a free monthly with seasonal news and listings on sports and recreation in the area.

There are scores more free publications piled on the floors of bookstores, bars and restaurants throughout the city. Pick up a few and see if you find one you like.

Television
Chicago's local network TV affiliates are little different from their counterparts in other large cities. WLS (channel 7, the ABC affiliate) is generally the ratings leader for newscasts with the latest murders and mayhem from the streets. WMAQ (channel 5, the NBC affiliate) is a ratings loser after a revamp of its newscasts in 1997 that bore a striking resemblance to the more apocalyptic aspects of the movie *Network*. WFLD (channel 32, the Fox affiliate) has a witty and inventive morning newscast with Bob Sirott that highlights any wacky or interesting events in town that day. The CBS affiliate, WBBM, is channel 2.

Other stations in town each have their own niches. WGN (channel 9) is owned by the Tribune Company. Its meteorologist, Tom Skilling, will tell you more than you could ever want to know about the weather, but that's good if you're traveling. The station also shows all the games played by fellow Tribune-empire denizens, the Cubs.

WTTW (channel 11) is a good public broadcasting station. *Chicago Tonight*, at 7 pm Monday through Friday, takes an in-depth look at one of the day's new stories. It's hosted by John Callaway, one of the best interviewers in the business.

WSNS (channel 44) is a Spanish-language station.

The Great Defender

After World War I the *Chicago Defender*, founded in 1905 by Robert S Abbott, was the most important black newspaper in the country and the most popular newspaper among Southern blacks.

A complex distribution system, which included Pullman sleeping-car porters throwing bundles off at every stop, meant each week's edition was read by hundreds of thousands of African Americans. So effective was the *Defender* that racist whites, fearing the paper's influence, murdered its readers and tortured its distributors.

The paper played a pivotal role in the Great Migration, the movement of millions of southern blacks to Chicago and other northern cities in the (see History in Facts about Chicago). Abbott knew that the influx of thousands of blacks into the city would increase the community's clout – and by sheer numbers alone, it did. Abbott, the city's first black millionaire, reveled in the Great Migration. By 1929, the *Defender*'s circulation was 230,000. After Abbott's death in 1940, however, the paper's influence steadily declined. Today it is but a shadow of its former self. ■

Radio

The highest-rated radio personality in town is morning man Bob Collins, on the Tribune's AM station, WGN (720). His bumpkin charm commands huge shares of the audience for his show, which is a mixture of news, calls, mutterings and other sundry information.

During some parts of the day (but not during Collins' show) WGN broadcasts from its street-level studio in the Tribune Tower overlooking Michigan Ave. You can press your nose up against the glass and make stupid faces at hosts such as the duo of Kathy O'Malley and Judy Markey, two irreverent delights.

National radio personalities who work in Chicago include Paul Harvey, the amazingly stalwart conservative fossil, and Jim Nayder, host of *The Annoying Music Show*, which plays such duds as Leonard Nimoy crooning 'Proud Mary' and the Brady Bunch demolishing 'American Pie.'

The radio spectrum screeches with a cacophony of local stations. Newcomers to the US will want to listen to talk radio on WLS (890 AM) for a few minutes to hear a succession of the kind of paranoid blabbermouths who give the nation a bad rep. For calmer, more reasoned chatter, WBEZ (91.5 FM, the National Public Radio affiliate) is the choice.

To find out within the first minute of listening whether war has broken out, WBBM-AM (780) blares news headlines all day long, with traffic reports every 10 minutes. The most interesting music is on WXRT (93.1 FM), a rock station that aggressively avoids falling into any canned format trap.

Besides the stations mentioned, other notables in Chicago are:

WMAQ –	670 AM, with news and traffic reports every 10 minutes
WMVP –	1000 AM, sports talk
WLIT –	93.9 FM, 'lite' rock
WXCD –	94.7 FM, classic rock
WBBM -FM	96.3, top 40
WFMT –	98.7 FM, classical
WOJO –	105.1 FM, Spanish
WGCI –	107.5 FM, urban contemporary

PHOTOGRAPHY & VIDEO

If you are from overseas and wish to purchase a video here, remember that the US uses the NTSC video format, which will look like so much static in the PAL format that's common elsewhere in the world. Check what will work in your country before you buy. Blank film and videotapes are readily available; see the Shopping chapter.

TIME

There's never enough, right? Chicago is in the US Central Standard Time (CST) zone. 'Standard time' runs from the last Sunday in October to the first Sunday in April. 'Daylight savings time,' when clocks are advanced one hour, runs from the first Sunday in April to the last Sunday in October and gives you that extra hour of light in the evening.

RYAN VER BERKMOES

Chicago is one hour behind Eastern Standard Time, which encompasses nearby Michigan and Indiana, apart from the northwestern corner of Indiana, which follows Chicago time. The border between the two zones is just east of the city. Note that

Indiana doesn't take a cotton to notions like daylight savings time. In the summer, with the exception of its northwestern corner, the state has the same time as Chicago; in winter it is one hour ahead.

The city is one hour ahead of Mountain Standard Time, which includes much of the Rocky Mountains, and two hours ahead of Pacific Standard Time, which includes California.

Chicago is six hours behind GMT/UTC (but remember daylight savings time).

ELECTRICITY

Electric current in the US is 110-120 volts, 60 Hz AC. Outlets accept North American standard plugs, which have two flat prongs and an occasional third round one. If your appliance is made for another system, you will need a converter or adapter. These are best bought in your home country. Otherwise, try a travel bookstore (see Books in the Shopping chapter).

RAY HILLSTROM
The view over Lincoln Park

LAUNDRY

Swank hotels will do your laundry for you, but it won't be cheap. Expect to pay $2 to $5 per item or more. You'll have to decide if the convenience of having someone haul your dirty duds away and bring them back sparkling clean is worth it. Dry cleaners abound, with one on almost every block. Coin-operated laundries are cheap and plentiful. A wash in a large machine costs about $1.50, with large dryers going for 25¢ for 10 minutes. Laundromats usually have machines dispensing little boxes of detergent and the like.

The simply named Coin-Op Laundry, 1868 N Damen (no phone; Map 9), is the best deal in town: you can wash 2½ pounds of your stinky duds for 75 cents; it's open 7 am to 7 pm. The neighborhood is filled with diversions where you can spend your savings while you wait.

Riverpoint Coin Laundry (☎ 773-549-5080), at 1730 W Fullerton in the Omni Shopping Center, features a 125-gallon fish tank complete with an exhaustive sign detailing the inhabitants. This upscale suds house is open 24 hours. They serve free coffee from midnight to 9 am. You can stock up on supplies at the huge Omni supermarket, in the same complex and also open 24 hours, while your clothes spin.

Saga Laundry Bar (☎ 773-929-9274), at 3435 N Southport in Wrigleyville (Map 7), has an attached sports bar and café for your entertainment. Other good bars and cafés are just across the street.

Laundries in the Spincycle chain are all over town They are clean, air-conditioned and have TVs. A call to ☎ 312-578-2233 will tell you the location closest to you.

WEIGHTS & MEASURES

The US continues to resist the imposition of the metric system. Distances are measured in inches, feet, yards and miles; weights are measured in ounces, pounds and tons.

Here are some common measurements you will encounter: Gasoline is sold in US gallons, which are 20% smaller than the Imperial version and the equivalent of

3.79 liters. Once you have that down it will become apparent what a bargain gas is in the US. Beer on tap in bars is often sold in US pints, which are three sips short of international ones. Sandwiches often have a quarter-pound of meats or cheese on them. Temperatures are given in degrees Fahrenheit. When it is 65 to 85 degrees outside, it's nice. Water freezes at 32 degrees. Your body is normally 98.6 degrees.

HEALTH

Chicago is a typical first-world destination when it comes to health. The only foreign visitors who may be required to have immunizations are those coming from areas with a history of cholera and yellow fever.

Excellent medical care is readily available, but if you are not properly insured, a collision with the US health care system could prove fatal to your budget.

Precautions

The water is fit to drink, and restaurant sanitation is high. The only health risks you face in Chicago are related to accident, violence or the weather. The first is somewhat preventable, the second easy to minimize by reading the later section Dangers & Annoyances. Weather can be almost entirely eliminated as a health risk by following certain rules. In the winter, when it's cold, bundle up. That sounds absurdly simple, and it is, but many people coming from perennially warm regions don't understand it. When the weather forecasters say there is a 'wind-chill factor' of fifteen or colder then you should not expose any parts of your body to the air. ('Wind-chill factor' is a calculation of the temperature your skin feels when the effects of the cold are multiplied by the wind.) Wear warm and solid footwear with wool socks to avoid frostbite. The key to preventing frostbite is to listen to your body. If your toes, ears or other easily chilled parts of you feel cold, numb or worst of all, painful, then you need to take action to warm them.

RICK GERHARTER
Wacker Drive sentinels

People from mild climates can have problems during the warm summer months also. Chicago is not in the tropics, but on a hot, sunny day fair-skinned people can burn quickly. Sunscreen is readily and cheaply available; use some with an SPF of 30 or more. Dehydration is also a problem; drink plenty of fluids. If the temperature is well into the 90s, those not acclimated to that kind of heat shouldn't spend all day in it. Spend time in air-conditioned places and don't overexert yourself.

Medical Kit

Most medications are readily available, and there's no reason to pack extras. If you require a certain medication, take an adequate supply with you and bring the prescription as well, in case you lose your supply. Other than that, you might want to pack the following:

Aspirin, acetaminophen or Panadol.
Antihistamine (such as Benadryl), which is
    useful as a decongestant for colds, to ease the
    itch from allergies, and to help prevent
    motion sickness.

Bismuth subsalicylate preparation (Pepto-Bismol), Imodium or Lomotil, for stomach upsets.

Rehydration mixture, to treat severe diarrhea, particularly important if you're traveling with children.

Antiseptic, mercurochrome and antibiotic powder or similar 'dry' spray, for cuts and grazes.

Bandages, for minor injuries.

Scissors, tweezers and a thermometer (airlines prohibit mercury thermometers).

Sunscreen and lip balm.

Insurance

Traveling to or within the US without health insurance is foolhardy. One small mishap can drain you of thousands of dollars. Visitors from abroad should carefully check to see what their national or private health insurance will cover. In many cases, you will need to purchase additional travel insurance; read the fine print and make certain that it will cover you for any activity you're likely to engage in.

Americans traveling within the US should check carefully to see what conditions are covered in their policy. This is especially true for HMO members, who may have to call a special number to get approval for health care away from home.

No matter who you are, save all receipts, records and anything else related to your treatment. You'll undoubtedly need them for reimbursement. When in doubt about your insurance, call your carrier no matter where you are and see what they recommend. Doing so could save you thousands of dollars later.

Medical Attention

If you are ill or injured and suspect that the situation is in any way life-threatening, call ☎ 911 immediately. This is a free call from any phone, and you don't have to make a deposit in a pay phone first. It will connect you to a Chicago emergency services operator, who will dispatch the appropriate people to assist you.

If you have a less serious malady, such as the flu or a sprained ankle, and just want to see a doctor, ask your hotel for a recommendation. Chicago is filled with clinics and doctors who will treat you. However, none of their services come cheap, so *have insurance*.

The following hospitals offer medical services through their emergency rooms. If your condition is not acute, call first, because many also have clinics that can see you in a more timely and convenient manner.

Northwestern Memorial Hospital – the most convenient to the Near North and Gold Coast. The emergency room is at 233 E Superior (☎ 312-908-2000; Map 3).

Illinois Masonic – 836 W Wellington, just west of Halsted in Lincoln Park (☎ 773-975-1600; Map 7).

University of Chicago Hospital – 5841 S Maryland Ave, just north of 59th St at the west end of campus in Hyde Park (☎ 773-702-1000; Map 11).

Howard Brown Health Center – 945 W George near the El (☎ 773-871-5777; Map 7); specializes in treating gay men, lesbians and bisexuals.

If you are broke and have no insurance, head to Cook County Hospital (835 W Harrison, one block south of the Medical Center El stop on the Blue Line; ☎ 312-633-6000; Map 10). If your problem is not life-threatening, you will be seated in a waiting room where you will do just that for perhaps 12 hours while you are surrounded by people sicker than yourself. However, if you have been shot, stabbed or injured in a horrific accident, you will come here by ambulance and will receive the best trauma care in the world. This is where the concept was invented, in 1966. The TV show *ER* was inspired by this place, although I've never seen anyone who looks like George Clooney prowling around.

TOILETS

When it's time to see a man about a horse, drop the kids off at the pool or whatever euphemism you prefer for bladder or bowel evacuation, you will face several challenges. In fact, perhaps you need to be your own nagging mom and repeatedly ask yourself before you set out each day, 'Are you sure you went?'

The main challenge faced by all is finding a place to go. Try shopping malls, department stores, large bookstores (the Borders at Michigan and Pearson has one in the basement), train stations and other large public places. Hotels often have downright swank facilities somewhere past the front desk, often by the phones. Museums usually place the toilets past where you pay admission. The Chicago Park District has begun a push to clean and sanitize the toilets in its parks and beaches. Many are now much improved and optimistically called 'comfort stations' on park district maps. In a dire emergency, no restaurant or bar should refuse you.

Foreign visitors face the additional problem of figuring out what goofy terminology is being deployed by the designers of your chosen establishment to indicate where the toilets are. Here are synonyms in a rough descending order of frequency: bathroom, rest room, facilities, men's/ladies'/women's room, little boy's/little girl's room, powder room, latrine, john, lavatory, way station, potty. Worse yet, this nonsense is often replaced by cryptic signs on the individual doors that bear little relationship to your immediate needs. Confronted by two doors, each with a non-gender-specific animal head on it, what do you do? Try the one on the left. If screams from the opposite sex result, try the one on the right.

WOMEN TRAVELERS

Women will be safe alone in most parts of Chicago, though they should exercise a degree of caution and awareness of their surroundings. The El is safe, even at night, though you might want to seek out more-populated cars or the first car, to be closest to the driver. Or you can take one of the buses that parallel many train lines.

In the commonly visited areas of Chicago, you should not encounter troubling attitudes from men. In bars some men will see a woman alone as a bid for companionship. A polite 'no thank you' should suffice to send them off. Chicagoans are very friendly, so don't be afraid to loudly protest if someone is hassling you. It will probably send the offending party away and bring helpful Samaritans to your side.

Women travelers face the extra threat of rape. The best way to deal with this threat is to avoid the same kind of risky situations that might leave you open to other types of violent crime. Be alert if alone in an elevator, if somebody seems to be following you to your hotel room or if someone is trailing you down a street. Conducting yourself in a commonsense manner will help you avoid most problems. Self-defense experts say that if you are attacked in any way, immediately start screaming as loudly as possible.

If you are attacked, call ☎ 911 from any phone. You will be connected with an operator who can dispatch the appropriate assistance to help you. The Chicago Rape Victim Emergency Assistance 24-hour hot line is ☎ 312-744-8418.

Santa Fe

GAY & LESBIAN TRAVELERS

Chicago has a large and vibrant gay and lesbian community. It is centered on North Halsted St between Belmont and Addison, but it's by no means confined there. Andersonville, Lincoln Park, Bucktown and other neighborhoods are gay- and lesbian-friendly. Outside of the Halsted neighborhood, however, open affection between same-sex partners often generates confused or disapproving stares.

Information

Horizons (☎ 312-929-4357), 961 W Montana, is a good social service agency for gays, lesbians and bisexuals. They can make referrals to social services and provide many other services as well.

For AIDS- and HIV-related questions, try the AIDS Foundation of Chicago (☎ 312-922-2322), 411 S Wells Suite 300, or the Illinois AIDS Hotline (☎ 800-243-2437).

Other information services include Chicago Black Lesbians & Gays (☎ 312-409-4917), PO Box 14811, Chicago, IL 60614 USA; the Chicago Women's Health Center (☎ 773-935-6126), at 3435 N Sheffield; the Horizons Lesbian & Gay Help Line (☎ 773-929-4357), which has taped messages about events in the community; or the Chicago Area Gay & Lesbian Chamber of Commerce (☎ 773-871-4190), PO Box 805, 3712 N Broadway, Chicago, IL 60613 USA.

Publications

The *Windy City Times* is the major local weekly newspaper with national and international news.

Several other publications can be found in stacks near the entrances of homosexual-friendly businesses. *Gay Chicago* is a weekly entertainment magazine with lots of listings. Other titles you may see are *Outlines*, *Nightlines* and *Blacklines*, all put out by Lambda Publications, which also publishes the free *OUT! Resource Guide*, a handbook covering Chicago area businesses, services, and resources for the lesbian and gay community.

As with all the alternative press, titles come and go; see what you find lying around and give it a read.

DISABLED TRAVELERS

Chicago is not an accommodating place for people with reduced mobility. The preponderance of older buildings means that doorways are narrow and stairs prevalent. Most of the El is inaccessible. If you do find a station with an elevator, make doubly sure that there's also one at your destination. You can get from O'Hare to the Clark and Jackson stations on the Blue Line in the Loop. From Midway, the Orange Line Library, Washington and Clark stations are accessible in the Loop.

Half the CTA buses are not equipped with wheelchair lifts. Of those that are, I have been aboard some that sped past people in wheelchairs because the driver didn't want to stop and work the lift. Metra and Amtrak trains are supposedly accessible, but boarding them is usually a major undertaking, so you're best off getting to the station early. Call ☎ 836-7000, preceded by the area code for whatever area of Chicago you are in – 312, 708, 847, 630 or 773 – for details on the CTA and Metra services; for Amtrak call ☎ 800-872-7245.

For hotels, you are best off with the newest properties. But call the hotel itself – not the 800 number – and confirm that the room you want to reserve has the features you need.

The Mayor's Office for People with Disabilities (☎ 312-744-6673, TTY 312-744-7833) is a good starting point for referral information for answers to questions about the availability of services.

Organizations

There are a number of organizations and tour providers around the world that specialize in the needs of disabled travelers.

In Australia, try *Independent Travelers* (☎ 08-232-2555), at 167 Gilles St, Adelaide, SA 5000.

In the UK, try *RADAR* (☎ 0171-250-3222) 250 City Rd, London, or *Mobility International* (☎ 0171-403-5688).

In the US, try Mobility International USA (☎ 541-343-1284, fax 541-343-6812), a program that advises disabled travelers on mobility issues and runs an educational exchange program. Write them at PO Box 10767, Eugene, OR 97440 USA. You also can try SATH (☎ 212-447-7284, the Society for the Advancement of Travel for the Handicapped), 347 5th Ave No 610, New York, NY 10016 USA.

Twin Peaks Press (☎ 360-694-2462, 800-637-2256) publishes several useful handbooks for disabled travelers, including *Travel for the Disabled* and *Directory of Travel Agencies for the Disabled*. Write them at PO Box 129, Vancouver, WA 98666 USA.

CHICAGO FOR CHILDREN

Chicago can seem like a big mean city to kids, but it doesn't have to be. Almost all the museums have installed special areas aimed at entertaining, amusing and even (don't let this one slip) educating them. Here are some of the major sites that work at being kid friendly (addresses and more information can be found in Things to See & Do):

Chicago Children's Museum – on Navy Pier, an obvious place to start, followed by the rest of the pier itself.
Art Institute of Chicago – has an excellent hands-on art area.
Field Museum of Natural History – dinosaurs everywhere!
Lincoln Park Zoo – has a special children's area where they can commune with rodents.
Museum of Science and Industry – a perennial favorite.
Shedd Aquarium – has lots of neat fish.

Child Care

Check with your hotel for baby-sitting recommendations. Also try the American Registry for Nurses & Sitters (☎ 773-248-8100), 3921 N Lincoln. They have been minding the little dears since 1950.

SENIOR TRAVELERS

Though the age at which senior benefits begin varies, travelers 62 and older (though sometimes 50 and older) can expect to receive discounts from hotels, museums, tours, restaurants, and other places. Some national advocacy groups that help seniors in planning their travels are:

American Association of Retired Persons (AARP), 601 E St NW, Washington DC 20049 USA (☎ 202-434-2277, 800-424-3410, in Chicago 773-714-9800)
Elderhostel, 75 Federal St, Boston, MA 02110 USA (☎ 617-426-8056)
National Council of Senior Citizens, 1331 F St NW, Washington DC 20004 USA (☎ 202-347-8800)

Grand Circle Travel (☎ 800-248-3737) has a brochure called '101 Tips for Mature Travelers.' Call and leave your name and address if you would like to receive it.

LIBRARIES
Harold Washington Library Center

The Harold Washington Library Center (☎ 312-542-7279, TTY 312-747-4314), 400 S State on the block bounded by Congress and Van Buren (Map 3), opened in

RAY HILLSTROM
Hoot owl on the Library Center

1991 after an architectural competition in which the citizens of Chicago were allowed to vote on their choice of several designs. This is a great free library, and you can while away hours wandering its nine floors. The basement has rotating historical and art expositions. The 2nd floor has the children's library. The main collections begin on the 3rd floor.

Here's a guide to some of what might interest you:

Third Floor – newspapers from all over Illinois and the US, and English-language papers from around the world; microfilm of old newspapers going back to the founding of the city.

Fourth Floor – foreign-language newspapers from around the world.

Sixth Floor – travel books and guides for the entire world, as well as atlases, maps, and comprehensive worldwide airline and train schedules.

Seventh Floor – special section devoted to Chicago authors.

Eighth Floor – section on Chicago architecture

Ninth Floor – winter garden atrium, a cheery place to read a book.

Copy machines are located throughout the building. Copies are 15¢ each, but if you buy a special card on the 3rd floor they're only 13¢ each. The collection catalog is on a database that you can search from computer terminals scattered all over the library. You can also access major information databases, as well as the Internet and Web, on other terminals.

The library is open Monday 9 am to 7 pm; Tuesday and Thursday 11 am to 7 pm; Wednesday, Friday and Saturday 9 am to 5 pm; Sunday 1 to 5 pm.

Other Libraries

The **Newberry Library** (☎ 312-943-9090), 60 W Walton (Map 5), is a huge research facility geared toward scholars. Its 1.5 million volumes cover specialties such as the Italian Renaissance, cartography and genealogy. The vast and diverse collection contains such inestimable gems as the papers of Ben Hecht. Visitors are welcome,

but remember that nothing circulates, so you can't take that first edition of the King James Bible home with you.

The **Gerber-Hart Library** (☎ 773-883-3003), 3352 N Paulina, is one of the nation's oldest and largest gay and lesbian libraries. Its more than 50,000 books are augmented by magazines and archives.

CULTURAL CENTERS

The Chicago Cultural Center (☎ 312-744-1424), 78 E Washington (Map 3), was once the Chicago public library. Now it's an amalgam of a number of draws, such as an art gallery, the Museum of Broadcast Communications, a visitor information center, special events, and a public space where you can get a muffin and coffee and chill out for a while.

Alliance Française (☎ 312-337-1070) is at 810 N Dearborn. The Goethe Institut (☎ 312-329-0915) is at 401 N Michigan.

LEGAL MATTERS

In a big city like Chicago, the cops usually have better things to do than hassle tourists. Usually. If at any time a police officer gives you an order of any kind (such as 'Get outta the road!' or 'Move on!'), do not, I repeat do not seize upon that moment for a debate. I have had good experiences with Chicago cops through the years; they've pulled me out of a few jams and averted their eyes when I messed up but seemed genuinely contrite. But I also have witnessed scores of cops showing zero tolerance for back talk. They'll happily throw you in a lockup for a few hours while you reconsider your argument.

Then again, if you have a problem or question, feel free to take it to the nearest cop. Often the response will be an entertaining spiel delivered in pure 'Chicagoeez.'

If you are arrested, you have the right to remain silent. There is no legal requirement to speak to a police officer if you don't want to, but never walk away from one until given permission. Anyone who is arrested is legally allowed (and given) the right to make one phone call. If you don't have a lawyer or friend or family member to help you, call your consulate. The police will give you the number upon request.

It's generally against the law to have an open container of an alcoholic beverage in public, whether in a car, walking down the street, in a park or at the beach. But during festivals and other mass events this rule is waived. If everyone else around you is having a beer and they don't look like candidates for a 12-step program, then join in.

The drinking age of 21 is pretty strictly enforced. If you're younger than 35 (or just look like it), carry an ID to fend off overzealous barkeeps and the like.

There is zero tolerance at all times for any kind of drug use.

See the Car & Motorcycle section in the Getting Around chapter for the scores of ways a car can get you in trouble.

DANGERS & ANNOYANCES

Parts of Chicago are as safe as you'll find in any American city; other parts are virtual killing fields, with several murders a day. Fortunately, there is little reason for you to go to the unsafe parts of the city, although you should be aware of their existence – not just for your own safety, but so that you have a balanced image of Chicago.

Unsafe Areas

Unless noted otherwise, the areas written about in this book are reasonably safe during the day. At night the Loop, lakefront, major parks (with the exception of Grant Park during any kind of festival or concert) and certain neighborhoods (especially south and west of the Loop) can become bleak and forbidding places. The Near North, Gold Coast, Old Town, Lincoln Park, Lake View and Wrigleyville neighborhoods are safe at night, especially on the busy commercial streets.

Be aware that neighborhoods can change in just a few blocks. Four blocks west of the Gold Coast and south of Old Town lie the Cabrini-Green housing projects, which are very unsafe and where schoolchildren are ordered to lie down under their desks when gunfire breaks out.

Scams

Destroy your credit-card carbons when you make purchases and don't give your card number out to anybody unless it is a business you have called.

If anybody offers you anything on the street (gold jewelry, sports tickets and the like) for absurdly low prices, you can assume that the goods are stolen.

You may be propositioned by urchins claiming that the money from the candy bars they're selling supports their sports team. The goods are usually from a vandalized container in the vast rail yards and the sports team or club nonexistent.

Chicago's winters make it an inhospitable place for the homeless. However, you will encounter people selling the newspaper *Streetwise* year round. This is a great worthy enterprise that provides health, housing and job-training services to its homeless vendors and requires them to follow a code of conduct.

Crime

Most of Chicago's violent crime is perpetrated by street gangs battling over drug turf. The gangs are often centered around public-housing projects, where 95% of the residents are honest people held hostage by the mayhem.

The kind of crime you should be most aware of in Chicago is the same type that exists throughout the world: pickpockets, purse or jewelry snatching, auto break-ins and bike stealing. Basically, if you leave something accessible to crooks, they will try to steal it.

Finally, use your common sense. If a neighborhood, street, El station or any other situation doesn't seem right or something about it worries you, don't stick around.

EMERGENCIES

Dial ☎ 911 for police, fire or ambulance services. Chicago emergency services have a good record of arriving within three minutes for life-threatening situations.

For any disaster in the lake, call the Coast Guard at ☎ 847-729-6190.

To report a picked pocket or other minor crime for which speedy police response is useless, dial ☎ 312-746-6000. You will need a police report in most cases to file for an insurance claim.

If your traveler's checks are lost or stolen, call the check issuer:

American Express – ☎ 800-221-7282
MasterCard – ☎ 800-223-9920
Thomas Cook – ☎ 800-223-7373
Visa – ☎ 800-227-6811

If your credit card is lost or stolen, call the card issuer:

American Express – ☎ 800-992-3404
Diners Club – ☎ 800-234-6377
Discover – ☎ 800-347-2683
MasterCard Emergency Assistance –
    ☎ 800-307-7309
Visa – ☎ 800-336-8472

BUSINESS HOURS

Office hours in Chicago are typically 8 am to 5 pm, although masters of the universe and their overworked minions often work many more hours than that.

Shops are usually open at least until 7 pm, and most keep Sunday hours. The Loop tends to close earlier than the Near North. During Christmastime, stores will often be open until 9 pm every night. You'll find plenty of convenience stores and supermarkets open 24 hours a day. Banks increasingly keep hours like stores, including First Chicago (☎ 888-963-4000), which has Sunday hours at several of its locations.

Movie theaters and many bars and restaurants are open every day of the year. Smaller restaurants are often closed one or two days a week, frequently early in the week. Most theaters for stage productions are dark on Monday.

PUBLIC HOLIDAYS

Christmas is one of the few holidays left for which most stores close. The following holidays are a combination of local and federal holidays. Those marked with an asterisk (*) are widely observed, with banks and businesses closed, few stores open and public transport operating on greatly scaled-back schedules. When some of these holidays fall on the weekend, they are celebrated on the following Monday. Some other holidays always fall on Monday.

*New Year's Day** – January 1
Martin Luther King Jr's Birthday – third
    Monday in January.
Presidents' Day – third Monday in February
Pulaski Day – 1st Monday in March
*Memorial Day** – Last Monday in May
*Independence Day** – July 4
*Labor Day** – first Monday in September
Columbus Day – second Monday in October
Veterans Day – November 11 (some celebrate it
    on the nearest Monday)
*Thanksgiving Day** – fourth Thursday in
    November
*Christmas Day** – December 25

The festive annual Christmas season traditionally runs from the Friday after Thanksgiving through the big day itself. Purists will be horrified to note that Christmas decorations – and even sales – start in September.

SPECIAL EVENTS

Dates of special events can shift from year to year, so if any these events are essential to you, confirm the dates with the Chicago Office of Tourism (☎ 312-744-2400) or check the city's Website (see the Internet Resources appendix) before you make your travel plans.

Music festivals in Grant Park are held at the Petrillo Music Shell – call the Chicago Office of Tourism for information.

January

Navy Pier Art Fair – displays by local artists all month.

Chinese New Year – massive celebration with millions of little firecrackers, a parade and more in Chinatown; exact date varies according to the ancient Chinese calendar.

February

Black History Month – displays and live events all month at Navy Pier.

Chicago Auto Show – Detroit, Tokyo and Bavaria all introduce their latest to the excited gearheads in a huge show mid-month at McCormick Place.

Winterbreak – a new event designed to fill a desolate period in the city's events calendar. Ice sculpture contests on the Mag Mile are but one of a hodgepodge of events that take place the first two weeks of the month.

March

St Patrick's Day Parade – a Chicago institution that snakes south on Dearborn St from the river, dyed green for the occasion. Look to see which politicians are jostling to be at the very front – the best part.

April

Spring and Easter Flower Show – zillions of blooms are at their best at the Lincoln Park Conservatory, just north of the zoo, and at the Garfield Park Conservatory.

Smelt Season – tiny bony fish swarm through near the lakeshore, to be snared by nighttime anglers, who then deep-fry 'em.

RAY HILLSTROM

The green sure doesn't mean Earth Day.

Earth Day – tree huggers and other good people gather on the fourth Saturday of the month at the south end of Lincoln Park for music, poetry, and liberal talk.

May

Art Chicago – a massive mid-month festival at Navy Pier featuring international artists.

Printer's Row Book Fair – thousands of rare and not-so-rare books on sale, plus author readings, on the last weekend of the month.

June

Chicago Blues Festival – a highly regarded three-day festival in Grant Park on the first weekend of the month.

57th St Art Fair – roving artists hawk their wares in Hyde Park.

Chicago Gospel Festival – the best gospel music for one entire weekend in Grant Park.

Old Town Art Fair – a wonderful event for strolling around and partying. The art is not always the best, but the mood is. Second weekend of the month.

Andersonville Midsommerfest – a traditional Swedish festival pegged to the longest day of the year has become a rollicking street fest north of Foster on Clark the weekend closest to June 21.

Country Music Festival – Grant Park is transformed into a hoedown the last weekend of the month.

Gay & Lesbian Pride Parade – a most flamboyant spectacle parades through Lake View, usually on Belmont and Broadway to Lincoln Park. The Dykes on Bikes are a perennial favorite, as are the Proud Parents, who cause more than a few eyes to go misty; usually the last Sunday of the month.

July

Taste of Chicago – an enormous festival that closes Grant Park for the 10 days leading up to Independence Day. More than 100 local eateries serve some of the greasiest food you've ever tried to rub off your fingers. Live music on several stages drowns out the rumble of the belches from the 3.5 million people who attend each year; an acquired taste.

Independence Day Concert and Fireworks – it's really the day before, on July 3, but the city pulls out all the stops for this concert, featuring a really long fireworks show and Tchaikovsky's '1812' Overture, played with gusto by the Grant Park Symphony Orchestra. For the best view, try the embankment east of Randolph and Lake Shore Drive.

Independence Day – the Chicago Historical Society focuses on the roots of the day around the Lincoln statue in Lincoln Park behind the museum.

Chicago to Mackinac Island Yacht Race – usually the third weekend of the month, this race holds near-mystic significance to its participants. The town is witness to the amusing antics of drunken sailors in bars the nights before the kickoff. Monroe Harbor is a good place to watch the boats depart.

World's Largest Block Party – a huge singles' bash sponsored by the savvy pastor of Old St Patrick's Church, in the West Loop. Tens of thousands of single, primarily Catholic Chicagoans drink beer and exchange Catholic grade school horror stories the third weekend of the month. The church is fully booked for weddings for months afterward.

Black Expo Chicago – businesses, volunteer groups and anybody else trying to reach African Americans take part in a McCormick Place exhibition the third weekend of the month.

Sheffield Garden Walk – ostensibly a chance to tour the lovely gardens of some of Lincoln Park's gentrified homes, but really an excuse for a huge street party with music, food and beer.

Venetian Night – late in the month, yacht owners decorate their boats with lights and parade them at night in Monroe Harbor to the adulation of the rabble; followed by a good fireworks display.

August

Gold Coast Art Fair – loads of booths centered on the blocks near State and Division, staffed by traveling artists on the second weekend of the month.

Bud Billiken Parade & Picnic – named after a merry and mythical figure in the black community, this huge parade is a local institution founded by the late John H Sengstacke; it runs south on Martin Luther King Jr Drive from 39th to 55th Sts, with a huge Washington Park picnic following. Usually the second Saturday of the month.

North Halsted Market Days – the street festival of the gay neighborhood features lots of people wearing costumes usually seen in S&M nightmares. Open to all, it's really quite an enjoyable event. The only Market it refers to is Meat.

Chicago Air and Water Show – your tax dollars at work: the latest military hardware flies past the lakefront from Diversey south to Oak St Beach. Aerobatic planes and teams perform all afternoon both days the third weekend in August. The water part of the show is always a dud, featuring a couple of speedboats most people can't see. The best views are those from high-rises overlooking the lake. Try to wangle an invite to one of them.

Chicago Jazz Festival – loads of national and local groups play, usually the last weekend of the month in Grant Park.

September

Around the Coyote – a once cutting-edge festival now gone mainstream, featuring all forms of art by local artists in their Wicker Park and Bucktown studios. There's something for everyone; try to find the worst and best of the performance art. It's usually the second weekend of the month, but the quarrelsome artists are always feuding on exact plans.

Viva! Chicago – Latin music festival in Grant Park, usually mid-month.

Mexican Independence Day Parade – colorful and loud event with lots of cute kids dressed to the nines on the second Saturday of the month.

Berghoff Oktoberfest – holds true to the traditional German dates in mid-September; it's hugely crammed and popular in front of the restaurant on Adams St during the week.

German-American Festival – A much more enjoyable Oktoberfest, in the heart of the old German neighborhood at Lincoln Square, 4700 N Lincoln. Third weekend of the month.

October

Chicago International Film Festival – scores of films compete during this weeklong event, which every year produces some sleepers and some stinkers.

Windy City Marathon – runners from all over the world compete on the usual 26-mile course. If there is such a thing as slacker runners, this is the marathon for them, because the city is dead flat.

November

Day of the Dead – the traditional November 1 Mexican celebration of spooks and souls, with displays at the Mexican Fine Arts Center Museum.

Magnificent Mile Lights Festival – the increasingly commercialized lighting of all 600,000 lights on the trees lining the streets takes place mid-month, after which the little fellas twinkle sweetly on Michigan Ave north of the river through January. Get hold of the program from a hotel or store; it lists all sorts of free events and giveaways.

Official Tree Lighting Ceremony – the city's Christmas tree lights up on Daley Plaza on Thanksgiving Day.

December

Carol to the Animals – a goofy event in which hordes of people sing Christmas tunes to perplexed zoo critters at the Lincoln Park Zoo. The question on all the inmates' minds: 'When's feeding time?' Second Sunday of the month.

Kwanzaa – the increasingly popular African American holiday celebration adds new events and locations each year.

RAY HILLSTROM

Who has the Lucky Charms?

Long-Term Events

Under the Picasso – local and visiting bands, dancers and other entertainers give performances almost every weekday, roughly between noon and 1 pm either inside or outside the Daley Center.

Skate-on-State – until some developer comes along, the empty block west of Field's in the Loop will be home to ice-skating from November through March; you can rent skates, drink hot chocolate and practice your double toe loops.

Grant Park Music Festival – June though August; see the Classical Music section in Entertainment for details.

Neighborhood Festivals

From May through September, just about every neighborhood has a street festival on one weekend. These usually feature live music, lots of beer and gourmet treats like corn dogs. They vary greatly in size and are worth checking out for excellent people-watching. Many festivals take on the ethnic character of their neighborhoods. In Lincoln Park that means everybody has new polo shirts on; in Pilsen it means that the tacos are excellent and cost less than $1. Check with the Mayor's Office of Special Events to see what's on where (☎ 312-744-3315).

WORK

Foreign visitors can always find work in the US if they are willing to work in low-paid menial jobs, such as cleaning hotel rooms or working at McDonald's or at even more frightful third-rate fast-food places with names like Peanut World II. However, you should know that from the first minute you accept a job in the US without a hard-to-get work visa, you become an illegal alien. If you are caught, the full weight of the anti-immigration sentiment in the US government will crash down on you. Expect to be immediately deported and barred from the US for at least five years. This is not be taken lightly, because the deportation can now occur the same day the INS finds you. There will be no time to gather belongings or notify friends or loved ones.

Getting There & Away

AIR

Chicago is served by two main airports. O'Hare International (ORD) is the world's busiest hub. Midway (MID) is much smaller and is primarily served by discount carriers. The Getting Around chapter has full details on the myriad options for getting from the airports to central Chicago.

O'Hare International Airport

Sixty-five million passengers a year – one quarter of the population of the United States – pass through O'Hare each year, continuing Chicago's historic role as a US transportation hub. Each day flights depart to 284 cities around the world, a figure unmatched by any other airport anywhere.

The place is huge. The best advice for navigating O'Hare is to tread slowly because, while the signs and maps aren't bad, the sheer scope of the place can intimidate even grizzled travelers. Domestic flights and international departures for domestic airlines depart from Terminals 1, 2 and 3. All international arrivals, as well as departures for non-US airlines, are in Terminal 5. There are some exceptions to this rule: Lufthansa, for instance, departs out of United's Terminal 1. The listing of airlines below gives terminal information.

United's **Terminal 1**, designed by Helmut Jahn, is the largest hub of the world's largest airline, hosting 840 flights a day. The soaring concourses and the underground New Age light show and tunnel between Concourses B and C are attractions in themselves. There are moving sidewalks and escalators galore, and for such a huge place it is really quite user friendly. United's partner Lufthansa departs from here.

Domestic airlines Continental, Northwest, US Airways and TWA are located in **Terminal 2**, the building right across from the Hilton Hotel. After United, the other major carrier at O'Hare is American Airlines, which operates a hub out of **Terminal 3**, a

facility whose cut-rate renovation a few years ago (the concourses have long walks unbroken by moving sidewalks) befits American's number-two status. Delta, Air Canada and Canadian are here as well.

Terminal 5 is the international terminal; all foreign airline departures (except Lufthansa's) and those to Canada can be found here. Built in the early 1990s, it is designed to minimize walks to and from the planes. Arriving passengers are treated to a large immigration and customs facility. They are also treated to a great collection of local art, but it's doubtful that the bleary-eyed arrivals notice the works.

Careful counters will note the lack of a Terminal 4; it was a temporary facility used while Terminal 5 was being built.

The terminals and the main long-term parking lot are linked by a people mover system. The service is frequent, quick and runs 24 hours a day. Be certain to get on the train going in the direction you want. Short-term parkers can use the main parking garage, a vast facility where the fee starts at $2 and increases by $1 an hour thereafter. Fees at the long-term parking lots are about $10 a day. On nice days, the top level of the main parking garage has good views of the runways and is a good place for some 'fresh' air if you are stuck between flights.

Information City-run information booths are located in the baggage claim areas of Terminals 1, 2 and 3. In Terminal 5 the desk is between the two customs exits. The employees have undergone training in courtesy from the Disney organization. The results have paid off: the red-jacketed people working these booths are not only polite but often enthusiastic. Many of them speak a range of languages. Unless you are familiar with Chicago, it's worth visiting these booths for advice and armloads of maps and brochures. You may have to look

---

What's an ORD? Who's O'Hare?

In 1942 fighter pilot Edward 'Butch' O'Hare shot down five Japanese planes that were attacking his ship, the *USS Lexington*, during the Battle of the Coral Sea. He became America's first fighter ace of World War II and was an immediate national hero at a time when the nation had few.

One year later, O'Hare himself was shot down and killed. The Chicago City Council moved to rename a small airport named Orchard Field, on the city's northwest side, in honor of the pilot, and O'Hare Airport was born.

At the time it had already acquired the three-letter code ORD, for Orchard. This technical designation has remained on international rosters and continues to adorn millions of bags every year.

During the 1950s, the world's busiest airport was Midway, on Chicago's southwest side. But hemmed in by houses on all sides, it couldn't be expanded for the new jets and huge growth in air travel that followed. Looking about for an alternative, Chicago settled on the still-sleepy O'Hare. Runways and terminals were built within just a few years, and O'Hare began its unbroken tenure as the busiest airport in the world, with 67 million people passing through in 1997.

For years, there was little information at the airport about why it's named O'Hare or who O'Hare might have been. That should have changed by the time you read this. A restored version of an F4F Wildcat fighter, the kind flown by O'Hare, is scheduled to go on display in Terminal 2. It will feature the complete story about O'Hare and how the vast airport came to bear his name. ■

---

carefully for them, since the directional signs are inconsistent.

Large boards between the exit doors provide hotel and motel information for hundreds of places that are all in the suburbs. Pass these right by.

Money Scores of ATMs accepting every card known to humankind can be found throughout the terminals. Full-time currency exchanges are in the arrivals area of Terminal 5 and Concourse K of Terminal 3, where the American Airlines flights to Europe depart. Some rather cheesy currency exchange carts operate near the departure gates for international flights.

Food & Drink There is no shortage of places for $8 sandwiches and $3 sodas. You'll never be more than a few meters from a place with greasy pizza, overcooked hot dogs, uninspired deli sandwiches and expensive fruit. There are also outlets for all the usual fast-food places. Concourse C and the departure level of Terminal 5 have food courts with wide selections of chow. Stands near the gates offer bags of snacks to supplement the meager and often unpal-

atable offerings aboard many domestic flights. Goose Island, an excellent local microbrewery, has bars in Concourses H and K in Terminal 3.

The food situation is set to improve because Host Marriott Services, the company responsible for the bad pizza and tough weenies, will be giving up almost half its space in 1998. In its place will be outlets from local favorites such as the Billy Goat Tavern, the Corner Bakery and Connie's Pizza. The Berghoff, a Loop legend, will open in Terminal 1.

If you have a long time to spend between flights, the Hilton Hotel in the middle of the terminals has a good sports bar and a fine Italian café. Take the pedestrian tunnels down from the baggage claim areas to get there.

Stores Unlike airports such as those in the cities of London, Amsterdam and Singapore, O'Hare limits its retail mostly to small shops selling travel goods, souvenirs and the like. There's no Harrods outlet here, although there is the Michael Jordan Golf store in Concourse B of Terminal 1. The British bookstore chain Waterstones has decent outlets in the concourses of Terminals 1, 2 and 3; buy your Lonely Planet guide to your next destination there. A huge omission is that O'Hare has no grocery store. If you want water for a long flight, you have to buy tiny bottles for an extortionate $1.95.

Other Services Terminal 2 has a large children's recreation area, a branch of the Museum of Broadcast Communications showing classic TV shows and, beginning in 1998, a huge exhibit dedicated to the airport's namesake (see What's an ORD? Who's O'Hare?).

The University of Illinois at Chicago operates a clinic (773-894-5100) in Terminal 2. Americans will be familiar with it as a 'doc in a box' general-service facility that can help with minor problems, such as the aftereffects of that bad food on the flight in.

Midway Airport
Home to cut-rate carriers such as Southwest, Midway has a suitably low-rent ambiance. The city has plans for a new terminal by 2003 to service traffic that is about one-seventh that of O'Hare. The existing facility dates from the 1950s, when Midway was the busiest airport in the world. It's worth pondering how far air travel has come when you look around at how small the place is.

Unless your flight is late, you won't have to spend much time here, and that's good.

Information A city information center is at the confluence of Concourses A and B in the main terminal. It offers transportation and accommodations information.

Services Scant. The café and newsstand near the information booth are about it. There is a bar, often filled with yahoos drunkenly preparing for their first flight, by Concourse C.

Within North America
Obviously there's no shortage of flights to and from most places within the US. Finding the best fare will take a lot of work.

The huge computer reservations systems used by the airlines record 10,000 or more fare changes a day. With fares changing by the minute, it's not too easy to be sure you've got the cheapest ticket. And in many respects no one will. Travel agents use the vast computer systems run by the major airlines. They often do not have access to the obscure carriers, like some of those found at Midway. Those same carriers may not advertise extensively, either.

So if you want to get to or from Chicago, it first will literally pay to find out all the carriers that fly your route. Try browsing some of the Websites listed in the Internet Resources appendix, or look in an *Official Airline Guide* at a library, and check the Sunday newspaper travel supplements for airfare charts. Then try calling each carrier to get a fare quote. You can try a travel agent, but commissions for discount tickets have been cut to the bone, and it doesn't really pay for them to spend much time looking for a cheap fare. Compare prices, watch the news for sudden fare specials that are often announced without warning, and when you feel you've got the best deal, buy the ticket. Chances are, no matter how hard you try, somebody on your flight will have found the same flight for a bit less.

It's important to keep in mind as well that the tickets with the greatest discounts are heavily restricted, which means that you will have to buy your ticket at least 14 days in advance and stay over a Saturday night. If you just want to get a one-way ticket, the cheapest option is often a heavily discounted roundtrip ticket. Fly on the one half, toss the other (you can't really give it away or sell it, because the airlines now check the identification of passengers for security reasons).

Airlines United may not always have the lowest fares, although its fares usually are competitive. This giant airline excels because of the sheer volume of nonstop flights it offers. I have flown close to one million miles on United in 30 years of traveling and can recommend them fully.

American is the other major carrier at O'Hare, though unlike United, its primary hub is not in Chicago. It doesn't offer quite as many flights to as many places as United, but it's an excellent airline in every other respect.

Unless you happen to be going to one of their hubs, keep in mind that all the other major carriers at O'Hare will likely route you through one of their hubs, which means changing planes someplace else.

At Midway, Southwest is the major carrier. It has frequent flights to many Midwestern cities at cheap fares (although if you can plan in advance, the major carriers usually match them). The airline has a flawless safety record, but I personally find certain aspects of its service a bit annoying: there's no advance seat selection, nothing beyond a beverage in flight and not much room between the seats. Check Southwest's flights to Detroit, Cleveland, Memphis, St. Louis, Louisville and Baltimore. Flying farther on Southwest will require one or more changes of planes. A $199 fare to California sounds good until you find out it's via St. Louis, Dallas and Phoenix, for an all-day aviation adventure.

Also at Midway, Kiwi has good prices to Newark (New Jersey), and Frontier has cheap fares to Denver. Be careful which cheap airline you pick, because many have only one flight a day, and if for some reason it's canceled, you might be stuck, since the bargain carriers don't sell tickets that other airlines will honor. Another consideration is that if your cheap airline goes out of business – which they do with alarming regularity – you can be stranded and your money gone.

Fares Here's a very rough idea of what you can expect to pay for flights using the most heavily restricted (and therefore cheapest) roundtrip tickets to and from Chicago:

Major cities within 500 miles	$150 to $300
The South and the East Coast	$250 to $400
The West and the West Coast	$350 to $550

As you try to make sense of all of the flight options, you can take heart that unlike many frequent flyers, you won't have to change planes at O'Hare.

To/From Abroad
International treaties keep fairly rigid controls on airfares to and from the US. But after you've tried to figure out the domestic morass, that can be a relief. Also, because international tickets pay decent commissions, you're much more likely to find a travel agent's ears perking up with interest when you make an inquiry about them.

Know, too, that there are options for ticket purchases outside of the regular avenues of airlines and travel agents. Called 'bucket shops' in the trade, they are given seats to sell by the airlines that otherwise would be empty. Since they exist outside the regular channels, they can sell the tickets for whatever the market will bear. But be aware that these tickets are highly restricted and may not leave you with many rights if your flight is canceled. These tickets are also advertised in the travel sections of major newspapers. Look for tiny ads that list inexpensive flights to major cities all over the world.

Visit USA Passes These are coupons good for flights within the US that non-US citizens buy in their home countries. They are a very good deal, so much so that I'm thinking I need to get a passport from some other country so I can take advantage of them. United has the most flights to the most places from Chicago, so here's their program: Three coupons cost about $350. That is a fantastic deal, because you can fly from Chicago to, say, Seattle, then to Los Angeles and then back to Chicago. You could never do that for so little with regular tickets. The coupons can be purchased in whatever amount you wish and get progressively cheaper the more you buy. Six cost about $600, which is a mere $100 a flight.

Round-the-World Tickets If you are coming from overseas, you may want to include Chicago on a round-the-world itinerary. These typically cover East or West Coast cities in the US, but you can usually get them to cover Chicago as well. They offer substantial savings over individual tickets in all three classes of service.

All the major airlines offer round-the-world tickets in conjunction with other major airlines. United, for instance, offers 31 itineraries and routings, and also offers a single-flight round-the-world service (one flight number and airline all the way around the world, the only service of its kind), which stops in Hong Kong, New Delhi and London.

The fares vary depending on how you want to go around the world. It's cheaper to go via the North Pacific, but then you miss the bounteous pleasures of the South Pacific. African options also exist, as well as some for South America and others involving various side trips.

Check the travel sections of major newspapers wherever you live to see which travel agents specialize in these routings. Try calling a few of the major international carriers, too.

Latin America American and United have flights via Miami, and United now has non-stop service to São Paulo. Continental has flights connecting through Houston. Fares from Brazil average $800 to $1000, from Mexico City $400 to $500.

Europe American, British Airways and United each have multiple flights a day to and from London's Heathrow airport; the flight takes about eight hours. Other major European carriers have nonstop flights serving their capitals, such as Swissair to and from Zurich, KLM to and from Amsterdam and Sabena to and from Brussels. American Airlines has its base for European flights at O'Hare; it serves Paris, Frankfurt, Stockholm and other cities. United has two flights a day to Frankfurt, as well as flights to Düsseldorf and Paris. In the summer, European service increases dramatically.

European fares follow a predictable pattern. Except for the Christmas season, flights from November through March are $400 to $600 roundtrip. During the 'shoulder' months of April, May, September and October, fares are $500 to $700. In summer and at Christmastime, expect to pay $700 to $1000 – if you can find a seat on the always jammed flights. Tickets bought in Europe are roughly equivalent to these prices, depending on the vagaries of exchange rates.

Check the back of the weekly entertainment magazine for the city you plan to travel from for ticket-discounter ads. In London, *Time Out* has several pages of them. Also try calling any of the following travel agencies:

Campus Travel
 174 Kensington High St, London W8
 (☎ 0171-938-2188)
 28A Poland St, London W1
 (☎ 0171-437-7767)
STA Travel
 117 Euston Rd, London NW1 2SX
 (☎ 0171-937-9962)
Trailfinders
 194 Kensington High St, London W8 7RG
 (☎ 0171-937-5400)
Travel Cuts
 95A Regent St, London W1
 (☎ 0171-637-3161)

Australia & New Zealand Service to and from down under requires a change of planes in either Los Angeles, San Francisco or Honolulu. All three cities make very attractive stopover points. Qantas and Air New Zealand have flights to Los Angeles and Honolulu. United serves Auckland and Sydney nonstop from LA and Sydney nonstop from San Francisco. With flights between the US and the South Pacific averaging 14 hours, the idea of a stopover becomes much more appealing. Fares from Sydney can vary widely with the seasons – by as much as $1200 to $1800.

The usual newspaper advice for finding cheap tickets applies to travel from these two nations. In Australia, the Flight Centre and STA travel agencies, in Melbourne and Sydney, have competitively priced tickets. STA also operates offices in Auckland, New Zealand.

Asia JAL, Northwest and United have daily flights to Tokyo. United also has seasonal nonstop service to Hong Kong (the longest scheduled flight in the world, a delirium-inducing 16 hours in the air) and has many connections through their Asian hub in San Francisco. Korean Air has flights to Seoul. The wealth of service to Tokyo keeps fares around $900. Hong Kong requires more shopping, with huge variations on fares through the year – anywhere from $1200 to $2000.

Airlines

Airlines serving Chicago include those on the list following. Note that, especially at Midway, scheduled service by low-fare airlines changes frequently. Also, most of the following airlines have at least one city ticket office, while United and American have scores. These are handy places for working out complex itineraries. Check the Yellow Pages for their addresses.

The letter M following the airline name indicates an airline serving Midway. The letters M, O indicate an airline serving both airports.

Aer Lingus	☎ 800-223-6537
Aeroflot	☎ 312-819-2350
Air Canada	☎ 800-776-3000
Air France	☎ 800-321-4538
Air Ukraine	☎ 800-857-2463
Alitalia	☎ 800-223-5730
America West Airlines (M, O)	☎ 800-235-9292
American Airlines	☎ 800-433-7300
American Trans Air (M)	☎ 800-435-9282
British Airways	☎ 800-247-9297
Canadian Airlines	
International	☎ 800-426-7000
China Eastern Air Lines	☎ 312-337-8008
Continental Airlines (M, O)	☎ 800-523-3273
Czech Airlines	☎ 312-201-1781
Delta Air Lines	☎ 800-221-1212
El Al Israel Airlines	☎ 312-516-3525
Frontier Airlines (M)	☎ 312-443-0063
Japan Airlines	☎ 800-525-3663
Kiwi (M)	☎ 800-538-5494
KLM	☎ 800-374-7747
Korean Air	☎ 800-438-5000
Lot Polish Airlines	☎ 312-236-3388
Lufthansa	☎ 800-645-3880
Mexicana Airlines	☎ 800-531-7921
Northwest Airlines (M, O)	☎ 800-225-2525

Reno Air	☎ 800-736-6247
Sabena	☎ 800-955-2000
SAS	☎ 800-221-2350
Southwest Airlines (M)	☎ 800-435-9792
Swissair	☎ 800-221-4750
TWA	☎ 800-221-2000
United	☎ 800-241-6522
US Airways	☎ 800-428-4322
Vanguard (M)	☎ 312-565-1065
Western Pacific (M)	☎ 800-930-3030

BUS

The striking, modern main bus station (☎ 312-408-5980; it's often referred to as 'the Greyhound station') is at 630 W Harrison between Des Plaines and Jefferson (Map 10). The Clinton El stop on the Blue Line is two blocks away.

Greyhound

The sole national bus line, called 'The Dog' by veteran riders, has dozens of buses a day departing in every direction. The seats are narrow but otherwise comfortable, the windows are big and the passengers are a polyglot lot. The buses also stop frequently – not because of the most important reason (since they all have toilets), but rather to pick up passengers from countless small towns that otherwise have no connection with the outside world except by car. That slows progress considerably, and the bus always takes longer than even an auto obeying the speed limit would.

But if conditions are not posh, neither are the prices. The eight buses a day to Memphis and the nine buses a day to Minneapolis, for example, charge a full fare of only $59. The bone- and butt-numbing journey to San Francisco, 48 hours straight, costs a mere $103. These fares are subject to a thicket of bargains and include the option of bringing a companion along free. If you buy your ticket more than 21 days in advance, no destination in the whole continental US costs more than $59.

Visitors to the US may become Dog-lovers when they see the prices for the Ameripass. Seven days of unlimited travel everywhere Greyhound runs cost $199. Prices climb to $599 for 60 days of riding.

If anyone takes advantage of this deal, please let me know the gory details.

Indian Trails

This is a regional line operating buses similar to Greyhound's. It serves Michigan from the main Chicago bus station for similar bargain-basement fares.

TRAIN

Visitors from Europe will be appalled at the state of train travel in the US. The quasi-government agency Amtrak is the sole provider of interstate service, and it provides very little.

Thanks to penurious government funders, trains in the US are slow and infrequent (Chicago's superb Metra commuter rail system is an exception). But if that keeps most Americans from using trains to get anywhere, it shouldn't stop you. The slow pace of the trains is perfect for sightseeing, and many of the routes run past magnificent scenery. In urban areas, the trains provide a view into residents' backyards, giving you an unvarnished look at how people really live. One thing that's immediately apparent is that Americans keep a lot of crap piled up.

Amtrak

Chicago is the hub for Amtrak's national and regional service, so it has more service than any other city. The trains themselves are very comfortable. Lacking speed and frequency, they are filled with amenities to lure people aboard: Dining cars and lounge cars dispense food and drink, and on long-distance trips special sightseeing cars have extra-large windows that encompass part of the roof, to make the good views even better. Sleeping cars come in a variety of sizes and budget levels, and even lowly coach class on long-distance trains has seats roughly equivalent to those in business class on long-distance flights. The lounge cars are a unique American institution. Selling cheap drinks well into the night, they are filled with convivial former strangers cheerfully chatting each other up.

Reservations During much of the year it's crucial to have your Amtrak journey reserved well in advance. In the summertime, sleeper space and even simple seats are gone weeks in advance. The same situation exists at holidays. The reservation phone system (☎ 800-872-7245) is often busy or plagued by mind-numbing waits. Try going in person to Union Station, 210 S Canal between Adams and Jackson (Map 3; there are entrances to the station on all three streets), where all the Chicago trains depart, or use Amtrak's interactive reservation system on the Web (see the Internet Resources appendix).

Fares Amtrak travel can be cheap. The three trains a day to Detroit have discount seats available right until departure for $20 to $29. That is about the same price as the bus, but the train is more comfortable and faster.

Some regular coach fares are: Milwaukee, $25; St. Louis, $48; New York, $148; San Francisco, $224. Sleeper prices depend on their level of luxury; a basic room for two can cost from $150 to $300. These accommodations can be a pretty good deal because they include all meals, some drinks and other treats, including coffee in bed.

Except during the summer and Christmas, Amtrak has Explore America tickets, which can be an excellent deal: The US is divided into four regions – the West, the Midwest (including Chicago), the East and Florida. The tickets allow you to make up to three stopovers on a roundtrip. Travel in one region costs $168; in two regions, $218; and in three or four, $278. Some itineraries from Chicago include these: New Orleans-San Antonio-Kansas City for $168; Boston-New York-Washington DC for $218; or a 4,000-mile trip through some of the best western scenery on the Seattle-San Francisco-Los Angeles route, for a ridiculously cheap $218. You have to make your plans in advance, and sleeping cars would cost extra, but these are really good deals.

Amtrak has a deal with United Airlines by which you can ride the train one way and fly back. This is a great deal because you can enjoy the scenery on your way to

RAY HILLSTROM
Amtrak rolls into Chicago.

someplace like Portland, but then avoid chugging back through the same sites on your return to Chicago. There is a special reservations number for this deal, imaginatively called 'Air-Rail' (☎ 800-437-3441).

The Trains Amtrak's three trains from Chicago to the West Coast can be vacation experiences in themselves. They utilize the line's cushy 'Superliner' equipment and have a full range of amenities. Each takes upward of three days and two nights to reach its destination. And don't plan any split-second connections: Amtrak is notoriously late, sometimes by several hours.

The *Empire Builder* goes to Seattle and Portland, passing through the beautiful northern Rockies and the 'big sky' country of Montana. The *California Zephyr* passes through dramatic canyons in the Rockies in Colorado and the Sierra Nevada in California. The *Southwest Chief* traces the route of the legendary *Super Chief*, once run by the Santa Fe Railroad. It speeds through the striking painted deserts of New Mexico and Arizona and usually carries

Native American guides to point out and describe the sights.

Other long-distance trains take one night and serve Texas, Washington DC, and Boston. The *Lake Shore Limited* to New York City makes a dramatic run at dawn along the old Erie Canal and Hudson River (unless it's late; then it's a dramatic mid-morning run). And the *City of New Orleans* covers the same route immortalized in the Arlo Guthrie song.

Short-distance trains run more than once a day and go to Detroit, St. Louis and Grand Rapids, Michigan. Five trains a day go to downtown Milwaukee in slightly more than 90 minutes, better than you can do by car.

CAR & MOTORCYCLE

Interstate highways converge on Chicago from all points of the compass. None is especially scenic or otherwise recommended, although if you are coming from the east, follow the Indiana Toll Road all the way to the border and then spring for $2 for the skyway. You'll save a good 30 minutes or more, compared to curving around on I-94.

Try to time your arrival so as not to arrive during the worst weekday rush hours, from 6 to 9 am and 4 to 7 pm. Your nerves and passengers will thank you. See the Media section in the Facts for the Visitor chapter for a list of radio stations that offer frequent traffic updates. Turn to the Expressways section of the Getting Around chapter to interpret what they're saying – roads in the Chicago area are referred to by their names rather than numbers.

HITCHHIKING

Hitchhiking in the US is dangerous and is no longer a common practice. All those bad movies that get made about American mass murderers on the road have their basis in sad fact. Less sensationally, if you hitchhike you open yourself up to robbery, physical abuse or rape. Most decent people are wary of hitchhikers, which makes the credibility of those who would stop extra suspect. I cannot recommend hitchhiking in the US.

That said, if you still insist on hitchhiking, it helps to follow a few guidelines. If you are a woman, even a group of women, don't. If you are a man, your chances of being picked up decrease with each additional person. Carry a neat destination sign and keep baggage to a minimum. Don't look like anyone you yourself wouldn't pick up.

WARNING

One final repetition of my advice about research is in order here. Travel prices are more volatile than those for ripening bananas – they change constantly. Treaties are signed, rules amended, sales start and end and a plethora of other factors affect prices. In addition, schedules change, service is introduced and canceled, companies go bankrupt and other changes occur that make the situation unpredictable.

There is simply no substitute for doing your homework, gathering information and carefully working with your airline, travel company or travel agent. The details in this chapter should be the basis for your own scholarship, not the substitute for it.

Getting Around

Often you will find that the best way to get around Chicago is by foot. It's flat and easy to navigate, and walking is the best way to get the flavor of the city. But when your feet need a break, public transit here is not bad by American standards. This is one of the few American cities you can fully enjoy without a car. In fact, having a car in Chicago would seriously *detract* from your enjoyment.

TO/FROM THE AIRPORTS

There is no best way to and from O'Hare and Midway. Each option discussed here requires a tradeoff between cost and convenience. Details specific to each airport are listed separately.

Cabs are plentiful around the clock at the airports and will always very happily take you anywhere in town. Their large trunks will swallow up all your luggage. But taxis are stuck with the same traffic jams as everybody else, despite your cabbie's best efforts to drive on the shoulder, maniacally switch lanes, etc. Cabs are the most expensive option, costing about $27 to $30 to the Loop from O'Hare and $15 to $20 from Midway, but they are the only option with direct door-to-door service.

During rush hours, which seem to occur on Chicago expressways for the majority of each day, the CTA El is the quickest way to and from the airports. At $1.50, it is also by far the cheapest. But the trains are not designed for people with luggage, and at the airport the stations are a long and sometimes confusing walk from the gates. The stations downtown have few escalators and fewer elevators, so be prepared to schlep your bags.

Shuttles leave at regular intervals from the airports to the major downtown hotels and vice versa. But they, too, are vulnerable to traffic woes, and unless you are the last aboard, you may have to spend a frustrating half-hour or more waiting as the shuttle collects or drops off passengers at various terminals or hotels. Shuttle fares fall midway between those for the CTA and taxis.

See the Driving section for details on reaching the city by auto, and see the Kennedy Expressway entry in the Expressways section for tips on how to reach O'Hare from the city.

O'Hare International Airport

You'll want to leave O'Hare as quickly as possible. Fortunately, your choices are many.

Taxi Each terminal has one taxi stand outside the baggage claim area that may require you to line up. As mentioned, the fare to the Near North and Loop runs $27 to $30, depending on tip (usually about 10% to 15%) and traffic (taxi meters keep running even when the car is stuck in a standstill). Extra passengers are 50¢ each. If there are other travelers heading downtown, it may make sense to use the Share-a-Ride program (some signs may read 'Share-a-Cab' or 'Ride Sharing'), by which a cab takes you to the city for a flat $15 per passenger. However, make certain you inform the driver you want to do that before you start off.

The El The CTA offers frequent train service on the Blue Line to and from the Loop. Unfortunately, the O'Hare station is buried under the world's largest parking garage. Finding it can be akin to navigating a maze like a rat – and there's no cheese waiting at the end to guide you. Directional signs are variously marked as 'CTA,' 'Rapid Transit' and 'Trains to City.'

From Terminals 1 and 3, look for the escalators down from the baggage claim areas. There you will encounter a vast curving corridor that will lead you via a series of moving sidewalks to the CTA station. From Terminal 2, take the escalator down from baggage claim to a corridor that runs under the Hilton Hotel. This leads to the station.

If you're coming from Terminal 5, prepare for an adventure. The journey takes 15 minutes and is a fair hike, involving several modes of transport. Exiting customs, proceed up two levels to the tram station. Take a tram going to the main terminals, and be careful which one you board: it's easy to go the wrong way and end up in a remote parking area. Get off at the first station, which is Terminal 3. Go up the escalator and turn left into the parking garage, not right to the terminal. In the parking garage, head to the elevator bank on the right. Ignore all the buttons bearing the logos of Chicago sports teams (a clever device to help drivers remember where they parked their cars) and take the elevator down to the level marked 'Hilton CTA.' Follow a narrow corridor to a much larger one, and you are on your way to the station.

At the station, it is a good idea to buy a fare card right from the start. (Full details on fare cards can be found in the CTA section.) Unless you are staying right in the Loop, you will have to transfer to another El or bus to complete your journey. For recommendations on which one to take, ask your hotel when you reserve your room. A good alternative is to ride the El as close as you can get to your hotel and then take a taxi for the final few blocks. Again, ask your hotel, or consult the neighborhood map in this book, to see which El stop is closest to your hotel.

Shuttle Airport Express has a monopoly on services between the airport and downtown. The fare is $15.50 per person, plus the usual 10% to 15% tip. Once downtown you may drive around while others are dropped off. You also may have to wait until the van is full before you leave the airport. If there are two or more of you, take a cab – it's immediate, direct and cheaper per person.

Limo Limos may sound expensive but they often are not. They easily hold four people and accommodate piles of luggage. They charge a flat $40 an hour no matter how many people ride, and the fee is prorated. So if your trip lasts 45 minutes, you pay $30. To arrange for a limo, look for the 'Pre-Arranged Ride Directory' in the baggage area of each terminal. Use the phone to find a company that can take you immediately. Most keep limos on standby at a vast holding area near the airport.

If you want to plan ahead, here are the numbers for four large companies:

American Limousine	☎ 630-920-8888
My Chauffeur Limousine	☎ 847-671-3600
One Magnificent Limousine	☎ 312-944-1317
Safe Limousine Co	☎ 773-275-7796

Regional Buses For trips farther afield, regional bus companies serve southern Wisconsin, suburban Illinois and northwest Indiana from the Bus/Shuttle Center, installed in the ground level of the central parking garage. Use the tunnels under the Hilton Hotel to get there from Terminals 1, 2 and 3. Terminal 5, the international terminal, has its own pickup area.

Midway Airport
Many of the transportation details for Midway are the same as for O'Hare. The differences follow.

Taxi The fare to the Loop is $15 to $20 plus tip. The Share-a-Ride fare is $12 plus tip.

The El The CTA Orange Line goes to Midway from the Loop elevated tracks. The trains go around clockwise on the inner set of tracks, so take the correct set of stairs. At the airport, you reach the Midway El station through a small entrance at the end of the Southwest Airlines baggage claim area. A very long and remarkably cheap walkway (there's only one measly pair of short moving walkways and no ventilation) connects the terminal to the station.

Because the Orange Line goes around the Loop elevated tracks, it is especially cumbersome to transfer from it to the Red Line, which in the Loop is in a subway.

Follow the directions carefully at the State St Station, where you obtain a free transfer to the subway.

Shuttle The Airport Express monopoly charges $11 per person (plus tip) to get you downtown.

Car To reach the city from Midway, drive north on Cicero Blvd, the major road in front of the airport exit, for two miles, until you reach the Stevenson Expressway (I-55). Veer right and head northeast into the city.

CTA

The Chicago Transit Authority (CTA) is the underfunded public transportation system serving the city. It consists of the El and buses. You will soon find that there are a dearth of helpful signs or maps for the El at its stops, so use the one here in the book or ask for a free map at the information booths in El stations. The system has its roots in a slew of private and competing companies that provided transit in the city before World War II. Almost 60 years later, the myriad routes are still not well integrated.

Bring something to read – even though the CTA has recently posted schedules for the El in the stations, they are really best-case scenarios and have little bearing on how long you will actually wait. Buses have no published schedules.

The system is fairly safe. Statistics show that crime is less prevalent on the CTA than on the streets as a whole. Avoid deserted El stations late at night, although those between the Loop and Addison, with the exception of North/Clybourn, are populated around the clock. Whether on the El or buses, watch out for pickpockets.

Information Bus drivers, El conductors and station attendants may give you detailed and friendly transit advice or they may tell you to hump off. Your best bet is to call ☎ 836-7000 – the information number for the CTA, Metra and the Pace bus company – preceded by the area code of whatever area of Chicago you are in – 312, 708, 847, 630, or 773. A loud screech will sound, followed by instructions on what to dial, if you don't need to dial the area code or have dialed the wrong one.

Fares The fare on a bus or the El is $1.50. Within the El system, you can transfer between as many lines as you like without paying extra. But to transfer between the El and buses or vice versa, or just between buses, you need to pay 30¢ for a transfer, which is good for two hours after you buy it. Note: *You have to buy your transfer when you pay your first fare.*

The CTA has introduced fare cards called Transit Cards, which on the El have replaced cashiers and ticket booths. Some turnstiles accept $1.50 in change, but the vast majority take only a transit card. These are bought from vending machines located in every El station for any value you wish between $3 and $100. Note that for every $13.50 in value you put on the card, you actually get credit for $15. A minor bargain! The El turnstiles automatically deduct the cost of your ride from the card.

On the buses you can pay your fare in exact change and cash (buses accept dollar bills) and buy a transfer good for another ride on the bus or the El, or if you have a transit card, you can use that by swiping it through a machine. (You cannot buy a transit card on the buses, however.) It knows if you are transferring and will deduct 30¢ from the card instead of the full $1.50.

So what happens when your card has some useless amount like 60¢ left on it? You add value to the card using one of the vending machines. Also, more than one person can use one card by having each rider insert it separately. Children younger than seven ride free. Those seven to 11 ride at half price, but you have to prove their age to the bus driver or station attendant, a hassle.

Tourist Pass The CTA had a pilot program in 1997 under which tourists could buy an unlimited pass good for 24 hours for $5. It was sold at hotels, museums, visitor information centers and major El stations. However, whether the program would continue was not going to be

RICK GERHARTER

The El rumbles into the Loop above the Chicago River.

decided by the CTA bureaucracy until sometime in 1998. So all you can do is ask. If it is still in effect and you plan to ride more than three times during a 24-hour period, it's convenient and cheap.

The El

The CTA likes to call its train service 'Rapid Transit.' I've never heard anyone refer to it that way – everybody just calls it the El, whether the specific service they are referring to runs above ground, below ground or somewhere in between. For simplicity, this book does the same thing.

There are seven color-coded lines on the El: Red, Blue, Purple, Orange, Brown, Green and Yellow (you won't need to ride either of the last two). Most visitors should be able to use the system for almost all their transit needs, the exception being those going to Hyde Park, certain areas of Lincoln Park near the Lake and the area east of N Michigan Ave that includes Navy Pier.

Cars are air-conditioned as well as heated and have large windows for good viewing when above ground. (In fact, see An El of a Tour for an excellent tour of the city courtesy of the CTA.) During the day you shouldn't have to wait more than 15 minutes for a train. At night and on weekends, service varies. The Red Line and the Blue Line between the Loop and O'Hare operate 24 hours a day, but other lines and many stations may not run or may be closed.

On the North Side, the Sedgwick, Armitage, Diversey and Wellington stations are closed weeknights from about 9:30 pm to 5 am. On Saturday they close at 7:30 pm, and they never open on Sunday and holidays. This also applies to Brown and Purple Line service south of Belmont. The Brown Line runs north of Belmont through Wrigleyville every night until about 2 am except on Sunday, when it closes at midnight.

The Orange Line to and from Midway Airport is closed from 11:20 pm to 5 am, coinciding with the airport's operating hours. On the Red Line, the Harrison station, which is convenient to the South Loop, is closed after 10:30 pm weekdays and all day weekends.

An El of a Tour

For $1.50 you can see Chicago in its glory and despair and get an up-close tour of many of the city's most interesting neighborhoods. From your (usually) climate-controlled car on the El, you can get a vantage point on Chicago impossible from the street. You can see how neighborhoods have grown and declined while tracing the city's history.

Any of the lines pass interesting sights, but the following tour on the Orange and Brown Lines will give you the most varied experience. Station names are shown in boldface.

Start by boarding an Orange Line train at **Clark**, which is part of the bulbous glass monster known as the James R Thompson State of Illinois Center. At **State**, the next stop, look right. Next to the Chicago Theater is the Page Brothers Building, which has a cast-iron facade. Before the great fire in 1871, most of the Loop's buildings resembled this one.

The train turns south and runs above Wabash. Through the upper-floor windows of buildings on both sides, you can catch myriad glimpses of urban life that are denied pedestrians. This is one of the busiest stretches of the Loop tracks, which were opened in 1897 to unite the various elevated lines built by several different companies. The tracks have survived several proposals through the years to replace them, their longevity mostly thanks to a lack of public funding to build anything better.

As you leave the Loop, you penetrate what was once known as 'the Levee District,' a notorious area populated from about 1890 to 1910 by prostitutes, gamblers and other vice-seekers. Around **Roosevelt** you can see a housing development called Central Station, a vast project that will be under construction for the next decade. This is where Mayor Daley lives. The old warehouses in the surrounding blocks are undergoing renovation, and the area is quickly gaining popularity with artists and professionals.

After the tracks split, the Orange Line heads southwest and traverses acres of vacant land that were once used for railroad yards servicing the hundreds of daily passenger trains that made Chicago the rail transit hub of the country.

Continuing southwest, the line is hemmed in by the Stevenson Expressway and the Chicago River. Past the **35th St/Archer** station the tracks climb to their highest point for the best view of the skyline from anywhere on the El system.

Just before **Western**, look left to see a relic from the city's days as a major meat processor. The cattle ramps and holding pens look out of place today.

After **Kedzie** the line overlooks block after block of tidy bungalows before it reaches Midway Airport, where the planes take off above the trains. At **Midway**, which is the end of the line, cross the tracks and return downtown.

When you reach the Loop, the train will turn left, heading west, and stop at the new **Library** station. Two pioneer office towers flank Dearborn St, to the right of your train. On the east side of the street, the Fisher Building dates from 1896. Look for the terra-cotta fish and other seashore critters decorating the exterior. On the west side is the world-famous Monadnock Building, built from 1889 to 1893.

Seashore critters decorating
the Fisher Building

One block west of the Fisher and Monadnock Buildings on Clark St, the Chicago Metropolitan Correctional Center, built in 1975, cuts its unique angle to the left of the tracks. Housing people awaiting trial for federal crimes, the building's five-inch-wide plastic windows allowed a few inmates to escape before bars were added on the inside.

◁▽◁▽◁▽◁▽◁▽◁▽◁▽◁▽

The most delightful station out of a mostly dreary lot in the Loop is **Quincy**. Originally built in 1897, and restored by the city in 1988, it shows what all the stations once looked like.

Get off when you reach **Clark** and cross over the tracks to board a Brown Line train. One of Chicago's most famous views occurs right as the trains leave the Loop and cross the Chicago River.

Between **Chicago** and **Armitage** there used to be seven stations; now there is only one. This run gives a stark illustration of the disparities in wealth in the city. To the east is the Gold Coast, one of the nation's wealthiest neighborhoods; to the west, Cabrini-Green, one of the poorest.

The sharp turns at Halsted St, a daily annoyance to thousands of standing commuters, are a legacy of the free-enterprise roots of the El system. During the line's construction in the 1890s, the German farmers in the area held out for higher prices for their land. Instead of negotiating, the then-private El company simply went around them.

Beginning at **Armitage**, the tracks run north through gentrified Lincoln Park. After **Belmont** the line heads west for some of the most varied views in the city. The distant lakefront, numerous vintage buildings and industrial water towers all combine for constantly changing urban panoramas.

West of the **Western** station, which serves the old Lincoln Square German neighborhood, the line descends to ground level. There's a nice crossing of the Chicago River before the tracks terminate at **Kimball**, in Albany Park. From here you can explore the neighborhood, which has many Middle Eastern and Asian shops, or you can return to the Loop. Alternatively, take a No 81 Lawrence Ave CTA bus east to the **Lawrence** El stop on the Red Line. Here you can ride south past Wrigley Field back to the Loop. ■

◁▽◁▽◁▽◁▽◁▽◁▽◁▽◁▽

Bus

CTA buses go almost everywhere, but they do so on erratic schedules. The bus stops are clearly marked with signs on poles showing which routes stop there, but little else. Buses make frequent stops and don't go very fast. At rush hour you'll have to stand, and during the summer many are not air-conditioned (you can tell which ones are, because all the windows will be closed).

The following routes are of use to visitors and run from early in the morning until late in the evening.

22 Clark – runs north on Dearborn until Oak and then on Clark all the way to the north end of the city. This is a good bus for getting to the parts of Lincoln Park that are a hike from the Fullerton El stop, such as the zoo. It is also a good bus for shuttling up and down the North Side.

29 State – runs on State St through the Loop and River North, then east on Illinois to Navy Pier. These buses have large 'Navy Pier' signs on their fronts.

36 Broadway – mostly mirrors the 22 Clark route going north, until it reaches Diversey, where it veers off on Broadway. It's a good way to reach east Lake View.

72 North – runs on North Ave. It's a good route between Bucktown/Wicker Park and Lincoln Park.

73 Armitage – runs parallel to the 72, but four blocks north.

146 Marine-Michigan – runs from the Berwyn El stop in Andersonville south along the lakefront all the way to North Michigan Ave. It transits the Loop via State St, then cuts through Grant Park on Balbo and Columbus to the Museum Campus. This is a very tourist-friendly route. Note that on weekdays it runs express between Belmont and Michigan Ave.

151 Sheridan – runs from Union Station through the Loop and then up North Michigan Ave until Lake Shore Drive, where it takes local streets through the heart of Lincoln Park; there is a stop right in front of the zoo.

METRA

A web of commuter trains running under the Metra banner serves the 245 stations in the suburbs surrounding Chicago. Their primary riders are people who work in the city and live elsewhere. These customers don't tolerate delays, and the trains almost always run on time. The trains are clean and have two levels, with the second offering tight seating but better views.

RICK GERHARTER

Derived from the services once run by the many competing railroads in the region, the Metra's 12 lines depart from four stations ringing the Loop:

Union Station – This is a great and grand station that will make you wish the trains lived up to the grandeur of the main waiting area. Scores of restaurants and shops serve commuters. In addition to Metra services, all Amtrak trains depart from here. 210 S Canal between Adams and Jackson (Map 3; ☎ 312-655-2385).

Richard B Ogilvie Transportation Center – Formerly called Northwestern Station, a moniker it's bound to keep for most people, this airy station is built into the base of Helmut Jahn's 1986 re-creation of a 1930s radio. It also has many food stalls and shops. 500 W Madison at Canal (Map 3; ☎ 312-836-7000).

Randolph St Station – This station is in the midst of a multiyear reconstruction that has reduced amenities to a bare minimum. It is linked to the underground Pedway system that lets you walk past Marshall Field's to destinations in the central Loop without sampling Chicago's sometimes horrid weather. Besides the Metra electric service to Hyde Park and beyond, the station is the terminus for the South Shore trains to the Indiana Dunes and South Bend. Below street level at Randolph and Michigan (Map 3; ☎ 312-836-7000).

LaSalle St Station – As businesslike as the Chicago Stock Exchange above it, this station has a tiny waiting room and next to no shops. Trains depart for Joliet on the Metra/Rock Island District line. 414 S LaSalle between Congress Parkway and Van Buren (Map 3; ☎ 312-836-7000).

Information

Some of the Metra lines run frequent schedules seven days a week; others operate only during weekday rush hours. The four main Metra stations in Chicago have schedules for all the lines and other information. The Metra information line is an excellent service that can tell you what combination of CTA, Metra and Pace (a very limited suburban bus service) can get you from where you are to where you want to go. The information number is the same for all three transit services: call ☎ 836-7000, preceded by the area code of whatever area of Chicago you are in – 312, 708, 847, 630, or 773. A loud screech will sound, followed by instructions on what to dial, if you don't need to dial the area code or have dialed the wrong one.

Fares

Short trips start at $1.75 and go to $5 or more for long journeys. Tickets are on sale from agents and machines at major stations. At small stations where nobody is on duty you can buy the ticket without penalty from the conductor on the train; otherwise there is a $1 surcharge for doing this.

On weekends adults can buy a ticket good everywhere Metra goes for $5. The tickets are good on both Saturday and Sunday, and each holder can bring along up to three children younger than 12. This is an excellent deal – just make certain that the lines you want to take operate on those days.

Important Lines

Following are Metra lines of interest to tourists. The stations where the trains originate are listed in parentheses and are indicated on the Loop map.

Metra Electric (Randolph St, Van Buren St) – This is the best way to get to Hyde Park and the Museum of Science and Industry (15 minutes, $1.95). Trains run at least hourly every day. It's also an excellent way to get to and from McCormick Place (10 minutes, $1.75).

South Shore Line (Randolph St, Van Buren St) – This historic line with modern electric trains serves northwest Indiana. These trains are the best means for visiting the Indiana Dunes (75 minutes, $5.75) and South Bend (2½ hours, $9.40). They run every day, but not all of them travel the entire route, so definitely check schedules first. The ride through the Gary steel mills is a lesson in the brutal grandeur of 20th-century industry.

Metra/BNSF (Union Station) – These trains provide at least hourly service every day to the western suburbs, including the Hollywood stop, which serves the Brookfield Zoo (23 minutes, $2.75).

Metra/Union Pacific North Line (Northwestern Station) – The line provides frequent service all the way to the Wisconsin border, with stops at affluent North Shore suburbs, including Wilmette and Winnetka, on the way.

CAR & MOTORCYCLE

In most cases, once you are in the city, you can forget about your car. Whether it's for the day or for a week, park it and forget it. Better yet don't bring it. Parking expenses will rapidly eat through your wallet. Riding a motorcycle is a good idea only during the temperate months, and finding secure parking for it is even more of a concern than for cars.

Driving

Chicago's streets, with their logical layout and numbering system, are easy to navigate, but drivers do not take dawdlers lightly, and horns are sounded with little provocation. If you can possibly avoid it, don't drive during rush hours (6 to 9 am and 4 to 7 pm), when circulation becomes an artery-clogged nightmare, conditions that mimic the heart attack you may suffer while jammed in frustrating traffic. Weekends, when residents are out trying to run errands, can be even worse.

Fuel Note that gas bought in the city is subject to reams of taxes. If you're embarking on a big journey out of town, wait until you're well clear of the city before filling up. You'll easily save 30¢ or more a gallon.

Rules & Regulations The wealth of Chicago nightlife is a good excuse not to drive for two reasons. First, the blood-alcohol level considered legally drunk is now only .08, the equivalent of about four beers. Cops love to toss drunk drivers in jail overnight. Second, there still are plenty of drunk drivers out there, and you're far better off not tangling with them.

Anyone driving or riding in the front seat of a car must wear a seatbelt. Motorcyclists are not required to wear helmets, leaving them free to suffer the kinds of head trauma that keep ERs busy.

Parking Trying to park your car will soon make you wish it would be stolen. In the Loop and Near North there are plenty of parking garages, but they charge $15 a day or more. The lots are usually secure, even the ones where the attendant asks you for the keys, so he or she can move your car about through the day. If you are staying in a hotel, find out what the parking charges are before you commit; otherwise that bargain room may be $20 a day or more extra. Conversely, during slack times hotels may offer free parking to entice you.

RICK GERHARTER
Street scene on the Near Northwest Side

Some parking garages, hotels and many restaurants offer valet parking. You pull up and a person in a red cap takes your key and drives away. The fees vary widely, but remember to tip the person who retrieves your car at least $1.

In the Near North area most streets have parking meters. Competition for these spaces, which average 25¢ for 15 minutes, is heated. Parking enforcers patrol constantly and will cheerfully slap a ticket on your windshield within seconds of the meter expiring. You can toss the ticket away, but the city is adept at tracking down in-state and out-of-state offenders. Don't think a rental car will shield you, either. The rental company will simply put the charge on your credit card a few months later.

The situation is no better in the neighborhoods. If it's a neighborhood you want to park in, then there is probably some sort of permit scheme in force to prevent you from doing so.

Finally, if you do find a place to park, make certain that it is not a tow zone. Both the city and private companies make big profits from snatching illegally parked cars. The city charges a cool $110 plus the cost of the parking fine to retrieve your car. In fact, most people who report cars stolen later find them in city or private auto pounds. If you suspect your car has been towed, check the place where you parked to see who has jurisdiction over towing there; if it was a public street, call the Chicago Police Department at 312-744-6000 to find out which lot to check with (there are several).

Expressways

People accustomed to numerical designations, such as I-80, for US highways will be in for confusion in northern Illinois, where the roads are more commonly identified by honorary names rather than numbers. Many people you ask for directions will know the highways only by their names, not their numbers.

Even the designation for highways can be confusing. Roads without tolls are called expressways, not freeways. Those that charge money are called tollways or toll roads. To add further stress, the Illinois

---

Lincoln Bandits

You need to run into a store for some simple item. You can't find a place to park, but then you spy an empty space in an alley. You leave your car for a moment, complete your business, come back and find your car gone. Was it thieves? Possibly, but more likely it was the zealous trolls working for Lincoln Towing (☎ 773-561-4433), a private firm with contracts to police most of the private parking lots, alleys and other places that might tempt you to leave your car.

Employing dozens of spotters and commission-based drivers, Lincoln Towing snatches scores of cars every day, towing them – often with car alarms shrieking like an animal caught in the jaws of a predator – to its lot at 4882 N Clark. The frustration of the hapless car owners is evident in the office area: the entrance bears traces of fires, graffiti and possible assault on a vehicle; the employees work behind heavily scarred bulletproof glass. The anger on the part of car owners stems partly from the inconvenience and expense ($105) of retrieving one's car, but it is greatly compounded by the Lincoln Towing personnel, who revel in abusing their 'clients' with a stream of invective. When I called to ask about the pricing structure, this was the response I got from the representative on the phone: 'When your car gets towed, get your ass up here and I'll let you know what it will run you.'

Oh, and if you think your car was towed by mistake, tough luck. Short of evidence you can use in court – numerous witnesses, photos, etc – you can forget getting the fee waived. Pay your money (cash only!), check carefully for damage and avoid these vultures like the plague. ■

An Express Guide to the Expressways

Here's how to get out of central Chicago for major destinations, using the Interstate designations. Be aware that roads may start and stop and you may merge with others, but keep following the numbers. Entering the city is usually easier because all you have to do is keep following the Chicago signs. (Praying for clear weather so you can see the skyline helps, too.)

Destination	Route
North Shore, Wisconsin, Minnesota	West I-94
Schaumburg, Rockford	West I-90
O'Hare International Airport	West I-90 to I-190
Oak Brook, Naperville and western Illinois	West I-290 to West I-88
Iowa and west all the way to San Francisco	East I-90/I-94 until just south of the Loop, then South I-55 to West I-80
Springfield, St Louis, the South and Southwest	East I-90/I-94 until just south of the Loop, then South I-55
Champaign-Urbana, Southern Illinois and the Southeast	East I-94 to South I-57
Indiana and the East	East I-90
New Buffalo and Michigan	East I-94

Department of Transportation has some of the worst signs in the nation, and roads will be designated East I-94 even when they are going due south. So don't use your compass.

The solution is a good map and the following guide to highway names, going counterclockwise from the north.

Edens Expressway (I-94) Named for a minor political figure, William G Edens (known as 'the father of the Illinois good roads program,' though he never owned or drove a car), this expressway serves the North Shore communities and is a major link in the route to and from Milwaukee. It runs between the Kennedy Expressway and the Tri-State Tollway.

Tri-State Tollway (I-94/I-294) This is the designation for the toll road that begins at the Wisconsin border and sweeps south through the Chicago suburbs before heading east to Indiana. Coming south from Milwaukee, the I-94 designation breaks off to become the Edens Expressway, which heads toward the city center. The road then becomes I-294 as it continues its suburban journey to Indiana. Tolls are frequent, often cause huge backups and require you to repeatedly dig into your pocket for 30¢.

Northwest Tollway (I-90) Beginning at O'Hare International Airport and the Tri-State Tollway, this is another highly annoying toll road, with frequent stops for change. It serves Schaumburg and points west.

Kennedy Expressway (I-90/I-94) Oh the confusion! This is the major expressway from Chicago to O'Hare, but watch the numbers. *Don't* follow the I-94 signs when the Edens Expressway branches off for the North Shore. Stay on I-90 until you see the Cumberland Rd exit; at that point get all the way over to the rightmost lane and take the I-190 exit for the short hop to O'Hare. Getting to the city from the airport is easier – just follow the Chicago signs. If it's daylight, look for the Sears Tower; if you see it somewhere in your frontal vision, you're okay. One more note on the Kennedy: it features reversible express lanes. In the morning they go into the city, reversing in the afternoons. If you are heading to O'Hare in the afternoon, these are a good choice. There is no toll between the city and the airport.

Eisenhower Expressway (I-290) The area's first highway, it serves close-in Oak Park and the western suburbs. It loses its name when it reaches the Tri-State Tollway. I-290 continues northwest to Schaumburg. However, the major portion of the road and traffic are linked with the East-West Tollway.

East-West Tollway (I-88) This road serves Oak Brook, Naperville, Aurora, and various less developed Illinois cornfields.

Stevenson Expressway (I-55) This begins just south of the Loop; you can access it off of Lake Shore Drive or the Dan Ryan Expressway just south of the Loop. Widely reviled as the worst-maintained road in the region, this is the main route toward Midway airport. Exit at Cicero Ave. The bumpy drive continues southwest toward Joliet, where it links up with I-80.

Dan Ryan Expressway (I-90/I-94) North of the Loop it is the Kennedy; this is the name south of the Loop. The busiest highway in the world, this 14-lane monster requires careful navigation. Shortly after I-55 branches off, the Dan Ryan divides into express and local lanes. The latter are clogged with trucks banned from the express lanes, which you can take if your journey extends beyond the city. If you are going east to Indiana, get in the local lanes at 55th St and take the Skyway/Indiana Toll Road exit. I-90 branches off here. At 95th St, the Dan Ryan splits. To the right, the unnamed I-57 heads south to I-80 and southern Illinois. To the left, I-94 continues on as the Calumet Expressway, which links up with the eastern portion of the Tri-State Tollway.

Chicago Skyway (I-90) This boondoggle of a road built by the city has been bankrupt and bumpy almost since it opened 40 years ago. You pay $2 for the privilege of riding on a five-mile elevated road and bridge linking the Dan Ryan Expressway with the Indiana Toll Road.

Kingery Expressway (I-80/I-94) The eastern portion of the Tri-State Tollway takes this name when it is joined by I-80. When the road leaves Illinois for Indiana, it becomes the Borman Expressway.

Car Rental

If Chicago is your first stop on a tour of the Midwest, then wait to pick up a rental car until you are ready to leave the city. If you are staying in Chicago and just need a car for a couple of days, try to time your rental for the weekend, when the rental lots are full of cars unwanted by business travelers. As with hotels, there will usually be a variety of deals on offer. Most are in force from about noon on Thursday until Monday morning.

All the major car rental companies have outposts at the airport and in the city. For the best deals, you may have to go to the airport to pick up your car from one of the vast lots out there. The best way to get there is to take the El to the airport and then transfer to one of the free car rental shuttle buses, which frequently make runs out to the station. You'll have to weigh the convenience of in-town rental against the savings of a trip to O'Hare.

Reservations Make them in advance to ensure the best deal, and shop around carefully to get a good rate. Be aware of any deals you might get from various credit card, frequent flyer or even employer tie-ins.

Here are the numbers to call for firms with offices at O'Hare; most, but not all, also have offices downtown and at Midway:

Alamo	☎ 800-327-9633
Avis	☎ 800-831-2847
Budget	☎ 800-686-6800
Dollar	☎ 800-800-4000
Hertz	☎ 800-654-3131
National	☎ 800-227-7368
Thrifty	☎ 800-367-2277

Rates Midweek rates for a compact car are $45 to $60 a day. Weekly rates can be much cheaper, at $135 and up. Weekend deals for $29 a day can be found. As you ponder these figures, add in the special city and state car rental tax of 18%.

American car renters will cheer the lack of usurious collision and loss or damage insurance that in other states average another $10 a day. These extra fees are illegal in Illinois and are replaced by insurance coverage and a standard deductible built into the rental rate. Check with the agency for its exact details. Your credit card may give you some coverage as well, but check *very* carefully with your card issuer, because many have numerous hoops that make getting reimbursed for a claim an ordeal.

Rentals almost always include unlimited mileage, but again, it's well worth double-checking.

Age & Credit Requirements The minimum requirements are usually 25 years of age with one good credit card. Beware of firms that put a huge hold on your card, leaving you with no credit line and in deep doo-doo when you try to check out of a hotel. Renting a car without a credit card is conceivable but requires advance planning with the company. Renting a car when you are younger than 25 is also possible with some companies, but sometimes they charge you an extra fee.

Fuel Costs As mentioned before, try to buy gas out of town to avoid noxious city taxes. But also remember to return your car with a full tank to avoid even more noxious refueling surcharges, which the rental companies just love to add.

You will probably be offered the latest car rental scam by the brightly smiling counter clerk when you pick up the car: a chance to 'buy' your full tank of gas at a going rate. A good deal? I quote my friend Nick Selby, author of Lonely Planet's *Miami* guide, among other titles: 'Unless you're the kind of person who can calculate exactly how far a tank will get you, and

you run on fumes all the way back to the airport, this is a bad idea, because there are no refunds on unused fuel: if you bring the car back half full, you've just paid twice the going rate for the gas.'

Buying a Used Car

Only if you are from another country and planning to spend a long time in the US, say several months, would I recommend buying a car. Eventually you'll save money over a rental, but in between you have the hassle of finding a car you can trust and finding a mechanic you can trust to check it out. There are mandatory registration and insurance fees, and then you have to unload the thing when you're done with it.

Furthermore, the only kinds of used cars that are priced low enough to make this work financially are real junkers, at least in Illinois. All that ice and snow are combated by equal amounts of road salt that soon dissolves bodies, transmissions, frames and other vital organs. If you are on a major tour, wait until you are someplace warm and dry to buy a car. The odds of it leaving its entrails strewn on the highway are much lower.

TAXI

Taxis are easy to find in the Loop and north through Wrigleyville. Raise you arm and one will promptly cut a few cars off and zip over to the curb to pick you up. In other parts of the city, you can either call a cab or face what may be a long wait for one to happen along. When the cab's top light is on, it means it is ready for a fare (although many of the lights are broken and remain on even when the back seat is full).

The major cab companies are:

Yellow Cab	☎ 312-829-4222
Checker Cab	☎ 312-243-2537
Flash Cab	☎ 773-561-1444

The first two companies have the same owners and are responsible for the majority of cabs on the streets. Flash is very popular with locals because it has a reputation for hiring older, more experienced drivers. Flash is worth calling first. When hailing a cab, there is no reason to get picky.

Driving a cab is hard work, with very long days and some risk of robbery. Many cab drivers are people new to the US job market and may have limited English skills and knowledge of the city. However, most are fairly polite and will do what you ask, such as turning on the air-conditioning on a hot day or turning down overamped talk radio. Cases of meter-fraud are not common.

Fares are $1.50 when you enter the cab and $1.20 for each additional mile; extra passengers are 50¢ per passenger. Drivers expect a 10% to 15% tip. A ride from the Loop into Lincoln Park will cost about $9, including tip. The same underpublicized Share-a-Ride program that is in place for airport passengers also applies at McCormick Place: a ride to or from the vast convention center from downtown or Near North costs $5 per person. Make certain you explain to the driver that you want to ride-share before you set off in a cab.

BICYCLE

Curbs are the highest mountains you'll find in Chicago, making the town ideal for biking. The 18½-mile lakefront path, from Hollywood Ave in the north to 71st St in the south, is very popular and has its own traffic jams on warm weekends. The path is an excellent way to see the city from top to bottom, and in the hot weather the lake offers cooling breezes.

Lincoln Park is another good spot for biking, with paths snaking around the small lakes and the zoo. Chicago streets themselves, while flat, are not terribly accommodating: bike lanes don't exist, except in a couple of places, where they have become de facto double-parking zones, and many streets are just wide enough for speeding traffic and parked cars. And it's both illegal and bad form to ride on the narrow sidewalks. One way to beat cars is to take small side streets in the neighborhoods, which are less hectic and more pleasant.

Finally, lock your bike, lock your bike, lock your bike. Oh, and did I mention to lock your bike? And choose a busy location. The number of broken supposedly thief-proof U-locks you see in the gutters should tell you about the kind of opposition you're up against.

RICK GERHARTER

Bike path bliss

Rentals

Bike Chicago (☎ 312-944-2337; 800-915-2453) is one of those cool companies deserving of praise and business. From April 15 to October 15 they rent Trek mountain bikes, big cruisers with fat tires, bicycles built for two and kids' bikes. They are at Navy Pier, 500 E North, and also operate out of trailers, when the weather is nice, at Oak St Beach, Lincoln Park Zoo and Buckingham Fountain. As part of the deal, you can pick your bike up at one location and return it to another for no extra charge. Their free maps show the 18-mile lakefront path in detail, and they include locks and helmets in the deal.

If you rent for an entire day, Bike Chicago will bring the bike by your hotel in the morning. Rates are $8 an hour and $30 a day, with significant reductions for additional days. Here's one of the coolest offers: each day they lead 15 riders on a two-hour tour. It's free and is open to people who didn't even rent from Bike Chicago. To join a tour, all you have to do is call and secure your place in advance. They also rent in-line skates at lower rates than for the bikes.

In Lake View, the Bike Stop (☎ 773-868-6800), 1034 W Belmont, two blocks west of the El stop, rents mountain bikes and in-line skates.

WALKING

Except when huge chunks of windblown sleet are smacking you in the face, the best way to see the city is on foot. (When the aforementioned weather conditions are in force, I recommend fantasizing about the city while sitting next to the fireplace in a cozy bar.)

The city is flat and very simply laid out – you know that by now, right? Walking the sidewalks, you can discover for yourself the myriad little shops, cafés, corner pubs, architectural gems and scores of other treats that make Chicago such a surprising and interesting place for residents and visitors. Just walking the residential streets on the North Side in Lincoln Park and Lake View can yield unexpected delights, such as clever details added to exquisitely restored Victorian homes or somebody's lovingly nurtured wildflower garden.

Streetwalking

Wandering the streets of Chicago is one of the city's greatest pleasures. There are no points awarded for doing so in the Near North – it's fun and fascinating, but you won't need any guidance there; just start walking.

This book offers self-guided architecture walks of the Loop, the University of Chicago and Wicker Park; it also has sculpture tours of the Loop and Grant Park. (See the special Architecture section for the Loop tour, Things to See & Do for the rest.) But I can't stress enough that you should find some area or site you like the sound of and then just start walking. The maps in this book will guide you, and the number of routes is infinite.

Following are four ideas to help you get started. See the appropriate sections in the Things to See & Do and Shopping chapters for guidance to sights. The Places to Eat and Entertainment chapters will have ideas for refreshment and frolic. Use these streets as starting points. Wander off them in any direction and see what you find.

Wells Street and Lincoln Avenue The walk north from Division St to Diversey Parkway covers the heart of Old Town and Lincoln Park in 2.3 miles.

Clark Street The 3.4-mile trek north from North Avenue to Irving Park Road goes from gentrified Lincoln Park through lively Lake View and Wrigleyville.

Lincoln Park Start where Dearborn St ends at North Avenue and head north; when you reach Diversey, head east to the lake and you can keep going all the way to Hollywood Ave, 1.7 to 5.4 miles. This is the most bucolic long walk in the city.

Loop to the Museum Campus Take South Michigan Ave south from Madison St to Roosevelt Rd and east to the Museum Campus, 1.8 miles. This walk encompasses the grandeur of Michigan Ave, Grant Park and the museums. ■

Don't let winter put you off, either. After a fresh snow, the sounds of traffic are muffled and the fresh flakes make a seductive crunch-crunch under your feet. Of course, once the snow gets old, dirty, and slushy, then you're better off back by the fireplace.

The Organized Tours section suggests some guided walking tours. But I can't emphasize enough that you'll have the best time on your own. The Streetwalking sidebar has some ideas to get you started in your explorations.

For advice on neighborhoods to avoid in your rambles, see Dangers & Annoyances in Facts for the Visitor. At night in any neighborhood, it's good to stick with the major streets with commercial activity.

ORGANIZED TOURS

There are myriad ways to see Chicago on a guided tour. Especially in the warmer months, you can go by land or lake. The choice of bus versus boat depends on the experience you want. You cover more territory on a bus, but you can't duplicate the views from the water. If nothing else, boats let you see how badly the undersides of the city's bridges need paint, and they show you the lock into Lake Michigan, the canyon effect of the buildings along Wacker Drive and the occasional dead fish. Also, for whatever reason, the friendly citizens of Chicago wave constantly at people on boats. When you're on the bus, nobody waves at all.

Buses excel at covering a lot of territory, especially the longer tours. Heading north and south, you get away from Michigan Ave and the Loop and get a chance to see more of Chicago's diversity. For in-depth tours, there are several walking tours that offer detailed information on selected areas.

Bus Tours

Buses have the advantage of operating throughout the year.

American Sightseeing (☎ 312-251-3100) departs from the Palmer House and other downtown hotels. The buses are of the big air-conditioned and tinted-glass variety. You are definitely insulated from the sights

RAY HILLSTROM
Double-decker squeeze

you see. There are two tours: North covers the Loop, the many commercial pleasures of River North, Lincoln Park and Wrigley Field. South includes Grant Park, Hyde Park and historical areas of the city that few people take the time to see, such as Prairie and Woodlawn Aves. Each tour lasts two hours and costs $15 (children $7.50). Take both for $25/$12.50. Specialized tours on black Chicago and other topics are sometimes available. American Sightseeing operates similar tours under the Gray Line brand name (☎ 312-427-3107).

You can't help but notice the double-decker buses of the Chicago Motor Coach Co (☎ 312-922-8919). Although they don't cover a lot of territory, these buses do have the feature of making pickups and drop-offs all day at their 10 stops in the Loop and Near North, including the Water Tower, Sears Tower, Art Institute and Field Museum. You can use them to work your way from one tourist spot to the next. The charm of these buses are the breezy open upper decks and their unobstructed views of tall buildings. But there is no charm in the cramped seating, which makes long-term riding untenable. The entire tour lasts

90 minutes, but most people will want to get on and off, if for no other reason than to take a break from the spiel the driver delivers at each stop. The tour costs $10 for one circuit, $3 more to transfer all day. The buses run about every 15 minutes.

Okay, it's a personal opinion, but I always think that the people bouncing around the city's streets on the fake trolleys run by the Chicago Trolley Co (☎ 312-663-0260) look like nitwits. These gas-powered vehicles, which have both open and air-conditioned areas, are pretty cheesy looking. The service itself is not a bad idea, though: you pay one price and ride the trolleys all day, hopping on and off at all the major tourist attractions over a good portion of the city. If you opt for this ride, on-and-off tickets are $15. Call to find out the stop closest to you.

Boat Tours

Chicago has two main boat-tour companies offering similar 90-minute tours of the river and lake for $11. The guides are often perfunctory, offering bad jokes and limited information. Be aware that passing through the lock to and from the lake can take up a fair part of the tour.

Mercury Chicago Skyline Cruises (☎ 312-332-1353) depart from the southwest corner of the Michigan Ave Bridge and the river (Map 3). Wendella Sightseeing Boats (☎ 312-337-1446) depart from the northwest corner of the Michigan Ave Bridge and the river (Map 3). Both also offer other tours and night cruises.

About the only factor that you should consider when deciding between Wendella and Mercury is which side of the river you're on. They're that similar. The Wendella boats don't place you under as much blue plastic as Mercury's, but that can be a bad thing on a breezy ride. One thing you'll notice about the locks while waiting: seemingly every seagull in the Midwest lives on the breakwater there, and seagulls foul their nests. It stinks.

For a much more learned approach to water touring, take the Chicago Architecture Federation River Cruise (☎ 312-922-3432).

For more detail on these 90-minute, $17 tours, see the Architectural Tours portion of the Architecture section.

Shoreline Sightseeing (☎ 312-222-9328) offers 30-minute lake-only tours for $9 (children $4). You miss the river, but avoid the lock. There are lots of postcard views on these tours, which leave from Navy Pier, the lake in front of Buckingham Fountain and the Shedd Aquarium. You can get a ticket that lets you use the cruise to get from one site to the next. Printed translations of the narration are available in 12 languages, including French, Spanish, German, Polish, Arabic, Japanese and Hindi. The same company also runs handy water-taxis that link the Sears Tower (the pier is on the river across the street), Navy Pier and the Shedd Aquarium.

Navy Pier The south side of the pier has a row of tour and dinner-cruise boats that avoid the time-consuming locks into the Chicago River, but also miss the close-up views of a river tour. Schedules change with the seasons, so confirm them in advance. Also, the air over Lake Michigan can be pretty cold, even when the city is warm, so bring a sweatshirt or jacket.

RAY HILLSTROM
Brave a boat tour in winter.

The *Odyssey* (☎ 630-990-0800) is a sleek cruise boat that looks like a huge yacht. Two-hour cruises, which sail throughout the year, include a meal and music. The experience isn't cheap, and the company suggests that you should dress up for the experience. Brunches and lunches are $36 to $41. Dinners are a pricey $71 to $83. A moonlight cruise during the summer is $27 and leaves at midnight.

During the summer it's not uncommon to hear the loud, annoying drone of a cigarette boat zipping along the shore, piloted by some yahoo showing off. Groups can now enjoy the same sensation on the Seadog boats (☎ 312-822-7200), which are huge cigarette boats (cigar-boats?) that seat 149 people and zip across the lake at 30 miles per hour or faster, their throbbing exhausts reverberating off the shore. Adults pay $13, children $8.

The *Spirit of Chicago* (☎ 312-836-7899) offers slightly down-market lunch and dinner cruises (wear what you want), departing year round, except when the lake is frozen. Lunch cruises cost about $32, dinner about $62 and various party cruises (no chow) about $25 to $35. The boat has lots of open space on deck for enjoying the view.

When the wind blows, which is most of the time, the *Windy* (☎ 312-595-5555), a 109-foot, four-masted schooner, plies the lake. Ninety-minute tours are $25 for adults, $15 for kids from May to September. Passengers can play sailor by helping to raise and lower the sails. A better deal is to play skipper by trying your hand at the wheel. With only the sound of the wind in your ears, the *Windy* is the most relaxing way to see the skyline from offshore.

Walking Tours

The Chicago Architecture Federation (☎ 312-922-3432) offers a long list of walking tours. See Architectural Tours in the Architecture section for details. See the Things to See & Do chapter for some self-guided walking tours.

Special Interest

You can find a tour for every taste, from cultural to off-beat to weird.

Chicago Neighborhood Tours (☎ 312-742-1190) were an immediate hit when they were started by the city's Department of Cultural Affairs in 1997. Nine tours are held throughout the year every Saturday, with one a week on a rotating basis. Among the neighborhoods explored are Bronzeville, Humboldt Park, Uptown, Devon Ave and Pilsen. Each tour lasts four hours, is hosted by local experts and gives a detailed look at one or two neighborhoods. Local businesses contribute free food and gifts. I highly, highly recommend these tours. Call to confirm the details, but in 1997 you had to be at the Chicago Cultural Center, Randolph and Michigan, at 9:30 am for the 10 am bus departure, and the tours cost, on average, $26.

Black CouTours (☎ 312-233-8907) has 2½-hour bus tours that focus on African American history in Chicago with a generous dash of soul. This an excellent way to see parts of the South Side ignored by major tours. Tickets are $25.

Chicago Supernatural Tours (☎ 708-499-0300) offers five-hour tours every day in the summer and on weekends the rest of the year for $28. The ghoulish itinerary takes in murder sites, cemeteries, supposedly haunted houses and all sorts of other places with some kind of spiritual connection (at least in the minds of the tour leaders).

Horse-drawn carriages depart from the Water Tower throughout the year, day and night. You can choose a route or let the driver pick one for you. These are popular with suburban teens who are in town for a prom and want to smooch. Rates are $30 for a minimum of 30 minutes, with another $30 for each half-hour thereafter. Drivers will hope for a tip, whether they give witty commentary or leave you to your romance.

Pedal-powered rickshas are a feature at Chicago street fairs all summer long. Twelve actors led by the delightful

Matthew Furlin will take you virtually any-place you want to go while giving you the kind of running patter you'd expect from out-of-work actors who never know when their passengers might turn out to be casting directors. These guys are great fun; to find them, drop by one of the festivals such as the Sheffield Garden Walk (held in mid- to late July in the blocks surrounding Sheffield and Webster; see Facts for the Visitor for a list of other festivals). Say hi to Matt for me. He let me pedal his ricksha late one night; it's hard work. Rates are very negotiable.

Untouchable Gangster Tours (☎ 773-881-1195) offer comic tours of gangland Chicago in an old bus. See the sidebar Capone's Chicago in Facts about Chicago for other tours.

Transit Tours

On the CTA, there's no canned spiel except for that provided by the loony guy in the next seat. The following two self-guided bus tours take advantage of regular CTA routes. See the sidebar An El of a Tour, ear-lier in this chapter, for a detailed tour of the city by train.

At only $1.50, the following two bus routes give very good tours. They are sim-pler than the complex El tour because you get on once and then sit.

For a typical tourist experience, take the No 146 Marine-Michigan bus which starts at the Adler Planetarium and heads north through Grant Park, the Loop, the Magnif-icent Mile and Lincoln Park.

A more adventuresome alternative is offered by the No 50 Damen bus. On its 11-mile run from Bryn Mawr Ave south to 35th St, the bus cuts through the heart of Chicago. In a little over an hour, riders get a tour of the city in all its diversity. Some highlights: classic two-flats and bunga-lows north of Belmont, trendy Bucktown south of Fullerton, Wicker Park and its green-haired habitués, the United Center and the burgeoning west side, and lively Pilsen south of 18th St. As a bonus, the views of the skyline as the road soars over the north and south branches of the Chicago River are picture perfect. Travel in either direction between the Damen El stop on the Brown Line (North Side) and the 35th St/Archer El stop on the Orange (South Side).

Things to See & Do

Chicago is a vast place with enough to keep you busy for a few years. Places of interest, museums, sights and other diversions are listed in this chapter by neighborhood. Recreational activities are at the end.

LOOP

The Loop is the historic center of the city, drawing its name from the elevated tracks that circle it. It's a fascinating place to walk around, and its buildings constitute a virtual textbook of American architecture. During the daytime it hums with shoppers, office workers and tourists. At night things get much quieter, but recently there have been signs of life after dark.

Through the 1960s, the Loop was both the commercial hub and the entertainment center of Chicago. Grand movie palaces, chic restaurants and nightclubs drew the masses. The 1970s and 1980s saw much of the focus shift to the Near North, Gold Coast and other neighborhoods. A disastrous effort that turned State St into a pedestrian mall in 1979 proved a 15-year failure that primarily benefited exhaust-belching buses. Most of the remaining theaters and entertainment venues closed or moved. At night the streets needed only a few urban tumbleweeds to complete the bleak tableau.

But during this same period, the city doggedly kept trying to resuscitate the area. Tax breaks were offered to developers, and State St eventually was attractively remodeled – with new street lamps, El entrances and other classical details – and reopened to traffic.

Now the long-closed Oriental Theater, at 20 W Randolph (Map 3), is set to reopen in 1998 as a live theater venue. The Palace Theater, 171 W Randolph (Map 3), is also set to reopen in 1998 for productions. Disney has taken over the refurbished Chicago Theater, at 175 N State (Map 3), and will be staging its crowd-drawing live productions there. In 2000 the Goodman Theatre, now part of the Art Institute complex (Map 3), will be moving to rebuilt old movie theaters at 180 to 190 N Dearborn.

This theater district is already luring new restaurants and nightlife to the Loop. Bolstering the action, developers have hit upon innovative schemes for some of the older office buildings: Previously these architecturally significant buildings would have been torn down, because their small floors, low ceilings and other details make them unsuitable for modern offices. Now, however, developers have realized that those small floors are perfect for residences and hotels.

RAY HILLSTROM

Disney's Chicago pied-à-terre

The landmark Reliance Building, with its terra-cotta details, 32 N State St, is set to become a European-style lodge; the Chicago Building, 7 W Madison St, has been converted to artists' lofts; condos are on sale at the McCormick Building, 330 S Michigan; and many more projects are in the works.

See the Architecture section for a Loop architecture walking tour.

Chicago Cultural Center

Galleries, exhibitions, beautiful interior design and a permanent museum all make the block-long Chicago Cultural Center (☎ 312-744-6630), 78 E Washington at Michigan Ave (Map 3), in the city's former main library, an interesting place to wander around. The exhibitions on three floors change frequently, so take a moment as you enter on either Randolph or Washington Sts to find out the schedule of events. The grand staircases at both of these entrances are works of art: the one on the Randolph side is decked out in pink

RICK GERHARTER

The Reliance Building

marble and complex mosaics; the one on the Washington side is clad in white marble, and its classical lines appear to hang in space.

The center is open Monday to Thursday 10 am to 7 pm, Friday 10 am to 6 pm, Saturday 10 am to 5 pm, Sunday noon to 5 pm; closed holidays. Guided tours take place Tuesday and Wednesday at 1:30 pm; check with the tourist information center in the building for more specifics.

Bad-Weather Refuges

Some aspect of Chicago's weather that never turns up in tourist brochures rears its head. What do you do? Eventually, shopping, museums, eating, drinking and other indoor pursuits lose their charm. And you don't want to go back to the hotel room. If it was nice, you'd sit in the park, but the present storm makes that an untenable option. Here are two places where you can just hang out, catch your bearings, and plan for your next adventure.

Chicago Cultural Center Home to the main tourist office, the Cultural Center (☎ 312-744-6630), on Michigan Ave between Randolph and Washington (Map 3), has a few galleries and museums to explore. But best of all is the large area inside the Randolph St entrance, where you can relax on comfortable chairs, write post cards at tables or stare at the wall. An outlet of the Corner Bakery provides battery-recharging refreshments. Open Monday to Thursday 10 am to 7 pm, Friday 10 am to 6 pm, Saturday 10 am to 5 pm, Sunday noon to 5 pm.

Harold Washington Library Center Sure, there are more books than you can count. But within this vast building (☎ 312-542-7279), 400 S State between Van Buren and Congress (Map 3), you'll find a good ground-floor coffee bar and scores of nooks and crannies where you can kick back. Floors 3 through 8 have quiet sitting areas along the exterior walls. Some of the alcoves have windows and tables. The 9th-floor winter garden has more comfortable chairs, but you can't take any library books there – which may be the point. Open Monday 9 am to 7 pm; Tuesday and Thursday 11 am to 7 pm; Wednesday, Friday and Saturday 9 am to 5 pm; Sunday 1 to 5 pm. ■

Loop Sculpture: From Historic to Incomprehensible
The arrival of the Picasso sculpture to what's now the Richard J Daley Civic Center in 1967 inspired a modern-day wave of Loop sculpture placement that was further strengthened in 1978, when the city council decreed that such works should be part of new or renovated public buildings.

Here are a few of the notable works in the Loop, from north to south.

Michigan Ave Bridge In 1928 the four bridge towers were given sculptured relief panels celebrating Chicago's early history. On the northeast, *The Discoverers*, by James Earl Fraser, shows explorers Louis Jolliet and Jacques Marquette and others. On the northwest, *The Pioneers*, also by Fraser, shows John Kinzie, a fur trader. On the southwest, Henry Hering's *Defense* shows the 1812 Fort Dearborn massacre; note the odd looks on the faces of the Potawatomi Indians as they prepare to wield their hatchets. On the southeast, Hering's *Regeneration* shows the rebuilding of the city after the 1871 fire.

The George Washington-Robert Morris-Haym Salomon Memorial In this 1941 Lorado Taft and Leonard Crunelle sculpture, two little-known early American patriots are shown with Washington. Both played a vital role in raising the money for the American Revolution.

Splash This brightly hued 1986 aluminum free-form work is by Jerry Peart.

Freeform Richard Hunt's 1993 free-form aluminum sculpture is 2½ stories tall, on the facade of the Illinois State Office Building, at 160 N LaSalle.

Monument with Standing Beast French sculptor Jean Dubuffet created this characteristic collection of blobs in 1984 for the state's James R Thompson Center, 100 W Randolph.

Sound Sculpture Henry Bertoia's 1975 metal sculpture recalls fields of wheat and makes various noises in the wind. It's on the east side of the Amoco Building, 200 E Randolph.

Arts and Science of the Ancient World: The Flight of Daedalus and Icarus This large 1991 mosaic by Roger Brown, over the entrance to 120 N LaSalle, shows dad and son escaping the Labyrinth of the Minotaur.

'The Picasso' Officially it's untitled, but Chicagoans soon adopted their own no-nonsense name for the huge work made out of Cor-Ten steel (the same material that clads the Daley Center, behind it). Bird, dog, woman – you decide. The base makes a great slide for kids.

Being Born Commissioned by the tool and die industry, this 1983 stainless steel sculpture by Virginio Ferrari symbolizes both precision, with its two fitted rings, and economic growth, through the open outer ring.

Dawn Shadows This is a black-painted 1983 steel sculpture by Louise Nevelson, inspired by the configuration of the El (maybe after a wreck).

Miró's Chicago Tucked into a dark plaza across Washington St from Daley Plaza, this 39-foot sculpture, made with various metals, cement and tile, was fashioned by Joan Miró in 1981. It is meant to evoke, in Miró's words, the 'mystical force of a great earth mother.'

The Four Seasons Russian-born Marc Chagall loved Chicago and donated this grand 1974 mosaic on the Dearborn side of First Chicago Plaza in 1974. Using thousands of bits of glass

RICK GERHARTER
The Picasso

and stone, the artist portrayed six scenes of the city in hues reminiscent of the Mediterranean coast of France, where he kept his studio. Chagall continued to fuss with the work, such as updating the skyline, after it arrived in Chicago. Recently, the bank built a roof over it to protect it from the elements.

Flamingo Alexander Calder's soaring 1974 free-standing steel sculpture provides some much needed relief to the stark facades of the federal buildings around it. Actually, a flock wouldn't be a bad idea.

The Town-Ho's Story This 6½-ton work, made of industrial junk, is in the lobby of the Ralph H Metcalfe Federal Building, at 77 W Jackson. Part of artist Frank Stella's 'Moby Dick' series, the sculpture seems to depict what would have happened if Moby had swallowed a garbage scow and later felt ill.

San Marco II Inspired by the four horses that grace the facade of St Mark's Basilica in Venice, artist Ludovico de Luigi created this stone sculpture. ■

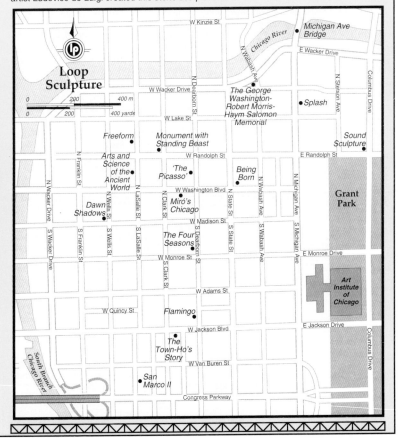

Museum of Broadcast Communications In the early days of television, most shows were produced live at the individual stations rather than picked up from networks. Chicago had a long tradition of live programming that extended back through the radio era.

This fascinating museum (☎ 312-629-6000), filled with memories for many Chicagoans, is a trip back to simpler days, before there was digital broadcasting and a choice of hundreds of channels. Radio is recalled with such local stars as Fibber McGee and Mollie, Edgar Bergen and Charlie McCarthy.

The TV area displays clips of shows that bring wistful smiles to adults who grew up with *Garfield Goose* and *Kukla, Fran and Ollie*. Famous local moments are also replayed, including the Kennedy-Nixon debate of 1960, which many argue Nixon lost because on television his shifty eyes and heavy beard made him look like a crook. (Who says TV lies?)

Visitors can view tapes from a large library of shows. They can also pose as a newscaster on an old WGN set and buy a videotape of their sensational performance for $19.95.

The museum is open Monday to Saturday 10 am to 4:30 pm, Sunday noon to 5 pm; closed major holidays. Admission is free; the fee for unlimited videotape viewing is $2. The museum is near the Washington entrance on the main floor of the Cultural Center (Map 3).

Sears Tower
It may be the world's tallest building, or it may not be (see the Tower Envy sidebar), but there's no doubt that the Sears Tower (☎ 312-875-9696), 233 S Wacker (Map 3), has become a symbol of Chicago. It has the kind of stats that make good grade-school presentations: 43,000 miles of phone cable, enough concrete to build an eight-lane highway five miles long, 2232 steps to the roof.

Much of what's inside the 110-story, 1454-foot building is mundane office space. But the lure of the world's highest observation deck draws more than 1.5 million people a year. You can join the mobs on the Skydeck (☎ 312-875-9696) or visit my preferred choice, the John Hancock Center Observatory (see below). The Skydeck entrance is on the Jackson Blvd side of the block-size building, which is also

---

Tower Envy
The Sears Tower was the undisputed size champ in the tallest-building category until the 1996 opening of the Petronas Towers opened in Malaysia. But the matter wasn't that simple. The 88-story Petronas Towers were shorter than the Sears Tower until two 111-foot decorative towers were added, topping the 110-story Sears Tower by 20 feet.

Civic boosters licked their erectile wounds until the Council on Tall Buildings and Urban Habitat, the international group that certifies tall buildings, came to the Sears Tower's rescue. In 1997 the council expanded the categories of tallest buildings from one to four:

• height to structural or architectural top
• height to the highest occupied floor
• height to the top of the roof
• height to the top of antenna

Under this scheme, Petronas wins the first category, Sears takes the second and third and the taller of New York's World Trade Center towers garners the fourth. So, thanks to the Council on Tall Buildings and Urban Habitat, Chicago and the Sears Tower still win two out of four. ■

RICK GERHARTER

Still a record breaker: the Sears Tower

More lines after the film mean that any lingering nausea will subside before the 70-second elevator ride to the top in the world's fastest elevators. Your ears will definitely pop on the way up. Once there, you're bound to think the view was worth the price paid in money and patience: The entire city stretches below, and you can take the time to see exactly how Chicago is laid out. You should be able to pick out most of the major features on the maps in this book.

There are usually lines of visitors waiting to descend in one of the two elevators, but you'd can linger as long as you like at the windows. Sunsets can be quite stunning, and the emergence of lights at twilight is charming.

The Skydeck is open daily 9 am to 11 pm March through September, 9 am to 10 pm the rest of the year. Admission is $6.75 for adults, $4 for children. Military personnel in uniform get in free. A one-hour film developer near the ticket windows will have your photos ready by the time your visit is over.

Trading Floors

Like polychromatic riots, but ones where the anarchists' goal is profit, Chicago's trading floors are fascinating places to observe. Hands fly, shouts are exchanged and a few shoving matches break out in these chaotic scenes, as traders compete to

bounded by Wacker, Adams and Franklin. Your journey to the top starts with a slow elevator ride down to the charmless waiting area where the visitors queue for tickets. A sign will give you the waiting times to the top. On busy days it can be an hour or longer, so this is a good time to confirm the visibility – before you invest your time and money. Even days that seem sunny can have upper-level haze that limits the view. On good days, however, you can see for 40 to 50 miles, as far as Indiana, Michigan and Wisconsin.

A dark series of rooms follow the ticketing area and are cleverly designed to never let you see the full scope of the waiting line. Eventually, you reach a theater (on my most recent visit, a saddened child whined: 'Do we have to go in there? Can't we just go to the top?'), where you have to watch a film titled 'Over Chicago.' Political junkies will be reminded of 'Morning in America,' the short film about a mystical America that Ronald Reagan used for his election campaign in 1984. The syrupy narration of the aerial footage of Chicago seems endless, but the film lasts only 15 minutes.

Trading Nothing

Hand signals flash, papers fly, voices frantically call out. The purpose of the din and confusion is money in sums that defy comprehension. It's the Eurodollar trading pit at the Chicago Mercantile Exchange, where each day contracts worth more than $450 billion are traded. Annual volume of the pit: $1.16 followed by 14 zeros. Try writing that. It's the hottest futures market in Chicago, which is the world center for futures trading. Brash, rough-edged, never refined, the Chicago markets have elbowed their way to a dominant position in global finance.

In the trading pits, contracts can be purchased for almost anything with a fluctuating value, such as metals, foreign currency, grains, bonds and much more. But whereas futures contracts on grain or even bonds represent something that you could conceivably hold in your hand, Eurodollars represent the ultimate embodiment of the legalized gambling that is futures trading: nothing. They don't exist; you can't hold one in your hand. They are the exchange value of US money held in foreign banks. The futures traders are betting on what that value will be at some distant date. If they're right, they make money, maybe a fortune. If they're wrong, they can lose their shirts.

It's a high-stakes business that favors the young and manic. When trading gets heated, brawls and mayhem can erupt. A badge of honor among the mostly male traders is a scar on the cheek caused by accidental pencil jabs from others frantically signaling in the pits.

The whole wild business began after the Civil War, when the Chicago Board of Trade revolutionized the way grain prices were set by instituting a uniform and dependable system. It soon became common to trade 'futures,' in essence, speculative bets based on the future price of commodities such as wheat. Farmers were guaranteed set prices, which reduced their risk. However, the suspicion has always lingered throughout the Midwest that the traders in Chicago somehow manipulate prices at the expense of the farmer. ■

buy or sell commodities and options for the best price. When a split-second's miscalculation can cost $10,000 or more, the stakes are as high as the energy levels. These people take caffeine to relax.

The two main futures trading organizations have free viewing areas overlooking their trading floors. Both take commendable steps to explain the impenetrable world of futures trading, where people make money by spending money they don't have on goods they can't buy and which really don't exist. It's a fascinating show.

The Chicago Board of Trade's 1930 main building (☎ 312-435-3590), at 141 W Jackson at LaSalle (Map 3), is a beautiful place with a four-story lobby decorated in marble, brass and platinum. It's open weekdays 8 am to 2 pm.

The Chicago Mercantile Exchange (☎ 312-930-8249), 10-30 S Wacker Drive between Madison and Monroe (Map 3), is in a modern

building with a good view of the river. It's open weekdays 7:30 am to 3:15 pm.

Admission to both is free. You can meet the traders after work (usually starting about 3 pm), when they begin their energetic decompression from their incredibly high-pressure jobs at the legendary Alcock's Inn (☎ 312-922-1778), 411 S Wells (Map 3). Some of the patrons are newly rich and others newly broke, but most of them are drunk.

For more information about futures trading and watching the action, see the sidebar Trading Nothing.

Chicago Athenaeum

The design of buildings, cities, products, fashion and more is the focus of the Chicago Athenaeum (☎ 312-251-0175), which has moved to new and expanded quarters in the old Montgomery Ward office building at the northwest corner of Madison and Michigan (Map 3).

The rotating exhibits have included shows on German industrial design; historical consumer products made in Illinois, such as Philco radios and Zenith TVs; computer chips; Chicago landmarks; and personal photos of Frank Lloyd Wright from his personal collection. The athenaeum's board is made up of local designers known for their cutting-edge work, so future shows should continue to be nontraditional and interesting.

It's open Tuesday to Saturday 11 am to 6 pm, Sunday noon to 5 pm. Admission is $3 for adults, $2 for children. A gift store, which shares the museum's main entrance off Madison, has assorted items whose design reflects the ethos of the museum. Some of the items will leave you asking, 'Is that a salt shaker or a lamp?'

Art Institute of Chicago

One of the world's premier museums, the Art Institute of Chicago (☎ 312-443-3600), Adams St at Michigan Avenue (Map 3), has found generous patronage among Chicago's wealthy. Their money has funded a collection that spans 5000 years of art from around the globe. Sculpture, textiles, painting and furniture are just a few of the wide-ranging media represented. The museum's collection of Impressionist and Postimpressionist paintings is second only to collections in France; it represents the purchased booty of generations of touring patrons, led by the indomitable Bertha Palmer.

Here's a brief rundown of the types of art you'll find: African and ancient American art; American art from the 17th century through 1955; ancient Egyptian, Greek and Roman art; architecture; Chinese, Japanese and Korean art, beginning 5000 years ago; European decorative arts since the 12th century; European painting and sculpture from 1400 to 1800; 19th-century European painting; photography; prints and drawings; textiles; 20th-century painting; and sculpture.

The main entrance is the original 1893 Allerton Building, where Adams St meets Michigan Ave. The bronze lions flanking the steps are Chicago icons. The Art Insti-tute decorated them with giant Bears football helmets in 1985, during that team's championship season. Purists cried foul, but everyone else enjoyed the gesture. The steps themselves are one of the city's prime rendezvous points on fair days.

The modern 1977 Rubloff Building, accessed via the Columbus Drive entrance, houses the School of the Art Institute, where the number of pierced body parts far exceeds the student body. The Rice Building was added in 1988.

The Art Institute is huge but not unmanageable, given the scope of its works. See the accompanying sidebar, The Art Institute in 90 Minutes, for a 90- to 120-minute tour that covers both major and interesting minor works. Excellent color maps of the institute are available free at the many information booths in the museum. You can use them to plot a visit that concentrates on specific aspects of the collection or leads to a grand tour. The quality of the documentation with the works gets better each year, as the curators share more of their wisdom about the displayed pieces.

RICK GERHARTER

Chicago stalwart

The Art Institute in 90 Minutes

Here's an eclectic and highly personal tour that takes in the greatest works of the Art Institute while giving an idea of the breadth of the collections. Give yourself 90 minutes if you follow this closely, more if you use it merely as a starting point to begin your own explorations. It starts with sculpture, pottery, and other physical works from all ages worldwide before beginning a backward march through the history of painting.

Pick up one of the color floor plans from an information desk and note that some pieces listed here may move from time to time, as curators try new groupings. If you can't find something, ask the omnipresent guards – they are usually quite knowledgeable.

After clearing the entrance gates on the Michigan Ave side, take the stairs down to the lower level. **Room 11** contains the Thorne Miniature Rooms, a fascinating series of 68 small rooms showing the progression of interior design from the 13th century to 1940. These are intricately detailed works of art in their own right. Kids love 'em too. Look for A30, a Georgia double parlor that needs only a dotty aunt to be complete, and A37, a California hallway right out of a Raymond Chandler novel.

Room 1 holds temporary photo exhibits that are always worth a look.

Return to the 1st floor and head up the first set of four steps to the Asian collections

Chinese water ewer (He),
Eastern Zhou dynasty

on the right. Pass through rooms 131A and 131B to **Room 132**, where bronze works date from 2000 BC. The detailing is both artful and witty; look for the water vessel with the arched cat used as the handle. Cut through Room 133 and take a right into **Room 105**. The stunning statues all around you are funeral earthenware from the Tang Dynasty (618 to 907 AD). These vibrant and animated figures may have been seen but once – during the funeral procession – before being placed in a tomb. Horses were highly prized. Note the quiet dignity the artists gave both human and beast.

Exit back the way you came and turn right outside Room 131A into Gunsaulus Hall, the link over the train tracks. Much of the room and the crowd's attention is devoted to the suits of armor, which have the same metallic charm as the scores of other, similar suits in museums worldwide. Along the right wall are much overlooked examples of European decorative arts. The Italian wine cistern dating from 1553 leads the brilliant collection of majolica, a tin-glazed earthenware with bright colors and animated decoration.

Once through Gunsaulus Hall, you descend into a hall called Room 150; turn right into the Rice Building and climb to the 1st floor. Pass forward through the sculpture court and into **Room 167**. Companion portraits of Daniel Hubbard and his wife were completed in 1764 by John Singleton Copley, a self-taught portrait painter from Boston who was known for his careful detail. Quiet, intelligent Mrs Hubbard contrasts with her smirking husband, who looks like he swallowed a canary. Imagine this pair bad-mouthing the British amid the early American furnishings in the next few rooms.

Moving closer to the modern age, **Room 177** is highlighted by a 1906 Vienna Secessionist coffee set in gold, blue, red and black. Exit the 1st floor and go to the lower level of the Rice Building.

Mrs Daniel Hubbard
John Singleton Copley

The star of this area, which is devoted to European decorative arts from 1600 to 1900, is the 1640 Augsburg Cabinet in **Room 71**. There's more to this ebony and ivory masterpiece than meets the eye. You'd never know it (which is the idea), but the cabinet has a bevy of hidden drawers and cubbyholes. Five medicine canisters and 22 drug-related utensils were secreted away. Move through Rooms 66 and 65 to **Room 64** for a hidden gem that is a favorite of the curator. Unlike many of its contemporaries, the French chest of drawers from 1770 has large drawers that would actually hold things, and delicate floral inlays. Imagine keeping your yearly change of underwear in that.

Paris Street; Rainy Day
Gustave Caillebotte

Exit the Rice Building and take a well-deserved rest on the benches in **Room 150**, facing the azure windows donated to Chicago in 1977 by artist Marc Chagall to honor America's bicentennial and Mayor Richard J Daley, who had only recently died.

Walk to the right of the stained glass and enter Room 159, passing through **Room 157**. The Ayala altarpiece is one of the best-preserved works of its kind and dates from 1396. It shows the kind of vanity art popular in the 14th century, with members of the commissioning Spanish family from Castille making guest appearances in scenes from the life of Jesus.

Through the windows you can see the shady McKinlock Court Garden, with fountains and a café serving above-average food. A jazz band performs on Tuesday evenings, making this one of the classiest places in town for a casual date.

Continue around the courtyard in Rooms 156 through 153, which house various ancient arts from Egypt, Greece, and Southeast Asia. Many guidebooks urge you to make a detour at **Room 153**, to the Chicago Stock Exchange Trading Room, which dates from 1893-94. This admittedly spectacular space is almost all that survives of its namesake building, demolished in 1972 despite having earned recognition as one of the most significant buildings in the city. Displaying this fragment of a willfully destroyed masterpiece is, to me, akin to putting the heart of a dead person in a jar and displaying it because the person 'had a good heart.' There's something ghoulish about the whole thing.

An exquisite collection of Indian and Asian art starts in **Room 152**. The 12th-century granite Buddha seems about to come to life, thanks to the skill of the Tamil carvers.

Proceed back around to Room 150 and the stairs leading up to the 2nd level, where a procession of masterworks begins. Just to the left, **Room 247** holds a work of art that rivals the Mona Lisa for the number of times it has been bastardized by marketers: *American Gothic*. Grant Wood's 1930 fanciful study of a fictional Iowa farm couple looks to Flemish Renaissance art for its formal composition. The image has been altered so many times that now even the real thing borders on self-parody, so take time to study the long faces Wood gave to the models: his sister and dentist.

A lively contrast is provided by the exuberant nightclub studies by Archibald J Motley Jr. His *Nightlife* (1943) explodes in neon colors.

Room 246 has several works from Pablo Picasso's familiar classic period. But notice Marc Chagall's 1943 painting *The Juggler* and try to interpret what this chicken-headed fellow is up to.

Nightlife
Archibald J Motley Jr

Continued on next page

An interesting early Picasso work in **Room 243**, the 1921 *Mother and Child*, becomes fascinating when you read the Art Institute's posted commentary on how Picasso altered the photo to give the originally pictured father the boot. Once you've read this, you'll realize that the kid isn't reaching for mom, but rather a fish that the father had been holding.

Continue three rooms forward and hang a left into **Room 231A**. Gifford Beal's *Puff of Smoke* (1912) captures the raw power and destruction that industry rapidly brought to the United States. Another icon awaits in **Room 236**: *Nighthawks* (1942), Edward Hopper's study of four isolated people in an anonymous diner, which has become one of the best-known images of 20th-century painting. Hopper said he wasn't trying to convey bleakness in the scene, but that 'unconsciously, probably, I was painting the loneliness of a large city.'

Next door, in **Room 237A**, is a painting with all the subtlety of bathroom graffiti. All but the dimmest bulbs will get the symbolism of Salvador Dalí's 1930 *Anthropomorphic Tower*. The challenge: count the penises.

A questionable call by the curators has put several Monets in dark **Room 234B**. Maybe it was this gloomy when Claude Monet painted *Parliament* (1889), but the light surely had to be better for his 1906 version of *Water Lilies*. This room is merely a warm-up for **Room 206**, where six examples of Monet's original 15 *Grainstacks* (1890-91) line the walls. Often called *Haystacks* or *Wheatstacks*, the works show Monet's impression of sustenance and survival caught in nature's temporal cycle.

Georges Seurat predated process color printing by decades with *Sunday Afternoon on the Island of the Grande Jatte*, his painting of Parisians enjoying a day in the park. Consider the number of dots Seurat painted and you'll see why it took him from 1884 to 1886 to complete the sofa-size work in pointillist style. He spent six months in the park just sketching possible subjects.

At the center of this, the Allerton Building, **Room 201** houses brooding paintings of Paris that convey more feeling than any photograph. Gustave Caillebotte's 1876-77 *Paris Street: Rainy Day* shows the artist's view of then-modern and bleak Paris. It moodily prefigures Seurat's work. Monet's 1877 *Arrival of the Normandy Train* is but one of 12 studies he did of this scene. In contrast to the bleak Paris streetscape, Pierre Auguste Renoir luminously captures *Two Sisters (On the Terrace)*, an 1881 work that is regularly voted a favorite of Art Institute patrons. Certainly Renoir's *Jugglers at the Circus Fernando* (1878-79) was a favorite of Mrs Potter Palmer, the original purchaser: she kept it with her at all times, even on trips, before it found a permanent home here.

Head down the hall past Rooms 226 through 223 to **Room 222**. This gallery shows the diversity of European painting in the 1800s before Impressionism. Joseph Mallord William Turner shows the insignificance of humans in the face of nature in *Fishing Boats with Hucksters Bargaining for Fish* (1837-38). Look at how he captured the roiling waves. Across the room, Alberto Pasini's 1880 *Cicassion Calvary* evokes strong emotion, and Constant Troyon shows his mastery with cattle in *The Road to Market* (1858).

Walk back through European art until you reach the 16th century in **Room 215**. Spanish master El Greco, who earned the named because of his Grecian birth, painted *Assumption of the Virgin* (1577) as his first major commission after arriving in Spain. The Virgin rises from her tomb and seems almost ready to burst from the canvas in an explosion of color. Match the holy men below with the following emotions: awe, excitement, disbelief and confusion. The mounting was added by the Art Institute in 1987 to recreate the feel of the painting's original setting and possibly to keep Mary from heading right on up through the roof.

Return to the central stairs and descend to the point where your tour began, safe in the knowledge that with just several more hours you could see everything. ∎

Many – but not all – of the Impressionist paintings are displayed in luminous skylit rooms. If your visit will coincide with dusk, head to these rooms before dark.

The institute is open every day of the year except Thanksgiving and Christmas: weekdays 10:30 am to 4:30 pm (Tuesday till 8 pm), Saturday 10 am to 5 pm, Sundays and holidays noon to 5 pm.

Admission is a recommended $7 for adults, $3.50 for children. Technically you can give less, but nobody does. The Art Institute directors deserve full praise for making Tuesday – the day with the longest hours – free all day.

GRANT PARK

After Montgomery Ward saved the marsh that was to become Grant Park from developers (see the sidebar The Man Who Saved the Lakefront), the Olmstead Brothers architecture firm published plans for the park to be developed along the formal lines of Versailles.

Executing the plan would take more than 20 years. It was completed just in time for the 1933-34 Century of Progress exposition, on the lakefront near where Soldier Field and McCormick Place are today. The park, often called 'Chicago's front yard,' has suffered deprivations over the years more befitting a back yard. Through much of the 20th century commissioners bowing to the tyranny of the auto allowed Lake Shore Drive, Columbus Drive and Congress Parkway to be developed into major thoroughfares, robbing the park of many of its best open areas. (Every year the huge Taste of Chicago festival closes Columbus and Congress for two weeks, and the world doesn't come to an end.)

Somnolent care from the Chicago Park District saw the entire place give way to weeds, dead trees and other neglect. The sad situation changed dramatically in the early 1990s, when Soldier Field was named the site of the opening ceremonies for the 1994 World Cup. Realizing that

The Man Who Saved the Lakefront

When Chicagoans frolic at the lakefront's vast expanse of beaches and parks, they should thank Montgomery Ward, founder of the department stores bearing his name, who led an impassioned crusade to save the shore from development.

For two decades, beginning in 1890, Ward invested a good chunk of his fortune in legal battles to block various projects that would have used a little bit of the shoreline here and a little bit there until all that would have separated the city from the lake was a wall of buildings. Although he was up against the three forces that have shaped the city – greed, power and corruption – Ward steadfastly defended the Chicago's original charter, which stipulated that the lakefront should remain 'forever open, clear and free.' Although his many critics thought of him as a populist dilettante, Ward saw the parks as a 'breathing spot' for the city's teeming masses.

After Ward's death in 1913, many others continued fighting for his cause. They had their work cut out for them, as a steady stream of politicians saw developing the empty real estate of the lakefront and beaches as 'progress.' For example, during the 1960s, Mayor Richard J Daley and his cronies hatched schemes that would have put huge overpasses and cloverleaves at both Oak St Beach and 57th St Beach. Fortunately, both schemes died after massive protest.

The one major loss of lakefront occurred in the 1950s, when the *Chicago Tribune* decided it wanted a mammoth convention center on the lake. McCormick Place is named after its sponsor, Col Robert R McCormick, editor of the *Tribune*, who used his newspaper to get the complex built on 34 acres of lakefront property, far from hotels and transportation. ∎

thousands of impressionable visitors would stroll through Grant Park on their way to the stadium, the city began an ambitious program to spruce up the place.

Hundreds of new trees have since been planted, sidewalks have been replaced, Buckingham Fountain has been repaired. Grant Park is looking much better and is an

Chicago's Front Yard

Grant Park is looking its best in 60 years thanks to restoration efforts begun in the early 1990s. The main text of this chapter contains sections on the following features: the Wild-flower Works, the Art Institute of Chicago, the Petrillo Music Shell (see the Special Events section in Facts for the Visitor for information on performances) and Buckingham Fountain. Here's a guide to additional features and pleasures.

Statues

This larger than life bronze statue of American politician **Alexander Hamilton**, by Bela Lyon Pratt, was placed in the park in 1918 to commemorate the state's centennial.

Large Interior Form, a free-form bronze suggesting the human figure, was created by British sculptor Henry Moore in 1983.

Edward Kemeys' bronze **lions** have become Chicago icons since their placement flanking the entrance to the Art Institute in 1894.

Architect Daniel Burnham's observation that no one had ever personified the Great Lakes inspired Lorado Taft to create **Fountain of the Great Lakes**, a large bronze work, in 1913. Partially hidden by surrounding shrubs, it is worth seeking out. Here's the artist's description of what the five conch-shell-holding women are up to: 'Superior on high and Michigan on the side both empty into the basin of Huron, who sends the stream to Erie, whence Ontario receives it and looks wistfully after.' This progression duplicates that of the Great Lakes.

The '**Sitting Lincoln**,' Chicago's second sculpture of Abraham Lincoln, the 16th US president, by Augustus Saint-Gaudens is a contrast to the artist's more animated study in Lincoln Park. In this 1908 statue, President Lincoln shows the isolation of his office as he sits alone in a chair.

The **Theodore Thomas Memorial** depicts a 15-foot bronze woman straddling a globe and listening to a chord on her lyre. This 1923 work by Albin Polasek honors the founder of the Chicago Symphony Orchestra.

The Bowman and the Spearman by Ivan Mestrovic comprises two 17-foot-high bronze figures of Native Americans. Both created in 1923, they symbolize the struggle between Indians and whites as the latter moved west and settled there. Both are in the act of using their weapons, which are left to the imagination of the viewer. Originally much closer together, they were separated by the 1956 intrusion of Congress Parkway into the park, which destroyed the grand steps that once led to a plaza beyond.

RICK GERHARTER

Ivan Mestrovic's *Bowman*

Other Features

In warm-weather months, visitors can play a set at Grant Park's tennis courts. In winter they can skate at **Daley Bicentennial Plaza** (see Activities for more about tennis and skating).

Continued on page 142

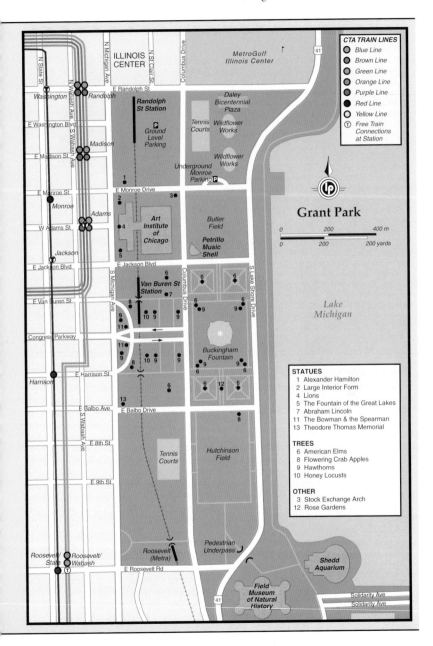

Grant Park

CTA TRAIN LINES
- Blue Line
- Brown Line
- Green Line
- Orange Line
- Purple Line
- Red Line
- Yellow Line
- Free Train Connections at Station

STATUES
1 Alexander Hamilton
2 Large Interior Form
4 Lions
5 The Fountain of the Great Lakes
7 Abraham Lincoln
11 The Bowman & the Spearman
13 Theodore Thomas Memorial

TREES
6 American Elms
8 Flowering Crab Apples
9 Hawthorns
10 Honey Locusts

OTHER
3 Stock Exchange Arch
12 Rose Gardens

From page 140

The **Stock Exchange Arch** is a relic amputated from the great building when it was demolished in 1972. The *AIA Guide to Chicago* calls it 'The Wailing Wall of Chicago's preservation movement.'

The Park's **Rose Gardens** are home to 150 varieties best viewed from mid-June to September.

To watch Chicagoans at a favorite pastime, stop by **Hutchinson Field**, where scores of amateur league softball games are played each summer.

Trees

Replanting is restoring the diversity of native and imported trees that once grew in the park. The following species are listed in ascending order of size; the original designers of the park intended for the trees to become gradually larger as the rows progressed away from open spaces.

The small flowering crab apples blossom throughout May and are later covered with fruit. The small, thorny **hawthorns** that flower in May and are native to the area. Honey locusts, another native species, are used to line streets because they seem impervious to salt, dogs, barbecue embers and other urban hazards.

When the park was built, its designers planted elms, long considered the most graceful of shade trees. More than 75% of the original 3000 elms have died from Dutch elm disease. Their replacements are less graceful but much more resilient hybrid American elms. ■

RYAN VER BERKMOES

The 'Sitting Lincoln'

excellent place both to visit and travel through on your way to and from the Museum Campus. (See Chicago's Front Yard for details on the sites not listed here.)

Buckingham Fountain

Kate Sturges Buckingham, a wealthy widow, gave the magnificent fountain to the city in 1927 in memory of her brother, Clarence. She also wisely left an endowment to maintain and operate the fountain.

It's twice the size of its model, the Bassin de Latone at Versailles. The central fountain is meant to symbolize Lake Michigan, the four water-spouting sea creatures the surrounding states. The fountain presents a subtle show rather than randomly spraying its 1.5 million gallons. Like so much in life, the spray begins small. Each successive basin fills, stimulating more jets. At the climax, the central fountain spurts up to its full 150 feet. The

crowd sighs in awe and is thankful that smoking is allowed.

At night the fountain is illuminated by colored lights that are timed to match its moods. The effect is both melodic and stimulating. At the four corners of the gravel expanse that surrounds the fountain, pavilions have toilets and sell refreshments. The fountain is turned on daily from 10 am to 11 pm, May 1 to October 1. It climaxes once an hour. The mood lighting begins every night at 8 pm, with 9 pm being the best time.

Wildflower Works

Up until 200 years ago, much of the land in northern Illinois was prairie, a vast undulating expanse that bloomed with a rainbow of wildflowers through the growing season. Early settlers who crossed it said it was like sailing in an ocean of color.

With farming and development, this delicate ecosystem was lost as nonnative plants muscled their way in to the region. In 1985, artist Chapman Kelly received permission to plant 1.5 acres near the Daley Bicentennial Plaza with native wildflowers. With a team of dedicated volunteers, Kelly found seeds for the long-forgotten plants. Often they had to go to rural rail lines, where land between tracks had for the most part been left alone, to harvest seeds.

The first few years were difficult for the group – the wildflowers were laggards when it came to germination and would have lost out had invading wind-borne seedlings not been uprooted by hand. It was very hard work. I was a volunteer then and crawled around picking out weed seedlings about the size of a bean sprout. The toughest part was differentiating between the good and bad plants. I'm afraid in my zones, the slaughter may have been indiscriminate.

More than 10 years later, the Illinois wildflowers are much better established. Their scores of seeds and root systems make outside invasion much more difficult. From April through October a constantly changing panoply of flowers in all shapes and sizes takes its turn on Kelly's stage. Take some time here to wander around, listen to the bumblebees and imagine the flowers in front of you stretching as far as the eye can see.

SOUTH LOOP

The South Loop resurged in the 1980s with the renovation of the Chicago Hilton & Towers, the success of the Dearborn Park development and the emergence of Printer's Row as a gentrified district of converted lofts. It is expected to continue to prosper as its vibrancy spreads south and the Museum Campus, to the east, draws more and more visitors.

RICK GERHARTER

Buckingham Fountain shows its stuff.

Printer's Row

Chicago was a center for printing at the turn of the century, and the rows of buildings on Dearborn from Congress south to Polk (Map 4) were the heart of publishing in the city. By the 1970s, the printers had left for more economical quarters elsewhere, and the buildings were either empty or barely making it on the feeble rents of obscure nonprofit groups.

In the late 1970s savvy developers saw the potential in these derelicts, and one of the most successful gentrification projects in Chicago began. It saw virtually every building renovated into mid-price and luxury rentals and condos. The following describes some of the notable buildings going from north to south.

A snazzy renovation of the **Mergenthaler Lofts**, the 1886 headquarters for the legendary linotype company at 531 S Plymouth Court (Map 4), included the artful preservation of a diner storefront.

The **Pontiac Building**, a classic 1891 design by Holabird & Roche at 542 S Dearborn (Map 4), has the same flowing masonry surfaces as the firm's Monadnock Building, to the north.

A massive and once-windowless wreck, the **Transportation Building** (1911) enjoyed a 1980 restoration that assured that the neighborhood had arrived. It's at 600 S Dearborn (Map 4).

The **Second Franklin Building**, a 1912 factory at 720 S Dearborn (Map 4), has a tiled facade showing the history of printing. The roof slopes to allow for a huge skylight over the top floor, where books were handbound, for this building went up long before fluorescent or high-intensity lamps existed. The large windows on many of the other buildings in the area are there for the same purpose.

Once the Chicago terminal of the Santa Fe Railroad, the 1885 **Dearborn St Station**, at 47 W Polk (Map 4), was the premier station for trains to and from California. Today it merely sees the trains of parent-propelled strollers from the Dearborn Park neighborhood, built on the site of the tracks to the south.

Museum of Contemporary Photography

Located in one of the many buildings of Columbia College, this museum (☎ 312-663-5554), 600 S Michigan at Harrison (Map 4), focuses on American photography since 1959. Once primarily a venue for student work, it has won widespread support and is now the only institution of its kind between the coasts. The permanent collection includes the works of Debbie Fleming Caffery, Mark Klett, Catherine Wagner, Patrick Nagatoni and 500 more of the best photographers working today. The rotating permanent collection is augmented by special exhibitions.

The museum is open weekdays 10 am to 5 pm (Thursday until 8 pm), Saturday noon to 5 pm; closed Sunday, holidays and all of August. Admission is free.

Spertus Museum

An excellent small museum devoted to 5000 years of Jewish faith and culture, the Spertus (☎ 312-922-9012), 618 S Michigan (Map 4), has an equally excellent corps of volunteers. The museum's exhibits juxtapose aspects of Jewish life and religion to convey the diversity of both. The Zell Holocaust Memorial has oral histories from survivors who emigrated to Chicago, as well as the names of Chicagoans' relatives who died.

The museum mounts well-curated special exhibitions that cover topics as diverse as Biblical images in classic art and Jewish humor in the US. The basement is devoted to a children's area called the 'ArtiFact Center,' where kids can have their own archeological dig for artifacts of Jewish life.

The museum is open Sunday to Thursday 10 am to 5 pm, Friday 10 am to 3 pm. Admission is $4 for adults, $2 for children, free on Friday.

Other Highlights

Architect Bertrand Goldberg followed up his famous Marina City project 20 years later with the much less famous **River City**, 800 S Wells (Map 4). The undulating

1985 buildings reflect the course of the river and have their own marina. Plans to expand the development by a factor of 10 have yet to materialize – which is what you'd expect Captain Kirk to do in these futuristic confines.

Rarely has a public building been placed in a more appropriate place: the **Chicago Fire Department Academy** (☎ 312-747-7239) stands on the very spot where the 1871 fire began – 558 W DeKoven St, between Clinton and Jefferson (Map 10). Although there's no word on whether junk mail still shows up for Mrs O'Leary, the academy trains firefighters so they'll be ready the next time somebody or some critter kicks over a lantern (see the sidebar Don't Look at Me – It Was the Cow, in Facts about Chicago).

If you call in advance on weekdays, they'll let you know what training exercises you can watch.

MUSEUM CAMPUS

The Museum Campus is a recent Chicago creation that brings together institutions devoted to land, sea and sky. The institutions are long established, but until 1996, when the northbound lanes of Lake Shore Drive were moved west of Soldier Field, the area was bisected by a constant roar of traffic. People familiar with the old setup can only smile now, as they stroll from the Field Museum to the Shedd Aquarium and the Adler Planetarium without fear of becoming a hood ornament on a speeding sedan.

A new pedestrian underpass makes the campus either a 15-minute walk east from the Roosevelt El stops or a longer but very enjoyable sojourn through Grant Park and along the lakefront from the Loop. Alternatively, the No 146 bus makes the run from N Michigan Ave and State St in the Loop. Parking is easy for once, as the commodious lots around Soldier Field have plenty of room (except during Bears games and huge conventions).

Field Museum of Natural History

Mummies, stuffed animals, Native American artifacts, and dinosaurs and more dinosaurs are part of the 20 million artifacts in the collections of this old and storied research institution (☎ 312-922-9410), at Roosevelt Rd and Lake Shore Drive (Map 4). Only about 4% of the specimens are on display; the rest fill countless storage areas.

The museum has been doing an excellent job of replacing its musty exhibits with fascinating interactive ones over the past 15 years. (For an example of how things used to be, take a gander at the orderly rows of display cases in the Indians section, then flee.)

The Building Money for the building was donated by Marshall Field, who decreed that he wanted 'a grand museum of natural history.' Constructed on marshland from 1915 to 1921, it has a 706-foot-long colonnaded facade of Georgia marble.

RAY HILLSTROM
The Field Museum's grand main hall

Entrances on the north and south sides lead to the dramatic 300-foot-long, two-story-high Stanley Field Hall. The scope becomes apparent when you see how small the life-size skeleton of the Brachiosaurus looks. And the two huge stuffed elephants look almost pint size in the space, which is often used for gala benefit dinners. (Being seated at a table under the elephants' rumps is a sign that you definitely have not arrived and a source of frequent protest.)

Most of the museum's displays radiate off the main floor of the hall or are on the floor overlooking the hall or the basement below it.

The Collections Few feet, especially little ones, can hope to survive a visit dedicated to seeing every last Maori bead and stuffed marmot. Following are some highlights. Use the cheerfully distributed maps to find your favorite. Note that in March 1999, a huge new exhibit will open dedicated to underground animal and insect life.

A recently opened ambitious walk-through exhibit on **Africa** attempts to capture the scope of the continent by taking visitors from the streets of Dakar to Saharan sand dunes. Aspects of life in the bush are explored before the path leads through the hold of a slave ship, with its grim shackles and collars.

A clever blend of the fanciful with a large amount of Field artifacts and other details, the **Inside Ancient Egypt** exhibit re-creates an Egyptian burial chamber on three levels. The mastaba (tomb) has 23 actual mummies and is a reconstruction of the one built for Unis-ankh, the son of the last pharaoh of the Fifth Dynasty, who died at age 21 in 2407 BC. The bottom level, with its twisting caverns, is especially cool. The reeds growing in the stream are real.

One of the first exhibit areas to open after the Field adopted a more user-friendly approach – but before the museum got clever with its names – **Maritime Peoples of the Arctic & Northwest Coast** is a very well thought out combination of life-size models and dioramas showing the precarious lives of the people native to the far north.

The head honchos at the Field read *Variety* and know the business *Jurassic Park* did. In recent years a series of dinosaur-related special exhibits have boosted attendance at the Field by up to 40%. The permanent **Dinosaur Hall** is filled with real and replica skeletons of a range of the beasts who measure their age in the tens of millions. A DinoStore has opened, selling anything that can possibly be pegged to dinosaurs. But the Field's most dramatic move came in October 1997, when it paid $8.4 million for a Tyrannosaurus rex named Sue. Found a few years earlier by a less-than-savvy rancher who sold it to a neighbor for just $5000, it is the best-preserved skeleton of the fierce meat-eater yet unearthed. Before it goes on permanent display in the main hall in 2000, visitors will be able to watch it being cleaned. Fears that the Field may be taking dino-mania a few steps too far in the evolution of commercialization were fueled by the museum's bidding partners for Sue, who will sponsor the new exhibit: McDonald's and Disney.

Other displays worth your time are Gems, Plants of the World, Traveling the Pacific and Messages from the Wilderness, an exhibit showing the perils of pollution and extinction.

Visiting the Field can cause extinction of even the most burning enthusiasm. The oversize rooms seem deceptively manageable. Just trying to navigate the Life Over Time exhibit will take the better part of a day if you try to absorb all the details, and it will certainly feel like a lifetime. At the west end of the 1st floor, the Rice Wildlife Research Station is a refuge where you can sit on comfortable chairs while you sort out your Albertosaurus from your Parasaurolophus.

The Field Museum is open every day except Thanksgiving, Christmas and New Year's Day from 9 am to 5 pm. Admission is $5 for adults, $3 for children; the DNA to Dinosaurs exhibit costs extra. A simple deli and a McDonald's (can Dino-burgers® be far off?) are in the basement.

Shedd Aquarium

The world's largest assortment of finned, gilled, amphibious and other aquatic creatures swim within the marble-clad confines of the John G Shedd Aquarium (☎ 213-939-2438), 1200 Lake Shore Drive (Map 4).

Most of the 8000 species represented are in fairly small tanks that pale in comparison to the flashy, shark-infested aquariums in other cities. However, the Shedd has built a spectacular draw, the controversial Oceanarium.

Further additions call for a huge Amazon River exhibit to be completed within the old building in May 2000. An entirely new structure, called 'The Ocean Kingdom,' will host five species of crowd-pleasing sharks and open in May 2002. A long, long overdue exhibit devoted to Lake Michigan and Illinois rivers (some would have thought those would be priorities, given Shedd's location) will open sometime thereafter.

The Building The original 1929 building houses 200 tanks in a compact octagonal shape. Waves and shells are repeated throughout the building's detailing, both large and small. Note Neptune's trident atop the dome. The 1991 Oceanarium is a spectacular space where the huge mammal pools seem to blend into the lake outside the floor-to-ceiling windows.

The Collections The aquarium has made a commitment over several years to change its tanks in the original building from those you might find in an upscale dentist's office to miniature ecosystems where fish swim amid the plants and bugs that they'd be hanging with in the wild.

Long popular, the centrally located 90,000-gallon **coral reef** tank is home to 500 tropical fish, from placid nurse sharks to less-neighborly moray eels. The water swirls create a current. Divers frequently pay visits with food to keep some of the more cannibalistic residents content. The entire display is undergoing a renovation that will bring more light into the tank and will equip the divers with video cameras to

allow visitors to watch the feeding frenzies up close on video monitors. Completion is set for September 1998.

Among the highlights in the darkened **galleries** of the original building, by gallery number, are (1) colorful Caribbean fish, (2) even more colorful warm-water Pacific fish, (3) a recently built northwest Pacific tidal-surge zone, (4) playful river otters, (5) a 50-year-old snapping turtle that comes up for air once an hour, and (6) well-fed piranhas and a river ecosystem from Thailand that no longer exists in the wild. In the same gallery, check out the employees' favorite fish, a wonderfully homely 60-year-old Australian lungfish.

With its huge windows and seemingly seamless transition to the lake beyond, the multilevel **Oceanarium** seeks to replicate the northwest coast of North America through real and fake foliage, geographic features and some native inhabitants.

Most controversial are the three female 1200-lb beluga whales, who were plucked from their Arctic homes and brought to Chicago, where they get to exhibit 'natural behavior' in return for fish. Ethics of their capture aside, they are remarkably cute creatures who come from the pint-size end of the whale scale. Their humped heads and natural 'smiles' have an eerily human look. Also on hand are Pacific white-sided dolphins, harbor seals, sea otters and penguins (who come from the Southern Hemisphere, but let's not quibble, okay?). Don't linger only on the main floor – you can go underneath the cement seats and watch the mammals from below through viewing windows.

The Shedd is an easy place to navigate. The original building is compact and radiates out from the coral reef tank. The Oceanarium has proven enormously popular, and you need a separate ticket for it, which gives you a specific entrance time.

The food court and sit-down restaurant can get mobbed on busy days at lunchtime. To avoid the fast-food chow and the crowds, you might want to time your visit to allow for eating back in the Loop or elsewhere.

From June through August the Shedd Aquarium is open daily 9 am to 6 pm; the rest of the year it's open weekdays 9 am to 5 pm and weekends 9 am to 6 pm. It's closed Christmas and New Year's Day.

The Shedd is no bargain. To see the entire place costs $10 for adults, $8 for children. For advance-purchase tickets (and to reserve the best Oceanarium times) call ☎ 312-559-0200. On Thursday the original building is free, but you still need a reduced-price ticket for the Oceanarium.

Adler Planetarium

Hard on the lake at the end of Solidarity Drive, the Adler Planetarium & Astronomy Museum (☎ 312-922-7827; Map 4) has had a low-key existence, with most of the buildings below ground. But in order to keep up with its flashier brethren to the west, the Adler is in the midst of a vast expansion that will debut in mid-1998.

The new wing will include a digital sky show that will allow such cataclysmic phenomena as supernovas to be replicated. (Does anyone see the trend here? The Field discovers dinosaurs and expands, the Shedd discovers sharks and expands, and the Adler the big bang and expands . . .)

The Building To see the sky, you head underground. From the entrance to the Adler, you go below the 1930 building, which has 12 sides, one for each sign of the zodiac. The new 60,000-sq-foot addition will have one window taking advantage of the museum's lakefront location, with the requisite café and gift shops.

The Collections The planetarium does a good job planning special events around celestial occurrences, be they eclipses or NASA missions.

An old telescope and other stargazing artifacts occupy the bottom level of the Adler, which you reach from the street level. A multimedia display gives visitors an introduction to space phenomena before they ascend a curving escalator up to the Sky Theater, where a mechanical Zeiss projector can create huge varieties of nighttime sky effects.

RICK GERHARTER

Lakefront pleasures: the Adler Planetarium on the Museum Campus...

The Adler staff does a good job of creating new shows every year. One of the best recent ones was 'African Skies,' which showed how various stellar observations influenced folktales on the continent. Each year at Christmas the Adler re-creates the heavens as they would have looked at the time of the birth of Jesus, which allows visitors to search for scientific answers to such legends as the Star of Bethlehem.

The new wing will have the much ballyhooed StarRider digital theater; besides re-creating momentous events, it will also allow visits to various planets and heavenly bodies.

The Adler does a commendable job of involving visitors in astronomy. It has live video links to various telescopes around the world, and parts of the facility that are used for research are designed to be totally accessible to visitors. The sky-show programs last about 50 minutes. The whole place can be easily covered in less than two hours. A small cafeteria has all the usual stomach-filling burgers, sandwiches and such.

The Adler is open every day but Thanksgiving and Christmas: weekdays 9 am to 5 pm (Friday till 9 pm), weekends 9 am to 6 pm. From Memorial Day to Labor Day it's open Thursday till 9 pm. Admission is $3 for adults, $2 for children, free Tuesday. The must-see sky shows are another $3 each.

Other Sights

The stretch of grass on the lake between the Shedd and the Adler may be the setting for more amateur and post-card photos than any other place. One look toward the skyline will show you why: the view is good year-round; on clear days in winter, when the lake is partially frozen and steam rises off the buildings in the Loop, it verges on the sensational.

Near the entrance to the Adler, a 12-foot **sundial** by Henry Moore is dedicated to the golden years of astronomy, from 1930 to 1980, when so many fundamental discoveries were made using the first generation of huge telescopes. About 100 yards west in the median, the **bronze statue** of 16th-century Polish astronomer Nicolaus Copernicus shows him holding a compass and a model of the solar system. Near the western end of the median, the **Thaddeus Kosciusko Memorial** honors the Polish general who fought on the winning side of the American Revolution and then returned

. . . and the open fields near Montrose Beach

Lakefront Parks & Beaches

The lakefront parks and beaches are certainly Chicago's most democratic institutions. It's not uncommon to find extended African American families having their huge reunion barbecues under one tree, while a white yuppie couple fusses over their perfect baby in a stroller that cost what a small bungalow once sold for under another, and a Hispanic amateur soccer club competes on the grass.

The water fountains always run because it would cost too much to turn them on and off each year, and this way their pipes don't freeze. Besides, the lake threatens to engulf the lakefront every few years, so every bit drained away helps. (The notable parks along Chicago's lakefront are covered separately in their corresponding neighborhood sections.)

Chicago's beaches stretch like a string of pearls along the lake, making the city the Miami of the Midwest, if only for a few months each year.

There's a beach for every taste, from vast, steamy meat markets to quiet secluded coves. All are fine examples of democracy in action: on hot days immigrants in underwear mix with sleek youths in Spandex. People from every one of Chicago's ethnic groups, rich and poor alike, can be found near the cooling waters of Lake Michigan on hot summer weekends.

From late May until early September, the Chicago Park District provides lifeguards. However, a usual amount of prudence is all that's really required for safe swimming, since the Lake Michigan surf is usually measured by the inch. Take note: the water temperature can vary dramatically, depending on a variety of factors; one day it will be in the 80s, the next in the 50s. Finally, all of Chicago's beaches are free, in contrast to those in some nearby suburbs. Selected city beaches, from north to south, follow.

More than eight blocks long, from North Shore Ave to Touhy Ave, **Loyola Beach** has one of those upscale wooden playgrounds for kids. It's fairly close to the Chicago International Hostel and the Loyola El stop.

Montrose Beach (Map 1) is a great wide beach with a curving breakwater. There's ample parking, but the walks to the beach can be long. The Montrose Harbor bait shop sells ice for coolers. It's easily reached by the bus No 146 or No 151.

It isn't really a beach, but **Belmont Rocks** (Map 7) is a popular gathering point for gays from nearby Lake View. It is just south of Belmont Harbor at Belmont Ave.

Zoo day-trippers and Lincoln Parkers fill **Fullerton Beach** (Map 6). The narrow beach can get jammed on weekends, but a five-minute walk south from Fullerton yields uncrowded vistas.

The closest thing Chicago has to a Southern California beach is **North Ave Beach** (Map 6). Countless volleyball nets draw scores of beautiful people wearing the latest skimpy neon-hued togs. The steamship-inspired beach house may soon be demolished or renovated. A short walk out on the curving breakwater anytime of the year yields postcard views of the city from a spot that seems almost a world apart.

Fabled **Oak St Beach** (Map 5) lies at the north end of Michigan Ave, less than five minutes from the Water Tower. The hulking Lake Shore Drive condos cast shadows in the afternoon, but this beach remains the place to go for those who spend the winter at the health club and in the tanning booth, preparing for summer.

Nestled between Lake Shore Drive and Navy Pier, **Ohio St Beach** (Map 3) is convenient for those wanting a quick dip or a chance to feel some sand between sweaty toes. Hidden east of Meigs Field and south of the Adler Planetarium, **12th St Beach** (Map 4) is a great break from the myriad sights of the Museum Campus. Its out-of-the-way location gives the narrow enclave an exclusive feel.

Just across Lake Shore Drive from the Museum of Science and Industry, **57th St Beach** (Map 11) has an expanse of clean, golden sand. A bit farther south, **Jackson Park Beach** (Map 11) has a stately, recently restored beach house with dramatic breezeways. This beach next to the yacht harbor has a charm lacking at the beaches with more modern – and mundane – facilities.

Venture behind the golf course and the elegant South Shore Cultural Center at 71st Ave and South Shore Drive and you find a hidden treasure: **South Shore Beach**. The medium-size beach is set in a cove with trees along one side. ■

to help in his nation's fight for freedom. The last two monuments inspired the city to rename the street Solidarity Drive in 1980 to honor the Lech Walesa-led movement in Poland.

The huge hulk to the south of the Field Museum is **Soldier Field**. Built from 1922 to 1926, the oft-renovated edifice is better-looking outside than in, which is the reason the Bears are in a perennial battle to win not just a game but a new taxpayer-subsidized stadium.

The planes overhead come from nearby **Meigs Field**, used almost exclusively by corporate jets, commuter flights to and from Springfield for politicians and lobbyists and the occasional pilot-tourist. Mayor Richard M Daley has attempted to close the airfield to convert it into a park, but the state bureaucrats who like the airfield's proximity to the Loop have successfully kept it open.

The **Burnham Park yacht harbor** completes this increasingly bucolic picture. During the summer, people work in the Loop by day and sleep on their moored sailboats by night.

NEAR NORTH

West of N Michigan Ave between the river and Chicago Ave there was once an assortment of warehouses, factories and association headquarters – until the 1970s. After that, the neighborhood known as River North rapidly changed. The grimy old users were sent packing and were replaced by galleries, trendy shops, hotels and the highest concentration of restaurants in the city.

The neighborhood north of the river to Chicago Ave has several distinct areas. Most people are already familiar with the upscale shopping heaven of N Michigan Ave, known as the Magnificent Mile. Nordstrom, the Seattle-based department store chain deified by shoppers, is the one major national department store without a location on the Mag Mile. In the fall of 1997, Nordstrom announced that it would be part of a complex to be built on several blocks just north of the Marriott. Thankfully, this project will also demolish much of the hideous lower portion of the Marriott.

Also north of the river, art galleries in renovated warehouses are concentrated in the area around Superior and Huron Sts and near the El tracks.

The area east of Michigan Ave is named Streeterville in honor of one of the city's great characters, George Wellington Streeter. A skipper who would have been at home on *Gilligan's Island*, Streeter and his wife were sailing past Chicago in the 1880s purportedly on their way from Milwaukee to the Caribbean (!) when they ran aground on a sandbar near what is today Chicago Ave and Lake Shore Drive. Streeter built a little causeway to the mainland and convinced developers to dump excavated dirt on the site. Soon the area had grown to several acres, and Streeter seceded from the city and Illinois.

Not surprisingly, the city was not impressed. Various efforts to evict Streeter and a band of loyal squatters who had joined him ended in fiasco. The entire matter was finally laid to rest in the courts

The Best Place to Stand Your First Day in Town

Sunset on the west side of the Michigan Ave Bridge: The last rush of workers are scurrying home and the first couples are beginning to stroll. The sun glints off the row of office towers lining the Chicago River. Their many panes of glass sparkle amid a kaleidoscope of reflections. To the south, Michigan Ave stretches to infinity, its traffic signals winking a sea of reds, yellows and greens. Above you, great buildings proclaim the city's architectural splendor. The Wrigley Building's shadow climbs the face of the Equitable Building. The gold-leafed dome atop the Hotel Inter-Continental glistens behind the Gothic spires of the Tribune Tower. Closer yet, each of the heroic sculptured reliefs on the four bridge pylons traces part of Chicago's history. If you're lucky, a street musician's tune will rise above the din of speeding cabs and tooting trucks on Lower Wacker. ■

in 1918. Streeter lost. Today Streeterville has some of Chicago's most valuable property and is home to hotels, expensive high-rise condos and offices.

The blocks surrounding Ohio and Ontario west of Michigan are home to the increasingly notorious zone of theme restaurants and nightclubs. During the weekends and all summer long the sidewalks crawl with Chicagoans and out-of-towners visiting the place of the moment and usually leaving with a bulging stomach and even more bulging bag from a gift store. A city spokesperson has compared the area to Las Vegas and Disney World.

The Hard Rock Cafe and the Rock & Roll McDonald's opened their doors in the mid-1980s; now the area is exploding with development, as entertainment conglomerates race to establish themselves. Disney is building a high-tech theme park called DisneyQuest across Rush St from the block-square Marriott and has plans for an ESPN sports bar nearby. Steven Spielberg has lent his name to an electronic game palace designed by Universal Studios and Sega Entertainment for the corner of Dearborn and Ohio. And David Copperfield is pulling a magic-theme restaurant out of his hat across the street.

River Esplanade

Beginning with the oddly proportioned curving staircase at the northeast tower of the Michigan Ave Bridge, this carefully detailed walkway (Map 3) extends east along the river past the Sheraton Hotel. The views of the river are great, the only sour note being struck by the multilevel roadways at Illinois Center.

Where the sidewalk meets McClurg Court, Centennial Fountain burbles away peacefully for most of the hour. But on the hour, from 10 am to 2 pm and again from 5 pm to midnight, it shoots a massive arc of water across the river for 10 minutes, much to the delight of spectators ashore and the concern of those adrift on tour boats. The entire exercise is meant to commemorate the reversal of the Chicago River in 1900, which stopped sewage from flowing into the lake, where it was sucked into the intake pipes that supplied the city with water.

RICK GERHARTER

Shadows grow long on the River Esplanade.

As the neighborhood east of here rapidly develops, plans call for the esplanade to be extended past Lake Shore Drive to Navy Pier.

North Pier

An utter fiasco, the renovation of this old warehouse off Lake Shore Drive near E Illinois (Map 3) was meant to create a lively mélange of goofy shops, restaurants, nightclubs and the like. It had some success in the early 1990s, before its customers and tenants were lured east to Navy Pier and west to River North. The surviving food court serves neighborhood office workers and is a good spot for lunch, with sunny indoor tables and nice seating along the quiet dock.

Navy Pier

From 1918 to 1930, Navy Pier (☎ 312-595-7437; Map 3), more than half a mile long, was the city's municipal wharf. Later it was the first home of the University of Illinois at Chicago. During the 1970s and 1980s it was like a dead 800-pound gorilla: huge, difficult to dispose of and with no obvious use.

After Mayor Richard M Daley was elected in 1989, plans that had been drawn up by his rich political ally John Schmidt were quickly enacted. Some $200 million in public funds later, the entire length of the pier had been massively rebuilt into a

RAY HILLSTROM
Navy Pier at dusk

combination amusement park, meeting center and food court. The result has proven to be a hit, with 5 million people trekking out to the pier each year. Many of them are booked into the exposition space that covers half the pier and which is managed in conjunction with McCormick Place.

A visit here can easily consume half a day, much of it spent wandering the great length. Grab a free map at the entrance to navigate. The views from the very end are excellent, and there's no charge to just wander around or get wet in the fountains. However, costs can mount perilously if you start taking advantage of the amusements, boat tours, souvenir stands and restaurants.

Fountains At the entrance to the pier, it's as much fun to watch the kids as the fountain itself; scores of water jets squirt at unpredictable intervals, and everyone's encouraged to get wet. The upper-level Crystal Gardens fountains feature delightful water jets that appear out of nowhere and lazily arc over the heads of the unsuspecting.

Top 10 Destinations

Here are Chicago's favorite sites and their number of visitors in 1996:

Navy Pier	5.5 million
Lincoln Park Zoo	4 million
Art Institute	2.37 million
Shedd Aquarium	1.78 million
Museum of Science and Industry	1.76 million
Sears Tower Skydeck	1.51 million
Field Museum	1.21 million
Chicago Children's Museum	600,000
Chicago Cultural Center	566,000
Adler Planetarium	458,000

Amusements The 150-foot Ferris wheel ($3 per ride) moves at a snail's pace, but that's good for enjoying the views. Not so good is the insipid piped-in narration that reminds you that McDonald's sponsors the ride. The merry-go-round ($2) is a classic, with bobbing carved horses and organ music.

A variety of acts appear through the summer at the Skyline Stage (☎ 312-595-7437), a 1500-seat rooftop venue with a glistening white canopy. The IMAX Theater (☎ 312-595-0090), $8.75 for adults, $5.50 for children, shows films less scientifically oriented than those at the theater at the Museum of Science and Industry.

Shops The front of the main building has numerous shops, most of which sell the kind of nonsensical knickknacks that fill closets for decades. The exception is the branch of Barbara's Bookstore, which has good, serious fiction.

Places to Eat The pier's food court and seven restaurants range from an expensive McDonald's to expensive sit-down places.

The cuisine is as elegant as the decor at *Widow Newton's Tavern* (☎ 312-595-5500), at the entrance to the pier. The food is high quality, albeit pricey (onion rings, $4.75). The zodiac spread across the ceiling is a valuable study aid for those stumped by 'What's your sign?'

The view's the thing at *Riva* (☎ 312-644-7482), an ambitious place about midway along the dockside promenade. The food's not bad, but for the money you might want to go to some of the highly recommended spots inland.

The much trumpeted beer garden near the end of the pier is not worth the walk. Some aging picnic benches are grouped around a stand selling Miller-brand beers (if you can call the stuff beer).

Tours A flotilla of competing tour boats line the dock. For the skinny on what's available, see the Organized Tours section of the Getting Around chapter for details.

RAY HILLSTROM
Navy Pier's famous Ferris wheel

Getting There & Away If you're driving, take the Grand Ave exit from Lake Shore Drive. There's parking on the pier itself or, when it's full, in lots to the west. It's about a 15-minute walk from Michigan Ave.

As for CTA bus, the No 29 State is the most frequent. It runs on State St through the Loop until it takes a right on Illinois in River North. The No 56 Milwaukee runs from Milwaukee Ave, past the newly renamed Metra Northwestern Station and on through the Loop to Navy Pier.

The lakefront bike path goes right past the entrance. In the summer, Shoreline Sightseeing (☎ 312-222-9328) runs a water taxi between Navy Pier, the river near the Sears Tower and the Shedd Aquarium.

From May through September, the pier is open Monday to Thursday 10 am to 10 pm, Friday and Saturday 10 am to midnight, Sunday 10 am to 9 pm; the rest of the year it's open Monday to Thursday 10 am to 9 pm, Friday and Saturday 10 am to 10 pm, Sunday 10 am to 7 pm. Note that individual restaurants and attractions may have different hours.

Chicago Children's Museum

The target audience of this attraction will love the place. Designed to challenge the imaginations of kids age one through 12, the colorful and lively museum (☎ 312-527-1000), near the main entrance to Navy Pier, has numerous politically correct exhibits.

The Stinking Truth about Garbage teaches recycling during a trip to an imaginary landfill. **Grandparents** teaches kids to love guess who (it's evidently assumed that the immediate older generation is beyond redemption) in a family-tree-building game.

An exhibit with a game-show motif, **Face to Face** teaches the young ones how not to grow up into jerks by cautioning against prejudice and discrimination. Designing your own flight of fancy is the goal at the build-your-own-airplane **Inventing Lab**. Other exhibits let kids get wet just when they've finally dried out from the Navy Pier fountains.

The museum is open Tuesday through Sunday 10 am to 5 pm, and on Monday in the summer and on some school holidays. Admission is $5.

RAY HILLSTROM
A fountain and museum for the kid in you

Terra Museum of American Art

Amid the commercial confines of the Mag Mile, this modest little museum (☎ 312-664-3939), 666 N Michigan (Map 3), displays an overview of American art since 1800. Founded by Daniel J Terra, a self-made millionaire, the museum has its own custom-built stairway and entrance building, which serves the galleries in renovated space next door.

The collection includes lesser works by Winslow Homer, James Whistler, John Singer Sargent, Mary Cassatt and others, including a passel of works by Andrew Wyeth. Special exhibitions focus on American artists at work abroad and at home. The museum's low profile on the Chicago cultural landscape was expected to rise substantially after highly regarded curator John Hallmark Neff was hired in 1997 to oversee the collection. This is a good place to take a break from acquisitive pursuits and learn something about American art. It's open Tuesday noon to 8 pm, Wednesday to Saturday 10 am to 5 pm, Sunday noon to 5 pm. Admission is $4, free on Tuesday.

Holy Name Cathedral

It's ironic that in a town with so many grandiose churches, the Chicago Archdiocese would call this modest Gothic church home (☎ 312-787-8040, 735 N State just south of Chicago Ave; Map 3). The irony is greater with the knowledge that the archdiocese has had to close some of its most beautiful churches because of declining membership in some parishes.

Built in 1875 to a design by the unheralded Patrick Keeley, the cathedral has twice been remodeled in attempts to spruce it up. The latter effort in fact covered up bullet holes left over from a Capone-era hit across the street.

The cathedral does provide a quiet place for contemplation, unless the excellent choirs are practicing, in which case it's an entertaining respite. The cathedral is open most of the day and has frequent services.

Other Sights

Many additional sights are covered in the appropriate sections in the Places to Stay, Places to Eat and Shopping chapters.

Whales Not the living kind, but life-size nonetheless, these whales cavort on the east wall of the Hotel Inter-Continental, 505 N Michigan, part of a mural unveiled late in 1997. The 25-story painting is by Wyland, a uni-named artist whose paintings of marine life have made him a millionaire many times over. The Chicago mural is his 73rd in a series of 100 he is donating worldwide.

Floor Clock The floor for this clock is part of a city block. Its hands – the minute hand is 20 feet long – run on tires as they make timely cruises past gigantic numbers. The best way to appreciate this work by Vito Acconci is from a room at the Sheraton. The clock is on the block bounded by Columbus and Illinois St east of the NBC Tower and north of the Sheraton (Map 3).

Tribune Tower Rocks These are not the ones in the writers' heads but rather the ones implanted all around the base of the Tribune Tower, at 435 N Michigan (Map 3).

RICK GERHARTER
Bits of the world at the Tribune Tower

Eccentric owner Col Robert McCormick both collected and had his overworked reporters send rocks from famous buildings and monuments around the world. See how many you recognize.

Chicago Sun-Times Presses With all the appeal of an aluminum can, the headquarters of the most-read paper in the city, at 401 N Wabash (Map 3), does not lure admirers. But on any weekday, you can cut through a long hallway running the length of the main floor from the Wabash entrance to the east door and have a publisher's-eye view of a working museum of printing technology. The *Sun-Times* presses are ancient and are on full view through picture windows. Watching the various editions race through the ink-smeared rollers is reminiscent of one of those 'breaking news' scenes from an old movie. The show won't go on forever, however: the paper is building a new state-of-the-art press on the city's southwest side.

Between the east side of the *Sun-Times* building and the back of the Wrigley Building, one of the most pleasant plazas in the city overlooks the river and the Loop skyline. Trees, lawns you can sit on and many, many benches make this a wonderful spot to rest your weary dogs on a decent day. A branch of the ubiquitous McDonald's and a small grocery store provide sustenance.

American Medical Association Designed by Japanese architect Kenzo Tange and opened in 1990, the headquarters of the AMA, at 515 N State (Map 3), is proof that all that glitters is not gold. Managerial miscues and blunders have helped drive membership in the association to record lows. Now less than 40% of American doctors belong. Perhaps some of the AMA's woes can be traced to a certain hubris at the top. Note the distinctive four-story cutout at the top of the building's profile and then consider that upon the building's opening, employees were told that the hole would help them find the building. This conjured visions of AMA staffers dopily wandering the city asking: 'Have you seen the building with the hole?'

Anti-Cruelty Society The facade facing LaSalle St – the formal address is 159 W Grand (Map 3) – was designed to resemble a basset hound. The building's architect, Stanley Tigerman, is known for his witty creations. His parking garage in the Loop at 60 E Lake looks like an old Bentley.

Tree Studios These fascinating artists' spaces were built during the World's Columbian Exposition in 1893 in an effort to encourage artists to remain in Chicago. The facade, on the east side of State St between Ontario and Ohio (Map 3), is very well preserved. Above the small artist-related ground floor stores, loftlike studios are still rented out to artists. The most interesting detail is hidden from the street: huge greenhouse windows on the back of the building, overlooking a lovely enclosed courtyard.

GOLD COAST

In 1882 Potter and Bertha Palmer were the power couple of Chicago. His web of businesses included the city's best hotel and a huge general merchandise store later sold to a clerk named Marshall Field. When they moved from Prairie Ave north to a crenelated castle of a mansion at what's now 1350 N Lake Shore Drive, the Palmers set off a lemminglike rush of Chicago's wealthy to the neighborhood around them. Showing the kind of shrewd judgment that had made him a millionaire, Palmer purchased much of what later became the Gold Coast *before* he moved there. He later subdivided his land and quadrupled his money.

Development centered on Astor St, and within 40 years most of the plots were covered with grand mansions. After WWII, surging demand for lake-view apartments led to the wholesale slaughter of mansions on Lake Shore Drive; in their place some of the most hideous high-rises in Chicago were erected and quickly filled. As the wave of construction threatened to move inland, preservationists managed to save most of the blocks from development, although the occasional 1960s high-rise

draws attention to the bankrupt aesthetic values of that era. Today most of the district has been placed on the National Register of Historic Places.

While the area east of Clark prospered, the area west was a notorious slum known as Little Hell. European immigrants who arrived in the 19th century were later joined in the tenements by blacks from the South. After WWII, two projects dramatically altered Little Hell's future: The city cleared the slums west of Orleans and built the Cabrini-Green housing project. The first units built were simple two-story townhouses, but in the late 1950s, because of budget woes, 15 high-rises from 7 to 19 stories were built. Meanwhile, just to the east, a huge middle-class development known as Sandburg Village mixed townhouses and high-rises on the blocks between LaSalle and Clark north of Division.

Little did anybody know, the latter would prove an effective lure for young college-educated professionals. Soon demand for space spread to Old Town and Lincoln Park, two neighborhoods that were in

RAY HILLSTROM
Ghosts of lost mansions haunt Lake Shore Drive.

tatters. Some urbanologists have gone so far as to say that Sandburg Village saved the North Side of Chicago, because it proved there was demand for inner-city housing among the middle class at a time when developers were bulldozing cornfields and carving out suburbs as quickly as they could.

The lesson of the Cabrini-Green projects has been unremittingly grim. Rundown and crime-ridden, they are the legacy of a Chicago Housing Authority that, until Harold Washington's election in 1983, was controlled by whites with little regard for black tenants. Instead of being affordable homes for the working poor, they became warehouses for the chronically underemployed and unemployed. Single mothers – and the vast majority of CHA households are headed by single women – found it impossible to supervise their kids playing 15 stories away. Gangs soon took over many of the buildings.

By the early 1990s, the CHA had given up on them; the agency is now slowly demolishing the high-rises. Many of them have been empty for years, illegally populated by drug dealers and gangs. They are now surrounded by gentrification on all sides, and developers are visibly licking their chops at the prospect of covering the land with expensive townhouses. The city, desirous of the tax revenue, is sending the poor residents to live in other parts of town.

A visit to Cabrini-Green, which runs east of Orleans and north of Chicago, is a bad idea day or night. Sniper gunfire regularly rings out in a place as much a Little Hell as it was 100 years ago.

Water Tower

It's hard to believe that the 154-foot Water Tower, at 806 N Michigan Ave (Map 5), a city icon and focal point of the Mag Mile, once dwarfed all the buildings around it. Built in the late 1860s, the Water Tower and its associated building, the Pumping Station across the street, were constructed with local yellow limestone in a Gothic

RAY HILLSTROM

The Water Tower

style popular at the time. This stone construction and lack of flammable interiors saved them in 1871 when the great Chicago fire roared through.

The complex was obsolete by 1906, and only concerted public outcry saved it from demolition three times. Whether Oscar Wilde would have joined the preservationists is open for debate: when he visited Chicago in 1881, he called the Water Tower 'a castellated monstrosity with salt and pepper boxes stuck all over it.' Yet by 1883 his attitude had somewhat softened: 'It was not until I had seen the water-works at Chicago that I realized the wonders of machinery; the rise and fall of the steel rods, the symmetrical motion of the great wheels is the most beautiful rhythmic thing I have ever seen.'

A major restoration in 1962 ensured the tower's survival. It is surrounded by a pleasant park and is host to a tourist information office and a branch of Hot Tix, the discount theater-ticket vendor.

Museum of Contemporary Art

The MCA (☎ 312-280-2660), 220 E Chicago Ave (Map 5), has been on a roll since its new building opened in 1996. Visits are up substantially, and the museum now has four times more space for exhibits than it did in its old location in a converted bakery. From being a second-rate facility with a limited catalog, the MCA is rapidly building its permanent collection with works by major artists and promising lesser names.

The Building Designed by Berlin architect Josef Paul Kleihues, the boxy MCA and its imposing entry stairs from the sidewalk have been likened to the works of Albert Speer, Adolf Hitler's architect. You decide.

The metallic exterior panel is designed to age to a sort of dull gray. Inside, things are much brighter. A curving staircase on the north side of the building presents an invitation few can refuse. They are rewarded by four galleries on the top floor with soaring barrel-vaulted skylit roofs. The café overlooking Lake Michigan has quickly become popular as much for its fine views of the sculpture garden and lake beyond as its creative food.

The Collections The MCA generally believes that 'modern art' covers works since 1945. The permanent collection includes Franz Kline, René Magritte, Cindy Sherman and Andy Warhol. The displays are arranged to show the gradual blurring of the boundaries between painting, photography, sculpture, video and other media. The MCA also mounts large special exhibitions, among them one devoted to the brilliant desert photos of Richard Misrach.

Anyone who has ever found themselves staring at some noted modern work and wondering what the hell it is will appreciate the copious curator's notes that accompany the exhibits. For instance, wall panels give maximum explanation of artistic movements such as Minimalism. The MCA is open Tuesday to Sunday 11 am to 6 pm (Wednesday till 9 pm); closed Monday, Thanksgiving, Christmas and New Year's Day. Admission is $6.50 for adults, $4 for children, free on Tuesday.

860-880 N Lake Shore Drive

This is where the International Style of high-rises got its start. Built from 1949 to 1951, the twin towers (Map 5) were the manifestation of designs architect Mies van der Rohe first put forward in 1921. The idea of high-rises draped only in a curtain of glass and steel was so radical at the time that psychologists speculated about the impact of living in a transparent home.

At the buildings' opening, few guessed at how easily Mies' precepts would be bastardized by legions of untalented architects. The aesthetic nightmares just up the road are immediate examples. How their boneheaded architects managed to screw up Mies' design tenets is remarkable. Of course, maybe this kind of building was simply meant to be taken in small doses.

John Hancock Center

The world's tallest mixed-use building, the Hancock, 875 N Michigan (Map 5), is the third tallest overall in Chicago, at 1127 feet. A recent remodeling of the plaza below street level added a nifty fountain whose curtain of water muffles traffic noise above.

Observatory Much less popular than the Sears Tower's Skydeck, the John Hancock Observatory (☎ 312-751-3681) benefits from having shorter lines and no sappy film. The friendly employees guide you to the fast – 23 mph – elevators for the 40-second ride to the 94th floor. In many ways the view here is better than at the Sears, because from the Hancock you can see the Sears and appreciate just how tall it is compared to the rest of the Loop skyline.

Another way the Hancock tries harder is with an outside area that, while screened to prevent mischief, lets you hear the sounds of the city. When you're that far above the street, there's something almost lyrical about the dull roar of traffic punctuated by jackhammers, sirens and the like.

RICK GERHARTER

The John Hancock tower (at center) dominates the Gold Coast skyline.

The observatory is open every day, 9 am to midnight. Admission is $7 for adults, $5 for children. Look for some of the clever details built into the waiting area, which evoke the original Hancock construction site. Hint: one of the workers didn't like pickles.

Fourth Presbyterian Church

This 1914 church (☎ 312-787-4570), on Michigan between Chestnut and Delaware (Map 5; the official address is 126 E Chestnut) belongs to one of the city's wealthiest congregations. It brings to mind a bunch of dons in some old Gothic school guzzling port and eyeing the choirboys. Lurid fantasies aside, it provides a welcome break from the commercial blocks and is a reminder of how, not so long ago, the neighborhood was dominated by low-rise mansions. There are occasional organ recitals in the splendid sanctuary.

Astor St

This street of mansions has retained the grandeur lost to high-rises elsewhere. For a quick idea of what Lake Shore Drive once looked like, trot over to the lake and check out Nos 1250, 1254 and 1258. All three narrowly averted the fate of their brethren.

Astor St is lined with gems; take your time strolling and be sure to note the following standouts, all on Map 5.

Originally four, now three, the 1887 homes at **Nos 1308-1312** have a lovely sculptured quality that extends to the turrets, gables and dormers. The architect, John Wellborn Root, was so pleased with his efforts that he moved into **No 1310**.

Once one home, now several apartments, the 1887 mansion at **No 1355** represents the full flower of Georgian revival. Note the alternating skulls and animal heads above the windows.

While he was still working for Louis Sullivan, Frank Lloyd Wright designed the large but only 11-room Charnley House, at **No 1365**, and he proclaimed with his soon-to-be-trademarked bombast that it was the 'first modern building.'

A late arrival on the street but in keeping with its elegance, the 1929 Russell House, at **No 1444**, is Art Deco French at its most refined.

The official address of the 1880 mansion that is the **archbishop's residence** is 1555 N State, but it spans the entire block to Astor. Built in the Queen Anne style that later became known generically as 'Victorian,' this comfortable place looks like it would provide solace to any archbishop pondering the sins of the flock.

Other Notable Buildings

Walking south from State St and North Ave, look for the following buildings, all on Map 5.

French elegance came to Chicago in a manner as humble as Napolean's ego with the 1912 apartment house at **1550 N State**, which once boasted a mere one unit per floor.

The sexual revolution perhaps started in the basement 'grotto' of the otherwise unremarkable 1899 mansion at **1340 N State**, which belonged to *Playboy* impresario Hugh Hefner in the 1960s and '70s. Later a dorm for the School of the Art Institute (imagine the pickup lines!), it was gutted in 1993 and turned into four very staid apartments.

A stunning 1919 flamboyant Gothic courtyard building, **Archbishop Quigley Preparatory Seminary** holds the magnificent Chapel of St James (☎ 312-787-8625), 831 N Rush, which was ambitiously modeled after Sainte-Chapelle in Paris. With 45,000 panes of glass in its impressive windows, it comes close. In the summer it's open Monday to Saturday 11 am to 3 pm; the balance of the year it's open Monday, Tuesday, Thursday and Saturday noon to 2 pm. Local choral groups often perform in the chapel, a recommended and ennobling treat.

The **St Benedict Flats** at 42-50 E Chicago are an unusual example of French Second Empire architecture. I once lived here briefly. I hope my millions of roach roommates were eradicated during the recent complete renovation.

International Museum of Surgical Science

An eclectic collection of surgery-related items, the Museum of Surgical Science (☎ 312-642-6502), 1524 N Lake Shore Drive just south of Lincoln Park (Map 5), has an odd and often poorly marked assortment that at first makes the museum seem like nothing more than a place to escape a vicious lake squall. But start exploring and you will soon be rewarded with fascinating thematic displays, such as the one on bloodletting, the act of bleeding patients to death to 'cure' them. The undeniable gems of the collection are the 'stones,' as in 'kidney stone,' 'gallstone,' etc. All of the spectacularly large specimens were passed by patients who may have wished instead for a good bloodletting. The museum is open Tuesday to Saturday 10 am to 4 pm, Sunday 11 am to 5 pm. Admission is free!

Washington Square

A center of 1855's beer riots (see the Beer Riots sidebar in the Entertainment chapter), this park has had a colorful and tragic history. In the 1920s it was known as 'Bughouse Square' because of the communists, socialists, anarchists and other -ists who gave soapbox orations there.

In the 1970s, when it was a gathering place for young male prostitutes, it gained tragic infamy as the preferred pickup spot of mass-murderer John Wayne Gacy. Gacy took his victims back to his suburban home, where he killed them and buried their bodies in the basement. Convicted on 33 counts of murder (although the actual tally may be higher), he was executed in 1994.

Washington Square is a rather plain park across from the Newberry Library and is bounded by Walton, Clark, Delaware and Dearborn (Map 5).

Dave & Buster's

This 60,000-sq-foot dining and entertainment bazaar (☎ 312-943-5151), 1030 N Clark (Map 5), is a playground for young single guys with too much disposable income and few obligations. The Chicago branch of this national chain has a sports bar, bowling, pool, shuffleboard, electronic golf, 3-D interactive games and a whole lot more. Open daily from about 11 am to 1 am.

OLD TOWN

This once simple neighborhood of wood houses was one of the first in the city to gentrify in the 1960s. The original artist residents, with plenty of late 1960s inspiration, made the neighborhood Chicago's funky hippie hangout with the requisite string of head shops on Wells St.

Today the neighborhood is one of the city's most affluent. The old wood houses have been fixed up and modified in ways their builders never would have imagined. But those are the lucky ones; many other simple old homes have been demolished by greedy owners whose replacement houses fill the lots to bursting in all their extravagance. The only haze over Wells St now comes from cigar-puffing swells at the many swank restaurants that line both sides of the street.

Wells St north of Division is safe, although the neighborhood to the west calls for caution. North of North Ave and west of Wells is a jumble of narrow streets that are perfect for wandering. The area bordered by North, Wells, Lincoln, Armitage and Larrabee is safe and filled with surprises.

The facades of the 1890 vintage apartments of **Crilly Court**, a single block off Eugenie St (Map 6), are charming stone variations of Queen Anne architecture, but the real surprise is the back of the units, which line a private alley between St Paul and Eugenie. They have wrought-iron porches right out of the French Quarter in New Orleans.

RAY HILLSTROM

A stately Old Town home

The **Henry Meyer House**, at 1802 N Lincoln Park West at Menomonee (Map 6), gives you a rare look at how Chicago's houses appeared before the 1871 fire. This one was built right afterward – the flames roared through here – but just before legislation was enacted banning wood structures in the area devastated by the fire.

At 1838 N Lincoln Park West (Map 6), the **Frederick Wacker House** is another good wooden example built during the same brief window of opportunity as the Meyer House. Imagine whole blocks of these homes and you'll start to get an idea of the horror of the fire.

LINCOLN PARK

Chicago's most popular neighborhood is alive day and night with people in-line skating, walking dogs, pushing strollers and driving in circles for hours looking for a place to park. The humble origins of most of the blocks away from the lake have been lost under the waves of renovation and gentrification that began in the mid-1970s. Notable highlights are few, but the entire neighborhood, which stretches roughly from North Ave north along the lake to Diversey and west to Clybourn and Ashland, is a pleasant place to stroll about. The Places to Eat, Entertainment and Shopping chapters are littered with ideas to get you started.

Lincoln Park Proper

The neighborhood gets its name from this park, which at six miles in length is Chicago's largest. Its 1200 acres stretch north from North Avenue to Diversey, where it narrows along the lake and continues until the end of Lake Shore Drive. The park's many lakes, trails and paths make it an excellent place for recreation. Cross-country skiing in the winter and sunbathing

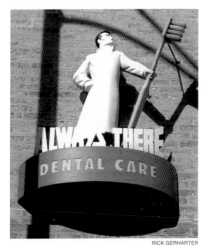

RICK GERHARTER
Lincoln Park detail

in warmer months are just two of the activities Chicagoans enjoy in Lincoln Park. Many buy picnic vittles from the markets on Clark St and Diversey Parkway.

Most of Lincoln Park's pleasures are natural. A few highlights are listed here; major sights have their own sections, following.

In contrast to his 'Sitting Lincoln' in Grant Park, sculptor Augustus Saint-Gaudens in his **Standing Lincoln** shows the 16th president deep in contemplation right before he delivers a great speech. Saint-Gaudens based the work on casts made of Lincoln's face and hands while Lincoln was alive. The statue is in its own garden east of the Chicago Historical Society (Map 6).

Near the southeast corner of LaSalle Drive and Clark St (Map 6), the **Couch Mausoleum** is the sole reminder of the land's pre-1864 use: the entire area was a municipal cemetery. Many of the graves contained hundreds of dead prisoners from Camp Douglas, a horrific prisoner-of-war stockade that was on the city's south side during the Civil War. Trying to move all the bodies proved a greater undertaking then the city could stomach, and today if you start digging at the south end of the park you're liable to make some ghoulish discoveries.

From a little dock in front of pretty Cafe Brauer, a 1908 Prairie School architectural creation, you can rent two-person **paddleboats** and cruise the South Pond, south of the zoo (Map 6). A more bucolic cruise can be had on the North Pond, which doesn't have the zoo crowds; rent boats from the little boathouse east of where Deming Place meets the park (Map 6). The rental season at both ponds is roughly May through September.

Chicago Historical Society

The Lincolns, Capones, Daleys and other notables are here, but the focus of this well-funded museum (☎ 312-642-4600), 1601 N Clark at North Ave (Map 6), is on the average person. The role of the commoner in the American Revolution sets the tone for the humanistic exhibits. One, titled

Fort Dearborn and Frontier Chicago, shows how settlers and Indians changed each other's lives. The Pioneer Court gives hands-on demonstrations in the intricacies of making candles, weaving blankets and knitting clothes. None of the work was easy.

Much of the 2nd floor is devoted to Chicago's development and history. The roles of immigration and industry are addressed, as are the problems of slums and the lives of the rich. Special exhibitions are the museum's strong point, covering such diverse topics as how bungalows allowed almost every family to afford a home, and how WWII affected the average family.

The museum is open Monday to Saturday 9:30 am to 4:30 pm, Sunday noon to 5 pm, closed major holidays. Admission is $3, free on Monday. The Big Shoulders Cafe serves creative soups and sandwiches.

Lincoln Park Zoo

The zoo (☎ 312-742-2000) is one of Chicago's most popular attractions not just because admission is free, but also because of its wide range of exhibits, featuring 1600 animals on a compact 35-acre setting. The official address is 2200 N Cannon Drive (Map 6), but in reality it is easily reached from most parts of the park; there are entrances to it on all sides.

Founded in 1868, the zoo enjoys considerable community support. Wealthy patrons, including Joan Kroc, wife of McDonald's founder Ray Kroc, have donated millions of dollars over the last three decades to renovate

RICK GERHARTER
Diptych: Parent and child

old facilities and build new ones. The following tour starts at the main, west entrance on N Cannon Drive and proceeds around the zoo in a clockwise direction. There are maps of the zoo on several signs there.

Once inside you encounter the crowd-pleasing antics of the sea lions, who are frolicsome day and night. Especially at night: I once lived across the street and can attest to their boisterous antics in the wee hours.

Penguin/Seabird House Take a trip to Antarctica. Eighteen penguins from three species stoically stare out from their refrigerated quarters. The big ones are kings.

Turn left as you leave and follow your nose.

Joseph Regenstein Large Mammal Area Here's where you find ever popular Bosie and the rest of the elephants. Look for Shanti, the first elephant born in Illinois. Nearby is Jambo Twiga, a young giraffe whose name is Swahili for 'hello giraffe.' The tapirs, although severely lacking in the cuteness department, are notable because they have existed almost unchanged in South America since prehistoric times. And note that the rhinoceros horn is actually made of matted hair. Regardless, poaching has almost eliminated all the rhinos from the wild in Africa because of a belief in some parts of the world that the 'horn' can be used to treat such human maladies as impotence.

Exiting the mammal house, you'll find the polar bear exhibit. The two huge white beasts spend much of the summer in their pool. To see them at their best, drop by in January.

Head south past the exhibit of the other bears, which seem to be in year-round hibernation.

McCormick Bird House This can be one of the most rewarding exhibits at the zoo, but you have to work at it. Visitors in a hurry won't see a majority of the species on display, because the birds take time to locate among the natural foliage in the 10 habitat areas.

RICK GERHARTER

Storks at play outside the Lincoln Park Conservatory

Contrary to popular belief, not all birds sit in trees; many spend their lives wandering the ground. An example you can see at the zoo is the cape thick-knee, a relative of the roadrunner that stalks about in the savanna exhibit. In the tropical river area, look for the green imperial pigeon, which has gold feathers on its neck that stand up during breeding.

Regenstein Small Mammal-Reptile House Opened in 1997, this glass-domed building is home to scores of beady-eyed rodents, amphibians, and other critters. The curving walkway snakes through open and glassed-in areas designed to give the animals a natural habitat while giving visitors a close look. Among the highlights: huge monitor lizards, Galápagos turtles, naked mole rats, fruit bats and spiders. Arachnophobes beware!

The koalas are very popular but are about as active as your teddy bear at home.

Skirt the lion house for now and continue south.

Helen V Brach Primate House This building, renovated in the early 1990s, is a far cry from its earlier days, when the animals were kept in sterile cages. To get a feeling for what it may have been like for them, sit in the metal seat of Bushman the gorilla (dead since 1951 and stuffed at the Field Museum) and stare out through the bars. The crowd-pleasers here are the white-faced gibbons, which like to come right up to the glass to inspect visitors. Also look for two small holes in the big stump in the lemur area. They're part of a system that releases termites into the exhibit for the animals to track down and eat.

Lester E Fisher Great Ape House The zoo has been a world leader in gorilla breeding, with more than three dozen born here since 1970. There are two distinct family groups of gorillas living in the building. The chimp and orangutan populations are much smaller. All the primates enjoy private areas far from the prying eyes of Homo sapiens.

Rather than walk quickly through this circular building, derisively comparing the primates' behavior to those of relatives, stop and watch their complex interactions as family groups. The facial expressions and eyes of the animals show a range of emotions that is almost eerie.

Look for 350-lb Frank. In the past 15 years, he has adopted almost a dozen baby gorillas into his family – behavior that's rare for his species. Although gorillas are usually good parents, its not uncommon for mothers to abandon a baby or, worse, for lead males to kill the infants of young females joining the group. Another stellar ape is Debbie, who has helped raise several infants.

If you're lucky, the chimpanzees will be drawing on poster board with crayons. Some of their works have been shown in galleries.

Walk past the hoofed-animals area toward the small pond. Continue around until you see the apocryphal vision of an Illinois farm, south past Cafe Brauer.

Farm in the Zoo The place where many urbanites first learn that milk comes from cows instead of cardboard containers, this area, south of the zoo, has a full range of barnyard animals in a faux farm setting (Map 6). There are frequent demonstrations of cow milking, horse grooming, butter churning and other chores. The exhibits don't make any bones about the ultimate fate of most livestock. For instance, those cute piglets head to the slaughterhouse only 4 to 6 months after birth.

Head back north past the flamingo pond to the roar of the big cats.

Kovler Lion House There's no posted feeding time here; the animals – there are tigers as well – receive food at various intervals throughout the day. Watching a 600-lb Siberian tiger devour a hunk of horse meat is an eye-opening experience. Also note the white spots on the back of the tiger's ears; they're the signals baby tigers use to follow their mothers through grasslands.

Revisit the sea lions and veer left to the low-slung brown building.

Pritzker Children's Zoo There's the usual lineup of furry creatures such as guinea pigs for kids to cuddle in the Children's Zoo. There's also the zoo's nursery behind a glass wall. Although visitors thrill to the sight of baby animals in cribs, zoo keepers don't. Animals end up in the nursery only if there has been a problem with their natural parents' ability to care for them.

Other Sights Just north of the zoo are two other worthy sights that keep the same hours. Near the zoo's north entrance, off Stockton Drive, is the **Lincoln Park Conservatory** (☎ 312-742-7736; Map 6), two gardens first planted in 1891 that bloom year-round under three acres of glass. The 1887 statue *Storks at Play* outside the conservatory has enchanted generations of Chicagoans.

The **Zoo Rookery** is a 1937 creation with stone walls reminiscent of the stratified canyons of the Wisconsin Dells. When not overrun with people, it is a magical setting, especially in winter. Planted with native Midwestern species, it's at the north end of the zoo near Fullerton (Map 6).

The Lincoln Park Zoo is open daily 9 am to 5 pm, and admission is free. CTA buses Nos 22, 36 and 151 all pass close by. Parking is among the worst in the city. Crowds are a problem on sunny weekends, but during colder months a visit can be an almost intimate experience. One note: the animals eat far better than visitors; don't lunch here.

Chicago Academy of Sciences

Always a snoozer, this museum slumbered for more than 100 years in a building near the zoo. It was never the powerhouse research institution envisioned by its founders (that role was usurped by the Field Museum). It offered nature exhibits as dry as the dust on its taxidermy collection.

In the early 1990s the academy began showing some signs of life under a management that hatched a deal with the Chicago Park District: the perennially office-space deprived zoo could have the academy's musty old building at Armitage and Clark, near the zoo entrance, if the academy could have space in the park for a new building. A classic win-win situation.

The new Chicago Academy of Sciences is set to open in the spring of 1999 across Fullerton from the north side of the zoo (Map 6). Preliminary indications suggest that it will be a winner. Plans are to focus on the natural environment around Chicago, past, present and future. A huge outdoor nature area will re-create five local environments, and a large atrium will hold 10,000 butterflies.

Perhaps the most interesting exhibit will let visitors take water from the adjoining North Pond and examine it under a microscope. Considering that I once passed a floating French tickler in my rented paddleboat there, the results should be interesting. A phone line (☎ 773-871-2668) has details about the construction, opening date and temporary exhibits and programs around the city.

Other Lincoln Park Sights

Elks Veterans Memorial The once hugely popular men's social club has fallen on hard times all over the US, but during its heyday it built this impressive memorial building (☎ 773-528-4500), 2750 N Lakeview, to honor members killed at war. It's open daily 9 am to 4 pm; admission is free.

St Clement's Church The restored Byzantine mosaics gracing the dome of this 1918 Catholic church (☎ 773-281-0371) were inspired by Istanbul's Hagia Sophia. When the Notre Dame football team loses, Sunday masses are a sea of red eyes in this parish, which caters to young, single college grads. The church is at 646 W Deming Place, a street lined with gracious mansions with extra-wide front lawns.

Reebie Storage & Moving Company So taken by Chicago that you want to move here? You might consider hiring this firm (☎ 773-549-0120), 2325 N Clark, for its legacy of wit alone. The 1923 building carries its King Tut-inspired theme right down

to the hieroglyphics below statue of Ramses II on the right, which read, 'I give protection to your furniture.'

Oz Park Bounded by Geneva, Webster and Halsted (Map 6), this public park is celebrating its name thanks to the generous donations of neighborhood's rich. The Tin Man stands at the northeast corner of the park, wondering which passersby might have a heart for him, while a yellow brick sidewalk stretches from that same corner into the park. Those neighborhood dollars also bought Oz the best playground in the city.

RYAN VER BERKMOES

John Dillinger

Unlike Al Capone, John Dillinger wasn't part of Chicago's criminal mobs. He was a bank robber whose daring exploits throughout the Midwest made him a celebrity. Many Midwestern towns have a bank once robbed by Dillinger. Despite being on the FBI's 10 Most Wanted List, the wily criminal was able to evade police time and time again. The following example comes from William J Helmer, Chicago gangster expert and coauthor of *Dillinger: The Untold Story*:

> Dillinger didn't confine his thrill-seeking to robbing Midwestern banks. During his leisure time, the Chicago resident liked the thrills of the rides at the old River View Amusement Park at Belmont and Western Avenues. While partaking of these pleasures on a spring day in 1934, Dillinger was alarmed when suddenly all the power to the park was shut off and patrons told to leave through one exit. Fearing he'd been recognized by the police, the 31-year-old robber ran up to a woman who was loudly complaining about the shutdown and said, 'Hey, they've got Dillinger trapped by the roller coaster.' The woman began screaming this news about Chicago's most wanted criminal. In the ensuing hubbub, Dillinger slipped past the waiting police and into an unattended police car. Roaring out the gates of the park, he encountered more cops and yelled, 'Hey they got Dillinger, I'm going for reinforcements.' Making good his escape, he ditched the car and vanished.

It was later that year, on July 22, that Dillinger was betrayed to the cops by the infamous 'lady in red' and gunned down by the FBI outside the Biograph Theater, in Lincoln Park at 2433 N Lincoln (Map 6). ∎

RICK GERHARTER

Never see movies with women in red.

DePaul University Stretching east and west of the El south of Fullerton (Map 6), the campus is charming, efficient or ugly, depending where you are. Chalmers Place is a scholarly square east of the El. The row houses were built for a seminary that has since been absorbed by DePaul.

West of the Fullerton El stop, the Academic Center and the University Center were built in 1968 and 1978, respectively. Their architectural style is the aptly named 'Brutalism': both monstrosities seem to have been designed as last redoubts in case of urban assault. The 1992 library marks a new era of DePaul design that is vastly improved. Notice how they've tried to camouflage some of the Academic Center.

LAKE VIEW/WRIGLEYVILLE

These neighborhoods have become just as popular as Lincoln Park, to the south, but are younger and have more of an edge. Specific sights are few, but strolls along Halsted, Clark, Belmont or Southport can be both entertaining and surprising. Sojourns on the side streets can yield their own delights.

Lake View begins at Diversey and stretches from the lake to Ashland. Near Addison, what was North Lake View has adopted the name of the Cubs stadium, thanks mostly to the efforts of Realtors.

The Belmont and Addison El stops serve the area well, with able bullpen support from the Diversey, Wellington, Southport and Sheridan stops. Check the map for details.

Dunkin' Donuts

At 3200 N Clark (☎ 773-477-3636; Map 7), this 24-hour shop serves the same deep-fried calorie bombs found in scores of other Dunkin' Donuts branches around the city. However, this one is famous for more than its cheap coffee: its parking lot is the center of Chicago's punk and otherwise disaffected youth scene. On Friday and Saturday nights scores of tattooed and black-clad teens congregate here and on the surrounding blocks. There is a dark side to the scene, though: many of the teens are runaways, spending their days begging for change. Several charitable groups operate in the area, trying to help them sort things out.

The parking lot boasts the fastest tow times in the city. Don't even pause to tie your shoe.

Wrigley Field

At 1060 W Addison at Clark (Map 7), Wrigley Field draws tourists who pose year-round under the classic neon sign over the main entrance. See the Entertainment chapter for details about watching a game. If you don't have tickets or don't want to see the Cubbies lose, stroll over to Sheffield and chat with the guys who hang around all day, waiting for a ball to be hit out of the park. Notice, too, how the surrounding three-flats have adapted their roofs for watching games.

RAY HILLSTROM
Just looking for a hit

Alta Vista Terrace

Chicago's first designated historic district is worthy of the honor. Developer Samuel Eberly Gross re-created a block of London row houses on Alta Vista Terrace in 1904. The 20 homes on either side of the street mirror each other diagonally. Each building is exquisitely detailed, and the individual owners have worked hard at maintaining the spirit of the block. Individuality isn't dead, however: head to the back of the west row and you'll notice that every house has grown to the rear in dramatically different fashions.

Reaching the block can be a challenge; use Map 7 to trace your way one long block east of Clark along Grace or the one long block north of Wrigley Field on Seminary.

Graceland Cemetery

Why go to Memphis to see ostentatious memorials to the dead when you can go to Graceland right in Chicago? The local version (☎ 773-525-1105), at 4001 N Clark at Irving Park Rd (Map 7), a 10-minute walk west from the Sheridan El stop, is in much better taste and is the final resting place for some of the biggest names in Chicago history. Most of the notable tombs are around the lake in the northern half of the 121 acres. Buy one of the 25¢ maps at the entrance to navigate the swirl of paths and streets.

Many of the memorials relate to lives of the dead in symbolic and touching ways: National League founder William Hulbert lies under a baseball, hotelier Dexter Graves is under a work titled *Eternal Silence*, and George Pullman, the railroad car magnate who sparked so much labor unrest, lies under a hidden fortress designed to prevent angry union members from digging him up.

Daniel Burnham, who did so much to design Chicago, gets his own island. Photographer Richard Nickel, who helped form Chicago's nascent preservation movement and was killed during the demolition of his beloved Chicago Stock

Exchange Building (the 1972 accident was unrelated to the demolition), has a stone designed by admiring architects. Other notables interred here include John Wellborn Root, Louis Sullivan, Ludwig Mies van der Rohe, Marshall Field and Potter and Bertha Palmer.

The cemetery is open daily from 8 am to 4:30 pm.

ANDERSONVILLE

Once little more than celery farms, Andersonville grew up around the turn of the 20th century. It was a heavily Swedish neighborhood, a legacy that continues today in the names of many of the stores, such as the Swedish Bakery (see the Places to Eat chapter). Andersonville kept its traditional residents long after other neighborhoods had undergone rapid ethnic turnover; as a result, it remained one of the city's most stable enclaves.

Now most of the residents are Swedish only by chance. The blocks surrounding Clark St from about 5000 North through Bryn Mawr Ave have become popular with young professionals. The once-low rents attracted graphic artists and other creative types in the 1980s and 1990s. Many lesbians have found a home among the widely varied residents.

Even today, the shopkeepers and condo owners routinely sweep their sidewalks each day, as per Swedish tradition, although now they are as likely to be Lebanese or gay as they are the stolid older Nordic residents.

The Berwyn El stop on the Red Line is a 10-minute walk east of Clark St. Simply walk up Berwyn Ave. The No 22 Clark bus also cuts through the heart of Andersonville.

Swedish-American Museum Center

The permanent collection at this small storefront museum (☎ 773-728-8111), 5211 N Clark (Map 8), focuses on the lives of the Swedes who originally settled Chicago. In that sense it reflects the dreams and aspirations of many of the groups who have poured into the city since it was founded. Look at some of the items people felt were important to bring with them both because they thought they would need the items and because they wanted to remember their homeland: butter churns, traditional bedroom furniture, religious relics and more.

Among the occasional programs for kids is the delightful fair 'Vikings R Us.' The museum is open Tuesday to Friday 10 am to 4 pm, Saturday and Sunday 10 am to 3 pm. Admission is $2 for adults, $1 for children.

Lakewood-Balmoral Neighborhood

These residential blocks draw their name from the two streets they are centered on. You can explore this area when you are walking to and from the El. It is an integral part of Andersonville and lies midway between Clark St and the El (Map 8).

The houses here all date from the turn of the 20th century. They are quite large and were built as single-family homes for upper-middle-class families who often employed Swedish servants. Among the variety of designs: 5222 N Lakewood, which looks like something out of 'Hansel and Gretel'; 5347 N Lakewood, an example of the Craftsman style that emphasized careful detailing; and St Ita's Church, at 1220 W Catalpa, which is in the 13th-century French Gothic style.

WICKER PARK/BUCKTOWN

For more than 100 years these were working-class neighborhoods where generations of Central European immigrants lived in simple wood-frame homes (the 1871 fire didn't come through here, so wood houses were still legal).

In the 1980s, Bucktown was discovered by yuppies and artists, who quickly gentrified the area on the blocks on either side of Damen north of the railroad tracks that bisect the area at 1800 North. Wicker Park, south of the tracks and surrounding the namesake park, retains an edge, as yuppies, artists, musicians, Hispanic immigrants

and others all mix in a mostly harmonious manner. Gen-X cafés, exquisite restaurants and dives peddling brain tacos for a buck line Milwaukee Ave.

In both neighborhoods a stroll down the residential streets will reveal scores of houses built before the Chicago street level was raised. They have yards below the sidewalks and stairs leading a half-flight up to what once was the second floor.

With a dome modeled on St Peter's in Rome, the huge **St Mary of the Angels Church** (☎ 773-278-2644), 1850 N Hermitage at Cortland, dominates both Bucktown and the view from the Kennedy Expressway. Built with money from Polish parishioners prodded by a zealous pastor, the church features angels on the parapet, in the nave and possibly in the heavens above as well. Certainly the church is blessed, because after only 60 years from the time it was completed in 1920, it was headed toward an early death. Maintenance costs were through the holey roof; the heating bill alone was beyond the means of the diminished flock.

A grassroots campaign arose to save the church, drawing support from the community and people across the city. In 1992 the repairs, which cost more than the original construction bill, were completed, and the invigorated parish has many new members.

Wicker Park, a triangular park south of the Damen El stop, is the focus of the neighborhood and has buffed bods walking pedigreed dogs past retirees playing chess. The neighborhood's inherent energy is expressed in the facade of the promisingly named Fun Church (☎ 773-489-7601), 1903 W Schiller at the southeast corner of the park (Map 9).

The **Nelson Algren House**, a three-flat one block south of the park at 1958 W Evergreen (Map 9), is where the writer created some of his greatest works about gritty life in the neighborhood (see the Nelson Algren sidebar in Facts about Chicago). You can't go in, but you can admire it from the street.

Wicker Park Walking Tour

The streets northwest of Wicker Park have been called 'the ethnic Gold Coast.' German and Scandinavian immigrants who made it big in the late 19th century built their mansions there. Although they could have built their grand homes on Prairie Ave or the Gold Coast, they preferred to live where the people they ran into on the streets spoke the language of the old country.

From the Damen El stop on the CTA Blue Line, walk two blocks northwest on Milwaukee Ave to Caton St. Turn left and begin the tour.

RICK GERHARTER
Wicker Park Victorian

Nos 2138-2156 W Caton St This is an 1891 minidevelopment of five large homes, each with a different exterior design and theme. Among the variations: No 2142, Queen Anne; No 2146, Swiss; No 2152, Renaissance. No 2156 is the stone-and-brick home of Norwegian Ole Thorp, who built the houses.

2159 W Caton St This large 1891 mansion is a good example of Queen Anne style.
The next two buildings are across from where Caton meets Leavitt.

1644 & 1658 N Leavitt St To fit in with nearby mansions, these upscale apartment flats were built using high-quality materials such as limestone, ornately carved wooden details and cut glass.
Go south on Leavitt.

2156 W Concord Place This is an 1893 mansion with a proud conical tower.
Continue south; cross North Ave and turn east on Pierce Ave.

2146, 2150, 2156 W Pierce Ave Three similar houses, these date from 1890. Note how the limestone 2150 has held up better than the sandstone 2156 and 2146.

2138 W Pierce Ave See all that woodwork? You'd never guess that the original owner, John D Runge, owned a wood-milling firm. Notice the Masonic insignia under the eaves of the dormer.

2135 W Pierce Ave There's more detail in pressed metal, wood and brick than the eye can soak up on this 1889 house. The side porch overlooking a garden was a popular detail in the neighborhood.
At the end of the block, turn south onto Hoyne Ave.

1520 N Hoyne Ave Germans liked sculpted figures of women, as seen on this 1886 house, which was actually built for a Russian lumber baron.

1521 N Hoyne Ave The porch of this 1895 turreted Queen Anne house has wood carved to resemble lace.

Wicker Park Lutheran Church At Hoyne and LeMoyne, this 1906 church was built using granite salvaged from an upscale Levee District brothel.

1417 N Hoyne Ave This 1879 Italianate house has a typical side porch.

1407 N Hoyne Ave This proud French Second Empire mansion, dating from 1879, has a cast-iron porch.
Turn east on Schiller St and cross Damen.

1941 W Schiller St This 1891 house is a prime example of Queen Anne architecture in all of its styling.
Rest up after your tour across the street in Wicker Park. ■

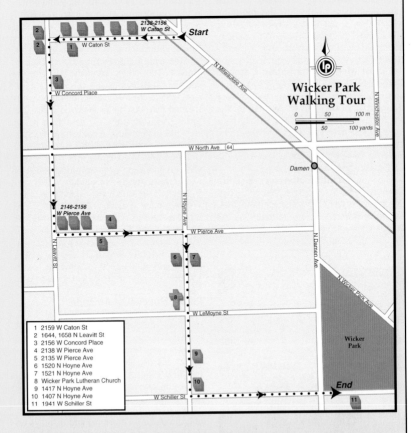

Wicker Park Walking Tour

1   2159 W Caton St
2   1644, 1658 N Leavitt St
3   2156 W Concord Place
4   2138 W Pierce Ave
5   2135 W Pierce Ave
6   1520 N Hoyne Ave
7   1521 N Hoyne Ave
8   Wicker Park Lutheran Church
9   1417 N Hoyne Ave
10   1407 N Hoyne Ave
11   1941 W Schiller St

UKRAINIAN VILLAGE

This ethnic enclave is still heavily populated with its original residents or their descendants. The No 66 Chicago Ave bus runs through the heart of the neighborhood.

Inside a bright white storefront, the **Ukrainian Institute of Modern Art** (☎ 773-227-5522), 2320 W Chicago Ave (Map 10), displays works by artists of Ukrainian descent. The growing permanent collection rotates through one gallery, while special mixed-media exhibitions occupy the others. The fall of the Soviet Union has opened up the Ukraine and that has added new vitality to the museum, which now sponsors the work of native Ukrainians. It's open Tuesday to Sunday noon to 4 pm (in July and August, weekends only). A donation is requested.

The **St Nicholas Ukrainian Catholic Cathedral** (☎ 773-276-4537), 2238 W Rice, one block north of Chicago on Oakley (Map 10), is the less-traditional of the neighborhood's main churches. Its 13 domes represent Christ and the Apostles. The intricate mosaics were added to the 1915 building in 1988 and are inspired by the Cathedral of St Sophia in Kiev.

The new **Saints Volodymyr & Olha Church** (☎ 312-829-5209), 739 N Oakley (Map 10), is attended by the traditionalists. Liturgical differences led the traditionalists at St Nicholas to build this showy edifice in 1975. It makes up for its paucity of domes –

St Nicholas Ukrainian Catholic Cathedral

only five – with a massive mosaic showing the conversion of Grand Duke Vladimir of Kiev to Christianity in 988 AD.

WEST SIDE

The flat expanse west of the Loop and affluent lakefront is a patchwork of ethnic neighborhoods, urban renewal, blight, gentrification and a lot of sleepy areas that defy description.

The area west of Milwaukee Ave, the Loop and S Halsted St has always been a working-class area. Neighborhood names such as Greek Town, Little Italy and others reveal the origins of their early residents. The far West Side neighborhoods that radiate out from W Madison St, such as Lawndale, are some of the worst in the city.

After Martin Luther King Jr was assassinated in 1968, this part of the city literally went up in flames during several nights of rioting that saw the destruction of the commercial districts, businesses and many factories. As is so often the case with urban riots, the rioters destroyed their own neighborhoods. After the fires were put out, the rioters were much worse off than before and any hope of new capital investment had literally gone up in smoke.

Safety is definitely a consideration when visiting many sites on the West Side. The areas discussed here are okay during the day, and some are okay at night as well. Individual cautions are given for each area.

Transportation options are also covered in each neighborhood section. If you have a car, you can cover the entire area in an afternoon.

Polish Museum of America

Rather than focusing on Poles in America, this large museum (☎ 773-384-3352), 984 N Milwaukee at Augusta (Map 10), focuses on Poles in Poland. Its heyday was during the decades after WWII, when the museum sought to portray Poland's long history of art, culture and science, a heritage largely ignored by the Communists.

The exhibits mix art, artifacts (such as ubiquitous suits of armor) and displays on the lives of such notable Poles as Chopin, Copernicus and Pulaski. The last, who has a major Chicago street and a city holiday named in his honor, was a Polish general who fought with the Americans in the Revolutionary War. One of his greatest achievements was covering the retreat of George Washington from a battle gone bad. He died fighting the British in 1779.

The museum is open daily 11 am to 4 pm; closed on major Catholic holidays. Admission is $2. The Division El stop on the Blue Line is three blocks north of the museum on Milwaukee.

Museum of Holography

Now that they're on every Visa card, holograms don't evoke the same sense of wonder they did a decade ago, but that shouldn't stop you from visiting this museum (☎ 312-226-1007), 1134 W Washington (Map 10), which will show you how a three-dimensional image is recorded on a cheap piece of Mylar.

The human images are especially fascinating in that the process faithfully records everything, right down to the smallest unclipped nose hair. The portrait of Mike Ditka invites disturbing comparisons to the awful horror movie *They Saved Hitler's Brain*. The museum is open Wednesday to Sunday 12:30 to 5 pm; closed major holidays. Admission is $2.50.

United Center

Built for $175 million and opened in 1992, the United Center arena, 1901 W Madison (Map 10), is home to the Bulls and the Blackhawks, and is the venue for special events such as the circus. The most notable thing about the building is its huge size; the interior is similar to other huge stadiums.

The statue of an airborne Michael Jordan in front of the east entrance is a lively tribute to the man whose talents made the financing for the edifice possible. The center, surrounded by parking lots, is okay by day but should be avoided at night – unless there's a game, in which case squads of cops are everywhere.

For the 1996 Democratic Convention at the United Center, the city remodeled Madison St all the way from the Loop. The

RICK GERHARTER
United Center tribute

new planters and streetlights have definitely helped the area's appearance and have sparked the first signs of gentrification.

Haymarket Riot Monument

On May 4, 1886, striking factory workers held a meeting at Haymarket Square, at Randolph and Desplaines Sts west of the Loop. Toward the end of the meeting a mob of police appeared, things quickly degenerated into chaos, and a bomb exploded, killing seven cops. Eight anarchist leaders were convicted of inciting a murder, and four were hanged.

Public sentiment worldwide was with the striking workers, who were demanding an eight-hour workday and were the victims of efforts by the factory owners and their police lackeys to discredit them.

In memory of the seven dead cops, a statue was erected on the spot some years later: a stilted officer standing with arm upraised, commanding peace 'in the name of the people of Illinois.' The statue has since had a history almost more violent than the event it commemorates. Seen as representing antilabor forces, it was long a focus of protest. The plaques at its base were stolen several times, and shortly after the turn of the 20th century a bus driver rammed it, claiming to be sick of seeing it every day. In 1928 it was moved several blocks west, to Union Park, where it stood peacefully until the uproarious 1960s, when it was blown up twice. Repaired yet again, the statue has found a home in the courtyard of the Chicago Police training center, at 1300 W Jackson (Map 10).

Old St Patrick's Church
A Chicago fire survivor, this 1852 church (☎ 312-782-6171), 700 W Adams at Desplaines (Map 10), is the city's oldest and one of its most successful, based on the shrewd strategies of its politically connected pastor, Friar Jack Wall. A year-round calendar of social events for single Catholics boosted its membership from the tens to the hundreds in the 1980s. Many of them are now married and producing new parishioners.

The domed steeple signifies the Eastern Church; the spire signifies the Western Church. Call to find out when the church is open so you can see the beautifully restored Celtic-patterned interior, which was originally built by parishioners well over a century ago.

Bat Column
No, not the Bat Cave nor the Bat Mobile, it's the . . . oh, just go see for yourself. This is an excellent example of your federal tax dollars at work in public art. Artist Claes Oldenburg gives full value for his commission with this 100-foot work in front of the regional Social Security office, at 600 W Madison (Map 10).

Little Italy
The area south of the Eisenhower Expressway to Roosevelt Rd was a thriving Italian community until the 1950s, when several blows almost killed it. The expressway itself was rammed through the most vibrant part

of the neighborhood; the surviving commercial area was demolished for the campus of the University of Illinois at Chicago, and several public housing projects were scattered through what was left. Many people still suspect that the old Mayor Daley was behind the entire scheme as retribution for the schemes of rival politicians.

Perhaps out of sheer stubbornness, the Italian residents hung on. The commercial focus centered on Taylor St. Meanwhile, professionals drawn to the university and the fast-growing Chicago Medical Center to the west discovered the tree-lined streets of the neighborhood. Beginning in the 1970s, gentrification transformed old homes and added new townhouses. The remaining blighted housing projects, however, require that visitors to the area should take care to avoid stretches that go from safe to grim in a block.

The CTA Blue Line serves the northern portion of the neighborhood. The Racine and UIC-Halsted stops are the most convenient. Be extra careful around the blocks between Racine and Loomis on Taylor, west of Damen and south of Roosevelt.

Taylor St preserves many old Italian family businesses. Mario's sells painfully fresh Italian ice and lemonade from May to September at 1066 W Taylor (Map 10). Conte di Savola (☎ 312-666-3471), 1438 W Taylor (Map 10), sells everything an Italian cook could hope for, including scores of imported rarities and wines. Open the door and take a sniff.

Six-acre **Arrigo Park** (Map 10), one block west of Racine and bordered by Cabrini and Loomis Sts, faces to the north the affluent townhouses of the gentrified neighborhood west of the university. To the south it faces the Jane Addams Homes, a 1930s housing project that's as faded as the dreams of its idealistic builders.

University of Illinois at Chicago
UIC used to be a much more interesting place to visit for all the wrong reasons. Noted Chicago architect Walter Netsch created a design that at best can be called eccentric. When the 55-acre campus opened

in 1965, it usually provoked extreme protests from those who saw it.

Netsch proclaimed that it was his goal to re-create the sense of wonder one feels when exploring an Italian hill village, but the only emotion he stirred was anger. The area lacks hills, so he designed a double-deck campus where all the buildings were linked by upper-level elevated walkways. The focus was a vast amphitheater area in the heart of the campus. The looming 28-story administration and faculty building, at 601 S Morgan, was meant to be the campanile.

The realities of Netsch's design were unremittingly grim. The elevated walkways cast a gloom over the muddy landscape below, the amphitheater became a windblown tundra in the winter and a sun-baked desert in the summer. (Netsch lives in Chicago; you'd think he would have known better.)

By the mid-1980s the whole place was ugly, falling apart and despised by its 30,000 students and faculty. In 1990 a massive rebuilding program began that eradicated much of Netsch's hill town. His voice of protest was lone. The University Center Housing and Commons, 700 S Halsted, is an attractive undergraduate dorm that welcomes people onto the campus and was the first major building to break with the past. The campus is now a pleasant place to go to school, but there's no reason to make a special trip there.

Jane Addams Hull House In 1889, at age 29, Jane Addams founded Hull House at 800 S Halsted (Map 10), in an 1856 home donated by philanthropist Charles Hull. At the time the area was a densely packed neighborhood of recent European immigrants who worked for menial wages and lived in horrific tenements.

With several other women professionals, such as Ellen Gates Starr, Addams provided day-care facilities, a kindergarten, an employment bureau and many other social services to masses of exploited and hopeless people. She also provided space where the burgeoning labor unions could meet.

Jane Addams

Addams fought for and saw passage of laws regulating child labor and requiring public education. She was also active in the international peace movement and won the Nobel Peace Prize for her efforts in 1931. She died in 1935, but Hull House continues her work at locations around the city.

UIC has preserved Addams' house, along with the 1905 dining hall where neighborhood residents could come for hot meals (☎ 312-413-5353). At its peak, the complex had 13 buildings, which included the city's first public baths, playground, swimming pool, adult-education school, and many other service facilities.

A 15-minute slide show on the second floor of the dining hall details Addams' work. Displays document the struggle for social justice waged by Hull House and others in the first half of the 20th century. The first floor of the hall has been restored to appear as it did when hundreds found sustenance here daily. The house itself also has been restored to its appearance when Addams and Starr took it over. Many of Addams' possessions, such as her writing desk, are on display. Quiet today, the house was the social and administrative center for the whole complex at its peak.

The house and dining hall are open weekdays 10 am to 4 pm, Sundays in summer noon to 5 pm. Admission is free.

Elsewhere on the West Side

Cook County Hospital At 1835 W Harrison St (Map 10), this huge, gray dinosaur of a hospital dates to 1913. Patients whom profit-minded institutions won't accept come to this publicly funded facility. Care is widely variable, but it does have one of the best emergency-care programs in the world.

Set up in 1966, the trauma unit was the nation's first and caters to patients critically injured in accidents and violence. Unfortunately, the doctors get all too much practice with victims of shootings and other mayhem. Hundreds of doctors working in emergency rooms worldwide have trained in trauma care at County during the past three decades. More than one famous doctor has told me that if they were ever shot, they'd want to go to here. The hit TV series *ER* is based on County.

In the surrounding blocks are several more medical institutions, including two more hospitals and several medical schools. Together the facilities are known as the Chicago Medical Center and comprise the largest collection of health-care facilities in the world.

Maxwell St Police Station Fans of the TV show *Hill Street Blues* will instantly recognize the exterior of this old police station – it graced the opening of every episode of the series, which was based on a gritty fictional neighborhood not unlike this one. It's at 943 W Maxwell, two blocks west of Halsted, one long block south of Roosevelt (Map 10).

Holy Family Church This huge Catholic church (☎ 312-738-4080), at 1080 W Roosevelt, was dedicated in 1860. At times its survival seems to have occurred only through the notoriously strong wills of the Jesuits who run it. Almost demolished a few years ago, it is now being recon-structed – a process that can't happen too quickly, given that the weight of the slate roof has already pushed some of the Gothic pillars out of plumb by 18 inches.

Neighboring St Ignatius Prep School is one of the premier Catholic coeducational high schools in the city, where the Jesuits run a very tight ship. The original building was opened in 1870.

PILSEN

Pilsen has been the first stop for immigrants to Chicago for more than 100 years. First it was the Czechs, who gave the neighborhood its name (Pilsen is the second-biggest town in the Czech Republic). Later it was home to Poles, Serbs and Croats. In the 1950s Hispanics began arriving in great numbers, drawn by the low rents for both residential and commercial space, which encouraged small businesses.

Today the streets pulse with the sounds of salsa music, the cries of food vendors with carts and the chatter of a thousand conversations. The focus of the area is 18th St, with its scores of taquerias, bakeries and small shops selling everything from devotional candles to the latest CDs from Mexico. If you pay more than $1 for a taco, it had better be extra good.

Much of the charm of a visit to Pilsen is getting caught up in the culture of the neighborhood, rather than specific sights. A stroll east on 18th St from the El stop yields a thorough dose of Hispanic life. However, traces of previous residents remain as well. Beyond the colorful signs and details are traditional Chicago three-flats and storefronts with distinctive Central European details. And outside of summer, the weather is unlikely to make you think you're in Mexico or Puerto Rico.

Pilsen is easily reached from the Loop. The 18th St El stop on the Cermak branch of the CTA Blue Line puts you in the center of the action. The station itself sets the tone for the neighborhood: every surface has been covered with murals inspired by Mayan, Aztec, and modern-day Mexican art.

Mexican Fine Arts Center Museum

Founded in 1982, this vibrant museum (☎ 312-738-1503), 1852 W 19th St (Map 10), is in a renovated and expanded old field house in Harrison Park. The two large exhibition spaces are used for temporary exhibits of work by Mexican artists. The media is mixed, from painting to sculpture to textiles, and is always among the best, owing to the museum's high profile in North America. A big new addition due to open in 1998 will triple the museum's exhibit space and allow for the installation of permanent exhibits. The museum also sponsors readings by top authors and performances by musicians and artists.

If you are in town during the fall, be sure to check out the exhibits and celebrations relating to November 1, the Day of the Dead, a traditional Mexican holiday that combines the festive with the religious. The events take place for a month on either side of the day.

The museum is on the south side of Harrison Park, about a five-minute walk from the 18th St El stop. It's open Tuesday to Sunday 10 am to 5 pm, closed Mondays and most holidays. Admission is free.

St Adalbert Roman Catholic Church

One block north of 18th St, at Paulina (Map 10), this 1914 church has 185-foot steeples that are almost impossible to appreciate, given the narrow streets. This is a good example of the many soaring churches built by Chicago's ethnic populations through thousands of small donations from parishioners, who would cut family budgets to the bone to make their weekly contribution. The interior is rich with ornamentation glorifying Polish saints and religious figures.

St Pius Church

The Poles had St Adalbert's; the Irish had this Romanesque Revival edifice, one block south of 18th St at 1901 S Ashland (Map 10). Built between 1885 and 1892, its smooth masonry contrasts with the rough stones of its contemporaries. Catholics of one ethnic group never attended the churches of the others, which is why this part of town, with its concentration of Catholic immigrants, is thick with steeples.

José Clemente Orozco Academy

The exterior wall of the academy (☎ 773-534-7215), at 1645 W 18th Place, one block south of 18th St (Map 10), is the canvas for a tile mosaic begun in 1991 showing a diverse range of Mexican images, from a portrait of farmworker advocate Dolores Huerta to the Virgin of Guadalupe. Each summer art students add more panels.

Lozano Public Library

In a neighborhood where most of the structures were built by immigrants hailing from countries distant from those of today's residents, this large branch library (☎ 312-746-4329) celebrates the current realities with decorative tile inspired by pre-Columbian buildings in Oaxaca, Mexico. The building has a prominent spot at the intersection of 18th, Blue Island Ave and Loomis St.

Thalia Hall

Named for the Greek muse of comedy, who casts a bemused gaze from a spot in the arch over the entrance, this large stone 1893 building, at 1807 S Allport just south of 18th St (Map 10), was home to the Bohemian side of the Czech immigrants, who used it for theater and music productions. It's now home to various offices.

BRIDGEPORT

Bridgeport is more important for its historical role in the city than as a tourist sight. The stockyards were once a major attraction, but they are long closed and their land is being rapidly covered by new warehouses and industry. The traditional home of Chicago's Irish mayors, Bridgeport remains an enclave of descendants of Irish settlers. A few Chinese and Hispanic people have moved in, but the perception is strong that African Americans, who live to the south and east, are not welcome. That image was reinforced in 1997 when a black

RICK GERHARTER

Pilsen's artful and colorful 18th St El stop

teen on a bike was savagely beaten by three white teens when he entered their neighborhood. Many residents say that Bridgeport is more tolerant now than in its past, but it will probably never live down its role in the 1919 race riots, when neighborhood thugs went on a killing spree after a black youth on a raft floated too close to a 'white' beach.

Halsted St from 31st south to 43rd is Bridgeport's rather uninteresting main drag. Most of the neighborhood lies west of the huge train embankment that itself is west of Comiskey Park. However, Bridgeport extends north of the park all the way to Chinatown and makes for a good walk after a game if you're in a group and don't stray east of the Dan Ryan Expressway.

Bridgeport's dearth of concentrated sites makes for a visit best accomplished by car. Safety depends somewhat on your ethnicity, although the neighborhood is mostly safe during the day.

Bubbly Creek

Your first thought standing on its litter-strewn bank is 'God, I hope I don't fall in.' Little life moves in the stagnant black water, and dead fish rot in the sun, surrounded by murk. This putrid pool, at 37th St and Racine Ave a few blocks west of Halsted, is a remnant of the notorious Bubbly Creek. Some 90 years ago, Upton Sinclair in *The Jungle* documented this open sewer of Chicago's stockyards. Today the worst section has been covered over and the packing plants that fouled it are long gone. But bubbles still rise from the depths, fed by the tons of waste still rotting on the bottom, a legacy of Chicago's role as 'hog butcher for the world.'

Other Sights

The derelict **International Amphitheater**, 4220 S Halsted, hasn't been as much fun as it was during the disastrous 1968 Democratic Convention, when Mayor Daley's thugs beat Dan Rather while Walter Cronkite cried foul from the broadcast booth. Another low point came when the mayor openly shouted a racial epithet at liberal Connecticut senator Abe Ribicoff, combining a maternal reference with a vulgar term for sex (12 letters, you figure it out). Ribicoff had just used his nomination speech for George McGovern to condemn the 'Gestapo tactics' of the Chicago police.

A tiny vestige of the stockyards stands at 850 W Exchange Ave, just west of Halsted. The **Union Stockyards Gate** was once the main entrance to the vast stockyards where millions of cows and almost as many hogs met their ends each year. The value of those slaughtered in 1910 was an enormous $225 million. Sanitary conditions eventually improved from the hideous levels documented by Upton Sinclair, although during WWI the greatest number of casualties suffered by American doughboys were due to bad cans of meat from the Chicago packing houses. The cow immortalized at the top of the 1879 gate is Sherman, a prize-winning steer.

The most crime-free place in town is still at **3526 S Lowe**, where Mayor Richard J Daley's widow, 'Sis,' still lives and where Mayor Richard M Daley grew up. A police car is always outside and a huge station house is just down the block. The block itself is three blocks east of Halsted and is typical of middle-class blue-collar neighborhoods all over the city.

One of many Pilsen murals

NEAR SOUTH SIDE

One hundred years ago, the best and worst of Chicago lived side-by-side south of the Loop. Near the lake around Prairie Ave, the top millionaires of the day, such as Marshall Field and George Pullman, lived on 'Millionaire's Row,' between 16th St and 20th St (now called Cullerton).

In contrast, four blocks to the west was the Levee District, an infamous area known for its saloons, brothels, opium dens and virtually any other vice that money could buy. With four major train stations near the neighborhood, Chicago became the sin capital of the Midwest. Legend has it that the 'Mickey Finn' knockout cocktail was invented here as the first of generations of conventioneers came to Chicago itching for fun and left with merely an itch.

Corrupt politicians ran the ward. 'Bathhouse' John Coughlin and Michael 'Hinky Dink' Kenna staged annual Levee District orgies that attracted scores of politicians, business leaders and police. The bacchanalia lasted for days. Eventually this drunken spectacle became too much even for the city government, and the area became a warehouse district. Meanwhile, the crooked politicians took their vices to City Hall, where they began the long Chicago government tradition of shakedowns and kickbacks.

A taste of the district's past returned in the late 1920s, when Al Capone set up shop at the Lexington Hotel, at the corner of Michigan and Cermak. This location achieved fame again in 1986, when pompous talk-show host Geraldo Rivera opened a supposedly 'secret' vault on live TV and discovered nothing.

Today the entire area is undergoing a renaissance. The Dearborn Park neighborhood has become home to 15,000 people on the site of the old Santa Fe rail yards south of Polk St to 15th St. The Central Station neighborhood is being built on the old Illinois Central yards east of Michigan Ave and south of Roosevelt Rd. Mayor Daley caused a minor uproar when he moved here in 1994 from his traditional Bridgeport home. The once musty warehouses are fast being renovated into lofts, and businesses are beginning to move into the area. Many people predict that Central Station will be the 'hot' Chicago neighborhood by 2000.

The Roosevelt El stops on the CTA Red and Green Lines serve the north end of the neighborhood. Otherwise, the No 3 King Drive bus starts at Chicago Ave and N Michigan Ave and stays on Michigan all the way south to Roosevelt, where it shifts one block east to Indiana and covers the length of the neighborhood. The area is improving, but the streets can be quite bleak and empty at night.

American Police Center & Museum

You have to be touched by the sincerity of the people who started this museum in 1974 as an antidote to the practice of calling cops 'pigs.' The displays are hopelessly hokey, but that just adds to the museum's charm. Some of the highlights: 'Parade of Police Patches,' which shows the patches used by more than 45,000 US police departments, and 'Gangster Alley,' which includes a disused electric chair named the Texas Thunderbolt (the display placard urges visitors to 'note the fingernail marks on the chair's arms').

Some especially unconvincing mannequins are threaded throughout the museum's displays; they have the same wooden faces as the puppets did on the old *Thunderbirds* TV series.

A sobering note amid the kitsch is the display honoring Chicago police officers killed in the line of duty, complete with portraits. The museum is located at 1717 S State (☎ 312-431-0005; Map 4). It's open weekdays 9 am to 4:30 pm. Admission is $3.

Prairie Ave Historic District

By 1900 Chicago's crème de la crème had had enough of the scum de la scum over in the Levee. Potter Palmer led a procession of millionaires north to new mansions on the Gold Coast. The once pristine neighborhood fell into quick decline as one mansion after another was demolished for warehouses and industry.

In 1966 the Chicago Architecture Foundation was formed to save the Glessner House and other survivors from demolition. The area's fortunes slowly improved thereafter, accelerating in recent years. Streets have been closed off, making the neighborhood a good place for a stroll. A footbridge over the train tracks links the area to Burnham Park and the Museum Campus.

John J Glessner House The Glessner House (☎ 312-326-1480), 1800 S Prairie (Map 4), is the premier survivor of the neighborhood. Famed American architect Henry Hobson Richardson took full advantage of the corner site for this beautiful composition of rusticated granite. The arched motif over the doorways is a classic that invites a third and fourth look.

Built from 1885 to 1887, the L-shaped house surrounds a sunny southern courtyard, prefacing this modern urban design element by a century. Much of the interior looks like an English manor house, with heavy wooden beams and details. More than 80% of the current furnishings are authentic, thanks to the Glessner family's penchant for family photos. The Glessners lived in the house for more than 50 years and by every indication loved every minute of it.

Tours of the house are given Wednesday to Sunday on the hour from noon to 4 pm. Admission is $5 or $8 for a combined tour of the Glessner House and the nearby Henry B Clarke House.

Henry B Clarke House When Caroline and Henry Clarke built this imposing Greek Revival home in 1836, the vogue in Chicago residential architecture was still log cabins. Built on what were then sand dunes, the house was considered a country home far from downtown. The Clarke House was built to last, and that it has; it is the oldest structure in the city. The sturdy frame also paid off, because over the past 160 years it has been moved twice to escape demolition. The present address, 1855 S Indiana Ave (Map 4), is about as close as researchers can get to its somewhat undefined original location.

The interior has been restored to the period of the Clarkes' occupation until 1872. The tall, narrow windows make the simple rooms bright and airy. The children enjoyed a bed made to look like a sleigh. Other period toys are arranged throughout the rooms. Given what the area looked like when the house was built, one expects to see a sand pail and shovel as well.

Hours and phone number for the Clarke House are the same as for the Glessner House. The Chicago Architecture Foundation runs the tours for both houses.

Other Houses Generally, visits to the following houses are not possible, but you still can admire them from the outside. Modeled after 15th-century French chateaus, the **William K Kimball House**, 1801 S Prairie (Map 4), was built for the organ maker from 1890 to 1892. Sadly, it can't help looking like a French post card in comparison to the Glessner House, across the street.

The **Joseph G Coleman House**, 1811 S Prairie (Map 4), is a more restrained Romanesque style than the Kimball House. Limestone puts a glitzy facade on the brick **Elbridge G Keith House**, 1900 S Prairie (Map 4), an early 1870 home that is now home to a first-floor art gallery. A house restorer looking for a huge challenge can find a life's work at the remains of the **Marshall Field Jr House**, 1919 S Prairie (Map 4). The hulk you see was once a 44-room mansion; it awaits a few million dollars and months of work.

Hillary Rodham Clinton Women's Park Dedicated in October 1997, this park is now little more than some fenced-in grass and uncleared rubble from demolished mansions. But the city has plans to turn it into a public space honoring Chicago's women; it may include flower and herb gardens, reflection areas, a walk honoring creative women and other features to be selected by an advisory committee.

Fronting on Prairie Ave, with the Glessner House to the north and the Clarke House to the west (Map 4), the four-acre park is named for First Lady Hillary Rodham Clinton, who grew up in suburban Park Ridge and is a lifelong Cubs fan.

The park already has a notorious past. An 1893 sculpture, *The Fort Dearborn Massacre*, shows the events thought to have occurred on this very spot in August 15, 1812: Potawatomi chief Black Partridge is shown rescuing settler Margaret Helm from a tomahawk-wielding brave in mid-chop. A less fortunate settler dies at their feet, while a child reaches out for help.

Second Presbyterian Church Designed by James Renwick, the architect of St Patrick's Cathedral in New York and Washington's original Smithsonian Institution building, the 1874 church (☎ 312-225-4951), 1936 S Michigan (Map 4), is a Neo-Gothic limestone celebration rich with Tiffany stained glass.

National Vietnam Veterans Art Museum Opened in 1996, this museum (☎ 312-326-0270), 1801 S Indiana at 18th St (Map 4), displays the art of Americans who served in the military during the Vietnam war. On three floors in an old commercial building, it has a 500-piece (and growing) collection of haunting, angry, mournful and powerful works by veterans expressing their emotions and reactions to their service.

Cleveland Wright's *We Regret to Inform You* is a heartbreaking look at a mother in her kitchen at the moment she learns of her son's death. Ned Broderick's *VC Suspect* shows the bleak future of a prisoner. Joseph Fornelli's *Dressed to Kill* is a sculpture-commentary on the role of the average grunt in Vietnam.

The museum plans to add a floor devoted to the Huey helicopter that has become an enduring symbol of the war. Other areas will relate the history of the war and the role of the American draftees sent to fight it.

The museum is open Tuesday through Friday 11 am to 6 pm, Saturday 10 am to 5 pm, Sunday noon to 5 pm; closed Mondays and holidays. Admission is $4 for adults, $2 for children. Cafe V serves innovative and healthful foods.

Chess Records

From 1957 to 1967, this humble building at 2120 S Michigan Ave (Map 4) was a temple of blues and a spawning ground of rock and roll. The Chess brothers, both Polish Jews, ran the recording studio that saw – and heard – the likes of Muddy Waters, Bo Diddley, Koko Taylor and others. Chuck Berry recorded four top-10 singles here, and the Rolling Stones named a song '2120 S Michigan Ave' after a recording session in 1964. (Rock trivia buffs know that the Stones named themselves after the Muddy Waters song 'Rolling Stone.')

Today the building is owned by Willie Dixon's Blues Heaven Foundation, a nonprofit group set up by the late musician to promote blues and preserve its legacy. A gift store should soon open in front, and refurbished studios will be upstairs and archives will be in back.

McCORMICK PLACE

Called the 'mistake on the lake' for its prime location in Burnham Park, the McCormick Place convention center (Map 4) is an economic engine for the city's hotels, restaurants, shops and airlines. 'Vast' isn't big enough to describe it, nor 'huge,' and 'enormous' doesn't work, so settle for whatever word describes the biggest thing you've ever seen. The 2.2 million sq feet of meeting space are now spread over three halls.

RICK GERHARTER
McCormick Place

To the east, on the lake, the original building interrupts the sweep of the lakefront. (For the *Chicago Tribune*'s disgraceful role in this episode, see the sidebar The Man Behind the 'World's Greatest Newspaper' in Facts for the Visitor.) It was completed to replace the original fireproof McCormick Place, which burned down in 1967. This building is now called the Lakeside Center. The North Building is a barn of a place erected with huge cost overruns in 1986. The newest addition, the South Building, was finished in 1997. The best of the lot, it features the Grand Concourse, a bright and airy hall linking all the buildings.

In a place this big, any of the four million people who visit annually can get lost easily. The distances and the scale of the halls combine to make you feel you have the significance of a bug. Escaping the place for a stroll along the lake or north to the Museum Campus is a challenge. When I tried that in 1997, several employees were stumped at how to actually get out. I finally found out, but only at a loss of hours spent wandering endless and windowless carpeted halls.

Here's how to flee: Go to Level Two of the Lakeside Center (the East Building) and proceed north to the 'Burnham Park Parking' exit. You'll emerge in a small park overlooking the yacht harbor; the museums are a 15-minute walk north.

The main McCormick Place telephone number is ☎ 312-791-7000. The Chicago Convention and Tourism Bureau is the public relations arm of McCormick Place, handling all convention and show questions at ☎ 312-567-8500.

Getting There & Away

It's easy to get a cab to McCormick Place, but much harder to get one leaving at, say, 5 pm, when everyone is trying to get one. The scene can get quite chaotic. Try arranging a Share-a-Ride for $5 a person. A great insider's tip is the 23rd St Metra train station, hidden in the lowest level of the North Building. Signage is not great, so ask at the information booths. Trains to and from the Randolph St and Van Buren St stations, in the Loop, are frequent at rush hour. Midday Monday through Saturday they depart from Randolph St at 20 minutes past the hour and take 7 minutes to reach McCormick Place. On Sunday the trains run about every 90 minutes. The fare is $1.75.

Parking can be a hike from the buildings and is expensive. The walk through Grant Park and the Museum Campus is pretty. From Michigan Ave and the river, it's a little over three miles. The main entrance is now on Martin Luther King Jr Drive, just north of the Stevenson Expressway. A towering new Hyatt Regency hotel is set to open at the complex in summer 1998 (☎ 312-567-1234).

Conventioneers have whined about the quality and prices of food and drink at McCormick Place for decades. There's no reason to stop now. I had a $3 cookie before setting off to find the lakeside exit. It stunk.

CHINATOWN

The charm of Chinatown can best be enjoyed by wandering its streets and browsing in its many varied small shops. Wentworth Ave south of Cermak is the retail heart of the neighborhood. Other interesting parts include Cermak itself and Archer just to the north. The neighborhood is one of the city's most vibrant, and its affluent residents are developing land in all directions even as more immigrants continue to arrive.

The Cermak-Chinatown El stop on the CTA Red Line is just to the east of the action. East of the stop itself is a dicey area dominated by a housing project. The busy streets of Chinatown itself are generally safe.

The **On Leong Building**, 2216 S Wentworth, was once home to various neighborhood service organizations and has also been the scene of some spectacular police raids on illegal gambling operations. It now houses the Chinese Merchants Association. Built in 1928 and also known as the Pui

RICK GERHARTER
The On Leong Building

Tak Center, the grand structure is a fantasy of Chinese architecture that makes good use of glazed terra-cotta details. Note how the lions guarding the door have twisted their heads so they don't have to risk bad luck by turning their backs to each other.

Much of the rest of Wentworth is a blend of typical Chicago and Chinese architecture. The characteristic arch near Cermak was added in the 1970s. Among the businesses you might want to check out are the straightforwardly named Woks N Things (☎ 312-842-0787), 2234 S Wentworth, with every kind of utensil and cookware you could want, and Sun Sun Tong (☎ 312-842-6398), 2260 S Wentworth, which has hundreds of varieties of tea and herbs.

Over on Archer Ave where it meets Cermak, the continually growing **Chinatown Square** was begun in 1992 and combines ground-floor shops with upper-level apartments for their owners.

SOUTH SIDE

South of the Stevenson Expressway and east of the Dan Ryan Expressway, Chicago's South Side has had a tough time since WWII. Whole neighborhoods vanished as crime and blight drove residents away. Among Chicagoans of all colors, the area's reputation is not the best.

The construction of the vast wall of housing projects along the east side of the Dan Ryan created huge impoverished neighborhoods where community ties were broken and gangs held sway. The Chicago Housing Authority has begun a demolition campaign to try to remake the projects into mixed-income communities. But the news isn't all bad: some parts have remained vital, others are being rediscovered and still others, such as the large area from 26th St south to 31st, have been successfully redeveloped.

Illinois Institute of Technology

A world-class leader in technology, industrial design and architecture, IIT was formed in 1940 by the merger of two earlier institutions. The campus owes much of its world-famous look to legendary architect Ludwig Mies van der Rohe, who fled the Nazis in Germany for Chicago in 1938. From 1940 until his retirement in 1958, Mies designed 22 buildings for the campus that all reflect his tenets of architecture, which combine simple metal frames painted black with glass and brick infills. This 'International Style' was endlessly copied throughout the world for the next three decades.

The star of the campus and Mies' undisputed masterpiece is SR Crown Hall, appropriately home to the College of Architecture. The building appears to be a transparent glass box floating between its translucent base and suspended roof. At night it glows from within like an illuminated jewel. The building is near the center of campus, at 3360 S State St.

The 35th/Bronzeville El stop on the CTA Green Line is at the south edge of the campus, which is best explored by simply wandering around and seeing how all the Mies buildings interrelate. Private police ensure that the campus itself remains safe during the day.

Bronzeville

Once home to Louis Armstrong and other notables, Bronzeville is the unofficial name for the neighborhoods radiating from 35th St and Martin Luther King Jr Drive. From 1920 until 1950 it was the vibrant center of black life in the city and boasted economic and cultural strength that matched that of New York's Harlem.

Shifting populations, urban decay and the construction of the wall of public housing along State St – including the Robert Taylor Homes, the worst project in the nation – led to Bronzeville's decline. In 1997 attention again focused on the neighborhood when the Black Metropolis Convention and Tourism Council succeeded in plans to have the neighborhood designated a Historic Landmark District by the city council.

The same forces that led to the neighborhood's decline make visiting the area a cautious endeavor. During the daytime it's best to take a friend along. The 35th/Bronzeville El station on the CTA Green Line is on the western edge of the area, which is also bordered by IIT.

Many of Bronzeville's grand houses have been restored ahead of the commercial districts. Two blocks on Calumet Ave between 31st and 33rd Sts, known as 'The Gap,' are especially significant. Among the buildings are Frank Lloyd Wright's only row houses, the **Robert W Roloson Houses** at 3213-3219 S Calumet.

Gospel music got its start at **Pilgrim Baptist Church** (☎ 312-842-5830), 3301 S Indiana. Built as a synagogue from 1890 to 1891, the classic exterior only hints at the vast and opulent interior.

Other notable buildings are listed below. Note that many are in miserable shape and are not inviting of more than an inspection of the exterior.

At the corner of 35th and King Drive, the **Supreme Life Building**, a nondescript 1930s office building, was where John H Johnson Jr, the publishing mogul who founded *Ebony* magazine, got the idea for his empire, which also includes *Jet* and other important titles serving African Americans. Plans are for the building to become a visitor's center.

In the median at 35th and King, the **Victory Monument** was erected in 1928 to honor black soldiers who fought in WWI.

The long, low **Alco Drugs** building, on the southwest corner of 35th and King, is slated to reopen in 1998 as a jazz club, restaurant and bank.

The landmark **Eighth Regiment Armory** (1915), a former National Guard building on the east side of Giles, just south of 35th, awaits funds for a planned conversion into an ROTC school by the Chicago Public Schools. It will also house a museum of African American military history.

The **Chicago Defender Building**, the headquarters of the paper from 1921 to 1960, is a three-story structure built in 1899 as a synagogue. From here, legendary publisher Robert S Abbott chronicled and promoted the vast black migration to Chicago from the South. The roof of the building collapsed in 1997, and its future is in doubt.

Other Bronzeville buildings included in the historic designation are the Overton Hygienic/Douglass National Bank Building, 3619-3627 S State; the Chicago Bee Building, 3647 S State; the Wabash YMCA, 3763 S Wabash; Unity Hall, 3140 S Indiana; and the Sunset Cafe/Grand Terrace Cafe, a legendary venue for great entertainers such as Armstrong and Jelly Roll Morton (it's now a hardware store), 315 E 35th St.

HYDE PARK

Hyde Park is an enclave within the city's South Side. Much of its existence is owed to the University of Chicago, a school where the graduate students outnumber the undergrads. The bookish residents give the place an insulated, small-town air in stark contrast to the rough neighborhoods to the west and south. The streets are densely lined with trees, the dead ones quickly replaced by mature specimens.

The major attraction for most visitors to the neighborhood is the Museum of Science and Industry, but west of the train tracks the university and the neighborhood itself also are well worth a stroll (see the University of Chicago walking tour).

Hyde Park isn't just isolated in spirit; it's isolated transit-wise as well. The best link to the center of town is the Metra electric service from the Loop's Randolph St and Van Buren St stations. Two trains an hour – one local, one express – serve the neighborhood. The local is slower than the express by just a few minutes, and it serves the convenient 55th-56th-57th St station. Use the 57th St exit for the most convenient route to the museum and the campus. The express train goes to 59th St station, from which it's a 10-minute walk to the museum. Schedules are freely available; nab one so you can plan your return. A one-way trip from the Loop is $1.95.

Bookstores

Not surprisingly, the home to the University of Chicago has several good bookstores. The University of Chicago Bookstore (☎ 773-702-7712) is at 970 E 58th, at Ellis (Map 11), in a red brick 1902 building. Gussied up under the management of Barnes & Noble, it still stocks textbooks on everything you can imagine (the color titles in the medical section will put you off smoking, drinking, meat and perhaps even life itself), plus many more titles penned by faculty and students. On the 2nd floor they have a souvenir and paraphernalia section.

The Seminary Cooperative Bookstore (☎ 773-752-1959), 5757 S University Ave (Map 11), is the bookstore of choice for several University of Chicago Nobel Prize winners, including Robert Fogel, who says, 'For a scholar, it's one of the great bookstores of the world.' The store carries more than 100,000 academic and general titles.

Three blocks away, 57th Street Books (☎ 773-684-1300), 1301 E 57th St (Map 11), has a vast selection of general-interest titles spread over the basement of two buildings. The travel section has a commendable choice of Lonely Planet guides, a table and chairs for careful choosing and a chilled water dispenser to cool the sweaty tourist.

The tone of O'Gara & Wilson Ltd (☎ 773-363-0993), 1448 E 57th St (Map 11), is set by the leaded glass in the oaken door. Ladders run on tracks along the walls amid the used and obscure titles, which lean toward American and English literary criticism.

Everything African can be found at Freedom Found Books (☎ 312-288-2837), 5206 S Harper, in Harper Court (Map 11). A good place to catch the likes of Toni Morrison when she's in town, it has an inspirational pile of self-published revolutionary journals by the door.

Washington Park

Designed in 1871, this classic lakeside park (Map 11) is linked to Jackson Park by the Midway Plaisance. Located at the junction of the Midway Plaisance and Washington Park, the **Fountain of Time**, a 1922 concrete Lorado Taft sculpture, commemorates 100 years of peace between the US and England. It's in dire need of repair, its original meaning all but lost. But the hooded figure of Time continues to watch over the rising and falling waves of humanity, inspired by the phrase 'Time goes, you say? Ah no! Alas, Time stays we go . . . ' This is one of the city's most moving monuments and is well worth seeking out.

DuSable Museum of African American History

Located in a peaceful part of Washington Park, the DuSable Museum of African American History (☎ 773-947-0600), 740 E 56th Place in Washington Park (Map 11), is named after Chicago's first permanent settler, a French-Canadian of Haitian descent, Jean Baptiste Point du Sable. The permanent collection includes 90 works of African American art and permanent exhibits such as Up from Slavery, which covers African Americans' experiences from slavery up through the Civil Rights movement.

The 1910 building has been a police lockup and a parks administration building. A new exhibit, Harold Washington in Office, re-creates the mayoral office of the charismatic Washington, who was elected in 1983 and 1987 and died on November 25, 1987. Most of the artifacts were collected by

RICK GERHARTER

Contemplate your mortality at the Fountain of Time.

Washington's half-brother in the decade after the mayor's death.

The museum is open Monday to Saturday 10 am to 5 pm, Sunday noon to 5 pm; from October to April it closes every day at 4 pm. Admission is $3 for adults, $2 for children (free on Thursday).

Kenwood

The neighborhood just north of Hyde Park is best toured by car. It is home to many large and imposing mansions and is a mix of middle-class and wealthy whites and blacks, including some famous names.

The **Kehilath Anshe Ma'ariv-Isaiah Israel Temple**, or 'KAM Synagogue,' a domed masterpiece at 1100 E Hyde Park Blvd at Greenwood (☎ 773-924-1234; Map 11), is in the Byzantine style. Its acoustics are said to be perfect. It's open weekdays and Sunday during the day; call for exact times.

A rarity in Chicago, **Madison Park** is a refined development east of the 5000 block of Woodlawn Ave (Map 11) set around a private boulevard. Most of the houses date from the 1920s.

Many classic homes old and new line the gracefully shaded **Woodlawn Ave**. A sampling, going north: **5132 S** (Map 11), the Isidore Heller House, is an 1897 Frank Lloyd Wright house with the characteristic side entrance. The house at **4944 S** (Map 11) was once home to Muhammad Ali. The bow-tied guards around the 1971 Elijah Muhammad House, at **4855** (Map 11), indicate that this is the present home of Nation of Islam leader Louis Farrakhan. And **4812** is a mostly unaltered 1873 house; before everyone else moved into the neighborhood, it was a lonely country villa.

Promontory Point

Hyde Park's best picnic and view spot, at the end of 55th St and Lake Shore Drive (Map 11), has a field house designed to look like a lighthouse. In summer neighborhood residents often congregate to sun and swim. Nearby you can still see traces of a 1950s cold war missile battery meant to defend Chicago from Russian bombers.

RICK GERHARTER

The erstwhile Palace of Fine Arts

Museum of Science & Industry

The main building of this vast and confusing place (☎ 773-684-1414, 800-468-6674, TDD 773-684-3323), 57 S Lake Shore Drive (Map 11), was the Palace of Fine Arts at the landmark World's Columbian Exposition in 1893. It was converted to its present use in the 1920s and is now in the midst of another renovation, which includes installing an underground parking garage in front and regrouping the exhibits into themed areas, a welcome but time-consuming change.

The MSI has grown into a hodgepodge of huge and small exhibits celebrating the technical aspects of life. Despite the free maps, it's easy to become disoriented as the scores of displays compete for attention. There are two ways people visit the museum: they either wander in, wander around in a daze and emerge hours later squinting into the sun, or they arrive, sit down with the map, plan which exhibits they most want to see and do their darned best to find them. Obviously you should try the latter.

The MSI is open every day but Christmas: weekdays 9:30 am to 4 pm, weekends, holidays and every day from Memorial Day to Labor Day to 5:30 pm. Admission is $6 for adults, $2.50 for children (free on Thursdays). The restaurants are uninspired. It might be worth a head-clearing walk down 57th St to the places along there.

Most of the exhibits are the products of joint ventures with industrial groups and companies. Some are up to date and fascinating, others are long in the tooth. Here's a guide to the most popular and interesting sights.

IMAX Theater Frequent travelers should be familiar with the concept behind these huge movie theaters; they're popping up in tourist attractions all over the world (there's another one at Navy Pier). The films are usually quite stunning, covering everything from nature *(Beavers!)* to space flight *(The Dream Is Alive!)*. If you want to see the movie, head here first to secure tickets, as the showings are popular and sell out quickly. Near the theater in the Henry Crown Space Center is the Apollo 8 command module, the spacecraft Frank Borman, Jim Lovell and Bill Anders used to become the first humans to travel to the moon and back. Think about spending seven days cooped in that tiny space and ponder the fact that at one point Borman was overcome with a fit of vomiting and diarrhea.

U-505 This was the only German submarine to be captured during WWII. A boarding team from the US Navy jumped into the sinking boat, which had been booby trapped and abandoned by the crew. The navy team closed the sea valves and unhooked the TNT, and the boat ended up here in 1954. Another tight squeeze for humans, 60 people lived in its minuscule spaces for months at a time. (You might want to see the movie *Das Boot* to get a sense of it.) This exhibit is always popular, so head here early in the day.

The Coal Mine This exhibit has finally gotten a long overdue update. Visitors ride the same equipment used by miners in a simulated mine where the walls are lined with Illinois coal. New additions include a computer control room and displays detailing various types of mining. Kids love the ride in the cage elevator.

Navy: Technology at Sea This is a rah-rah look at the workings of modern ships in the US Navy, including an aircraft carrier, an attack sub and a destroyer. Two F-14 simulators are always mobbed and give thrilling rides replicating bombing raids, dogfights and carrier landings. The last should give even the most jaded a respect for the people who land these things on the stamp-size decks of aircraft carriers in the ocean.

Flight 727 This is an old United Airlines plane that retired to its dramatic perch in the museum after almost 30 years plying America's skies. Its landing gear and flaps rotate through the positions used during flight.

Imaging: The Tools of Science This exhibit is better than its dry-as-dirt name suggests. It shows the tools scientists use to probe the secrets and mysteries of the body and universe.

Food for Life This exhibit gives you a nonflashy and mature look at what goes into getting food to the average supermarket. There are a lot of details here, and it is worth pondering what it takes to grow an ear of corn and get into the mouth of the happy cob-eater.

A chick hatchery shows what happens when an egg incubates to maturity. Should anybody worry, the chicks on display are not on the first stage of a one-way journey to the chicken-finger special in the restaurants downstairs. They are sent north to mature into chickens at Lincoln Park's Farm in the Zoo.

Body Slices In 1943 a dead man and woman were frozen and then sliced up in a manner not unlike deli pastrami. The resulting slices – vertical for the woman, horizontal for the man – show *every* aspect of the human body within their transparent, formaldehyde frames, hanging in the museum's blue stairwell. Dieters will find the exhibit useful before lunch.

Jackson Park

The setting for the 1893 World's Columbian Exposition, Jackson Park (Map 11) moldered for decades. But the overall revitalization of the Chicago Park District has been a boon for Jackson Park. The lagoons are the legacy of the 1893 fair, of which little remains beyond the heavily rebuilt Museum of Science and Industry.

An exhibition survivor and twice restored, the **Osaka Garden** is a peaceful refuge on an island in the reflecting pond (Map 11). The most recent restoration in 1981 gave it a new tea house. Take time to see the characteristic intricacy of the rocks, hills, plants, lanterns and bridges. The surrounding island has become a nature sanctuary.

At the intersection of Hayes Ave and Richards Drive in the middle of the park, **The Republic** is a smaller replica of a statue that celebrated 400 years of post-Columbus civilization at the 1893 fair. Its blinding brilliance arises from a 1992 restoration.

The simple wooden details and shingles of a former **Coast Guard station** evoke images of a much more rural setting for this charming building on the yacht harbor, a quarter-mile north of where Lake Shore Drive – formally called Coast Guard Drive at this point – meets Marquette Drive. It now holds a restaurant.

University of Chicago

Some universities collect football championships. The University of Chicago collects Nobel Prizes – 69 through 1997. In particular, the economics department has been a regular winner, with faculty and former students pulling in 18 prizes since the first Nobel for economics was awarded in 1969. Merton Miller, a U of C economics faculty member and a Nobel winner, explained the string of wins to the *Sun-Times*: 'It must be the water; it certainly can't be the coffee.'

The university's classes first met on October 1, 1892. John D Rockefeller was a major contributor to the institution, donating more than $35 million, which he called 'the best investment I ever made in my life.' The original campus was constructed in an English Gothic style. Since WWII new construction has been in the usual cacophony of styles, many quite ugly.

Robie House

The ultimate expression of Frank Lloyd Wright's Prairie School style is embodied in this masterpiece (☎ 773-702-8374), at 5757 S Woodlawn Ave (Map 11), which makes the otherwise charming surrounding houses look like so many dowdy old aunts.

The long, thin Roman bricks and limestone trim mirror the same basic shape of the entire house. The dominant feature on the prominent south side is the long row of carefully detailed windows on the first floor. The long and low lines, which reflect the Midwest itself, are ornamented solely by the exquisite stained- and leaded-glass doors and windows.

Birthplace of the Bomb

At 3:53 pm on December 2, 1942, Enrico Fermi looked at a small crowd of men around him and said, 'The reaction is self-sustaining.' The scene was a dank squash court under the abandoned football stadium in the heart of the University of Chicago. With great secrecy, the gathered scientists had just achieved the world's first controlled release of nuclear energy. More than one sigh of relief was heard amid the ensuing rounds of congratulations. The nuclear reactor was supposed to have been built in a remote corner of a forest preserve 20 miles away, but a labor strike had stopped work. The impatient scientists went ahead on campus, despite many who thought the thing might blow up and take a good part of the city with it. Places such as Los Alamos, New Mexico, and Hiroshima and Nagasaki, in Japan, are more closely linked to the nuclear era, but Chicago is where it began. ■

Univeristy of Chicago Walking Tour

This tour covers the campus' highlights and lowlights. It takes about an hour unless you dawdle along the way. When viewing the classic old buildings, keep looking up for the stone menageries of critters, fairies, monsters and other creatures that are carved into cornices, rooftops, entrances and windows. Follow the path on the accompanying map.

Robie House This is the starting point. For details see the Robie House section in the main text.
Walk south down Woodlawn Ave.

Ida Noyes Hall Built as a women's dormitory in 1916, it is now the student center. Note the woman's head carved into the entry arch. Inside, the lobby, lounge and library are richly detailed.
Cross Woodlawn.

RICK GERHARTER
Rockefeller Memorial Chapel

Rockefeller Memorial Chapel University officials sent themselves on junkets to England to ensure the authenticity of the main campus chapel, which was completed in 1928. Sculpture lovers will be in heaven: the outside has 24 life-size and 53 smaller religious figures. There are even more inside.
Walk west on 59th St, turning right into the courtyard just past Foster Hall.

Foster, Kelly, Green & Beecher Halls Listed south to north, these were the first women's halls, having been built in 1893 and 1899. Foster Hall has a pack of gargoyles on the turret overlooking the midway.
Continue north, walking between the Walker Museum, on the left (actually used for classrooms), and Pick Hall, on the right. Cross the Main Quad.

Eckhart Hall One of the last Gothic buildings built on campus, it was completed in 1930. The carved details honor the resident physics, astronomy and mathematics departments.
Pass into Hutchinson Court through the arched entrance to the left of Eckhart.

Tower Group Dominated by Mitchell Tower, which is modeled after Oxford's Magdalen College, these four 1903 buildings are linked by interior cloisters. The tower was the first purely aesthetic building at the university. It contains 10 bells, whose cacophonous chimes delight some and annoy others.
Exit Hutchinson by walking to the west, then turn right.

Hull Court Going clockwise from Culver Hall on the left are the 1897 Anatomy, Zoology and Biology Buildings. Look for the griffins atop Zoology. The pond was once stocked with exotic fish.
Continue north through Cobb Gate.

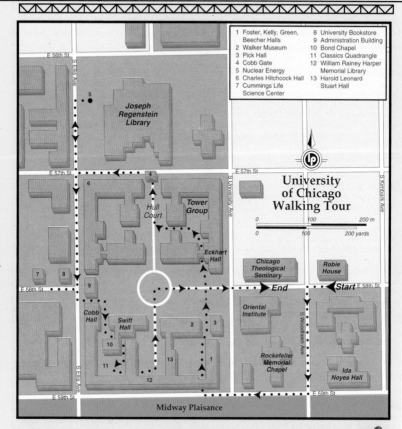

1 Foster, Kelly, Green, Beecher Halls
2 Walker Museum
3 Pick Hall
4 Cobb Gate
5 Nuclear Energy
6 Charles Hitchcock Hall
7 Cummings Life Science Center
8 University Bookstore
9 Administration Building
10 Bond Chapel
11 Classics Quadrangle
12 William Rainey Harper Memorial Library
13 Harold Leonard Stuart Hall

University of Chicago Walking Tour

0   100   200 m
0   100   200 yards

Joseph Regenstein Library

Chicago Theological Seminary

Robie House

End   Start

Oriental Institute

Rockefeller Memorial Chapel

Ida Noyes Hall

Hull Court

Tower Group

Eckhart Hall

Cobb Hall

Swift Hall

Midway Plaisance

Cobb Gate A university architect actually felt his style was cramped on campus, so he donated this ceremonial entryway in 1900 and let loose with his ornamental passions. The gargoyles struggling on the climb to the top are said to represent undergraduate students.

Turn west and face north.

Joseph Regenstein Library Walter Netsch, the architect whose notions of an Italian hill village cost the University of Illinois at Chicago millions to eradicate, brought Brutalism to the U of C in 1970. The vertical grooves and slit windows are supposed to help the library fit in with the classic structures to the south. The result actually fits in much the way the proverbial turd fits into the proverbial punch bowl.

Walk west along 57th St to Ellis Ave, turn right and walk a half-block north.

RICK GERHARTER

Continued on next page

Nuclear Energy A human skull and a mushroom cloud are combined in this 1967 bronze sculpture, which is on the exact spot where Enrico Fermi and company started the nuclear age (see The Birthplace of the Bomb).
Turn back south and go to the corner of 57th and Ellis.

Charles Hitchcock Hall The usual ornamental English posies are dispensed with on this 1902 men's dormitory. In their place are corncobs and other prairie flora.
Continue south to where 58th St ends, on your right; walk a half-block west.

Cummings Life Science Center A huge brick and limestone building and the tallest on campus, Cummings was built in 1973 and has 40 brick chimneys climbing the walls to provide ventilation for the many labs within.

University Bookstore This is the place to buy a T-shirt to forever remember your visit.
Head back east and pass between the Administration Building and Cobb Hall.

Administration Building The fact that no donor wants to be associated with this dud tells you all you need to know. Hand-wringing over the 'appropriateness' of Gothic architecture after WWII resulted in this unspectacular building, which the university's own public relations literature sums up by saying that it allows you to better appreciate its neighbors.

Cobb Hall The university's first building opened with classrooms and offices in 1892. The architect, Henry Ives Cobb, designed the next 18 buildings constructed on campus. The 4th-floor Renaissance Society has frequent art shows.
Walk diagonally southeast through the cloister joining Swift Hall and Bond Chapel.

Bond Chapel Built in 1926, this exquisite 300-seat chapel is the harmonious creation of the architects, sculptors, woodcarvers and glassmakers who worked together on the project. Look for the lute player on the cornice.
Exit the chapel and turn right into the courtyard.

Classics Quadrangle Starting at Cobb Hall and going counterclockwise are Gates, Blake and Goodspeed Halls (1892), the Classics Building (1915), Wieboldt Hall (1928) and Frederick Haskell Hall (1896). Among the ornamentation highlights are characters from Aesop's fables on Classics and noted authors on Wieboldt.
Pass through the archway between Wieboldt and Haskell.

William Rainey Harper Memorial Library The massive 1912 twin-towered building presents a grand facade both to the campus and the midway. The long row of arched, two-story windows bathe the third-floor reading room with light.

Harold Leonard Stuart Hall The 1904 law school building features the original law-giver on the roof. This Moses doesn't look like Charlton Heston.
Walk north.

Swift Hall The 1926 home of the Divinity School was placed in this prominent position to signify the importance of religion in education. In the basement there's a decent coffee shop.
Walk north to the center of the traffic circle; turn east and walk along 58th St.

Chicago Theological Seminary The red brick 1926 buildings provide a Tudor contrast to the university. The cloisters invite contemplation, and the beautiful Hilton Memorial Chapel invites prayer.

Oriental Institute See the section in the main text on the institute's museum.
Continue west to Robie House to complete the campus tour. See the main text for information about the building. ■

RICK GERHARTER

Robie House

Construction of the house was as revolutionary as the design. Poured concrete forms many of the floors and balconies, while the massively overhanging roof is supported by steel beams – a radical concept for residential construction.

The Robie family, for whom the house was built in 1909, lived there only until 1911, when the family bicycle business died right along with the couple's marriage. The Chicago Theological Seminary turned the house into a dorm, and conditions soon became hellish. By 1957 what the students hadn't destroyed was ready to be demolished. Designated a National Historic Landmark in 1963, it was taken over by the U of C, which allowed it to further molder until 1993. Since then, a joint agreement between the university and the Oak Park-based Frank Lloyd Wright Home and Studio Foundation has allowed plans to be made for a massive multiyear restoration. One look at some of the critical exterior details, such as the foundation, will hint at the urgency of this work.

Tours of the interior take in only the central living and dining room. But the sweep of the space, broken into its components by the fireplace, is alone worth the price of admission. Note that Wright, a control freak if there ever was one, used built-in furniture, windows and other details to prevent the owners from messing with his interior design vision.

Tours are given weekdays at 11 am, noon, and 1 and 3 pm; weekends they are continuous from 11 am to 3:30 pm. Admission is $8 for adults, $6 for children. A gift shop with books and other mementos operates in the garage.

Oriental Institute Museum

Artifacts from ancient cultures from Egypt to Mesopotamia are displayed at this fascinating museum (☎ 773-702-9521), at 1155 E 58th St in the heart of the campus (Map 11). The 'Oriental' in the name refers to the Near East, where University of Chicago archaeological work has been under way since 1919. In the museum's early years the exploits of its original curators were a bit like those of Indiana Jones. Today the museum continues work in Israel, Egypt, Jordan and Syria.

The often overlooked collection is getting new displays and signage, which left the museum closed for most of 1997. When it reopens in late 1998, take some time to examine the details of the almost 3000-year-old carved stone reliefs that once adorned the Assyrian city of Khorsabad when Sargon II was king.

At press time, admission and hours for the museum had not yet been decided.

David & Alfred Smart Museum

Named after the founders of *Esquire* magazine, who contributed the money to get it started, the official fine arts museum of the university (☎ 773-702-0200), 5550 S Greenwood Ave (Map 11), opened in 1974. Among the 8000 items in the collection are some excellent works from ancient China and Japan and a colorful and detailed Syrian mosaic from about 600 AD.

The strength of the collection lies in paintings and sculpture contemporary to the university's existence. Auguste Rodin's *Thinker* has a thoughtful place (hey it's a Smart museum), as do works by Arthur Davies, Jean Arp, Henry Moore and many others. The freakish 1929 painting *Four Arts Ball*, by Guy Pène Du Bois, has become something of a museum icon. As you study the groundbreaking Robie House dining-room set by Frank Lloyd Wright, you'll be forgiven if you wonder why it's not back in the original house three blocks away.

The museum is undergoing a major expansion so that more of the fast-growing collection of the well-endowed university can be displayed. It's open Tuesday to Friday 10 am to 4 pm, weekends noon to 6 pm; closed Mondays and holidays. Admission is free, making this one of the city's great bargains.

PULLMAN

George Pullman's dream community turned into a nightmare when idealism ran headlong into capitalism in 1894. The namesake town of the millionaire railroad car manufacturer had been started in 1880. His goal was to build a model town that would provide homes for his workers in a clean and wholesome environment. He built houses, apartments, stores, a hotel and churches, all of which were meant to return 6% on his investment.

Pullman earned kudos from both industrialists and social activists. The town's careful design was based on French models and had an aesthetic that was unknown in workers' housing then or now. But the 1893 depression hit Pullman's luxury railcar business hard. The firm laid off some workers and cut the pay of others. Rents and prices in Pullman's town stayed high, however, to insure that 6%.

Worker resentment grew and resulted in the Pullman strike of 1894. Violent clashes between the strikers and thugs hired by Pullman were finally settled when federal troops were sent in to force the strikers back to work. It was another turning point for the American labor movement, which had been fueled by the 1886 Haymarket Riot.

Pullman died a bitter man in 1897. The following year, the Illinois Supreme Court ordered the company to sell the town except for the factories. The sale was completed by 1907. The neighborhood has had ups and downs since then. The last part of the complex finally closed for good in 1981. The southern part of Pullman, which is where the higher-paid craftsmen and managers lived, was largely bought up by people determined to preserve it. North Pullman, with simpler housing for laborers,

is only now being appreciated for its underlying architectural qualities.

Thirteen miles south of the Loop, Pullman is easily reached by Metra Electric trains from the Randolph St Station. Get off at the 111th St station, which is right in the heart of the most scenic section. The fare is $2.75 one way. A side note: the double-decker Metra Electric trains were among the last passenger trains built by Pullman in Chicago.

If you're driving, take I-94 south to the 111th St exit. Pullman is a half-mile west.

Go in the daytime so you can appreciate the buildings. Start with the **Hotel Florence** (☎ 773-785-8181), at 11111 S Forrestville. Lavishly restored, the hotel is the official visitor's center for the neighborhood and has detailed maps available for walking and driving tours. Normally, they don't serve food except for a popular Sunday brunch; call to confirm hours.

The **Colonnade Apartments**, four matching curved 1892 apartment buildings at 112th St and Champlain Ave, surround the former market hall. The tiny bachelors' apartments upstairs were obviously not intended for men who expected company.

A rambling complex with varied rooflines, the **Pullman Administration Building and Clock Tower**, at 111th St and Cottage Grove Ave, are solidly French in conception. The state of Illinois is moving forward at a glacial pace with plans to restore the complex and create a railroad museum.

ELSEWHERE IN THE CITY
Garfield Park Conservatory

With 4½ acres under glass, the park district's premier conservatory (☎ 312-746-5100), 300 N Central Park Blvd, north of Lake St, is a significant bit of the Tropics on the west side. Built in 1907, the rambling glass structure houses one of the largest collections of indoor plants in the world. One of the original designers, Jens Jensen, intended for the 5000 palms, ferns and other plants to re-create what Chicago looked like during prehistoric times. Today the effect continues; all that's missing is a

RICK GERHARTER
The lakeshore in Evanston

rampaging stegosaurus. The Economic House has a fascinating range of plants that are used for food, medicine and shelter.

The conservatory is open daily 9 am to 5 pm. Admission is free. The surrounding neighborhood is unsafe at all times. Drive to the park, where parking is free and close to the conservatory door. The Garfield Park Conservatory Alliance (☎ 773-638-1766), a private support group, sponsors activities.

SUBURBS
Evanston
A clean and pleasant place 14 miles north of the Loop, Evanston combines sprawling old houses with a compact and very walkable downtown shopping district. Much of the town is dominated by Northwestern University, whose influence is felt in many ways.

The Methodists who founded the town in 1850 would be happy to see that today it is still hard to buy a beer here, a lingering effect of both the Methodist ethos and a rule once passed by Northwestern that forbade the sale of alcohol within 4 miles of campus. Lacking the grand vision of its rival, the University of Chicago, the NU campus holds more interest for its faculty and students than for visitors.

During rush hours you can ride the CTA Purple Line Evanston Express to and from the Loop. At other times, ride the Red Line to Howard and transfer to a Purple Line local. The Davis stop is in the heart of town and gown. Alternatively, you can take the Metra/Union Pacific North Line from North-

western Station, in the West Loop ($2.75 one way). The drive north from Chicago on Sheridan Rd is especially scenic.

Mitchell Indian Museum The lives of Native Americans in the Midwest, both past and present, are documented in this large regional museum (☎ 847-866-1395), 2600 Central Ave. Artworks, pottery, textiles, clothing, baskets, quilts and other items show aspects of the Indians' daily existence. Special displays let visitors handle traditional everyday objects, such as the stone tools used to make cornmeal. You'll never eat a corn tortilla so nonchalantly again – it's wrist-killing work.

Many Native Americans who live in the area take an active role in the displays, temporary exhibitions and lectures that the museum hosts. In late 1997 the entire 3000-piece collection moved to the former home of the Terra Museum of American Art. The much larger quarters are expected to allow for greatly increased activities.

The old museum location was open several hours a day every day but Monday. The new location is expected to have expanded hours; call to confirm. The old admission of $1 may continue.

North Shore
Chicago's northern suburbs on the lake are pleasant and gracious places that are worth every dollar the residents pay in property taxes. Quiet yet urbane, they became popular in the late 1800s with the carriage set, who were sick of Chicago's fires, riots, tainted water and other big city excitements.

RICK GERHARTER
Watch your step on the North Shore beaches.

If you have a car, a Sunday drive any day of the week through the North Shore communities provides a pleasant glimpse of the beautiful homes and stately gardens. Head north from Chicago on Lake Shore Drive. When it ends turn right on Sheridan Rd, drive north through Rogers Park to Evanston and you're on your way on a classic 30-mile drive following Sheridan through towns that include Kenilworth, Wilmette, Winnetka, Glencoe, Highland Park and the apex of the drive and social standing, Lake Forest. Just be sure to watch the signs, as Sheridan twists and turns. Return via I-94.

Baha'i House of Worship You may have seen this huge white-domed edifice as you flew over Wilmette on the way in. Completed in 1953 by members of the Baha'i faith, a Persian sect, the temple is a glistening white showplace and one of seven major houses of worship the faith has worldwide. The grounds in summer are ablaze with flowers, providing colorful contrast to the white cement.

Wilmette is the last stop on the CTA Purple Line. Catch an express in the Loop during rush hours, or take the Red Line to Howard and transfer to the Purple. The temple is a short walk east from the Linden station.

Chicago Botanic Garden The garden (☎ 847-835-5440) is actually in tony Glencoe, at 1000 Lake-Cook Rd, a half-mile east of the Edens Expressway (I-94). Featuring thousands of plants in 20 distinctive settings on 385 acres, the facility is run by the Chicago Horticultural Society. Among the leafy sights you'll see are a prairie garden, an herb garden, a Japanese garden and a rose garden. Frequent demonstrations show you how to try to replicate the gardens at home.

For fun, assign each member of the group a letter and see who can find the most plants beginning with that letter. For instance, the letter G will garner geraniums, grapes, ginkgo trees, gourds and, not be be overlooked, grass.

The garden is open 8 am to dusk daily except Christmas. Admission is free, but they employ the suburban scam of making you pay $4 for parking, knowing that the only people liable to walk there are those out of gas. Public transport is not an easy option.

Lake Forest
The toniest of the status suburbs is also the farthest north. Its downtown is a gracious place to wander, having been built in 1916 to designs inspired by English market towns, with other European influences. Considered by

Worth a trip: The Baha'i House of Worship

many to be the first suburban shopping area, its influences are difficult to detect in your average strip mall.

The reward for a Sheridan Drive cruise, Lake Forest is about 45 minutes to an hour north of the city, depending on traffic. The Metra/Union Pacific North Line has frequent service right to the heart of downtown ($3.90 one way).

Oak Park

Oak Park is the place to go to make a Frank Lloyd Wright pilgrimage. For ten years – from 1898 to 1908, when he took a surprise trip to Europe (see the sidebar 'He Was Not Morally Up to Snuff') – Wright worked and lived in a studio in Oak Park. Strolling the streets of this pleasant old town is like stepping back into one of those 1950s TV sitcoms, with

all its bland bucolic charm. Though native son Ernest Hemingway was unmoved – he called it a 'village of wide lawns and narrow minds.'

Wright's work is sprinkled throughout the town and is easily visited. The Oak Park Visitor Center (☎ 708-848-1500), 158 Forest Ave at Lake, boasts helpful, plain-talking volunteers and provides a wide variety of information. Ask for the architectural walking tour brochure, which comes with a useful map. The center is open daily 10 am to 5 pm.

Staff at the **Frank Lloyd Wright Home and Studio** (☎ 708-848-1976), 951 Chicago Ave, offer tours of the complex, the neighborhood and other Wright-designed homes between 11 am and 3 pm daily. Self-guided walking tours, including audio tours, are also available.

'He Was Not Morally Up to Snuff'

Oak Park may be home to a good portion of Frank Lloyd Wright's legacy, but you can't accuse locals of glossing over his checkered reputation. The title of this sidebar is a quote from the woman who was working in Oak Park's official visitor information center one afternoon when I went in. She had a variety of cutting comments about the acerbic and philandering Wright, who one day didn't go home to his wife and six kids at his Oak Park studio because he was on his way to Europe with Mamah Borthwick Cheney, the wife of a client.

Born in Wisconsin in 1867 and always a prodigy, Wright went to Chicago in 1887 to work for Louis Sullivan as a drafter. But in 1893 that relationship ended when Sullivan found out that Wright was moonlighting and not cutting the firm in on the profits.

After his European escapade in 1908, Wright worked from studios on a Wisconsin farm, where he lived with Cheney, although he was still married to his first wife. Public condemnation was harsh, and on Christmas Day, 1911, Wright held a press conference to explain his infidelity, proclaiming that he, as a 'thinking man,' did not have to follow the rules of 'the ordinary man.'

In 1914 Cheney was murdered by a deranged servant. Wright found consolation with Miriam Noel, who had sent him a letter of sympathy. They married in 1923 and divorced in 1927. In 1928 Wright married his third and final wife, Olga Ivanovna, with whom he had had a child in 1925.

Wright spent most of his later years working at his home in the Arizona desert, where he died in 1959 at the age of 90. His personal life notwithstanding, Wright was already rightfully recognized as the most original of all American architects when Wright died.

On the same day that the visitor's center staffer passed moral judgment, a touring architect outside the Moore House offered the following anecdote about his own run-in with the tart-tongued Wright: 'I was 19 and going to a small architecture school back East. Wright came and spoke. Afterward I tried to speak to him, because I admired him. He looked at me and said, "You'll never be an architect, because you go to school in a shoe factory." Then he hit me with his cane and drove away.' ■

RICK GERHARTER

The Wright home and studio

The studio is a fascinating place, filled with the unique sorts of details that made Wright so distinctive. Note how he molded plaster to look like bronze and stained cheap pine to look like rare hardwoods. Always in financial trouble, spendthrift Wright was adept at making the ordinary seem extraordinary.

The studio's bookstore has mountains of Wright-related paraphernalia. Unfortunately, all the books seem to have been written by supplicants, sycophants and adoring relatives.

One block away, the **Moore House**, 333 N Forest Ave, is Wright's bizarre interpretation of an English manor house. Tours depart from the front of the house when enough people have gathered, weekends noon to 4:30 pm from April to October.

The newly restored CTA Green Line and the Metra/Union Pacific West Line serve Oak Park with frequent and fast service. The CTA offers the more interesting ride. On either line, exit at the Oak Park stop, walk north one block on Oak Park Ave to Lake St, turn left, and walk west on Lake to the visitor center, which is five minutes from the Oak Park stop.

By car take I-290 west, exiting north on Harlem Avenue; take Harlem north to Lake St and turn right.

West Suburbs
Brookfield Zoo With 2500 animals and 215 acres, the Brookfield Zoo (☎ 708-485-0263), 8400 W 31st St, can easily gobble up an entire day. Much more commercially oriented than the Lincoln Park Zoo, it boasts several special attractions, some of which cost extra.

RICK GERHARTER

The Moore House

Because most visitors use the North Gate and tend to hit the attractions closest to it first, you can avoid some of the crowds by starting in the southern part of the zoo and working back north. You'll soon find that the exhibits have names invented by the marketing department. Some highlights follow.

Really three exhibits, the **Fragile Kingdom** comprises an indoor African desert scene, an indoor Asian rain-forest scene and an outdoor collection of big cats. The desert scene has the feel of an Indiana Jones movie set and includes jackals, monitor lizards and naked mole rats. Outside, the Wheel of Survival, a device that looks like something from a TV game show, illustrates that the odds of a big cat's catching a hapless gazelle are far less likely than television nature specials would have you believe.

The largest indoor exhibit at the zoo is **Tropic World**. It is divided into three areas representing rain forests in South America, Asia and Africa. Frequent showers douse the animals, sparing the visitors. Unfortunately, the walls are painted a sickly blue that contributes to the exhibit's overall gloomy feeling.

If walking with bats is your idea of a nightmare, skip the **Australia House**. Otherwise, the exhibit is well worth a stop. Couch potatoes and other critters with low metabolic rates will identify with the perpetually snoozing wombats.

Upstairs at the **Seven Seas Dolphinarium**, visitors can buy tickets for the 2000-seat amphitheater to see trainers putting dolphins through their paces. Downstairs, visitors can see the dolphins free through the underwater viewing windows. Watch the dolphins looking through windows into the kitchen where their meals are prepared.

Habitat Africa! is built on five acres and set in a mythical African game reserve called Makundi National Park. The level of detail used to create the exhibit is most effective in the kopje area, which represents a rocky outcrop rising from the African savanna. The next phase will open in 1999 and will feature a forest setting based on that found in Congo.

The newest attraction, **Living Coast**, models a portion of the coast of Chile and Peru where the world's driest desert meets one of the Pacific Ocean's richest breeding grounds. Sharks, turtles, penguins and 60 other species live in and around the huge tank of water.

The zoo is open daily 10 am to 4:30 pm; from May through September it's open daily 9:30 am to 5:30 pm. Admission is $4.50. On Tuesday and Thursday from April to September admission is $2.50; the rest of the year it's free on those days. Parking is $4.

The Metra Hollywood stop is near the main entrance and is served by frequent trains on the BNSF line from Union Station ($2.75 one way). By car the zoo is 14 miles from the Loop. Go west on I-290 to the 1st Ave exit, then south to 31st. Follow the signs to the zoo.

Morton Aboretum A private nature preserve on more than 1500 acres, the Morton Arboretum (☎ 630-719-2400) combines a wide variety of terrain and trees in one location. The settings range from manicured shrubs to special plantings of trees not native to the area to long stretches of local forest and prairie. Many of the trees are marked with small informational signs.

There are 25 miles of trails, but a realistic circular path covering most of the areas runs for 6 to 7 miles. Plan your course using the map you receive at the entrance. Parts of the arboretum are quite hilly, with paths that feel nicely rural. However, large sections of the park seem to have been designed with autos rather than walkers in mind. Many people tour the entire location without once leaving their cars, a situation befitting the park's suburban location. The park is fairly quiet in the middle, but toward the edges there's noise from I-88 and other busy roads. And there's those constantly touring automobiles . . .

The arboretum is open daily 7 am to 5 pm; from April to October it's open daily 7 am to 7 pm. It's 25 miles west of Chicago on Route 53, just north of I-88, in Lisle. This is a car-only trip. Admission is $6 per car ($3 on Wednesday).

South & Southwest Suburbs
Waterfall Glen Forest Preserve This 2200-acre park completely surrounds the Argonne National Laboratory, where research is done on nuclear bombs. The setting has some of the most diverse scenery in the area, including a waterfall, a deep limestone ravine, prairie, woods, marsh and a pond.

In the past the site supplied the limestone used for Chicago's Water Tower and was the location of a nursery where trees were grown for Lincoln Park. Although the lab is in the middle, it's almost impossible to see. It doesn't even glow. On the south side of the preserve is a large field popular with people flying radio-controlled planes.

The main hiking trail is one of the area's most beautiful walks; it is also – by local standards – hilly and strenuous. The 9-mile-long loop is an excellent way to explore the site. Maps are usually not available, so study the large one posted at the parking lot. The main trail is marked by brown plastic posts with orange circles. Follow them carefully, because it's easy to miss a turn and end up amid apartments or houses. The best way to proceed from the parking lot is counterclockwise, so that you'll get through the less interesting terrain first, saving the lake for the end. About four miles into the hike, the trail follows some old limestone walls under a thick canopy of trees.

The park is 20 miles southwest of Chicago, off Cass Ave, 1½ miles south of I-55. The trailhead is at the large map adjacent to the main parking lot.

ACTIVITIES
If you are staying at a hotel, definitely check with the concierge or front desk about arrangements the hotel may have with private clubs for any of the sports listed here. Many hotels can get you discounted indoor tennis time, health club access or day passes for pools or other facilities the hotel doesn't have.

Bicycling
Chicago is well suited for biking. The lakefront path is very popular and covers 18½ miles from Hollywood Beach to the South Shore Country Club, at 71st St. Every summer, progressive rock station WXRT hosts a midnight bike ride that starts at Buckingham Fountain and winds its way through the city all night long. It's a fun event, and survivors are treated to breakfast at the finish line. Check with the station (☎ 773-777-1700) for dates.

Bowling
Once called 'the opiate of the masses,' bowling is a distinctly Midwestern activity. People of all shapes, sizes and ages gather in boisterous groups to send balls crashing into pins. Talent is not a prerequisite, but the consumption of copious pitchers of cheap beer is. The lanes are most crowded during the cold months, when bowling is a great indoor sport (although the preponderance of beer bellies should tell you everything you need to know about the athletic aspect).

Diversey-River Bowl (☎ 773-227-5800), 2211 W Diversey; Waveland Bowl (☎ 773-472-5900), 3700 N Western Ave; and Marigold Arcade (☎ 773-935-8183), 828 W Grace, are big, cheap, open way past midnight, rent any equipment you'll need and are decorated in bright 1970s vinyl.

For bowling with charm, try Southport Lanes (☎ 773-472-1601), at 3325 N Southport in Wrigleyville (Map 7). This 75-year-old bar has four lanes with hand-set pins in the basement. The whole place has been beautifully restored and is in itself worth an evening out.

Gambling
In the years since 1991, when riverboat gambling began in Illinois, it hasn't become the embodiment of apocryphal Hollywood images. Visions of cigar-smoking, white-clad sharpies cheating the unsuspecting while 'Old Man River' plays in the background haven't come to pass, and the entire riverboat motif has turned out to be a sham: The riverboats have been refined to concentrate on the bread and butter of gambling – slot machines and blackjack. The boats rarely leave port and

instead are nothing more than small, somewhat cramped casinos.

There's no mistaking riverboat gambling in Illinois for that found in the mega-casinos of Nevada. The state's most popular casino, Empress Casino in Joliet, devotes a combined total of 36,200 sq feet to gambling on its two boats. In contrast, just one hotel in Las Vegas, the MGM Grand, devotes 171,500 sq feet to its casino.

Still, during an average month, $1.1 billion dollars is dropped into slot machines statewide and another $150 million is wagered at tables. Many of the customers are retirees who are lured to the 'boats' by cheap bus rides. But there's no question about who really wins: the average visitor to a riverboat casino leaves about $50 poorer.

The following casinos are all within an hour of Chicago. Unless you get a bus ride, expect to drive. Except for short closures in the wee hours, the casinos are open almost nonstop. Each casino offers 'departures' about every two hours. Patrons may board a half hour before 'sailing' and start gambling then. But even if the boat stays dockside, you can't board after the official departure time. Once the session has ended two hours later you can usually keep right on gambling into the next session unless it is sold out.

One advantage of having your boat stay dockside is that you can disembark anytime you want. If you're on the river and you want to leave early, you have to jump overboard.

Admission ranges from $2 in the morning to $10 on weekend nights. Often you can get various deals with the early cruises that include breakfast or lunch. Unlike in Las Vegas, however, there's no free booze for gamblers.

Empress Casino Joliet The Empress (☎ 888-436-7737), on the Des Plaines River near the confluence of I-55 and I-80 in Joliet, is a North African spectacle, with obelisks flanking the entrance to an extremely loose approximation of an Egyptian palace. Inside there's a large off-track

betting room with an array of video screens, as well as banquet facilities. The faux North African theme extends throughout the public areas. The Marrakech Market is a food court with such unlikely offerings as Wok Like an Egyptian (Asian food) and Omar's Pizza Oven.

The *Empress I* and *Empress II* are nearly identical sleek, modern-looking vessels. The boats are simply decorated and almost devoid of windows. Except for the unmistakable tinny sound under the carpeted stairs, it's easy to forget you're on a boat.

Harrah's Joliet Casino After ascending an escalator, visitors to Harrah's (☎ 800-427-7247), on the Des Plaines River in downtown Joliet, find themselves in a parklike place complete with robotic birds and animals. Harrah's boats are quite different from each other: The *Northern Star*, which was put in service when the casino opened in 1993, is a modern yachtlike craft. The *Southern Star II*, which premiered in November 1995, resembles an old riverboat complete with a big, working paddle wheel on the rear. Inside it has a large, open three-level gaming area with a tiny elevator.

Hollywood Casino Aurora The Hollywood Casino (☎ 800-888-7777), on the Fox River in downtown Aurora, has gone all out with its land-based operation, which includes a few knickknacks from Tinseltown. There's John Wayne's cowboy hat, Clark Gable's trousers and Joan Crawford's bustier. The Hollywood Casino also hosts big-name entertainment a few times a year at the nearby Paramount Theater. The Epic Buffet has outsize decor dominated by a big gorilla scaling the Chicago skyline.

Hollywood's boats, the *City of Lights I* and *II*, have a riverboat look sans paddle wheel. Inside, the gaming areas are rather opulent, with a brightly colored decor that reflects the Hollywood theme.

Grand Victoria Casino Operated by Circus Circus Enterprises – one of the

RICK GERHARTER

Find yourself a bicycle and join Chicago's monthly Critical Mass.

largest casino operators in Las Vegas – the Grand Victoria (☎ 847-888-1000), on the Fox River in downtown Elgin, has a large pavilion dominated by a 55-foot atrium with an 8-foot clock that's a historical nod to the Elgin National Watch Company.

The casino's one boat, the *Grand Victoria*, is a behemoth. At 400 feet in length, it is the largest floating casino in the United States. Almost all of the 1200 gambling positions are on one deck, giving the casino a look that approaches the spaciousness of some Las Vegas casinos. Although the exterior styling is meant to be reminiscent of an old side-wheeler, the huge size is like nothing that ever traversed Midwest rivers.

Trump Casino High-volume New York developer and self-promoter Donald Trump has crapped out with his big-ticket casino (☎ 888-218-7867) in Gary, Indiana, in a heretofore unknown and unnamed precinct 15 miles east of Chicago reachable by I-90 (take the Cline Blvd/State Road 912 exit and go north 3 miles). It's reasonably opulent and photos of Trump are everywhere, but the man *Spy* magazine once called a 'short-fingered vulgarian' has not been able to sway the Midwestern market. Even though he imperiously decided that his casino was no longer in Gary, one of the most blighted cities in the nation, and renamed its location 'Buffington Harbor,' few gamblers have shown up.

Golf

Chicago golfers stretch the season as far as possible in both directions. There's a certain macho pride in playing with neon-colored balls in the snow. Most courses are open from April to November. If it's a nice day outside of those months, phone the courses – they might be open.

The Chicago Park District has turned

management of the courses over to Kemper Golf, whose automated phone line (☎ 312-245-0909) has information about the courses, tee times, costs, directions and opening dates and will accept reservations.

Public Courses The district operates the Sydney R Marovitz Course (☎ 773-868-4113), in Lincoln Park at Irving Park Rd (Map 7). Commonly known as 'Waveland,' the nine-hole course has sweeping views of the lake and skyline. Its 1932 Gothic field house has a clock tower with chimes for the hours. Sadly, neighbors across Lake Shore Drive complained about the noise, and the chimes have been turned off. Obviously, they preferred the sonorous roar of traffic.

The course is very popular, and in order to secure a tee time, golfers cheerfully arrive at 5:30 am. You can avoid that sort of lunacy by spending a few dollars extra to get a reservation. Fees vary widely through the year, from $6 to $13, with extra charges for nonresidents and reservations. You can rent clubs there.

The district's only 18-hole course is the Jackson Park Golf Course (☎ 773-493-7085) at 63rd St and Stoney Island in Jackson Park. It is considered moderately challenging; fees range from $6 to $14. Reservations are recommended.

At the South Shore Country Club (☎ 312-747-2536), at South Lake Shore Drive and 71st St, the public course has a mere nine holes. The location is right on the lake and crowds aren't bad. And this is a favored course for cops, so crime is very low. The entrance is through the police stables at South Lake Shore Drive and 71st St.

If you just want to knock a bucket of balls, the Diversey Driving Range (☎ 312-281-5722), in Lincoln Park where Diversey meets the lake (Map 7), will let you whack away to your heart's content. It's open daily 7 am to 10 pm, and rental clubs are available; a bucket is about $6.

Private Courses In an inspired move, acres of vacant tracts of Illinois Center land have been turned into a golf course just east of the Loop. MetroGolf Illinois Center (☎ 312-616-1234) has a driving range, nine short holes with a complex green, chipping greens and a bar and restaurant. You can make reservations to get a round in ($20) before or after a big meeting. But finding your way to the course can be a tougher challenge than making par from a trap: its address is 221 N Columbus (Map 3), but Columbus is actually about 50 feet above the ground where the course is. From the Loop, you can get there by cutting through Randolph St Station; from River North, take Columbus Drive over the river and then every flight of stairs you can find out of the Illinois Center morass to the ground below.

Health Clubs
Hotels almost always have either their own facilities or agreements with nearby clubs. Otherwise, Lakeshore Athletic Clubs have pools, full equipment, jogging tracks and more in two convenient locations: 441 N Wabash (☎ 312-644-4880; Map 3), and 1320 W Fullerton, in Lincoln Park (☎ 773-477-9888). Day-use rates average $15 and don't include tennis.

Avoid the ubiquitous Bally Total Fitness Clubs, where commission-paid drones will dog you during your visit with increasingly desperate membership pleas, even if you're from out of town.

Ice Skating
The ice-skating season is depressingly long for sunbathers and even skaters. Skate on State (☎ 312-744-3315), across from Field's (Map 3), has skating from November through March. You can rent skates and drink hot chocolate from 9 am to 7 pm.

The Chicago Park District has a first-class rink at Daley Bicentennial Plaza (☎ 312-742-7650), on the south side of the 300 block of Randolph at the north end of Grant Park. The season runs from November to March. Skates may be rented. Call for hours; usually it's open several nights a week until 10 pm. Admission to both rinks is free.

'Spider Dan' Goodwin

Chicago may seem flat, but it has its own allure for mountain climbers, as Dan Goodwin proved in 1981 when he climbed the exterior of the 1454-foot Sears Tower. Media from around the globe made a folk hero of the man who climbed what was then the world's tallest building using suction cups and wearing a Spiderman costume. They even gave him a name: 'Spider Dan.'

For his next stunt, an assault on the 1127-foot John Hancock Center, the world's tallest residential building, Goodwin decided to forgo the Spiderman outfit and instead wore a wet suit. It proved prescient. As he neared the 37th floor, windows were punched out and a fire hose appeared. To Goodwin's amazement it was aimed at him, and on orders of fire commissioner William Blair, it was turned on. As Goodwin cowered under the deluge, Blair ordered his men to poke at him with pikes.

For the next two hours, Goodwin clung to the side of the Hancock while pictures of Chicago firefighters attacking him flashed around the world. An outraged Mayor Jane Byrne arrived on the scene and called a halt to the public-relations nightmare. She told Goodwin he could proceed at his own risk, and he did. That proved to be the last time he climbed a building uninvited. The city charged him with a variety of crimes, including performing an aerial act without a net. He received a year's probation and was ordered to engage in no more publicity stunts.

Goodwin now lives in California and writes novels and screenplays with, you guessed it, climbing themes. ■

In-Line Skating

At all the places you'd ride a bike, you can in-line skate. Many businesses, however, have clamped down on customers who try to act oh so cool by skating, say, to the bar for a beer or to the frozen foods section for a Lean Cuisine. See the bicycle section in the Getting Around chapter for sources of rental 'blades.

Running

As with biking, Chicago is well suited for running. The lakefront and Lincoln and Grant Parks are all popular with runners throughout the day. For information on organized races, try the Chicago Area Runners Association (☎ 312-666-9836, 312-922-4420).

Swimming

Lakefront beaches have lifeguards from late May through early September. However, you can swim at your own risk whenever you want, depending on what you think of the temperature. The water in August is usually in the 70s Fahrenheit.

In the summer the public pool at Holstein Park (☎ 312-742-7554), in the heart of Bucktown at 2200 N Oakley three blocks west of Damen (Map 9), is large and refreshing. You can rent a suit and leave your sweaty duds in a locker. Best of all, they have frequent adult-only hours, when squealing kids are sent packing. Admission is free.

Tennis

Chicago Park District There are several public tennis courts convenient to visitors. Some require reservations and charge fees, while others are free and players queue for their turns on the court. Place your racket by the net and you're next in line. The season runs from mid-April to mid-October.

At Daley Bicentennial Plaza, on the south side of the 300 block of Randolph at the north end of Grant Park (Map 3), there are 12 lighted courts, which charge fees (☎ 312-742-7650).

Waveland Tennis Courts (☎ 312-868-4132), in Lincoln Park where Waveland meets the park, on the east side of Lake Shore Drive (Map 7), has 20 lighted courts, which charge fees.

At Lake Shore Park, north of Chicago Ave near the lake, are two very popular lit and free courts.

In Grant Park, at 900 S Columbus about 300 yards south of Balbo (Map 4), are several courts. No reservations are taken, but fees are charged at peak times.

Private Courts The Lakeshore Athletic Club (☎ 312-644-4880), 441 N Wabash (Map 3), and the Mid-Town Tennis Club (☎ 773-235-2300), 2020 W Fullerton with 18 indoor courts, may offer day passes during off-peak hours.

Offbeat Activities

Catching fish has become a mayoral priority, and a special **Fishing Hotline** has been set up (☎ 312-744-3370) to answer questions about what to catch, when and how. Most of the lagoons in the parks are stocked in the summer, and charter boats now take anglers trolling on the lake.

Retrace the route of French trapper Louis Jolliet while you have an urban adventure by **canoeing the Chicago River**. Besides urban sprawl, you'll see deer, red foxes, beavers and birds. You'll also see parks and houses being built, showing that Chicago has finally discovered that the river is good for more bucolic pursuits than using it as a sewer. Chicagoland Canoe Base (☎ 773-777-1498), at 4019 N Narragansett Ave, will rent you a canoe for about $40 plus deposit. Owner Vic Hurtowy will give you tips on where to paddle. And fear not, the Chicago River is a lot cleaner than it used to be. Many species of fish have returned, and none have more than one head.

You can **windsurf** Lake Michigan (this *is* the Windy City) at Montrose Beach. Windward Sports (☎ 773-472-6868), with a year-round location at 3317 N Clark (Map 7), will rent you a board on the spot from June through August for $35 a day.

For an even bigger blow, Bill Gladstone's Chicago Sailing Club (☎ 773-871-7245), rents boats in several sizes and prices at Belmont Harbor (Map 7), the scenic haven on the North Side for hundreds of sailboats. If you don't know your jib from a poop deck, you can take lessons. Call for directions.

The many forest preserves surrounding the city have miles of **horse trails**. Glen Grove Equestrian Center (☎ 847-966-8032), 9453 Central Ave in Morton Grove, rents horses by the hour, starting at $40 an hour. They also offer organized rides in the woods.

When you've seen enough pigeons, call the Chicago Audubon Society (☎ 773-539-6793). The group organizes frequent and free **bird-watching** expeditions all around the area, and novices are encouraged to come along. Chicago is host to hundreds of bird species, from eagles to the rare white-breasted nuthatch, as well as Canadian geese passing through.

At Hinckley Soaring (☎ 815-286-7200) you can **sail in a glider** over the farms and prairies surrounding Chicago. There's corn as far as the eye can see, and it's a great way to see what most of Illinois really looks like. Hinckley Soaring is on US 30, 3 miles west of Hinckley, a tiny burg itself 30 miles west of the city. It charges $35 to $55 for sample rides.

Places to Stay

There are myriad lodging choices in Chicago, from world-class five-star hotels on North Michigan Ave to hostels far from the center. Your budget and your choice of neighborhood in which to lay your head should help you decide among them.

As the most popular convention city in the US, Chicago is well served with hotels. More than a hundred hotels of all types can be found in the Loop and North Side, offering more than 25,000 rooms. The conventions can attract tens of thousands of visitors, who fill up even the most remote locations and pay top dollar for the chance to do so. During one of the major shows (see Bad Dates in Facts for the Visitor) it might be better to skip Chicago entirely: the best restaurants and hotels will be packed.

But when conventions aren't in town, you can benefit from the hotels' desire to fill their rooms at almost any cost. All sorts of deals will be offered – especially on weekends – to lure you in. During off weekends in the winter, it's not unheard of to find deals in the best hotels for $99 a night, or even less. Package deals may include in-room treats such as champagne, as well as free theater tickets and parking. The latter can shave $20 a night off your bill.

Unless otherwise specified, the rates listed in this chapter are for singles *or* doubles, and they are the normal midweek rates. Use them for comparison purposes only, since they can vary so widely. Weekend or special rates are listed when they are fairly institutionalized by the hotel. Call and see what deals are on offer for the dates you want to visit. Frequently you can do better by calling chain-affiliated hotels directly than by calling their national toll-free numbers. Families should note that suite hotels can be a good deal; the kids can be exiled to the sofa bed while the adults take refuge in the real bed behind a closed door.

Beware of a nasty surprise you will find on your bill: the hotel tax is a gnarly 14.9%. Also, the more a hotel charges per night, the more likely it is to levy some sort of ridiculous fee on local calls. These can run $1.25 or more per call, so if you have a lot of business to conduct and you're paying your own bill, ask about these charges when making reservations.

Finally, in a city bursting with splendid food and drink options it rarely makes sense to eat or drink in your hotel. Most have restaurants and bars that are somnolent in quality and nightmarish in price. Hotels with worthwhile in-house consumption choices are noted.

HOSTELS

As in many towns, summer is the best time for availability of hostel rooms in Chicago. No hostels are in the heart of the Near North action, but several are in attractive locations.

Located near Loyola University, the *Chicago International Hostel* (☎ 773-262-1011), 6318 N Winthrop, three blocks south of the Loyola El stop on Sheridan, then two blocks east, is Chicago's major year-round hostel. It's housed in a 1960s building and its location is safe enough, but you're far from the action. The El takes at least 35 minutes to get you to Chicago Ave. A bed in the three- to six-person rooms is $13. Doubles with bathroom are $40. No credit cards.

In the heart of Lincoln Park, *Arlington House* (☎ 773-929-5380), 616 W Arlington Place, one block west of Clark St (Map 6), has an excellent location. Within the classic brick building, your room may be less than ideal if it's one of the basement four-, six- or seven-bed dorms. The hostel is open year-round, 24 hours a day. HI cardholders pay $15 for a bed, others $18. MasterCard, Visa and Diners Club are accepted. Private rooms may be available; ask when you reserve.

It's not quite a cloistered existence, but life at the women-only *Eleanor Residence* (☎ 312-664-8245), 1550 N Dearborn, just south of Lincoln Park (Map 5), is tightly regulated. Single rooms are $40 and include breakfast *and* dinner, making the place an excellent value – if you qualify in the gender department.

Artistic women should take note of the *Three Arts Club of Chicago* (☎ 312-944-6250), 1300 N Dearborn (Map 5). Since 1912 the club has tried to assist emerging women artists by providing inexpensive housing while they study in Chicago. For nine months of the year women students or practicing artists can stay here. During the summer the place goes coed and is a lot less picky about artistic and educational credentials. Nightly/weekly/monthly rates are $40/225/750 and include breakfast and dinner. Summer lovers and other couples can share a room from June to August for somewhat higher rates. Three Arts Club accepts all major credit cards except American Express.

During the summertime the *Chicago Summer Hostel* (☎ 312-327-5350), at 731 S Plymouth Court, one block west of State near the Harrison El station (Map 4), is a good choice that's fairly central in the Printer's Row district, in the South Loop. The 1897 building was one of the first homes of the giant RR Donnelley & Sons printing company. The building was restored in 1986 when the area became gentrified. Typically open from early June to early September, the dorm-style accommodations have two to three beds per room. Rates are $16 for HI cardholders, $19 for everybody else. MasterCard and Visa are accepted. For off-season information, call ☎ 773-753-2270.

The year-round HI-affiliated hostel is the *International House* (☎ 773-753-2270), 1414 E 59th St, a half block west of the 59th St Metra stop, in a 1932 Gothic building on the University of Chicago campus. Among the amenities are tennis courts, a game room, a weight room and a cheap cafeteria that serves meals you can eat in the sunny courtyard. Accommoda-

tions are in single rooms with shared baths. The rate for HI cardholders is $21; all others pay $34.50. They accept MasterCard and Visa. Note that if you don't plan to focus your stay on Hyde Park or the U of C, you'll spend a lot of time on Metra trains to and from the Loop.

B&Bs

Chicago has finally caught on to the bed-and-breakfast concept. *Bed & Breakfast/ Chicago* (☎ 312-951-0085, fax 312-649-9243, PO Box 14088, Chicago, IL 60614) books rooms at more than a hundred places throughout the city, most of them in the Gold Coast, Old Town and Lincoln Park areas. The units run the gamut, from bedrooms in upscale old graystones to whole apartments in elevator buildings where you are left to your own devices. The minimum stay at any of the places is two nights. The service provides you with a list of places based on your desires for price, location and proximity of the owners. Rates for singles and doubles range from about $65 to $150. This is an excellent opportunity to experience life in the more interesting neighborhoods.

Visitors from abroad will be especially welcomed by Sally Baker at the *Gold Coast Guest House* (☎ 312-337-0361), 113 W Elm St, just west of Clark (Map 5). Baker has been steadily refining her 1873 classic three-flat for 10 years. Her experience as a travel guide based in London helps her understand the needs of travelers new to the US or to Chicago. Guests in the inn's four rooms receive a bounteous breakfast and have access to the refrigerator at other times for sodas, beer and snacks. There's a walled-in garden in back that's a pleasant escape from the city. Rates range from $95 to $150.

HOTELS
Loop Area

Loop hotels are convenient to Grant Park, the museums and the central business and financial districts. They are usually no more than a 15-minute walk to River North and N Michigan Ave (and for those

10 Great Hotels
All the following are listed in this chapter.

Best Grand Experience
The Drake, Gold Coast, top end

Best No Expense Spared
Four Seasons, Gold Coast, top end

Best Convention Giant
Sheraton Chicago Hotel and Towers, Near North, top end

Best Family Hotel
Embassy Suites, Near North, middle

Best Pool
Hotel Inter-Continental Chicago, Near North, top end

Best Magnificent Mile Hideaway
The Raphael, Gold Coast, middle

Best Central Cheap Place
Cass Hotel, Near North, budget

Best Place for Loop Business
Westin River North, Near North, top end

Best for Nightlife
City Suites Hotel, Lincoln Park and North

**Best Place to Disappear
and Never Be Found Again**
Hyatt Regency Chicago, Loop Area, top end

---

near the river, much less). But despite several promising signs, such as the development of the theater district, the area is still a few years away from having its own hopping nightlife.

Middle The *Best Western Grant Park Inn* (☎ 312-922-2900, 800-472-6875), at 1100 S Michigan, three blocks from the Roosevelt El stop (Map 4), is not much to look at inside or out. It's got a great view, but the neighborhood is still in transition –

it's not bad, just dead. The hotel is close to the Museum Campus, though, and about a one-mile walk to McCormick Place. At night there's not much going on except at the Chicago police headquarters, a half block away. If you plan on getting in trouble, you'll have a short walk home from the pokey. Rates range between $86 and $155 for a single or double, and there are frequent specials.

Not much better than the Best Western, the *Essex Inn* (☎ 312-939-2800, 800-621-6909), 800 S Michigan (Map 4), is another tatty choice, but the prices aren't bad. Single/double rates start at $89/99.

As architecturally interesting on the inside as it is on the outside, the *Blackstone Hotel* (☎ 312-427-4300, 800-622-6330), 636 S Michigan (Map 4), is just a tad faded from when it hosted presidents and the like. Built in 1910, it is the birthplace of the phrase 'smoke-filled room': in 1920 reporters awaited word from such a chamber that Republican bigwigs had selected Warren Harding as their presidential nominee. The high-ceilinged rooms are simple, and the pricier ones in the front have good views of the lake and Buckingham Fountain. Say hi to the marble statues adorning the lobby. Guests receive muffins for breakfast. For entertainment without leaving the building, the long-running farce *Shear Madness* is in the theater; its jokes are almost as old as the building. Prices at the Blackstone start at $99/109 a single/double.

If you're on a group tour and you're reading this, don't despair if you're booked into the *Ramada Congress* (☎ 312-427-3800, 800-272-6232), 520 S Michigan (Map 4); you can spend lots of hours out of your room. Those not booked at the Congress may not want to penetrate the legions of tour buses stationed outside to find out what a dump it has become. It seems to have been on a downward slide since it opened in 1893. While working on this book I ran into a couple at the Billy Goat Tavern morosely staring into their beers and desperately trying to find *any* other place where they could stay on a fully booked convention weekend. I had to assure them repeatedly that I did not write the guidebook that had steered them there. Rates start at $125/145.

A moderate pick with nice-size rooms and good amenities, the *Hyatt on Printer's Row* (☎ 312-986-1234, 800-233-1234), 500 S Dearborn (Map 4), is the pick of the South Loop litter. On weekends, when the streets are tranquil (read: dead), it's an even better deal. Prairie is an excellent restaurant and a worthy destination in itself. Singles run from $139 to $164, doubles $164 to $189, but on weekends rooms go for $89.

Surrounded by asphalt and hard by the Kennedy Expressway, the *Quality Inn-Downtown* (☎ 312-829-5000, 800-221-2222), 1 S Halsted at Madison near Greek Town (Map 10), has little going for it. Even the guests can be a bit surly, given that this is the hotel where perennially late Amtrak sticks passengers who have missed connections. The hotel's main claim to fame is an event of a few years ago: a local sports figure went nuts in his room and threw everything out the window, including the toilet. Singles range from $79 to $109, doubles from $89 to $129.

The best thing about the *Clarion Executive Plaza* (☎ 312-346-7100), 71 E Wacker (Map 3), is the location right on the river. Rooms in front have excellent views of the North Side. Otherwise, this older hotel is undistinguished. Look for great deals on weekends and times when there are no conventions. Rates range from $106 to $199.

Top End When it was built in 1927, the *Chicago Hilton & Towers* (☎ 312-922-4400, 800-445-8667), 720 S Michigan (Map 4), was the largest hotel in the world, with close to 2000 rooms. A $225-million renovation in the mid-1980s brought that total down to a still huge 1543. Some of the resulting rooms now have two bathrooms, perfect if one member of a party locks him- or herself away for hours of ablutions. The public spaces are exquisitely grand, reaching a crescendo in the gilded ballroom, which is modeled after one at Versailles.

Even if you're not staying here, it's worth a peek. Another prime historical spot is the lobby bar overlooking Michigan Ave at the north end of the block-size building: Chicago police tossed protesters through the plate-glass windows here at the height of the riots during the 1968 Democratic Convention. The only riots today are in Kitty O'Shea's, the faux Irish pub at the south end of the ground floor: people get a $6 tab for one Guinness and scream in horror. Singles range from $145 to $250, doubles from $160 to $265.

Smack in the heart of the LaSalle St financial district is the *Midland Hotel* (☎ 312-332-1200, 800-621-2360), at 172 W Adams (Map 3). It aims to be a European-style hotel, the effort beginning with the black London cab parked outside the door and extending through the understated woodsy lobby. The building was built in 1929, but the rooms are nicely up to date. A distinctly non-European touch is the full American buffet breakfast served to guests every morning. Singles range from $175 to $235, doubles from $190 to $255. A $119-a-night deal is offered most weekends, when the moneyed neighborhood folks have gone home and you expect to find a tumbleweed or two rolling up the street.

Built in 1927, the *Palmer House Hilton* (☎ 312-726-7500, 800-445-8667), on 17 E Monroe on the block bounded by State, Adams and Wabash (Map 3), is the third incarnation of this hotel in 125 years. As in many hotels of its era, the Hilton's 1639 rooms vary greatly in size, so ask for a big one when you check in. Let those too mesmerized by the 21 murals on the lobby ceiling take the dinky, dark rooms. Up one flight on an escalator, the lobby is the stunning feature of the place. In addition to the recently restored ceiling, there's enough gilding to cover several lesser establishments. Duffers take note: the health club has a nifty golf simulator that lets you play the world's great courses without shelling out for green fees. Rooms normally start at $145/170 a single/double, though weekend deals are as low as $99 a night.

RICK GERHARTER

Lazing in the Loop

Tall people like me are thrilled with the extra-long beds at the *Fairmont* (☎ 312-565-8000, 800-527-4727), 200 N Columbus, in the depths of Illinois Center (Map 3). Less lofty-heighted souls will enjoy the spacious rooms, well-equipped work areas, opulent bathrooms and other luxuries provided by this San Francisco-based company. Rooms well up the hotel's 45 stories enjoy excellent views. The public spaces are equally grand, and overall the Fairmont would be among the elite of Chicago hotels if it weren't lost in the otherwise odious Illinois Center. Still, it's convenient to the museums and Grant Park, and they'll comp you at the nearby MetroGolf Illinois Center to lure you in. The Sunday buffet brunch is also excellent. The Fairmont charges $219 to $325 for a double. If you can snare a $129-a-night special on a weekend, you'll have a splendid bargain.

Next to advertising giant Leo Burnett, the *Renaissance Chicago Hotel* (☎ 312-372-7200, 800-468-3571), 1 W Wacker at

State and the river (Map 3), is a modern luxury hotel that's lavish in its decor and amenities. The public spaces are actually much nicer than the somewhat bland exterior would suggest, with ornate tapestries and other elegant touches. The rooms are large and have sitting areas, which will be appreciated by anyone who doesn't want to spend all their time in their room in bed. Bay windows give good views of the skyline and the river. Workaholics should go for the business traveler rooms, which have fax machines, modems and laser printers. The afternoon high tea in the lobby is an excellent and relaxing refuge during the winter. Singles cost $149 to $330, doubles $169 to $350. The hotel offers packages that include tickets to shows in Loop theaters.

A vast convention hotel with 2019 rooms, the *Hyatt Regency Chicago* (☎ 312-565-1234, 800-233-1234), 151 E Wacker, a block west of Michigan (Map 3), is best at being big. The slew of restaurants are okay, and so are the bars. But there's really no reason to seek the place out unless you want to be close to your meeting or you want to collect Hyatt frequent stayer points. They don't even have a pool. The whole joint is linked up to Illinois Center, which may be problem enough. Single/double rates are $209/234. They have lots of specials to keep all those rooms filled in off-peak times.

The *Swissôtel Chicago* (☎ 312-565-0565, 800-654-7263), 323 E Wacker on the eastern frontier of Illinois Center (Map 3), is easy to spot because it is in a striking triangular mirrored-glass high-rise. The 630 rooms are large, with the expected good views from the individual sitting areas. Separate showers and bathtubs mean that one can douse while the other dunks. The casual Cafe Suisse bakes its own bread and pastries, and the Palm is a notable steak house. Anyone wandering through can lay waste to the huge bowl of mini Swiss chocolates on the concierge counter. Singles range from $205 to $225, doubles from $225 to $245. On nonbusy weekends, it's $129 a night.

Near North

North of the river you can't go a block in any direction without finding a hotel. This is the neighborhood to stay in if you want to be near the center of Chicago's tourist action. Eating, drinking, shopping and entertainment are all here.

Budget Make your reservations quick at the *Ohio House Motel* (☎ 312-943-6000), 600 N LaSalle at Ohio (Map 3), before developers turn it into a trendy restaurant. This throwback auto-court motel, with its cement-block detailing, has remained resolutely unchanged since JFK was president. Rooms start at $67/75 a single/double.

Not much to look at inside or outside, the *Cass Hotel* (☎ 312-787-4030, 800-227-7850), 640 N Wabash (Map 3), won't give you much to look at in the bill department either. Rooms are very simple and rather small; in some the TV is on a shelf at an angle hard to see from the beds. The location, however, is excellent. Singles/doubles start at $59/64.

If you ever wondered what it would be like to actually stay on Mediterranean Ave when you play Monopoly, the *Hotel Wacker* (☎ 312-787-1386), 111 W Huron at Clark (Map 3), comes close. Actually, it's probably more like Baltic Ave. Rooms are clean and have TVs and air-con, but you need to leave a deposit for linen and your key. And note: budget motels and American slang notwithstanding, the hotel is named for Charles H Wacker, a great local brewer and preserver of the lakefront. So there. Hotel Wacker charges $42/47.

Straight out of your old family vacation in the minivan (or station wagon, if you have gray hair), the *HoJo Inn* (☎ 312-664-8100, 800-446-4656), 720 N LaSalle, a block south of Chicago Ave (Map 3), has free parking in a lot surrounded by a classic American motel. The only thing missing is a pool with a slide. Rooms cost from $63 to $85.

Middle The best thing about the *Holiday Inn Mart Plaza* (☎ 312-836-5000, 800-465-4329), 350 N Orleans (Map 3), is that when you're inside, you're not on the outside looking in. Located above the 17th floor of the downright hideous Apparel Center, the hotel surrounds a 1970s atrium lobby. Despite the building's prominent but unfortunate spot on the landscape, the views from virtually every room are sensational: south to the Loop, west to Iowa, north to Evanston and east to the Near North and the lake. The location seems out of the way, but it's actually within a five-minute walk of much of bustling River North. Singles range from $139 to $210, doubles from $155 to $226. The place crawls on weekends with bargain shoppers.

Don't be fooled by the fact that the *Courtyard by Marriott Chicago Downtown* (☎ 312-329-2500, 800-321-2211), at 30 E Hubbard at State St (Map 3), is part of a chain known for its moderate prices. This location is at the high end of the moderate range. However, unlike its hulking corporate brother a few blocks away on Michigan Ave, here you get what you pay for. Rooms on the high floors in the fairly new building have excellent views, and all have good work areas for travelers needing to pound away at the laptop. There's also a sun deck, whirlpool and indoor lap pool. Rather than have a couple of pedestrian restaurants in the hotel, management has cut deals with Shaw's Crab House and Tucci Milan, two excellent restaurants across the street, so you can put your meals there on your room account. Accommodations start at $129.

By the time you read this, the *Hampton Inn and Suites* (☎ 312-832-0330), 11 W Illinois at Dearborn (Map 3), should be open in a new building. Its prices and services should be similar to its immediate competitor, the Courtyard by Marriott.

They try harder at the *Best Western River North Hotel* (☎ 312-467-0800, 800-727-0800), 125 W Ohio, across from the Rock & Roll McDonald's (Map 3). The management aggressively markets the architecturally challenged motel as the choice for business travelers on a budget, or in this case no budget. Rooms all have coffee-makers, and some have refrigerators. The hotel charges $99 to $129 for singles, $117 to $141 for doubles.

One of the best values in the neighborhood is the *Best Western Inn of Chicago* (☎ 312-787-3100, 800-557-2378), at 162 E Ohio, a few doors east of Michigan Ave (Map 3). The building is older and the rooms aren't fancy, but you can't beat the location. Its rooms, costing from $79 to $149, are favorites with tour groups, so hold your breath as you pass all the buses idling outside.

Nearly generic, the *Holiday Inn-Chicago City Centre* (☎ 312-787-6100, 800-465-4329), 300 E Ohio (Map 3), is better than many of its namesake brethren, but still unremarkable in most respects. Views aren't bad, and you do get access to a health club in the same complex. Look for deals. The Holiday Inn charges $155 to $200 for singles, $175 to $230 for doubles.

Families can find good value at the *Embassy Suites Chicago* (☎ 312-943-3800, 800-362-2779), 600 N State, between Ohio and Ontario (Map 3). The Chicago outlet for this national chain has all the expected features, including the two-room layout with beds in one room and a sofa bed in the other. The kitchenette has a microwave, which means you can nuke up some sort of popcorn and pizza horror for the kids and then head down to Papagus, the excellent Greek restaurant on the ground floor. Not hungry? Work up an appetite at the indoor pool. There is also a free full – not continental – breakfast served in the lobby each morning. Rooms cost $195/249. Weekend and holiday deals are frequent.

Sometimes the beds fold down from the wall and none of the rooms are striking, but the location and prices of the *Lenox Suites* (☎ 312-337-7217, 800-445-3669), at 616 N Rush between Ohio and Ontario (Map 3), are hard to beat. Some of the suites are barely bigger than one room, but others are fairly sizable. Your free breakfast is delivered to your room. Rates range from $104 to $184 for singles, $114 to $194 for doubles.

Everything's a bit long in the tooth at the *Days Inn Lake Shore Drive* (☎ 312-943-9200, 800-325-2525), 644 N Lake Shore Drive on the inner access road (Map 3). This concrete high-rise was once a Holiday Inn, and the rooms are simple. However, its location away from other high-rises means that the rooms are sunny and the views of either the lake and Navy Pier or the city aren't bad. Low rooms on the Lake Shore Drive side suffer from traffic noise, and it's a hike west to Michigan Ave. Package groups are this place's bread and butter, so look for deals. Prices range from $90 to $189 for singles, $90 to $199 for doubles.

Those accustomed to the ratty roadside outlets of *Motel 6* will be surprised at the budget hotel chain's Chicago offering (☎ 312-787-3580, 800-621-8055), at 162 E Ontario (Map 3). Once a French-style hotel in a building from the 1930s, it has trappings you wouldn't normally expect, such as flowers in the lobby. But loyalists should fear not: any trace of the property's roots has been resolutely eliminated from the utilitarian rooms. Rates begin at $99/109.

Newly renovated, the *Radisson Hotel & Suites* (☎ 312-787-2900, 800-333-3333), 160 E Huron, a half block east of Michigan (Map 3), is an excellent value. There's a small heated pool and sun deck, and many of the rooms have microwaves and refrigerators. The furniture has a vague institutional feel, but it's too new to have any cigarette burns yet. Rates are an excellent $119, although they are scheduled to rise as the hotel begins attracting a clientele.

Top End Formerly the Hotel Nikko, the *Westin River North* (☎ 312-744-1900, 800-228-3000), 320 N Dearborn on the north bank of the river (Map 3), is little changed from its Asian self. The rock garden is still carefully raked each day, and Benkay is still an excellent Japanese restaurant. But fans of the Westin chain now have a viable place to stay in Chicago that is much better than its odious older sibling farther north (see below). Rooms are large, the views are good and the service is splendid. The lobby bar, with its clubby leather seats, is an excellent place to arrange a meeting. Single rates range from $265 to $335, doubles from $290 to $370. Regular weekend rates start at $179.

The best of the monster convention hotels is the *Sheraton Chicago Hotel and Towers* (☎ 312-464-1000, 800-325-3535), 301 E North Water St (Map 3), a bizarre address that means it is just behind the NBC Tower one block west of Michigan Ave along Columbus Drive. All 1206 rooms have excellent views, especially those on the river. The public spaces are vast but have huge plate-glass walls and nice fountains made with black granite. The hotel's lower level is on the bucolic River Esplanade, which runs east from Michigan Ave. The room decorations are typical of corporate hotels: nice but nothing special. Rates start at $175/195. There's usually a plethora of deals.

The *Hotel Inter-Continental Chicago* (☎ 312-944-4100, 800-628-2112), at 505 N Michigan (Map 3), has a split personality. The older portion, on the south side, dates from 1929 and was carefully restored a few years ago. Once a health club for rich men, it holds such classic details as a beautifully mosaicked indoor swimming pool in a setting worthy of William Randolph Hearst. The rooms got the same treatment and are at once elegant and convenient, with all the facilities business travelers expect. Just north, the cheesy aluminum addition had been devoted to the Inter-Con's budget chain. When reserving and checking in, be sure to go for the classic side. Rates range from $189 to $289. Swimmers should note that beyond the decor, the pool is also the largest inside any hotel in the city.

Barring a good deal, there's little reason to opt for the *Chicago Marriott Hotel* (☎ 312-836-0100, 800-228-9290), at 540 N Michigan (Map 3). If you're attending a meeting here, you can stay at several nicer places within a two-block radius. The hotel's outside looks like it was inspired by one of those huge Intourist monstrosities in Moscow; the inside isn't much better, with gloomy public spaces and so-so restaurants. The cracker-box rooms on the high floors have good views, and all rooms have coffeemakers and minibars stocked with $3 candy bars. Although it's only two decades old, the horribly ugly lower section is due

for a massive reconstruction as part of the planned Nordstrom complex. Rooms start at $149/159 a single/double.

One of the nicest properties on Michigan Ave, the *Omni Chicago Hotel* (☎ 312-944-6664, 800-843-6664), 676 N Michigan with the entrance just west on Huron (Map 3), is a modern all-suite hotel high above a retail and office building. The rooms are decked out in rich colors and cherry wood. The living room of each of the 347 units has an excellent work area with a two-line phone – perfect for leaving the boss on hold one while you talk nice-nice to a loved one on the other. There's an indoor pool, whirlpools and an exercise room. Celebrity watchers take note: Michael Jordan's agent is in the building, so keep your eyes open as you pass through the ground-floor elevator lobby. Rates range from $250 to $280, which is good for what you get. Weekend deals are usually about $169, but sometimes are lower.

Gold Coast
Home to many of the city's best hotels, the Gold Coast also has a few moderately priced gems.

Middle The *Raphael Hotel* (☎ 312-943-5000, 800-821-5343), 201 E Delaware (Map 5), is one of several boutique hotels in older buildings in this neighborhood near Water Tower Place. There aren't many amenities in the building itself, but the rooms are spacious, and many also have sitting rooms. There's a continental breakfast in the morning, and you can unwind at night in the quaint little bar downstairs or with the in-room honor bars. The Raphael has a very loyal following. Rates range between $110 and $185. A weekend 'suite' deal is just that: two nights with wine for a total of $240.

Another of the boutique hotels, the *Seneca* (☎ 312-787-8900), 200 E Chestnut (Map 5), is popular with people who want a nice room but don't need all the accouterments of a major hotel. The place has the feel of a well-maintained older apartment complex from the 1920s. Accommodations include voice mail, coffeemakers and refrigerators and range in size from one room to large suites. The published rates go up to $165, but rates of $89/99 are widely available, making the Seneca a splendid bargain.

The *Claridge Hotel* (☎ 312-787-4980, 800-245-1258), 1244 N Dearborn (Map 5), is a nicely renovated neighborhood hotel in the heart of the Gold Coast. Rooms range from tiny to spacious, so inquire carefully when you make your reservation and again at check-in. Parks, the lake and nightlife are all short strolls away. During slack times the Claridge offers many packages. Rooms cost $119 to $185.

Top End A tad less opulent in every way than its corporate sibling, the Four Seasons (see below), the *Ritz-Carlton* (☎ 312-266-1000, 800-621-6906), 160 E Pearson at Michigan Ave (Map 5), is perhaps a tad more discreet. One of the city's finest hotels, it occupies 32 stories above Water Tower Place. The lobby bursts with stunning floral arrangements but is otherwise understated. The large rooms are the embodiment of refinement, with antique armoires and floral prints. The concierges have earned a reputation for being able to conjure up the answer to any guest's demand. The health club is well equipped and includes an indoor pool. The eponymous Dining Room is an excellent French restaurant serving prix fixe and degustation menus, including vegetarian ones. The well-staffed kitchen rises to the challenge of special requests. Singles range from $260 to $295, doubles from $290 to $325.

The *Tremont* (☎ 312-751-1900, 800-621-8133), 100 E Chestnut, a half block west of Michigan Ave (Map 5), is the priciest of the neighborhood boutique hotels. Its rooms are fully wired with fax machines, VCRs, CD players and more. The decor is sort of whimsical European and is fairly bright for an older, somewhat staid building like this one. The clientele leans toward the tasseled-loafer lawyer set, who enjoy the speaker phones in the rooms. Cafe Gordon is an excellent casual restaurant off the lobby and is operated by Gordon Sinclair, progenitor of the famed Gordon restaurant in River North. The Tremont charges $205 to $225, $149 on weekends.

If your name regularly appears in the newspaper in bold type, you are a typical guest of the *Four Seasons Hotel* (☎ 312-280-8800, 800-332-3442), at 120 E Delaware, high above the 900 N Michigan building (Map 5). Regularly considered the best hotel in Chicago, the Four Seasons pampers its guests and firmly believes in the old maxim 'your wish is our command.' For instance, room service will endeavor to rustle up whatever you desire, whether it's on the menu or not, 24 hours a day. Each of the 343 rooms is unique, because the rugs and other decor are all handmade. Needless to say, there's an indoor pool, health club, whirlpool, sauna and just about anything else spa-related short of a mud bath. (On the other hand, if you wanted one . . .) Seasons restaurant serves superb American cuisine in a plush setting. The casual café is good as well. The commodious bar overlooking Michigan Ave is an excellent place to arrange to meet people. The hotel avoids being stuffy through clever touches such as the statue of the man hailing a taxi near the entrance. To be king or queen for a day, you'll pay $305 to $385 a single, $335 to $415 a double.

The *White Hall Hotel* (☎ 312-944-6300, 800-948-4255), 105 E Delaware, just west of Michigan (Map 5), benefited from a complete makeover in 1994. The 221 rooms in the 1920s building have been upgraded to include full PC-compatibility. The hotel has garnered a following of women business travelers who like the terry-cloth robes, hair dryers and makeup mirrors. Kids of any age will enjoy the video games on the TVs. The hotel's most famous regular visitor is media magnate Rupert Murdoch, who made himself at home while he tried to run the *Sun-Times* into the ground during his ownership of the paper in the 1980s. Rates range between $215 and $295. A $199-a-night weekend deal is a better value than it sounds, as it includes free valet parking (worth up to $20) and breakfast.

Let the record show that I've usually had excellent stays at Westin hotels the world over, but I would be hard-pressed to do so at the *Westin Hotel, Chicago* (☎ 312-943-7200, 800-228-3000), 909 N Michigan, with the entrance well east on Delaware (Map 5). This 740-room beast from the 1960s lacks any trace of charm. The run-of-the-mill nature of the place is exemplified by the rooftop swimming pool, which the management never bothers to fill. The rooms are big but usually stare out at another building, making them very dark. Because of the steady stream of groups plodding through, the staff tends to be abruptly expeditious. The parking garage attendants are known to lose cars for hours. To ensure business, management has cut deals with most visiting professional sports teams, leaving the lobby often thronged with groupies. The Westin charges $170 to $210 a single, $200 to $240 a double. Special deals abound – paying anything more than $129 a night is absurd.

Dysfunctional couples will love the *DoubleTree Guest Suites Hotel* (☎ 312-664-1100, 800-222-8733), 198 E Delaware, one block east of Michigan Ave (Map 5), where each room has two TVs, two phones and other amenities in pairs, including the freshly baked chocolate chip cookies. There's only one indoor pool, however. The striking modern lobby is a few notches above the usual hotel entry. The Park Ave Cafe and its casual cousin at street level, Mrs. Park's Tavern, are excellent outlets of the famous parent restaurant in New York. Rates during the week average $250. Bargains abound on weekends, when the corporate clients go home. A typical one offers the rooms for $125.

The grand hotel in Chicago, the *Drake* (☎ 312-787-2200, 800-553-7253), 140 E Walton St at Michigan Ave (Map 5), is ageless. Listed on the National Register of Historic Places, the hotel has hosted the likes of Gloria Swanson, Queen Eliz-

RICK GERHARTER

Dragon at the Drake

abeth, Bill Murray and other glitterati, as well as heavyweight politicians such as Helmut Kohl and Ted Kennedy, since opening in 1920. The hotel has a commanding location at the head of Michigan Ave and is convenient to Oak St Beach, a short stroll through the pedestrian tunnel under Lake Shore Drive. In fact, the Drake is really Chicago's undiscovered beach hotel. Rooms are built like bank vaults, with heavy old doors and marble baths. They are very quiet. The public places are suitably grand and the restaurants and bars many notches above the norm. The Cape Cod Room serves excellent seafood, and the casual Oak Terrace serves excellent Bookbinder soup, which my friend John ate every day for lunch when he worked across the street as an ad executive. Coq d'Or is one of the classiest bars in town and features the truly legendary Buddy Charles on the piano. Rates range from $245 to $325 a single,

$275 to $365 a double. Suites cost more, depending on the level of opulence. I stayed in a superb one once overlooking the beach; only the threat of the bill got me to leave.

The *Sutton Place Hotel* (☎ 312-266-2100, 800-606-8188), 21 E Bellevue at Rush St (Map 5), works hard at staying true to its European roots: it was built as a German-owned Kempinski Hotel in the mid-1980s and then was bought by the French chain Le Meridian in the early 1990s before adopting its rather anonymous name now. Electronics freaks will enjoy the rooms, which all come with CD players, VCRs and stereo TVs. When not exercising your finger on the remotes you can work out at the nearby health club or check in to the 'Aerobics Suite' and feel the burn. The contemporary decor is accented by Robert Mapplethorpe's lush floral photos (the controversial stuff is over at the Museum of Contemporary Art). Rooms cost $235 to $285.

Less famous than its former partner across the street, the *Ambassador West* (☎ 312-787-3700, 800-300-9378), at 1300 N State at Goethe (Map 5), is a good choice if they are running a special. The public areas are meant to evoke an old, woodsy English manor. The rooms are equally traditional, if a bit dark because of the small windows. Rates start at $149/169.

In Hitchcock's *North by Northwest*, Cary Grant gets to hang out at the *Ambassador East* (☎ 312-787-7200, 800-843-6664), 1301 N State (Map 5), with Eva Marie Saint before he meets that crop-duster in the Indiana cornfield. Your stay may lack the same glamour or danger, but you will still be in swank surroundings paced by the famous Pump Room off the lobby (see Places to Eat, Gold Coast). Grand touches abound, from the marble floors to the heavy woodwork. Rooms vary widely in size and style, with some seemingly untouched since Grant and Saint made eye contact. Aim for one of the large, bright ones. By chain affiliation, the hotel has added 'Omni' in front of its name and charges $145 to $185.

Lincoln Park & North

These hotels and inns are often cheaper than the big ones downtown and place you near a lot of the city's best nightlife. Daytime pleasures at the museums and in the Loop and Near North are a short El or bus ride away.

Once a flophouse called the Hotel Lincoln, the *Days Inn Gold Coast* (☎ 312-664-3040, 800-325-2525), 1816 N Clark (Map 6), has been upgraded to the low standards of Days Inn. However, it's clean and the furniture is much younger than you are. The best feature, besides the rate, is the excellent location across from the zoo and in the midst of Old Town. You can easily walk to many of the top destinations on the North Side from here. Rates start at $59 for singles and $69 for doubles.

With 122 rooms near the busy intersection of Clark, Diversey and Broadway, the *Days Inn Lincoln Park North* (☎ 773-525-7010, 800-325-2525), 646 W Diversey (Map 6), is well located and good sized. Otherwise, it's not the most charming hotel, situated in an old retail building above one of the North Side's 4 gazillion coffee bars. The free breakfasts include bagels. The hotel charges $74/84 and up.

A motel with parking! In the city! And it's not a dive! The *Comfort Inn of Lincoln Park* (☎ 773-348-2810), 601 W Diversey (Map 6), east of Clark, is right on enjoyable Diversey Ave and about five minutes' walk from Lincoln Park and the lake. The building was built in 1918 but was modernized in the 1980s to true anonymous Comfort Inn standards. Breakfast is free. Single/double rates range from $73 to $125 for singles, $99 to $175 for doubles. The motel is a good value at the lower end of that scale.

Location, location, location. The *City Suites Hotel* (☎ 773-404-3400), at 933 W Belmont, between Clark and the El (Map 7), definitely has it. You won't go hungry or thirsty or get bored in this stylish little place. Not all the rooms in this older building are suites, but they all have been brightly redone. This is one of my top recommendations in the city; it reminds me of the kind of place and neighborhood where I like to stay when I'm traveling in Europe. The same company, Neighborhood Inns of Chicago, also operates two other North Side hotels. The architectural pick of the trio is the *Surf Hotel* (☎ 773-528-8400), 555 W Surf, west of Broadway near Lincoln Park (Map 7). The very narrow property built in 1925 puts up an ornate terra-cotta facade. The lobby is small; the rooms are big and traditionally decorated. The *Park Brompton Inn* (☎ 773-404-3499), 528 W Brompton, just south of Addison (Map 7), is close to Wrigley Field and the Halsted Ave gay scene. The inside has a bit of a Laura Ashley feel. Rooms at all three hotels start at $76. Suites can often be had for $99.

O'Hare

Hotels near O'Hare International Airport don't offer any price advantage over those downtown, and you're stuck in the suburbs around O'Hare, places that might be nice for raising a family but are hardly of interest to visitors.

The hotels in Rosemont are mostly linked to an enclosed pedestrian walkway leading to the Rosemont Convention Center, a growing collection of buildings hosting trade shows and fairs for collectors of limited-edition plates and the like. If you're stuck at one of these places, you're probably within walking distance of the Rosemont CTA station for the 30-minute ride to downtown.

The airport hotels may come in handy if you have a very early flight. But remember, the same traffic that plagues the expressways around O'Hare will swallow up your hotel shuttle bus; many people instead use the CTA for its five-minute ride to O'Hare from Rosemont. If bad weather hits O'Hare – thunderstorms in the summer, snow in the winter – and you notice more and more flights being canceled, it can't hurt to call one of these hotels fast and secure a room. Otherwise you may end up bedding down in the concourses and be the subject of chirpy TV news reports about 'chaos at O'Hare.'

All the following places, except the first, have free shuttle service to and from O'Hare.

If you want a real airport hotel, you can't get closer than the *O'Hare Hilton* (☎ 773-686-8000, 800-445-8667), which is right in the middle of the airport, across from Terminals 1, 2 and 3. Underground tunnels link up with the terminals, the shuttle tram and the CTA. The rooms are large and soundproofed. There is an indoor pool, a sauna, a whirlpool and an exercise center. The restaurants aren't bad, either – definitely better than what you'll find in the terminals. Rates are $210 a room. Planespotters can enjoy weekend rates for about half that.

Suburban sprawl is embodied at the *Hyatt Regency O'Hare* (☎ 847-696-1234, 800-233-1234), 9300 W Bryn Mawr Ave, Rosemont. This ever expanding property has 1099 rooms, many with views of the expressway or the enclosed parking garage. It's across from the convention center. Rates are $119 on weekdays, $79 on weekends.

The pick of the O'Hare litter is the *Hotel Sofitel* (☎ 847-678-8488), 5550 N River Rd, Rosemont. A member of the friendly French chain of the same name, the hotel has its own bakery for especially flaky croissants and has an excellent Sunday brunch called a 'frunch' (get it?). Rooms are large and amenity filled. The Sofitel charges $180/195 a single/double.

The *O'Hare Marriott* (☎ 773-693-4444, 800-228-9290), 8535 W Higgins Rd, Chicago, is often home to bumped passengers. It's big and has a disco left over from the '70s, but is otherwise of little note. Rooms start at $154/169. On weekends all this and the huge parking lot are yours for $84. Just across the border, back in Rosemont, the *Marriott Suites Chicago O'Hare* (☎ 847-696-4400), 6155 N River, Rosemont, has much bigger rooms in a much newer building, averaging $179 on weekdays, $119 on weekends.

Pop-culture buffs will be keen to stay at the *Wyndham Garden Hotel* (☎ 773-693-5800), 5615 N Cumberland Ave, Chicago. This is where OJ Simpson checked in after his flight from California on the night of his ex-wife's murder. The broken glass and other memorabilia are long gone, as is the name of the place: in 1994 it was the O'Hare Plaza. The biggest question about this rather undistinguished hotel is, Why did OJ opt to stay here in the first place? Rates start at $139, $69 on weekends.

When I was a kid, the thought of a Holidome at a Holiday Inn – with an enclosed swimming pool and amenities such as the ever challenging shuffleboard – was enough to make me want to run away from home. The *Holiday Inn O'Hare International* (☎ 847-671-6350, 800-465-4329), 5440 N River Rd, Rosemont, has a Holidome and a whole bunch of other delights: an outdoor pool, whirlpools, arcade games and more. Best of all, it maintains an ambiance unchanged since my childhood, when Richard Nixon was president. Prices range from $89 to $169.

A favorite dumping ground for airline passengers whom the airlines don't like (nonfrequent flyers on dirt cheap tickets), but who still have to be put up for the night, the *Excel Inn of O'Hare* (☎ 847-803-9400), 2881 Touhy Ave, Elk Grove Village, is a simple motel located in the town that likes to boast that it's America's largest industrial park. Rates start at $57 for a double, more if you opt for interesting amenities such as VCRs and whirlpools.

The sleepy bear comes alive at the *Travelodge Chicago O'Hare* (☎ 847-296-5541, 800-578-7878), 3003 Mannheim Rd, Des Plaines. The aggressive management provides free in-room movies, cable TV, newspapers, coffee and more at the closest cheap hotel to the airport. The place looks like a throwback, but they really do aim to please. Rooms cost $52 to $62.

Elsewhere

Any of the following places should be considered only if you have a compelling reason to stay in their neighborhood.

West Side The *Hyatt at University Village* (☎ 312-243-7200, 800-233-1234), 625 S Ashland at Harrison (Map 10), is in the middle of the vast medical center complex and the University of Illinois at Chicago campus. Rooms are large and rather posh and cost $89 to $165 a single, $99 to $175 a double.

Midway Airport The El provides a fast and reliable link from downtown to the airport, but if you have to stay in this otherwise dull part of town, the closest lodging is the *Days Inn Chicago Midway Airport* (☎ 773-581-0500, 800-329-7466), at 5400 S Cicero, across the street from the main runway. Superlatives are unnecessary and unlikely for this purely functional two-story motel, which charges about $79/85 a single/double.

Hyde Park You won't hear the sound of the lake at the *Ramada Inn Lake Shore* (☎ 773-288-5800, 800-272-6232), a faded former Hilton at 4900 S Lake Shore Drive, on the inner access road. You will hear the sound of traffic. The whole place is in need of a refit, and it's not a good deal at $83 to $95 a single and $93 to $105 a double.

Evanston In another 30 years the *Omni Orrington Hotel* (☎ 847-866-8700), 1710 Orrington Ave, Evanston, will be classically old; now it's just old. But it is very well maintained and has a relaxed traditional feel. The Northwestern University campus begins one block north. Wunderkind Northwestern football coach Gary Barnett is the namesake patron of the lobby café. Rooms cost $165/185; $109 on weekends.

LONG STAYS

Hotels often have very attractive rates for stays of a week or longer, so you can start your hunt for a long-term stay with them. Another source is the Yellow Pages, under 'Apartments': several of the large management companies have placed advertisements of their furnished apartments, geared toward corporate clients.

Residence Inn by Marriott (☎ 312-943-9800, 800-331-3131), 201 E Walton St (Map 5), has apartment-size units available for the day, week or month. They provide breakfast every day, so you won't have to mess up your full kitchen. However, the nightly free drinks in the lobby seem more suited to the sterile suburban corporate neighborhoods where this chain usually operates than the bustling Gold Coast neighborhood just north of Water Tower Place. Rooms in the fairly new building are bigger than a typical hotel room and make good homes for the person stuck on the road. There's even a laundry room where you can wash your dirty duds. Studios, which sleep two people, cost $195 a night and $1,225 a week.

The *Habitat Corporate Suites Network* (☎ 312-902-2090) is run by the Habitat Company, managers of many of the city's upscale high-rises in the Near North. Their units are fully equipped, have cable TV and voice mail, and are in good locations, in buildings with door attendants. One note of caution: unless you want to be in a desolate part of the West Loop, avoid their Presidential Towers property.

Places to Eat

Visitors to Chicago regularly cite its restaurants as the city's top draw, ahead of other virtues such as museums or shopping. And these people aren't dumb. The breadth of dining options is breathtaking. The quality and value at all prices is often remarkable. Some of the most innovative chefs in the US are working in Chicago kitchens.

Best of all, you can have a memorable experience whether you wish to spend $5 or $150. Given its size, the Chicago restaurant industry is ruthless in its competition. Places that coast on their laurels, offer sloppy or indifferent service, charge outlandish prices or commit other crimes soon fade from existence. This competition also ensures that the staff at the restaurants – often just a few years out of college while they wait for their break in a creative pursuit like acting – are superlative in their efforts to satisfy customers. I have rarely encountered a rude or surly person at any of the successful places.

The restaurants in this chapter were selected both for their qualities and their uniqueness. I've tried to eschew chains, except where the local venue is especially notable or has become a major destination in its own right, such as the tourist-mobbed theme joints in River North.

Reservations are always a good idea, although not all places accept them. If you are staying in a hotel with a concierge, ask him or her to make your reservations for you. Concierges can often get you in to full places or secure reservations at places that don't 'officially' accept them.

LOOP

Most Loop eateries are geared toward the lunch crowds of office workers, but given the burgeoning nightlife and residential character of the area, more and more places are catering to diners well into the night. If your desires lean toward fast food, you'll be well served with scores of chain outlets dotting every block. You'll have no trouble finding 'extravalue meals' wherever you wander. However, there are many more choices that are either homegrown, cheap, especially good or all three. These are noted below.

When he opened *Printer's Row* (☎ 312-461-0780), 550 S Dearborn (Map 4), Michael Foley was ahead of two trends: the resurgence of traditional American foods and the revitalization of his Printer's Row neighborhood. That was more than 10 years ago, and the neighborhood no longer seems like a newly gentrified frontier. But Foley's restaurant still provides fresh pairings of primarily Midwestern foods. Venison direct from the woods and fish direct from the rivers are featured nightly. The menu changes with the seasons, but always expect to spend at least $40 a head before drinks for a memorable dinner. Service is at the smoothly professional level one would expect from a restaurant that has matured without losing an ounce of vitality.

A good casual outlet south of the Loop, especially if you're staying at the summer hostel, is *Edwardo's* (☎ 312-939-3366), 521 S Dearborn (Map 4). It serves justifiably famous stuffed spinach pizza, as well as thin-crust models, sandwiches and salads. Everything is fresh and cheap.

Prairie (☎ 312-663-1143), 500 S Dearborn (Map 4), is another long-time trendsetter whose name reveals its celebration of Midwestern food and ingredients. The dining room, in a prominent ground-floor corner of the Hyatt on Printer's Row, has the studied mannerism of Frank Lloyd Wright. The oak chairs are exact replicas of some of Wright's best-known designs. Featured items include Great Lakes denizens such as baby coho salmon and whitefish from Lake Superior. Corn can be found in many dishes, from the chowder to the muffins. Prices will again put you in the drinkless $40-a-head range.

Masters of the Universe are at home at *Everest* (☎ 312-663-8920). A ride up two elevators to the 40th floor of One Financial Plaza, 440 S LaSalle (Map 3), brings one to this temple of power and consumption. Corporate tigers can strut across the leopard-skin-patterned carpet while surveying their next conquest. The views and prices are both spectacular. You expect to find Gordon Gekko holding court in one of the private dining rooms. The food is American and French, with a slant toward the Alsace region, home of chef Jean Joho, who is also chef at Brasserie Jo (see listing in Near North). A seven-course 'degustation' goes for $80 a person.

The sign surrounded by light bulbs is the best feature of the *Artist's Snack Shop* (☎ 312-939-7855), in the Fine Arts Building at 410 S Michigan (Map 4). Otherwise, it's an updated diner with a better-than-usual selection of coffee and beer.

For a taste of Warsaw try the optimistically named *European Sunny Cafe* (☎ 312-663-6020), 304 S Wells (Map 3). Prices are pierogi-size at this simple lunchroom. A plate of homemade stuffed cabbage is only $3.50, and daily specials are even cheaper. The charming owners will cheerfully tell you in heavily accented English about how they fled the old country for Chicago.

You've got to like a place where the menu starts with detailed seven-step instructions on how to properly drink a shot of vodka. (Step 6: Say 'Oh Khorosho!' – 'It feels good!' Step 7: Repeat process in 10 to 15 minutes.) Clearly there's more than tea flowing at *Russian Tea Time* (☎ 312-360-0000), 77 E Adams (Map 3). The czar-worthy menu includes borscht, pelmeni dumplings, beef stroganoff and more. Russian folk songs complete the mood.

History abounds at the *Berghoff* (☎ 312-664-0780), 17 W Adams (Map 3). The building and the restaurant both date from 1898. It was the first place in Chicago to serve a legal drink at the end of Prohibition, and it is the only restaurant in town with its own carpentry shop employing full-time workers who maintain the antique woodwork and furniture. The menu carries

---

10 Great Restaurants
This was tough to do. Only 10! But here goes.

Best Historical Atmosphere
The Berghoff, Loop

Best Pizza
Leona's, Lake View/Wrigleyville

Best Family Italian
Tufano's, Vernon Park Tap, Little Italy

Best Breakfast
Lou Mitchell's, West Side

Best Bargain
Le Bouchon, Damen Ave

Best Inventive Asian
Yoshi's Cafe,
Halsted St in Lake View/Wrigleyville

Best Place to Use Up Your Change Before You Leave
Tecalitlan, West Side

Best Creative Kitchen
Topolobampo, Near North, middle

Best for Groups
Brasserie Jo, Near North, middle

Best Tourist Nightmare with a Huge Gift Shop
Rock & Roll McDonald's, Near North, budget

---

old-world classics such as sauerbraten and schnitzel, but it also features modern treats such as swordfish Caesar salad ($9). The creamed spinach is good for you and just plain good. The waiters are quick and efficient, whether serving the huge crowd of regulars or day-trippers from the 'burbs.

Next door, the *Stand Up Bar* (same phone number as the Berghoff) has changed little in a century, although women have been admitted for the past 30 years. Sandwiches are served from a buffet line at lunch, and frosty mugs of Berghoff beer, direct from the Wisconsin brewery, still line the bar. Look carefully toward the rear for federal judges from the courthouse next door.

RYAN VER BERKMOES
Sketch pad not necessary

A photo of your favorite dead celebrity can probably be found somewhere on the walls at *Miller's Pub* (☎ 312-645-5377), 134 S Wabash just north of Adams, next to the Palmer House (Map 3). This Loop institution has been serving remarkably tender and candy-sweet ribs ($15) for decades. The rest of the menu has the usual salads, burgers and the like. Open past midnight, it draws a post-theater crowd and some office trolls who are burning the midnight oil. Some of the celebrity photos are of people who you only thought were dead. See if you can count how many times Phyllis Diller appears.

It's three restaurants in one at the *Italian Village* (☎ 312-332-7005), 71 W Monroe (Map 3). The namesake *Village* is a bit like a Disney set, with twinkling lights and storefronts evoking the feeling of a southern Italian hill town. Old-style cuisine such as mastacholli with sausage ($14) is served from the very traditional red-sauce menu. The private booths are perfect for two, but you can't reserve them in advance so you'll have to hope your timing is good. *La Cantina* is a casual supper club with regional specialties such as cannelloni ($11.25) and seafood. A few distinctly American steaks make the cut here as well. *Vivere* is at the high end of the village, both in price and cuisine. The interior is a high-concept jumble of baroque design elements. The wine cellar is a high-content assortment of more than 1500 bottles. And the menu is a high-minded interpretation of standards such as veal scaloppine joined by unusual numbers such as bass-filled squid-ink pasta ($16).

Evidence that the nighttime revival of the Loop has begun can be found at *Voila!* (☎ 312-580-9500), across from the Shubert Theatre at 33 W Monroe (Map 3). It was opened by the same people responsible for the wildly good and wildly popular Bistro 110 (see the Gold Coast section), and the menu is drawn from its progenitor. Country French classics are joined by pizzettes and a wide range of salads. Prices are lower than at the original. I'm partial to the grilled marinated skirt steak with horse-radish potato cake ($15). A smoked salmon salad goes for $10, and a classic croque monsieur with frittes is $8.

LaSalle St bankers can try to lower their blood pressure at *Heartwise Express* (☎ 312-419-1329), 10 S LaSalle, although the entrance is off Madison (Map 3). Very slick and with the trappings of a fast-food joint, the menu offers veggie burgers for $3.25 and bags of carrot sticks for 75¢. The fat content of all the foods is listed.

RICK GERHARTER
Step back in time at the Berghoff.

Fast-food Italian with panache is the modus operandi at *Sopraffina* (☎ 312-984-0044), 10 N Dearborn (Map 3). Everything is fresh, including a bevy of salads such as chickpea, wheat berry and portobello mushroom and giardiniera. Sample your choice of three with focaccia for $7. There are also sandwiches, pasta and superthin-crust pizza. You can eat in or take out, but note that Sopraffina is open only until 4 pm. The concept has spread west to a branch in the AT&T Building, 222 W Adams, about two blocks from the Sears Tower.

With an excellent location right on Michigan Ave, *Boudin Bakery* (☎ 312-332-1849), 20 N Michigan (Map 3), serves good sandwiches on San Francisco-style sourdough bread. The veggie version goes for $4.69. Clam chowder is served in hollowed-out round loaves for $4. When you're done with your soup, you eat the bowl. White chocolate chip cookies are $1.35. The outside tables are perfectly situated for people-watching. Another outlet near the Sears Tower (☎ 312-855-1849), 216 W Jackson, is a much better choice than the humdrum places inside that behemoth.

Visit New Orleans without the hassle at *Heaven on Seven* (☎ 312-263-6443), 11 N Wabash on the 7th floor (surprise!) of the Garland Building (Map 3). Jimmy Bannos has carved out a busy empire by faithfully cooking up the classics of the Big Easy. Louisiana shrimp po' boys ($10), jambalaya ($9.75), sweet potato pie ($3.75) and more are served up every lunch hour to mobs of people. One of the most gratifying sights is the vast array of hot sauces lining the walls and tables. To get a seat without joining the besuited minions in line, drop by before 11:45 am or after 1:30 pm, but don't wait all day – they're not open for dinner.

If you're hopping on a Metra train at the Randolph St Station for McCormick Place or Hyde Park, you can grab a great snack at *Jacob Bros Bagels* (☎ 312-368-1181), 58 E Randolph (Map 3). The staffers are notoriously slow and have been known to confuse their own concoction of 'hummus and sprouts' for the unlikely duo of 'ham and sprouts,' so make sure you don't miss your train and you do get the right sandwich. At their location in the Monadnock Building, (☎ 312-922-2245), 53 W Jackson at S Dearborn (Map 3), the bagels are almost as substantial as the 6-foot-thick walls of this historic building, one of Chicago's first skyscrapers. For full rapturous praise of Jacob Bros peerless product, see the entry in the Gold Coast section.

Not picking up the check tonight? Then head to *Palm* (☎ 312-616-1000) in the Swissôtel, on the south side of the river at 323 E Wacker Drive (Map 3). The best lobster you've ever had goes for $18 a pound. Given that these crustaceans average about five pounds, you can see why you'll want to be sitting on your wallet and brimming with thanks at check time. Equally good and equally costly New York strip steaks are also about the best ever. Company accountant lax with expense reports? Have the surf and turf. Mike the bartender is affable, personable and sets the standard for his profession.

NEAR NORTH

The *Sun-Times* once dubbed the River North area 'Eaterville.' The name didn't stick, but it's more appropriate than ever. Literally hundreds of restaurants dot the area, from the river through the Gold Coast. From family-run snack bars to overhyped international theme cafés, from cheap vegetarian to haute cuisine, you can find it all here.

Because of the wealth of Near North choices, the listings in this section are broken into price groups based on the cost of a complete meal without drinks: budget runs less than $15 a person; middle, $15 to $30 a person; top end, $30 and up per person. The host of restaurants dotting Navy Pier are covered in the section on that attraction in Things to See & Do.

Budget

The gregarious old guys playing dollar poker up front (you use dollar bills as the playing cards, betting on the serial numbers) set the tone at *Boston Blackies* (☎ 312-938-8700), 164 E Grand (Map 3). One of the best of the usually excellent Greek-owned coffee shops, it serves up platters of burgers and sandwiches made with top-notch ingredients. The cheddar oozes out like volcanic magma under the chives and bacon bits on the $5 potato skins.

It's 5 am and you're ready for some broiled eggplant with Gorgonzola cheese. Where do you go? The *Cornerstone Cafe* (☎ 312-755-9540), 548 N Wells (Map 3), of course. This 24-hour deli has a menu groaning with unusual salads, sandwiches and Italian specialties for $4 to $7. Eat your meal in the plush dining area while the sun comes up. They also have a small grocery section.

The legend of Chicago-style pizza was started by Ike Sewell on Dec 3, 1943, at *Pizzeria Uno* (☎ 312-321-1000), 29 E Ohio at Wabash (Map 3). The well-worn building has been gussied up to resemble the franchised branches, but the pizza still tastes best here. Piles of cheese and an herb-laced tomato sauce are held by a light, flaky crust. The pizzas take a while, but stick to the pitchers of beer and cheap red wine to kill time, avoiding the salad and other distractions, to save room for the main event. The $11.99 classic lands on the table with a resounding thud and can feed a family of four.

There's a hidden patio with picnic tables in back of *Howard's Bar & Grill* (☎ 312-787-5269), 152 E Ontario (Map 3). The bar is about the narrowest in town. There really is a Howard, and he'll serve your beer in a frosted glass. The $4.75 cheeseburgers and other sandwiches come on paper plates and are served with potato chips. Pretzels are just a request away.

Buy a dog tag and get 25% off your booze at the *Brown Dog Tavern* (☎ 312-645-1255), 531 N Wells (Map 3). That and other gimmicks abound at this clever café cum bar. Sadly, you'll know you're in trendy River North the minute you see the gift stand. There's a range of salads, appetizers and sandwiches averaging $6 to $8. Entrées include comfort foods with an artful touch, such as the $13 wood-grilled buffalo meat loaf. On Fridays it's an all-you-can-eat fish fry for $10.

Like the Hamburgler on a feeding frenzy, the *Rock & Roll McDonald's* (☎ 312-664-7940), 600 N Clark, bounded by Ohio and Ontario (Map 3), has gobbled up its entire block. Inside the ever expanding mansard-roofed burgery is a rollicking museum of rock music from the 1950s and '60s. Album covers, posters and a life-size plaster re-creation of the Beatles' *Abbey Road* album cover are just some of the artifacts on display. The menu holds no surprises, with harried parents carting away plastic trays of Happy Meals by the score. And of course, there's a gift shop for those besotted with the golden arches.

Bijan (☎ 312-944-0445), 663 N State (Map 3), is an eccentric little café that serves French food until 3:15 every morning. The sparse wooden interior isn't much to look at, but this is the place to go for postmidnight plates of escargot ($6.50) and salade niçoise ($8.25). The front opens to the street much of the year, making for excellent people-watching.

Juice will run down your arms at *Mr Beef* (☎ 312-664-5496), 660 N Orleans (Map 3). The $4 Italian beef sandwiches are a local classic, complete with long, spongy white buns that rapidly go soggy after a load of the spicy beef and cooking juices has been ladled on. If you're not ready to ask for hot peppers (giardiniera), don't bother coming. Those not ready to bite into cow will enjoy the recent addition of deli sandwiches, including a roasted red pepper sub for $3.75. Past a sign marked 'Classy Dining Room' you'll find a decidedly unclassy porch with picnic tables and an odd selection of movie posters on the wall. The pictures of Jay Leno aren't fake – he regularly appears and eats two or three beef sandwiches.

Thai Star (☎ 312-951-1196), 660 N State (Map 3), sparked the affordable Thai food rage of the early 1980s. Now its legions of competitors have closed, and it continues to soldier on with excellent and inexpensive food served on plywood tables in a charmless corner location. Palate-scorching curries are the specialty, none costing more than $4.50. Once your eyes are watering, you're less likely to notice the lack of decor.

On crummy days one of the brightest places to eat lunch is amid the palm trees in the atrium winter garden atop Chicago Place. There are burbling fountains and a great view up and down the Magnificent Mile. Cuisine choices are mall food-court standards. The pick of the litter has to be the *Pita Pavilion*, on the 8th floor of Chicago Place, 700 N Michigan (Map 3), where a falafel pita sandwich is $4. Be sure to take the express elevator off Rush St to the top; using the escalators will expose you to depressing shop-free floors.

Big portions and small prices are the hallmark at *Mike's Rainbow Restaurant* (☎ 312-787-4499), 708 N Clark (Map 3). Open 5 am to 1 am every day, this classic Midwestern diner is *the* hot spot for cops and cabbies. Huge breakfasts come with real hash brown potatoes. Omelets start at $3.05. Act enthusiastic and you'll get a shot of ouzo. Now that's the hair of the dog!

The famous pizza at *Gino's East* (☎ 312-988-4200), 160 E Superior (Map 3), somehow tasted better before the concept was franchised in upscale malls from coast to coast. Oh well – if you don't have a local galleria, you'll have a good time here at the original. Every surface, except for the actual food, is covered with graffiti, left by generations of people who cheerfully endured the wait of 45 minutes-plus, first for a table and then for the pizza. The stuffed cheese and sausage pizza is a classic, oozing countless pounds of cheese over its crispy corn-meal crust. It's also a bargain, at $13.99 for a pizza that will feed two very hungry folks.

The best-smelling place in the world to get an espresso has to be *Della Robbia* (☎ 312-943-4059), 711 N State (Map 3). Primarily a flower shop, it sells various coffees and pastries, which you can eat at tables set amid the flamboyant floral displays.

Adorning the ugly orange interior of *Pockets* (☎ 312-664-4808), 75 W Chicago (Map 3), are scores of posters explaining why the doughy chapati bread is not a pita. Whatever they call it, the veggie, turkey and tuna sandwiches made from it are delicious and filling, and the hearty calzones are guaranteed to thwart any hope of a pro-

ductive afternoon back at the office. House dressing for the salads-in-a-loaf is creamy curry. The baked potatoes aren't as great as they might sound.

Although the hard-working journalists at *Business Insurance* magazine, right above, must live with the aromas wafting up all day, don't let guilt stop you from eating at *Giordano's* (☎ 312-951-0747), 730 N Rush, in the Crain Communications building (Map 3). The stuffed-pizza special stuffs two people for $13.50. Each pizza contains sausage, green peppers, mushrooms and onions.

There are no cheeseburgers and no gift store at *Big Bowl* (☎ 312-787-8297), also at 159 W Erie (Map 3). What they do have are big bowls of Asian noodles – an array the size of China. Wheat noodles with shrimp, black beans and snow peas is $9; barbecued chicken and noodles in broth are $8. The food is fresh, hot and different from anything else you've had. This place gets my just-invented four-spoon (out of four) rating.

Middle

Spectators (☎ 312-464-1000), in the Sheraton Chicago Hotel and Towers, 301 E North Water (Map 3), serves snacks, burgers and salads in a relaxed barlike setting. Rarely in Chicago should you bother with a hotel restaurant, but this one is a find, because the hotel's location, on a slight bend in the Chicago River, gives splendid views right out to Lake Michigan through the huge windows.

Politics keeps Americans from easily traveling to Cuba, but you can at least try the cuisine of the huge island at *Havana Cafe Cubano* (☎ 312-595-0101), 230 W Kinzie (Map 3). Run by local restaurant impresarios Roger Greenfield and Ted Kasemir, whose knack for creating trendy spots has left them loaded, the place is Caribbean, complete with wooden slat shutters and slowly twirling fans. The overstuffed chairs in the bar area will swallow you up before you've swallowed your second drink. A *Key Largo* Humphrey Bogart would be right at home here. The food consists of Florida seafood such as conch

Celebrity Restaurants

Chicago's love affair with celebrity restaurants ran its course in the 1980s. At one time, local politicians, DJs, sports figures and Oprah Winfrey all had their own eateries scattered throughout River North. But fading stars, as well as concept restaurants where the food was definitely not the star, spelled doom for most of them. At former Bears football coach Mike Ditka's place, the record crowds shrank with the team's diminishing number of wins, and even the lure of overdone pork chops wouldn't bring them back. The most entertaining fiasco was actor Steven Segal's restaurant, which generated such animosity from its initial customers for its bad food and lousy service that it closed before its grand opening.

There are two survivors of the fad, both of which remain successful because of savvy management and the inherent popularity of their namesakes. *Harry Caray's* (☎ 312-465-9269), 33 W Kinzie at Dearborn (Map 3), serves decent pasta and steaks, as well as its signature chicken Vesuvio; entrées range from $14 to $16. Caray was the long-time announcer for the Chicago Cubs known for his blubbery broadcast-booth antics, which included shouts of 'Holy cow!' when the Cubs did something good (his vocal chords were not taxed). Caray frequented the comfortable sports-bar area of the place whenever the Cubs were in town. He was both charming and very approachable, which endeared him to his legions of fans.

Unless you're a Martian, the continuing popularity of *Michael Jordan's Restaurant* (☎ 312-644-3865), 500 N LaSalle (Map 3), should come as absolutely no surprise. In Chicago, everything he is associated with, including his restaurant, attracts slack-jawed rapturous throngs. The food is based on Jordan's North Carolina upbringing and includes barbecued chicken ($14) and banana pudding. Every kind of clothing imaginable is sold in the gift shop, all of it in Bulls red and black and emblazoned with the number 23.

RAY HILLSTROM

Don't expect to break bread with Mike – he stops by once in a while but hangs out in a private dining room. Watching a Bulls playoff game in the sports bar is a memorable experience: your ears will ring for days from the shouting, and your eyes will see stars from the minicam lights. One cheesy but rather charming aspect of the place is that people driving Chevy Blazers – the gas guzzler Jordan shills for – park free. ■

melded with Cuban flavors. Black beans are liable to turn up anywhere. Entrées run about $10 at lunch, $16 at dinner.

The same owners run the adjoining *Club Creole* (☎ 312-222-0300), 226 W Kinzie, a more casual place whose name should leave no doubt as to the cuisine. There are lots of po' boy sandwiches, including an alligator sausage number for $7.

My favorite fish place in Chicago is *Shaw's Crab House* (☎ 312-527-2722), 21 E Hubbard (Map 3). Vaguely modeled on a Maryland seafood restaurant, the noisy, woodsy dining area wends its way through several rooms. To find out what's best and freshest, ask one of the friendly and efficient servers. They'll steer you to some can't-miss choices. The crab cake appetizer and the key lime pie make good bookends to the meal. The adjoining *Blue Crab Lounge* has oysters on the half-shell in an open and appealing bar area.

The worst thing about *Frontera Grill* (☎ 312-661-1434), 445 N Clark (Map 3), is that once you've eaten here you'll never be able to look at the slop most places pass off as Mexican food again. Chef-owner Rick Bayless has achieved celebrity status with his fresh variations inspired by south-of-the-border fare. His unusual pepper sauces are worth rolling around your palate like a fine wine. Hot tortillas made near the entrance hold tacos al carbón, which are filled with charred beef and grilled green onions. Chiles rellenos await converts to their succulent richness. Part of the reason the place is always mobbed is that you can have an incomparable meal here for less than $20.

Next door, at *Topolobampo* (same phone number as Frontera Grill), Bayless lets his creativity flow unfettered by cost restrictions. Compared to its rollicking neighbor, the mood at Topolobampo is serious as diners sample combinations of flavors most people never knew existed. The menu changes almost nightly; be prepared for a memorable experience.

The extended Ver Berkmoes family was once lured from our usual favorite (see Bistro 110, in the Gold Coast section) to *Brasserie Jo* (☎ 312-595-0800), 59 W Hubbard (Map 3). We were thrilled. This huge, open place serves wonderful food from Alsace, the French region near Germany that is the birthplace of owner Jean Joho. From the signature beer specially brewed by local microbrewery Baderbrau to the hot and fresh baguettes, all the details are right. The choucroute (smoked meats and sausages on sauerkraut) is great, as is the shrimp in a bag. The service is as bright and cheery as the decor.

Chinese food reaches new heights under the inspiration of Rich Melman at *Ben Pao* (☎ 312-222-1888), 52 W Illinois at Dearborn (Map 3). The high-ceilinged, dark interior, with its circular bar, is easily the most chic Asian restaurant in town. The menu has many twists, including five-spice shrimp satay, lemon-crusted chicken and Hong Kong spicy eggplant. Main dishes average $10.

RICK GERHARTER
The legendary Pizzeria Uno

One of the few restaurants on the Mag Mile itself, *Bandera* (☎ 312-644-3524), 535 N Michigan (Map 3), has reasonably priced American classics such as fried chicken platters, meat loaf and grilled fish for $12 to $15. If it's winter, the mound of mashed potatoes served with entrées will insulate you from the foul winds outside. Of course, you could always do what Richard Dreyfus did in *Close Encounters of the Third Kind* and make a sculpture.

Steaks bigger than the plate are the sizable feature at *Erie Cafe* (☎ 312-266-2300), 536 W Erie (Map 3). Housed almost on the north branch of the Chicago River in a renovated meat-packing plant, its menu harks back to the old Stockyards Inn, where the best of Chicago's prime meat was sold. Look for T-bones, filet mignons and lamb chops. A volcanic chicken Vesuvio erupting with garlic adds a touch of Italian. The steak fries will fill any gaps left by the meat, although such a need is unlikely.

One of the original outposts of the London-based chain, the *Hard Rock Cafe* (☎ 312-943-2252), 63 W Ontario (Map 3), opened in 1986. Tourists and suburbanites flock through the doors as fast as the $15 T-shirts fly out of the gift shop. Filled to the rafters with rock and roll memorabilia of varying importance, the two-level café serves a variety of moderately priced burgers, sandwiches and veggie offerings. Through numerous environmental messages adorning the menu, management urges patrons to think green. Cynics, noting the $225 bomber jackets, might suspect that management's green thoughts are more monetary than conservationist. A telling moment came a few years ago, when they chopped down a tree out front to build a bigger sign.

One of the city's original Japanese restaurants, *Hatsuhana* (☎ 312-280-8287), 160 E Ontario (Map 3), continues to excel. The hubbub of the city fades when you walk inside this very simple temple for sushi and sashimi. Natural wood, white walls, lanterns and paintings complement the long sushi bar. The tone is hushed and the food carefully prepared. A deluxe assortment is a good value at $20.

Carson's – The Place for Ribs (☎ 312-280-9200), 612 N Wells (Map 3), is a dream for cardiologists with cash-flow problems. Huge piles of fall-off-the-bone baby-back pork ribs are the specialty at this Chicago classic. The decor is dated, but you'll be gazing at your sauce-covered fingers anyway. Cole slaw, fries and rolls are mere sidelights to the main attraction, which costs $15. Fish swim at the bottom of the menu; leave them there.

The latest big-concept, big-event eatery/gift store/theme park is *Rainforest Cafe* (☎ 312-787-1501), 605 N Clark (Map 3). Built on the rubble of the defunct 'Capone's Chicago,' an unspeakable homage to the speakeasy, this 'café' takes the mall underpinnings of the theme-restaurant craze to new highs – or lows. Keep the following quote from one of its managers in mind as you enter: 'The restaurant drives traffic and the retail drives revenue.' That revenue comes from potions, lotions, T-shirts, stuffed vanishing species and more, all of it somehow linked to the concept of an endangered ecosystem as a marketing concept. Through shopping? The menu items include the pancontinental 'Rainforest Pita Quesadillas' and the 'Monkey Business,' coconut bread pudding that the menu says 'will make you go ape!' Robot animals prowl the plaster boulders, and every 20 minutes there's an electrical storm amid the fake trees. A family of four can easily drop $100 here. Donations to groups actually working to save rain forests are extra.

The battle for the suburban prepubescent dollar is a tough one in River North, and there's nobody tougher than the actress/waitresses at *Ed Debevic's* (☎ 312-664-1707), 640 N Wells (Map 3). It's hard to believe that 10 years ago this was a Rich Melman place that received rave reviews for its reborn American comfort food. Long since sold to people prepared to milk the concept for every dollar, it has become a parody of a place that was a parody of a 1950s diner. The quip-snorting waitresses don't seem to have quite the same sense of fun anymore either. The menu is as long as the runs in their nylons, with cheap burgers, chili, grilled cheese sandwiches and stalwarts such as meat loaf.

The 40-foot billboard exterior hints that you've found *Planet Hollywood* (☎ 312-266-7827), 633 N Wells (Map 3). Inside, banks of TVs blare trailers for future feature films. Here and there are artifacts from movies, and the fact that the first ones you see are from *Teenage Mutant Ninja Turtles* and *Mighty Morphin Power Rangers* should give you a clue as to who the target customers are. Somewhere deeper in this café cum carnival lurks detritus from *Batman*, *Waterworld* and other big-budget spectacles. Don't look for investors Arnold Schwarzenegger or Sylvester Stallone – they're busy opening a new outlet in Tashkent or someplace. As for the food, much of the buzz about the menu stems from the $6.50 chicken fingers breaded in ground-up Cap'n Crunch cereal. What's next? Fruit Loop fajitas?

On the spot of Oprah Winfrey's defunct 'Eccentric,' *Wildfire* (☎ 312-787-9000), 159 W Erie (Map 3), has taken off like its name by cooking with fire. A huge grill, rotisserie and wood-burning oven roast shrimp, prime rib, steak and ribs. Portions are generous, and prices hover in the $16 range – not bad for this comfortable and welcoming place. Hot fudge figures in several of the desserts, which, coupled with the long lines of folks who hang around outside, reading the blackboards listing the specials, prompts the thought, Does anyone miss Oprah's tiny, artful portions of nouvelle cuisine?

On the corner of the Embassy Suites, *Papagus* (☎ 312-642-8450), 620 N State (Map 3), is an excellent variation on standard Greek fare. Old faves such as taramasalata (cod roe spread), spanakopita (spinach and feta cheese in phyllo) and saganaki (the flaming cheese of 'Opaa!' fame) breathe new life thanks to the fresh touch in the kitchen. Prices are moderate, service is excellent and the whole place is like a *House Beautiful* version of a Grecian taverna.

Loop Cajun and Creole classic *Heaven on Seven* has opened a much more stylish and fancy outlet in the 600 N Michigan building, with the entrance at 600 N Rush at Ohio (☎ 312-280-7774, Map 3). For food details, see the Loop section. Otherwise, the difference here is that it is open for dinner and the prices are a bit higher. The decor is hot: one wall is nothing but colorful bottles of Louisiana hot pepper sauces.

At *Tuttaposto* (☎ 312-943-6262), 646 N Franklin, under the El tracks (Map 3), the bright flavors from around the Mediterranean are set off by the bright tile mosaics glinting under the sunlike lamps. Chef-owner Tony Mantuano performs magic in the open kitchen, which is ringed by special seats for those who want to watch the show. The changing menu combines elements from Spain, Greece, France and Turkey. Prices are modest for the experience: entrées hang in the $14 area. Early each Sunday evening, kids eat free.

The smell of baking baguettes hits you on the way into *Mango* (☎ 312-337-5440), 712 N Clark (Map 3). An American bistro with a European accent, it serves food as fresh and lively as its name suggests. Chef Steven Chiappetti features seafood such as shrimp along with meats like duck and pork. Mangos show up throughout the ever changing menu, sometimes as part of a duck prosciutto, other times as part of a dessert flan. Everything is prepared with care and is stylishly presented. Entrées rarely top $15, making a meal here an excellent value.

Can't get to one of those rustic supper clubs in the woods of Wisconsin this trip? Don't bother – *Blackhawk Lodge* (☎ 312-280-4080), 41 E Superior (Map 3), is prettier and has much better food. The hickory smoke wafting from the kitchen as you walk in tells you that good things are in store. Smoky corn chowder is a signature item; other choices vary with the season. I always enjoy the smoked trout as a starter. This is another good-value place for the quality – you can flee for $30 a head, not including drinks. And speaking of drinks, try the microbrew sampler.

Chef Barry Bursak is known for his creative use of organic foods. His latest creation in Chicago's food constellation is *Earth* (☎ 312-335-5475), 738 N Wells (Map 3). A favorite among the diverse appetizers and entrées is the house salad of nuts, legumes, sprouts and veggies on a mound of greens. Topped with a garlicky dressing, it is the antidote to your dietary sins. Prices run from $9 to $20. Grilled veggie skewers with brown rice and tofu curries are $15. In the morning they have organic juices and baked goods to go.

It looks hokey outside and it definitely is inside – plus it's a chain from Florida – but the *Crab House* (☎ 312-664-2722), 745 N Wells (Map 3), has one important quality: piles of well-prepared, fresh seafood priced cheap. The seafood and salad bar is bounteous and features lots of shrimp and other fishies. You can make a whale of yourself at this no-limits feast for $10 at lunch and $19 at dinner.

Happy diners look like kids in a candy store as they ponder their little plates of tapas at *Cafe Iberico* (☎ 312-573-1510), 739 N LaSalle (Map 3). Among the choices: salpicon de marisco (seafood salad with shrimp, octopus and squid, $4.75), croquetas de pollo (chicken and ham puffs with garlic sauce, $4) and vieiras a la plancha (grilled scallops with saffron, $4.75). Finish it off with flan. The large wine list has several $16 Riojas. The sherries run the gamut, from dry to rich cream. Tables sprawl through several tiled rooms.

Quirky and different – that's the *Paradigm Kafeteria* (☎ 312-337-2305), 735 N Clark (Map 3). The atmosphere is a cross between a coffeehouse and a bar, and

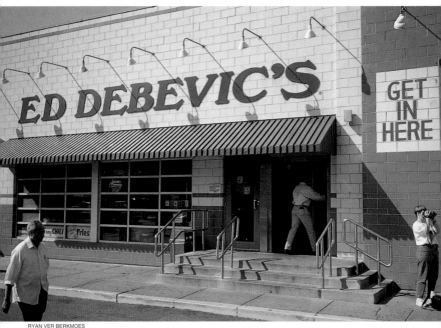

RYAN VER BERKMOES

Ed Debevic's still draws 'em in.

the menu is a cross between Asian and Mediterranean. Pot stickers share appetizer billing with bruschetta, and entrée linguine with clams costars with pad Thai. There also are steaks and sandwiches. Prices are reasonable. The help is prone to 'Hey man' as a salutation.

Top End

That *Gene and Georgetti* (☎ 312-527-3718), 500 N Franklin (Map 3), is Frank Sinatra's favorite restaurant in the Windy City should tell you everything you need to know about this half-century-old steak house. Old-timers, politicos and crusty regulars are seated downstairs. New-timers, conventioneers and – eek! – tourists are seated upstairs. The steaks are the same on both levels: thick, well aged and well priced. Out of place in the city, the old wooden building looks like it would be

more comfortable on a two-lane road in some farm town. Wear a pinky ring (this advice is for men) and act like a big shot and you may get better service. On the other hand, you might get mistaken for an alderman and served with a subpoena.

The biggest problem with *Spago* (☎ 312-527-3700), 520 N Dearborn (Map 3), is that, like so many other trendy places in River North, it isn't unique to Chicago. Nevertheless, the local edition of celebrity chef Wolfgang Puck's Hollywood original is thronged with the glitterati every night. The entrées are as pricey as the coifs on the patrons' heads. Food is from the fusion palette, which blends techniques and cuisines from every continent and has been trendy for a few years. Here, Asian food joins forces with European. Perhaps the most obvious element lacking here are the hordes of paparazzi who plague the entrance of the original. Bring your camera and provide your own flashes. The adjoining Spago Grill is toned down in atmosphere and prices. This the Grill is where you go for Puck's signature duck-sausage pizza.

For more than 20 years Gordon Sinclair has run one of Chicago's most original restaurants. Beginning at a time when most of the wine-drinking in the neighborhood was done from screw-cap bottles, *Gordon* (☎ 312-467-9780), 500 N Clark (Map 3), has set the pace for adventuresome eating for discerning diners. His chef alumni have gone on to open some of the best restaurants in town. This turnover in the kitchen has helped Gordon stay ahead of the times. Present chef Don Yamauchi excels at unusual combinations on the constantly changing menu. Diners in the know order the $59 five-course tasting menu to fully sample the kitchen's efforts. Desserts are memorable.

Direct from Milan, *Bice* (☎ 312-664-1474), 158 E Ontario (Map 3), provides an excellent chance to savor the delicately spiced foods of Northern Italy without the jet lag. Risottos are superb, as are the creamy pastas. Expect to pay $20 or more for an entrée. There's good people-watching from the outdoor tables. Make the rabble jealous by letting your tongue linger on the house-made gelato.

Veal is the specialty at *Avanzare* (☎ 312-337-8056), 161 E Huron (Map 3), a swank and cosmopolitan Italian nightspot in a contemporary building with high ceilings. The chefs are known for their light and artful touches with meals that begin with good crusty bread you can dip in exquisite herb-flavored olive oil. A perennial favorite and a dish that launched the restaurant's reputation is the tortellini with smoked chicken. Prices are not cheap: the signature veal chops are $26.25, and salmon over corn polenta is $22.50. Finish things off with the homemade gelati. Service is smooth and anticipatory. On nice days the outdoor café serves lunch with a lighter, cheaper menu in a pleasant, shrubbed setting.

Part of the Rosebud empire that started on Taylor St (see the Little Italy section), *Rosebud on Rush* (☎ 312-266-6444), 720 N Rush (Map 3), serves huge portions of familiar Italian standards. The prices and quality are both high. Veal in many forms is a specialty, with all the dishes priced at $20. You'll be unlikely to find enough energy to sing 'Chicago' as you and a companion attempt to plow your way through the 'Sinatra Abbondanza,' a massive $49 meal for two that seems to include half the menu.

GOLD COAST

Loads of restaurants crowd the streets of this affluent neighborhood, which is the first primarily residential neighborhood on the North Side as you head away from the Loop. Although some of the city's toniest addresses are here, many of the eateries and bars are still living off the area's nightlife reputation of 20 years ago. Beware. However, as the Gold Coast becomes less of a destination and more of an inwardly focused neighborhood, restaurants are springing up to serve its upscale denizens.

My mother's favorite restaurant in town is *Bistro 110* (☎ 312-266-3110), 110 E Pearson (Map 5). (In fact, my whole family likes the place.) Every time she goes to Chicago she wants to try a new place but is

RAY HILLSTROM
The Gold Coast skyline shelters many an eatery.

usually drawn back to this bright and bustling brasserie across from the Water Tower. She's got good reason. Shortly after you sit down you're given a sliced baguette, accompanied by roasted heads of garlic to spread on it. The roasted vegetable plate is heavily herbed and has surprises such as wild mushrooms – it's a big hit with my vegetarian sister. Dad likes the spicy pepper steak with frites. As for dessert, it's hard to tell who moans with delight more loudly between mouthfuls of the crème brûlée: me, or my wife. Entrées average about $13, a good price for the experience.

My wife, Sara, started every morning for four years with a whole-wheat honey-nut bagel from *Jacob Bros Bagels* (☎ 312-664-0026), 50 E Chicago, in the St Benedict Flats (Map 5). More than a few times she went back for lunch, often a sandwich on a 'celebrity bagel of the month,' such as sundried tomato or olive oil and fresh herbs. They refuse to toast their perfect, crispy on the outside, chewy on the inside creations at Jacob Bros, but they are happy to slather them with walnut-raisin or veggie cream cheese. Warning: if you happen by when a cinnamon-raisin batch emerges from the oven, resistance is futile.

The best $7 sundae you've ever had awaits at the *Ghirardelli Soda Fountain* (☎ 312-337-9330), 830 N Michigan (Map 5), an address that holds as much substance as the marshmallow topping, since the place is really several doors west of Michigan, on the less tony Pearson. The San Francisco-based chocolate company serves a calorie-counter's nightmare of elaborate and very good ice-cream creations in an 1890s marble and wood setting. The hot chocolate will chase away any winter chills pronto.

On sunny, warm days you'll be hard pressed to find a better lunch venue than *M-Cafe* (☎ 312-280-2660), 220 E Chicago in the Museum of Contemporary Art (Map 5). The patio of this eatery at the back of the new museum overlooks Lake Michigan. The food is upscale deli drawn from cuisines worldwide. A rotating selection of sandwiches, salads, soups and more is prepared by chefs from throughout Chicago.

It's worth penetrating *Foodlife* (☎ 312-335-3663), 835 N Michigan (Map 5), on the Mezzanine level of Water Tower Place. On the way in, pick up a magnetic card and have the staff reserve you a table. Then wander around and choose items from the stir fry, Mediterranean, Mexican, salad or rotisserie bars. Unfortunately, most portions are too large to sample lots of different cuisines. Your meal gets tallied up on the card, and you pay on the way out – probably more than you expected, because of the above-average prices and the service charge for the deserving, cheerful staff – but Foodlife is still a fun shopping break.

Not to be too extreme, but much of what's wrong with America can be found at the *Cheesecake Factory* (☎ 312-280-4080), 875 N Michigan, on the lower level in front of the Hancock Center (Map 5). Not that the food isn't any good – it is. And not that the prices are too high – they're not. But the entire place is dedicated to overindulgence on a Brobdingnagian scale. Here's a quote from one of its chirpy PR reps: 'Research shows that the average person can only eat two chicken breasts, that's why we serve three!' Conspicuous consumption aside, the food, including items such as the breast-laden Caesar chicken salad ($9), are all high quality. Topping off the excess, there are 40 cheesecakes to choose from. After the meal you may need a hoist to make it back up to street level.

The prices are predictably as high as the setting at the *Signature Room at the 95th* (☎ 312-787-9596), 875 N Michigan, near the top of the John Hancock Center (Map 5). (No points for guessing the correct floor.) For a place where diners spend more time looking out the windows than looking at their plates, the food is quite good. A steady procession of top-notch chefs through the kitchen ensures that you won't leave disappointed. Look for gourmet fare artfully presented. The Sunday brunch is a memorable event for families. But remember, the prices don't diminish when the weather diminishes the view, so pick your day carefully.

At the 900 N Michigan mall (Map 5) *Boudin Bakery* (☎ 312-649-3570), tucked away on the 5th level of the mall, makes for a good break from shopping. They also do their food to go for picnics at nearby Oak St Beach. The concept of a 1950s diner is getting a bit time-worn, but folks rave about the burgers at *Johnny Rockets* (☎ 312-337-3900), 901 N Rush, on the back side of the huge mall. The kitchen, eating area and servers are all clad in white. Kids like it, and it's not ridiculously expensive.

Lo-Cal Zone (☎ 312-943-9060), 912 N Rush (Map 5), is a veggie and budget haven in the midst of the Gold Coast's ritziest shopping. Situated in a tiny, tatty building that will last only until the next real estate speculator happens by, it offers twists on its namesake calzones, as well as veggie burgers, funky burritos (try the Cajun with turkey sausage and red beans and rice) and the creamiest, chocolatiest frozen yogurt anywhere.

Got a movie deal to close? *The 3rd Coast* (☎ 312-664-7225), 29 E Delaware, where Wabash runs out of steam (Map 5), is buzzing morning, noon and night. The people-watching from the sidewalk tables is so good that people pile on the layers to extend the season into November. Hip, trendy and stylish, the café serves up all the expected coffees, teas, scones and such. Reading material abounds. You'll fit right in with a copy of *Variety* and shades – especially at night. A second Gold Coast location (☎ 312-649-0730), 1260 N Dearborn, doesn't quite have the same cachet but is more relaxed.

Open 24 hours a day, *Tempo* (☎ 312-943-4373), 1 E Chestnut (Map 5), is good around the clock. Omelets, BLTs, soups, salads and more are moderately priced and above average in taste. The white interior borders on the stylish, definitely a few cuts above the usual all-night coffee shop.

Widely regarded as the best steak house in a town with a lot of competition, *Morton's* (☎ 312-266-4820), 1050 N State (Map 5), in the lower level of the Newberry Plaza high-rise, makes no compromises in its quest for the title. The meat is aged to perfection and displayed tableside before cooking. See that half a cow? It's the 48-oz

double porterhouse. Smaller but still quite dangerous if dropped on your toe are the filets, strip steaks and other cuts. The baked potatoes could be used in church foundations. The hash browns are superb versions of a side dish all too often ignored. The ambiance is clubby. This is the original location that sparked the famous sibling in Beverly Hills, scene of a thousand deals.

Three restaurants in a row serve the 30- and 40-something singles who live in the neighborhood. *PJ Clarke's* (☎ 312-664-1650), 1204 N State (Map 5), is named after the classic Third Ave bar in New York City. That's where the resemblance ends. It's not a bad place, and the burgers are quite good, but don't expect to make a lot of eye contact here – everybody's watching everyone else. After all, the grass is always greener . . .

Once people have made their match, they can go next door for their first date. *Yvette* (☎ 312-280-1700), 1206 N State (Map 5), has a jazzy piano player and a dance trio playing on weekends. Prices are high, even for the competent French bistro food.

Married? Third time? Doesn't matter. *St Germaine Bakery & Cafe* (☎ 312-266-9900), 1210 N State (Map 5), is the most relaxed of this troika, serving casual French café food such as quiche and onion soup for prices that won't hurt your alimony payments. The weekend brunch is the best in the neighborhood and costs a mere $10. This is where you go when the Sunday paper is proving increasingly more interesting than your partner.

Book yourself into Booth One at the legendary *Pump Room* (☎ 312-266-0360), 1301 N State, and you will have something in common with the pantheon of celebrity customers whose photos line the walls. Famous since the 1940s, this elegant restaurant in the Ambassador East Hotel continues its tradition of understated elegance. The food is American, with prime rib and roast duck the features. Real VIPs, or just lucky poseurs, sit in Booth One, a see-and-be-seen throwback to a previous, glamorous era. There's a dress code, but you won't need to loosen your tie for the cheek-to-cheek dancing most nights after dinner.

OLD TOWN

Trendy in the '70s, Old Town fell on hard times in the '80s as trends moved elsewhere. In the '90s the pleasant neighborhood centered on Wells St north of Division has stabilized and is home to a nice assortment of enjoyable eateries, some old, some new. It's a decent stroll or a $4 cab ride from River North.

One of the hottest eateries in Old Town is *¡Salpicón!* (☎ 312-988-7811), at 1252 N Wells (Map 6), which the linguistically aware will immediately recognize as a Mexican restaurant. Don't bother coming here if all you want is the Holy Trinity of T's – tacos, tostadas and tamales – this menu is several orders of magnitude away in creativity. Ceviche (raw fish marinated in lime juice) starts at $6.50 and includes versions made with lobster. Chiles rellenos (stuffed poblanos that are batter-fried) have been raised to an art and go for $13. Other items include some lovely marinated steaks and grilled shrimp in garlic. The building

has high ceilings and bold colors. Create your own bright colors in your head by trying some of the 60 tequilas, including some rare oak-barrel-aged numbers.

The *Fireplace Inn* (☎ 312-664-5264), 1448 N Wells (Map 6), has been serving up Chicago-style baby-back ribs (full slab, $16.50) for 30 years. Steaks, burgers and seafood round out the menu. The steak fries are perfectly crisp on the outside and tender on the inside. Blue-cheese lovers will want to spring for the extra 75¢ for that dressing on the side salad. The two-level dining room is heavy with wood – almost as much as the namesake fireplace burns up in a night. When the snow is blowing off the lake and the sidewalks are piling up with drifts, you can warm your cockles here.

The antipasto table is an olive-oil lover's delight at *Topo Gigio* (☎ 312-266-9355), 1516 N Wells (Map 6). Roasted peppers and grilled zucchini are just some of the treats that await at this faithful adaptation of a Roman trattoria. The linguini Cinque

RICK GERHARTER

Take a post-meal stroll in Old Town and admire the details.

Terre isn't just named for one of my favorite regions of Italy, it's also well priced ($13) when you consider the mound of shrimp that comes with it. This is an excellent choice for a relaxing evening of delicious, moderately priced Italian food.

On a warm day you can smell *O'Briens* (☎ 312-787-3131), 1528 N Wells (Map 6), before you see it. Clouds of cigar smoke waft away from the sizable outdoor garden at this Old Town institution. Whether that lures you in depends on your view of cigars. O'Briens' upscale

RICK GERHARTER
The view from Lincoln Park

clientele puffs away on hand-rolled specials that have prices measured in dollars rather than cents. The interior, which thankfully boasts high-powered ventilation, is dark and clubby. The food is old-boy American: steaks, chops and prime rib. This is the kind of place that trumpets its $16.25 'liver O'Brien.' The faces behind the cigars frequently belong to aging politicos reliving their days in smoke-filled rooms.

Pizza, ribs, Italian beef sandwiches and more may taste good, but eventually the traveler needs a break from the calorie-laden delights. Recharge your body with the 'kitchen sink' at *Fresh Choice* (☎ 312-664-7065), 1534 N Wells (Map 6): a glass of the fresh-squeezed juices of carrots, beets, celery, cucumbers, spinach and parsley. A 12-oz shot goes for $4 and is probably the healthiest thing you'll ingest in Chicago. Purists can choose less complex combinations and add forkable roughage to their diets at the salad bar.

My brother-in-law Danny, ace bartender and all-around great guy, swears by the baby-back ribs at *Twin Anchors* (☎ 312-266-1616), 1655 N Sedgwick, four blocks west of Wells (Map 6), and you will too. They don't take reservations, so you'll have to wait outside or around the neon-lit 1950s bar. The ambiance is like a supper club from that decade and is authentic right down to the almost all-Sinatra jukebox. Actually, the restaurant is even older, having opened in 1932. The meat ($17) drops from the ribs as you lift them. Choose from fries, onion rings and baked

potatoes for sides. The wait can be really long, so think about dropping by midweek.

There are many choices west of Old Town proper around the Halsted and North Ave intersection and the North/Clybourn El stop. *Bub City Crabshack & Bar-B-Q* (☎ 312-266-1200), 901 W Weed (Map 6), is perhaps the most popular. The ribs are good, and everybody is encouraged to make a big mess while going a little nuts. Live country music contributes to the cacophony most nights. Kids get to create their own cacophony on Sunday nights in their own supervised room.

LINCOLN PARK

Chicago's most pleasant and popular neighborhood is teeming with restaurants. A stroll down any of the commercial streets will yield a bounty of choices. The Fullerton El stop will put you within a 20-minute stroll of most of the places listed here. Cruising cabs are plentiful, parking is frightful and the streets are generally safe. See the Entertainment chapter for clubs and bars for post-meal joy.

Halsted St

Blue Mesa (☎ 312-944-5990), 1729 N Halsted (Map 6), has excellent southwestern cuisine at moderate prices. Much of the food has its roots in the corn-based dishes of Native Americans. The seemingly unnatural blue corn chips are a switch from the usual yellow ones. Several items made from this traditional blue grain dot the menu. The front-room fireplace burns real wood and is built in the motif traditionally used by Southwestern Indians for their ceremonial meeting spots. Slather your food with the smoldering New Mexican red chili sauce and you'll think the hot coals are in your mouth instead of the hearth. The Sunday brunch makes good use of the blue corn in muffins and features some really zingy omelets.

The name *King Crab* (☎ 312-280-8990), 1816 N Halsted (Map 6), says it all. The prices and the sartorial demands on the customers are modest. The portions of seafood are generous. Grilled prawns are $14, a half-dozen raw oysters are $5 and the blackened tuna is $15. The eponymous entrée is always available but is market priced, depending on how the big guys were clawing out in the Pacific.

A gathering spot for beautiful people who are too young for their first face lift, *Tilli's* (☎ 773-325-0044), 1952 N Halsted (Map 6), is jammed on weekends with yuppies whose growing salaries far outpace their ages. Actually, things are quite casual in this vast and noisy place, where the art of air-kissing is still being perfected. The menu bounces from Italy to Asia, with food such as goat-cheese pizza by the slice and chicken satay. Prices are moderate, which means you can keep saving for that first Chanel suit.

Chapulin (☎ 773-665-8677), 1962 N Halsted (Map 6), claims that its recipe for mole sauce comes from 'the Puebla nuns.' There's no word on who the nuns are or where they may be, but the thick and chocolatey sauce is certainly a good testament to these women. A version with chicken and poblano peppers is $12. Molotes de Tinga, homemade corn turnovers, are $5. The rest of the menu is equally interesting, and the dining room is bright and plant filled.

If you plan on kissing anyone after dinner at *Cafe Ba-Ba-Reeba!* (☎ 773-935-5000), 2024 N Halsted (Map 6), make certain they've dined with you. The garlic-laced sauces are worth licking the dishes for at this rambling, multiroomed tapas bar. The lineup of small plates of food would do the best bar in Madrid proud. The menu changes daily but always includes some spicy meats, marinated fish and a potato salad that will forever have you lambasting the gloppy American version. Prices are about $5 a plate. If you want a main event, order one of the nine paellas ($10 a person) when you get seated – they take a while to prepare.

Chef Ron Blazek's imagination is on full display at *Relish* (☎ 773-868-9034), 2044 N Halsted (Map 6). His unusual interpretations of American classics change with the seasons but can include entrées such as roasted duck breast with pea-sprout slaw. Prices reflect the care in the kitchen, averaging in the high teens for main courses. The deprived or the depraved will be intrigued by the 'very chocolate orgasm' for dessert. You may want extra napkins with this one. If the weather is nice, head out back to the secret garden, with its comfy wooden chairs; otherwise, enjoy the kaleidoscope of artwork inside.

Cleanse your previous night's sins with the oat-bran pancakes at *Nookies, too* (☎ 773-327-1400), 2114 N Halsted (Map 6). A full complement of eggs, waffles and sandwiches rounds out the choices at this popular brunch spot, which is open 24 hours on Friday and Saturday. The fresh-squeezed orange juice is pricey but worth it if your taste buds are already awake.

The pizzas fly out the door at *O'Famé* (☎ 773-929-5111), 750 W Webster, one door west of Halsted (Map 6). It's a booming carry-out and delivery business, but you can choose to enjoy one of these gourmet treats while seated inside. The usual ingredients are joined by basil and roasted red peppers, among others. A large thin-crust pizza runs about $12. Sandwiches, salads and pasta are other popular selections. You can get picnic versions of anything from the gleaming white-tile deli area to enjoy across the street at Oz Park.

Armitage Ave

Armitage west of Halsted to Sheffield is a wonderful microcosm of the North Side; casual eateries and ice-cream shops coexist with bars, funky shops and one of the finest restaurants in the world. CTA Brown Line trains stop at the Armitage station, right in

Charlie Trotter's

I was standing on Armitage Ave, admiring the grape leaves growing over the arbors next to the entrance to Charlie Trotter's Restaurant (☎ 773-248-6228), 816 W Armitage (Map 6). One of the valet parkers appeared at my elbow and asked me if I would like a menu. 'Sure,' I said. A short time later, the valet returned with a creamy sheet of paper listing the night's lineup. 'Please,' he said with a gentle and sincere smile, 'enjoy your evening.'

There I was, a grubby guidebook writer lurking on a sidewalk, when a valet anticipated my needs and sought out what I desired. There was no sign that I had or would ever have the means to part with the average of $125 a head needed to spend an evening in the rarefied air within. And yet there I was, menu in hand, departing with a big smile on my face.

Making people smile, that's the goal of the 30-something Trotter, who modestly says his dream is to run the finest restaurant in the world. It's a goal he's meeting: five stars from Mobil, five diamonds from AAA, a slew of culinary awards from experts, including French ones. This praise attracts diners from all over the world. One California gourmet has flown in more than 100 times since Trotter opened his temple for the tongue in 1987.

Part of the allure is the mystery and surprise that await each night. There is no regular menu, no signature dish. Rather, there is an ever changing lineup of dishes shaped by the seasons and the inspiration and ingenuity of Trotter and his artful staff. The kitchen's creations are as much for the eye as the palate. Architects could learn a thing or two from the complex constructions of food and sauces.

Diners are given a choice of the $70 prix fixe vegetarian menu or the $90 grand menu. Wines are selected from a 45-page list and a 40,000-bottle cellar. Requests are taken, but you're better off settling back and enjoying the ride. My valet-provided menu included the following: Maine lobster and artichokes with pickled papaya and preserved ginger, Illinois rabbit loin with braised collard greens, organic quinoa and meat juices, and goat cheese rice pudding with mission figs and walnut emulsion.

During my pause out front I read the poetic essays Trotter had written about late-summer Bing cherries, golden raspberries and other in-season delights. Walking away wearing that smile, I reflected on the prose of the season written for passers-by and on valets whose concerns extend beyond parking cars and thought, When you get the small details right, the big ones surely follow.

On better-dressed days I've had some splendid meals at Charlie Trotter's. For each meal I booked weeks in advance, and you should too. Make that months, if you want the kitchen table where four people can enjoy a ground-zero view of the action. ■

the middle of things, but only until about 9:30 pm. Cabs abound.

For a great neighborhood Italian bistro, try *Sole Mio* (☎ 773-477-5858), 917 W Armitage (Map 6). The small front room bustles with energy and crowds; quieter rooms are hidden in back. As is the case with most of the really good places in this book, make reservations. The menu has a full lineup of pasta and the like, with a few touches from France. The horse-radish dressing on the trout salad is an unusual treat. More conventional entrées, such as the penne primavera ($11), are well prepared and affordable. Finish the

meal off with tart and creamy raspberry zabaglione.

More conventional Italian fare can be found at *Espial* (☎ 773-871-8123), 948 W Armitage (Map 6). This is a classic Chicago steak and pasta joint, authentic right down to the El rumbling overhead. Order a heavy red wine to wash down the grilled beef. The pizza with garlic-sautéed spinach is worthwhile for vegetarians and carnivores alike. This is one of Chicago's growing legion of cigar-friendly places.

Make a bagel from *Jacob Bros Bagels* (☎ 312-248-9606), 953 W Armitage (Map 6), one of your five servings of grains a day.

Your stomach will thank you as much as your mother will. Full details on the Jacob Bros delights are in the Near North section.

The menu calls them 'swank'; what you call them depends on how many you have. The 'them' are the 200 cocktails listed on the drink card at *Bruno* (☎ 773-549-3586), 1008 W Armitage (Map 6). Lose yourself while you eat and drink in the vintage dark, heavily curtained booths. Those faces staring down at you from the walls aren't due to the drink; they're part of owner Dion Antic's collection of Indonesian and African masks. The fusion menu has the expected polyglot of influences: the intriguing – or frightening, depending on your attitude – 'paella crazy noodles' and the relatively more conventional Thai chicken noodles are each $14.

Lincoln Park West

The vintage pictures of waitresses that line the walls at *RJ Grunts* (☎ 773-929-5363), 2056 N Lincoln Park West, across from the zoo (Map 6), will take you right back to the swinging '70s, when Lincoln Park emerged as the young singles' neighborhood of choice. RJ Grunts is where famed restaurateur Rich Melman got his start in 1971. The fruit and vegetable bar and burgers are still the mainstays at this place. Don't even think for a second about the fact that some of the original customers are now grandparents.

The Belden-Stratford, 2300 N Lincoln Park West, is a classic grande dame of an apartment building overlooking the park. *Ambria* (☎ 773-472-5959; Map 6) occupies a large corner off the lobby and is perfect and oh-so-fittingly elegant. The cooking is careful and imaginative and the service refined and unobtrusive, in keeping with the quiet location away from the city's bustle. A grand five-course degustation goes for $64. A collegiate course's worth of vintage wines are resting in the wine cellar.

In the same building, *Un Grand Cafe* (☎ 773-348-8886) has been serving French bistro fare for more than 15 years. Seafood such as mussels predominates, but there is the de rigueur steak frittes as well. A four-course prix-fixe meal is $30.

Elsewhere in the Neighborhood

Little red peppers on the menu denote the mouth-sizzling quotient at *Asia Bowl* (☎ 773-348-3060), 1001 W Webster, at the corner of Sheffield (Map 6). This corner noodle shop is sleek, stylish and fast. The $5.50 Shanghai noodles get one pepper, and the Thai barbecue and rice gets the full four peppers (defined on the menu as 'Sign your tongue away'). Bottles of Thai hot sauce on every table let up the ante.

About every 10 years another generation discovers *John Barleycorn Memorial Pub* (☎ 773-348-8899), 658 W Belden, at Lincoln Ave (Map 6). Thus, this windowless tavern that dates from the 1890s is perpetually young. Amid the hubbub, a continuous-loop slide projector shows classic Western art, while somewhere under the buzz classical music plays. Model ships garnered over the years from old romantic ports of call in Asia adorn shelves along the walls. The menu is vast and comfortable, offering burgers, tuna melts, potato skins and the like. Outdoor seating started in the side garden and has spread right around to the front. The beer selection is good, but this is really more eatery than bar.

The Schiavarelli Brothers, ward politicians and record promoters, have turned *Demon Dogs* (☎ 773-281-2001), 944 W Fullerton, directly under the El stop (Map 6), into a shrine for their buddies in the band Chicago. The strains of 'Saturday, in the park . . . ' can be heard almost around the clock. The menu is short and celebrates another local institution, the Chicago-style hot dog: the poppy-seed bun is steamed, and the condiments, such as onions, cucumbers and celery salt, are piled on high.

Lindo Mexico (☎ 773-871-4832), 2642 N Lincoln (Map 6), cleverly rode the Mexican food trend through the '80s with big margaritas, 'El Chow' (cheap and tasty) and a staff that would clear out of the kitchen and surround the table of any birthday celebrant, singing appropriate songs. With each year the empire spread through adjoining properties. The culmination is a backyard patio evocative of a hacienda. Ever reflecting the latest trend, Lindo Mexico has recently carved a new restaurant out of its domain called *Cohiba*, which specializes in Cuban food and cigars.

'Order now or get the f*** the out!' screams the apron-clad man behind the counter while an addled patron tries to comply. It's 4:30 am at this Lincoln Park equivalent of a roadhouse, and the *Wiener Circle* (☎ 773-477-7444), 2622 N Clark (Map 6), has reached its frenetic and chaotic peak. Mobs of patrons displaced from closed bars are clamoring for cheap char-burgers and char-dogs to satisfy their munchies. The veteran staff glee-fully takes full advantage of their boozy delirium. A young woman clad in condi-ment-smeared sweats grills a cross-eyed woman in a cocktail dress about her pref-erences: 'Catsupmustardcelerysaltrelish-pickles?' It's a sobriety test more devious than any traffic cop could devise. The woman, her senses well beyond overload, casts her eyes wildly about and pro-claims, 'Huh?' The cheese fries make a perfect grease-soaking companion.

LAKE VIEW/WRIGLEYVILLE

Another restaurant-rich part of town, this area of the North Side offers a huge variety of eateries whose quality – but not prices – match that found closer to the center of town. The Belmont El stop is central to much of the area. Better transit bets are listed with the individual neigh-borhoods, below.

Smoked piles of meat are the order of the day at *Brother Jimmy's BBQ* (☎ 773-528-0888), 2909 N Sheffield (Map 7). Pork ribs come in a variety of styles drawn from var-ious regions of the US. I like the tangy Southern recipe, which is vinegar-based. The Northern is sweet and tomatoey. Several combo plates give you the chance to sample the offerings. The main room is like an old warehouse. At night it gets converted to a blues club, with decent bands taking the low stage. Feeling starved? On Sunday $18 gets you all the beer and ribs you can jam down. Kids under 12 get to eat free every day.

Thyme is a key ingredient of the sausage at *Pat's Pizzeria* (773-248-0168), at 3114

N Sheffield (Map 7). Combined with a few other toppings, it makes for a great thin-crust combo pizza. A frequent winner of *Chicago Tribune* competitions (which means that the *Sun-Times* regularly dumps on it), Pat's is a family place that still seems a bit overwhelmed by the huge changes in the neighborhood. If you're not here for a thin-crust, skip it.

In the early 1990s Dan Bacin bought an old bank, carefully restored it and reopened it as a restaurant. The name, *Bella Vista* (773-404-0111), 1001 W Belmont at Shef-field (Map 7), means 'beautiful view,' and that's what diners have from one of the five seating levels. The food is pretty bella too. The menu is a variation of rich Italian: the Gorgonzola and pepper mashed potatoes should tell you something. Pizzas with such sophisticated toppings as salmon and goat cheese ($9) cook in the wood oven, and scores of wines line the wine list and the walk-through cellar.

Ann Sather's Restaurant (☎ 773-348-2378), 929 W Belmont (Map 7), is the result of Tom Tunney's genius at work in the early 1980s. He took a long-time neigh-borhood coffee shop and gave it a trendy and quirky ad campaign that emphasized its good, basic food. Young professionals flock here for platefuls of reasonably priced chow served in stylishly friendly surroundings. At night Swedish standards such as meatballs and potato sausage are augmented by American classics such as salmon and meat loaf. Famous for break-fast are Ann Sather's warm and gooey cin-namon rolls, worth a trip in themselves.

Once I had a bad meal at *Leona's* (773-327-8861), 3215 N Sheffield (Map 7). I wrote a letter to the owner. He called me up shortly thereafter. Soon pizzas were being delivered to my door for free, and Sara and I were summoned to the restaurant to eat and drink ourselves silly. This place takes customer service very, very seriously, and it pays off. From this original location, outlets have spread all over town. Ninety-nine per-cent of the meals I've had at Leona's have been delicious and very reasonably priced. Sandwiches, salads and various entrées are huge. The pizza is justifiably famous and supports a full-time delivery staff of 250. For something really different, try an extrathin-crust pesto pizza. A medium for two runs about $10. Oh, and if there's a lengthy wait when you arrive, they give you lots of red wine to help pass the time.

It doesn't look like much from the outside and actually looks worse inside, but *Moti Mahal* (☎ 773-348-4392), 1031 W Belmont (Map 7), serves excellent Indian food. Everybody working here learned to cook in India, and it shows. The various legume curries are spiced just right. The 'Big Mix' combines a lot of everything – curries, tikkas and more – and tops the price list at $13. It's just about impossible to spend more per person. It's BYOB, which gives you infinite choice (1000 Liquors, a quirky late-night liquor store/bar, is across the street) and keeps the costs down even more.

Roscoe Village

The following restaurants are in Roscoe Village, a neighborhood a half-mile west of Ashland Ave with recently gentrified tree-lined streets and some excellent bars and restaurants. It's about a 10-minute walk west from the Paulina El stop on the Brown Line.

The homemade bread is reason enough to visit *Brett's* (☎ 773-248-0999), 2011 W Roscoe, a tidy little place that bans smoking from the door on in. American classics are given elegant touches, such as the garlicky scallops perched atop sautéed leeks. Everything is carefully prepared and artfully presented. Prices are moderate but unpredictable, since the menu undergoes a total rewrite every month. But you can count on excellent and creative work from the kitchen. You and your sweetie should try to save room for the two-person dessert sampler, which features five of the day's sweet offerings.

New Orleans comes to Chicago at *Crescent City Cafe* (☎ 773-472-7275), 2041 W Roscoe. Creole and Cajun treats abound in this 10-table operation just down the street from the jumbo Laundromat. The menu reads like Fanny Flagg, with fried green tomatoes, corn fritters, red beans and rice and superb fried chicken. The prices – $3 for starters, about $9 for main dishes – are as friendly as the service. Your budget also benefits from the BYOB policy, but plan ahead, as the neighborhood still needs a decent liquor store.

The worst thing about the *Village Tap* (☎ 773-883-0817), 2055 W Roscoe, is how good it really is. This neighborhood place does everything well: food, drink and atmosphere. And that's the problem – it can get crowded on Friday and Saturday nights. Otherwise, it's a real winner. The ever-changing lineup of Midwestern microbrews is carefully chosen, and free samples are available from the friendly bartenders. The kitchen turns out some great burgers, veggie burgers and chicken sandwiches, and the spiced pita chips are a nice touch. Out back the beer garden has a fountain; inside the tables have good views of the TVs for ball games. There are board games available so you and your friends can make your own fun.

Halsted St

Known as the heart of Chicago's gay community, Halsted St north of Belmont has many restaurants catering to all tastes and preferences. There may be a few more men than average, but the crowds are very mixed. Ride to the CTA's Belmont stop for the south end, Addison for the north.

'Comfort food' is the trendy term for the kind of rib-sticking fare that Midwestern moms have served for decades. When mom's not around to heat up the stove, your average Joe might resort to the frozen food section for his comfort. High-class Joes – or at least those with sophisticated palates – resort to *Erwin* (☎ 773-528-7200), 2925 N Halsted (Map 7). Here the homemade noodles come with rabbit, the fresh-baked bread with a white bean spread. Dishes on the rotating menu can include an onion tart with blue cheese for $6 and a roasted sweet pepper stuffed with seasonal veggies for $11. It's all imaginative, filling and comforting. Bring mom.

Yoshi and Nobuko Katsumura preside over one of the most innovative casual places in town at *Yoshi's Cafe* (☎ 773-248-6160), 3257 N Halsted (Map 7). The changing menu focuses on low-fat dishes with a Japanese flair. Grilled salmon and asparagus teriyaki is typical and goes for $18. The mushroom and brie soup is savory at $4.50. Other items can include soft-shell crabs with aioli, tuna tartare, barbecued chicken and grilled duck salad. The service is every bit as good as the food.

The wine at *Oo-La-La* (☎ 773-935-7708), 3335 N Halsted (Map 7), is as cheap as you want, since you bring your own. The menu is Italian with a sense of humor. The decor is stark, the patio out back shady. Standards such as calamari and veal piccata (each $16) are done with flair. This is a local joint that reflects the spirit of its neighborhood.

Obviously, with a slogan like 'Love animals, don't eat them,' you don't go to the *Chicago Diner* (☎ 773-935-6696), 3411 N Halsted (Map 7), for a steak. Large portions of fresh vegetarian food are the rule here, with salads, egg dishes and grilled sandwiches the order of the day. Breakfast tofu omelets for $6 are a hit. At night, entrées with varying amounts of grains and veggies are the norm. The whole place is quite dinerlike, with counter stools and booths. Vegans take note: even the pesto for the pasta can be had without a lick of cheese.

Arcos de Cuchilleros (☎ 773-296-6046), 3445 N Halsted (Map 7), avoids the upscale hype of some of the other tapas joints. The owners are from Madrid, and they have faithfully replicated one of that city's family cafés. The bar is long, the room is narrow and the furniture is dark wood. Small plates of classics such as sautéed lima beans, chickpea croquettes and tortilla espanola average $5 each. Don't keep track of how many pitchers of tangy sangria you drink, just keep ordering.

Carmen Miranda, of fruit-on-the-noggin fame, lives again at *Rhumba!* (☎ 773-975-2345), 3631 N Halsted (Map 7), where Brazilian cooking meets the flamboyance of Chicago's main gay strip in a salsa-hot atmosphere. Size up the kitchen from the sidewalk – you'll soon find yourself inside. Sopa de Felsao, rich with black beans and a shot of sherry, is $3.25. Entrées average $15 and feature lots of marinated meats, such as spicy pork ribs and skewered meats. This is the spot for the increasingly trendy caipirinha, a sugar-cane-based cocktail made with fresh limes. Oh, and under her skirt, Carmen's had a sex change.

Clark St

From Belmont to a little north of Wrigley Field are scores of moderate and budget-priced eateries serving food from around the world. Some are aimed squarely at the undiscriminating tastes of suburban day-trippers. Others offer excellent value with imaginative menus and are listed here. The CTA Belmont and Addison stops are close to either end of the strip.

For sandwiches and drinks, try *Alonti Cafe* (☎ 773-529-1155), 3201 N Clark, on the northeast corner of Belmont (Map 7). The creative menu includes unique items such as eggplant sandwiches and jambalaya pasta. Most items are $5 to $7. The cappuccino, iced or hot, makes a good take-along for strolling the neighborhood.

Mia Francesca (☎ 773-281-3310), 3311 N Clark (Map 7), is one of scores of small family-run Italian bistros in the city. It is also one of the most popular. Diners jam the large room, with its closely spaced tables topped with white tablecloths. A buzz of energy swirls among the patrons and arrangements of fresh flowers. The kitchen is open on one side, allowing full view of your food's preparation. The frequently changing handwritten menu features earthy standards such as caper-laced rigatoni siciliana for $10. I'm partial to the farfalle with ham, peas and wild mushrooms. They also do a good job with that often overlooked staple of Italian kitchens, polenta. Service can be harried because of the clamoring crowds.

If you want to become a part of the vibrant local theater scene, the best place to cut a deal is *Coffee Chicago* (☎ 773-477-3323), 3323 N Clark (Map 7). Located in

RICK GERHARTER

Cubs fans will appreciate the wealth of eateries near Wrigley Field.

the Organic Theater building, its big windows give a good view of the street. At any table you might find actors studying scripts, directors making casting decisions and a few hard-luck cases deciding that its time to chuck it all for another stint temping in the Loop. The pastries and baked goods aren't bad; neither is the coffee.

Tired of traveling? Do a good job working part time at *Jimmy John's* (☎ 773-244-9000), 3328 N Clark (Map 7), and they will set you up in business with your own outlet. If your commitment is more temporary, the sandwiches and subs are fresh, good and cheap: $3.25 to $4.25.

Some of the best Thai food in the city can be found at *PS Bangkok* (☎ 773-871-7777), 3345 N Clark (Map 7). The various fish tanks hint at the long list of seafood dishes, many of them the elaborate kind found at banquets in Thailand. The shrimp curries are hot and bursting with plump shrimp. The chicken satay leads the lengthy menu and comes with an excellent peanut sauce. Buried deep on the menu and worth requesting is the spinach oozing with garlic. Prices are in the $8 neighborhood for simple dishes but escalate rapidly for the seafood creations. If the place is jammed, as it often is, try *Thai Classic*

(☎ 773-404-2000), across the street at 3332 N Clark (Map 7). The menu is shorter and simpler, but the food is still quite good.

The Mexican food is only so-so at *El Jardín* (☎ 773-528-6775), 3335 N Clark, and its sibling *El Jardín Cafe* (☎ 773-935-8133), just up the street at 3401 N Clark (Map 7), but if you want a raucous evening focusing on tequila, then these are the places for you. One memorable sight was a patron just outside the door putting his complementary sombrero to use as a receptacle for overindulgence.

The *Texas Star Fajita Bar* (☎ 773-975-8008), 3365 N Clark (Map 7), isn't much better, but its doorway under the El tracks at the corner of Roscoe is famous as the location used for the explosion that killed the little girl at the beginning of the movie *The Untouchables*.

A half-block west of Clark and still under the El tracks, *Penny's Noodle Shop* (☎ 773-281-8222), 3400 N Sheffield (Map 7), counts as a certifiable phenomenon. Despite several other excellent Asian choices within a few blocks, the place is jammed most hours of the day and night and has people waiting outside in all weather, good and bad. Maybe these hapless hordes are drawn by the place's minimalist decor or the low prices. The cheap, tasty noodle soups ($4 average) are no doubt the main draw. Just remember, you can always head north a few blocks for several places that are as good and much less crowded.

A few doors south, *Le Loup* (☎ 773-248-1830), 3348 N Sheffield (Map 7), is a casual and friendly French bistro. The name means 'the wolf,' and you'll happily wolf down classics such as the $7 blue cheese salad and the $10 cassoulet, made with white beans, duck and sausage. The dining area is small and intimate. The adjoining garden, lushly planted with flowers and trees, comes alive in the summer.

Near the corner of Clark, *Manny's* (☎ 773-528-9890), 3418 N Sheffield (Map 7), is unadorned except for the wisecracking wait staff, who serve up vast platters of pancakes, omelets and other breakfast standards at dirt-cheap prices. Everything is authentic, from the waiters to the hash browns to the bottomless cups of coffee.

Long before travelers had anything as handy as Lonely Planet guides for advice, they traveled by such means as the legendary China Clipper flying boats of Pan American World Airways. During the 1930s these huge aircraft linked the world to the US on routes spanning the globe. Journeys were made in segments, stopping at company outposts in the Pacific and the Atlantic. The mother of Ted Cizma, one of the owners of The *Outpost* (☎ 773-244-1166), 3438 N Clark (Map 7), was a flight attendant for Pan Am during this era. Ted and his partners have created a warm, casual and chic restaurant that draws inspiration from the clippers' many ports of call. Dishes offered on the always changing menu are drawn from around the world. Examples include plantain fritters and grilled tuna for $17 and New Zealand venison for $20. The room is decorated with maps showing the clipper routes.

The wooden boat in the window hints at the fish-dominated menu at *Matsuya* (☎ 773-248-2677), 3469 N Clark (Map 7). This is one of the best-value Japanese restaurants in town. The lengthy sushi menu features standards such as California rolls on down to the square-shaped Osaka-style sushi. The octopus marinated in bean paste is an example of the depth of the rest of the menu. Less adventurous types will be happy with the teriyaki-marinated grilled fish. If the lines are long, *Tomodachi* (☎ 773-296-0857), 3468 N Clark (Map 7), is a modest alternative. Sushi neophytes will enjoy the full-color place mats that describe and show pictures of the offerings.

This dense thicket of Asian eateries also includes the very inexpensive *Pad Thai*, 3466 N Clark; the Vietnamese *La Paillotte*, 3470 N Clark; the brightly lit Japanese *Nagano*, 3475 N Clark; and the dark and simple *Sanko* sushi restaurant, 3485 N Clark (all Map 7). More will surely have opened by the time you read this.

One nearby place without soy sauce on the tables is *Arabesque* (☎ 773-348-5767), 3472 N Clark (Map 7). The engaging owners serve food drawn from across the southern Mediterranean. The maza platter offers five vegetarian appetizers for $9, among them smoky eggplant baba ghanoush and garlicky hummus. Kebabs and couscous dominate the menu and average $9. Have some baklava for me.

Jezebel (☎ 773-929-4000), 3517 N Clark (Map 7), is a cut above the budget nature of the strip. The richly decorated black and gold fixtures are matched by the black and gold fettucini ($19). The Italian menu spans that country. Have some pasta shaped like little ears: orecchiette with seasonal vegetables goes for $12.

There's a taste of Africa at *Addis Abeba* (☎ 773-929-9383), 3521 N Clark (Map 7). A nice change from the fare at the mobs of sports bars in the area, the foods of Ethiopia are served here in heaping portions. The dishes are fittingly somewhere between India and the Mediterranean – lots of legumes, grains, spices and vegetables. Everything comes atop injera, large spongy flatbread used for everything except paying the bill. Prices are cheap – you'll be out of Africa for $10 a head.

Although it's a chain from California, *Pollo Rey* (☎ 773-325-2500), 3545 N Clark (Map 7), is a good choice for budget Mexican. The vividly colored tile walls lean toward the sterile, making this more a fast-food eatery than a sit-down restaurant, but the quality is light years beyond the Taco Bell just around the corner. The chicken is grilled on rotisseries, and the salsa is made fresh all day. Burritos start at $3.89.

On the northwest corner of Waveland and Clark, across from the highly recommended Bernie's Tavern (see the Baseball Bars section in the Entertainment chapter) is *Tuscany* (☎ 773-404-7700), 3700 N Clark (Map 7), a branch of the well-known original on Taylor St in Little Italy. They have a wood-burning pizza oven and a real grill for the various steaks on the menu. Marinated pork chops cost $13. This place, although rather hoity-toity by Clark St standards, is still very casual.

The *Raw Bar & Grill* (☎ 773-348-7291), 3720 N Clark (Map 7), has a big tank of doomed live lobsters near the door. Fresh seafood is not one of Chicago's strengths, given the dearth of local seas, but what you get here isn't bad. After a Cubs game, the boozy fans boisterously slurping raw oysters are a show in themselves.

Southport Ave

In 1987 I lived near Southport Ave. It had a couple of bars, a few markets and no decent place to eat. Then word of its cheap rents, tree-lined streets and easy El access got out. In 1991 a Starbucks opened, and that was the beginning of the end of its mild-mannered days. Southport from Belmont to Irving Park is now one of the hottest neighborhoods for nightlife in the city. Take the CTA Brown Line to the Southport stop and you are in the heart of the action.

Zinc is the word at *Bistro Zinc* (☎ 773-281-3443), 3443 N Southport (Map 7). The namesake metal covers the bar. Classic French cooking is served in fair-size portions at fair prices – about $12 an entrée; the steak au poivre is $17. Just thinking about the leek tart filled with brie

has me ready to stop typing right . . . Okay, I'm back. Needless to say, the menu finishes with a full range of splendid desserts. If you find something smoother to put in your mouth than the chocolate mousse, don't tell me. Decorum wouldn't allow it. A takeout door on the side peddles picnic treats.

The health-conscious nature of Wrigleyville's young and affluent residents is reflected in the names of several restaurants that incorporate the marketing moniker 'lite' into their names. *Chinalite* (☎ 773-244-0300), 3457 N Southport (Map 7), promises all the standards without all the fat. Szechuan string beans ($6.90) and rice noodles with asparagus in a black bean sauce ($7.90) set the tone. You'll have to decide if the pork fried rice ($5.90) is in keeping with the theme.

The antifat theme continues at *Still Lite Cafe* (☎ 773-929-5090), 3647 N Southport (Map 7). Brown rice in various forms is both the main attraction and a principal sideshow. The menu changes often. Look for the $6 sesame-cilantro sandwich. A slew of outdoor tables lines the sidewalk.

Right next door, *Dish* (☎ 773-549-8614), 3651 N Southport (Map 7), is as small as the dress sizes of its well-buffed clientele. The imaginative menu features items such as portobello mushroom fajitas ($12) and vegetarian burritos ($10). It's a boisterous and cozy spot all winter long. In summer, tables stretch across the uncommonly wide Southport sidewalk.

Hi Ricky (☎ 773-388-0000), 3730 N Southport (Map 7), brings life to the west side of the street. Its long, inexpensive menu surfs through Vietnam, Indonesia, Thailand and China. Satays are the stars and come with prawn chips and an array of sauces. A sampler of all seven satay varieties is only $6. The interior is bright, cheerful and lacking in pretense. The clever logo seems destined to become the star of an as-yet-uninstalled gift shop.

Upscale bar chow predominates across the street at *Cullen's* (☎ 773-975-0600), 3741 N Southport (Map 7). The bar is meant to evoke an old Chicago classic, with lots of wood and tile. The whole place is the product of entrepreneur Michael Cullen, who has sunk a fortune into what was a humdrum haberdashery where I used to buy cheap underwear. Cullen is usually there, making certain that the crowds are having a great time. Baked artichoke appetizers go for $6, and marinated tuna sandwiches are $7. The beer list is long and interesting.

Typical, moderately priced Italian fare is featured at *Strega Nona* (☎ 773-244-0990), 3747 N Southport (Map 7). That hallmark of late-20th-century restaurant design – exposed brick – is the dominant element of the dining room, which opens onto the street.

Tango Sur (☎ 773-477-5466), at 3763 N Southport (Map 7), provides a beefy counterpart to the vegetarian-oriented menus of the street. This Argentine steak house smells great and has classic skirt steaks for only $11.90. Not in the mood for steak? Then kidneys await. Not in the mood for meat? Go elsewhere. Tables outside expand the seating from the very small and spare interior. This may be the only smoke-free steak place in town.

On the corner of Grace, *Banana Leaf* (☎ 773-883-8683), 3811 N Southport (Map 7), has a suitably leafy presence. The lush interior offers a lengthy Thai menu that is refreshingly free of the designer touches so commonplace elsewhere. Thai noodles, curries and basil dishes run about $7. The banana is a star at dessert, coming fried, roasted or steamed.

I once bought a can of soup at the grocery store that's now *Deleece* (☎ 773-325-1710), 4004 N Southport (Map 7), an upscale café. You can still catch a whiff of five decades' worth of ripening fruit, but now the predominant aromas are from the ever popular fusion of foods. Poblano peppers and cilantro add a Mexican touch, ginger chimes in for Asia and olive oil speaks for the Mediterranean. Prices reflect the grocery-store roots, and the soup is definitely not canned. Roasted chicken and mashed potatoes is $8; an asparagus and portobello brunch frittata is $6.

ANDERSONVILLE

The neighborhood is centered on Clark St from a block south of Foster to about five blocks north. It's a 10-minute walk west from the Berwyn El stop on the Red Line.

La Donna (☎ 773-561-9500), at 5146 N Clark (Map 8), is a casual, imaginative Italian place that seems to have the magic touch that eluded its many failed predecessors in this location, half a block south of Foster. Pastas for about $9 could include linguini with clams, pumpkin ravioli or the capellini puttanesca, a spicy concoction of tomatoes, capers, olives and garlic. Don't get too stuffed to try one of the marvelous microbrews next door at the Hop Leaf (see the Entertainment chapter for details).

Andersonville is also home to *Cousin's* (☎ 773-334-4553), a Turkish restaurant at 5203 N Clark (Map 8) with lots of vegetarian options, as well as chicken kebabs and roasted lamb; the entrées average about $7. You can make a great meal of warm pita bread, hummus and baba ghanoush. Lots of Chicago's finest stop by for the lunch deals – considered the ultimate endorsement at Windy City restaurants. There is another branch at 2833 N Broadway, in Lake View.

Although it looks old and authentic, *Ann Sather's* (☎ 773-271-6677), 5207 N Clark (Map 8), was actually opened in 1987. It's just as popular as its Belmont parent, and its cinnamon rolls are just as deliciously decadent.

Its hard to say anything bad about a restaurant where my name is displayed in huge letters next to a glowing review I once wrote for the *Sun-Times*. *Andie's* (☎ 773-784-8616), 5253 N Clark (Map 8), continues to deserve my praise. The much larger *Reza's*, next door, may get the yuppie hordes, but discerning Andersonville locals flock to unpretentious Andie's for smooth, garlicky hummus and more. Most of the cooking occurs up front, where the smell of grilling meat, eggplant and the world's best lentil soup fills the air. If you somehow manage to spend $15 a person, you'll either be drunk, bloated or both. Oh, and be sure to say hi to Andie for me.

If you're reading this at *Kopi, A Traveler's Cafe* (☎ 773-989-5674), 5317 N Clark (Map 8), then you better have paid for it! An extremely casual coffeehouse with a pile of pillows on the floor in the window, Kopi stocks a large range of travel books. However, lest a java catastrophe lay waste to the inventory, you're supposed to buy the books before you read them. Feeling cheap? They have piles of some of the most esoteric free weeklies in town, as well as travel magazines and brochures galore. The bulletin board has ads from people looking for trekking partners for Kazakhstan and the like. They have various sandwiches and desserts, although at times the help seems to be on a trip of their own.

You get free coffee in amazingly small cups at the Swedish Bakery (☎ 773-561-8919), 5348 N Clark (Map 8). But that's the only thing minimalist about the place, with its butter-laden breads, cookies and pastries. The coffeecakes will make you want to (a) buy one, and (b) go get a real cup of coffee.

The side-street location of the *Dellwood Pickle* (☎ 773-271-7728), just east of Clark at 1475 W Balmoral (Map 8), doesn't keep the hordes from seeking out their ultimate comfort food at prices that make you think you're back in Des Moines. Meat loaf and mashed potatoes are married in a New Orleans shepherd's pie ($7), while salmon and fresh pasta meet beneath surprising sauces. Fresh muffins and breads adorn the Sunday brunch, when the lines are long. Just sit back in a crumbling easy chair or browse other patrons' art for sale on the walls. BYOB.

You might wonder about the name *Tomboy* (☎ 773-907-0636), 5402 N Clark (Map 8), until you realize that Andersonville is a favorite neighborhood of Chicago's lesbian community. This fairly new restaurant has raised the street's fine-dining quotient by several notches. White tablecloths are a stark counterpoint to the natural-brick walls. The food is artful and filling, such as the grilled pork chops with Gorgonzola-topped potatoes. About half the entrées are pastas, many of which are vegetarian. Entrées average $14, and you can have a real gourmet bargain by bringing your own wine. Buy it from the liquor store three blocks south, at Foster and Clark – but watch your change.

You'll keep looking for your parents, or maybe your grandparents, at *Calo* (☎ 773-271-7782), 5343 N Clark (Map 8), an old-time red-sauce Italian joint. They were selling out of their wheel-size, tomato-stuffed focaccia when few people outside of Genoa had heard of the stuff. Middle-aged and older folks will all be chowing pasta, ribs and chicken cacciatore while catching the news or the Bulls game in the windowless den. That gives you all the more reason to go late at night – Calo keeps dishing up the spaghetti and garlic bread until 2 am (3 am on Saturday).

Fireside Restaurant & Lounge (☎ 773-878-5942), 5739 N Ravenswood (Map 8), has excellent American food such as Cajun burgers and ribs. There's a large and sunny beer garden that is an excellent place to linger over lunch. The bar has a vast selection of microbrews, and on many Saturdays they host a 'Brewmaster's Dinner,' where the actual brew masters for some of the beers lead tastings. Bite back the dog that bit you at the Sunday brunch 'build your own Bloody Mary' bar.

FAR NORTH

Two other North Side neighborhoods have heavy concentrations of ethnic restaurants and are further evidence of Chicago's vibrant immigrant communities.

Argyle St

Even the Argyle El station (Map 8) has an Asian motif in this dense neighborhood of restaurants and shops run by people from Southeast Asia. There's always someplace new on Argyle opened by a family in search of its dreams. The same holds true on the adjoining blocks of Broadway and Sheridan.

The children of the charming husband-and-wife owners of *Nha Trang* (☎ 773-989-0712), 1007 W Devon (Map 8), used to sit quietly in the corner and play cards with decks they'd made out of newspaper coupons. The kids are older now and have taken up official duties, which allow them to serve the excellent Vietnamese specialties in this very inexpensive and simple storefront. Various dishes come covered in fresh cilantro and are meant to be wrapped in sheets of rice paper. The sesame chicken is sweet and crunchy and is often ordered in multiple portions by regulars.

Devon Ave

India meets Israel along Devon Ave west of Western Ave. The two cultures coexist in a short four-block stretch. Shops selling saris alternate with kosher butchers. Now there's also an influx of Russian shops and cafés. The El doesn't come close to this area, so you'll have to drive, take a cab or ride the El to the Red Line's Morse Ave stop and transfer to the No 155 Morse Ave bus.

The premier Indian choice is *Viceroy of India* (☎ 773-743-4100), 2516 W Devon. There's a casual takeout side and a more formal white-tablecloth side. The menu comprises such common standards as tandooris and curries, all prepared with care. The $7 lunch buffet is a bargain and is a good break if you're exploring the street.

Items not found on most South Asian menus dominate at *Indian Garden* (☎ 773-338-2929), 2548 W Devon. Wok-like pans and simple iron griddles are used to prepare a lot of the items. Vegetables go beyond the soggy cauliflower in goopy sauces found at other, less inspired places. Wash it all down with a mango shake.

The Jewish businesses observe strict opening hours, so keep that in mind if you'd like to visit. *Kosher Karry* (☎ 773-973-4355), 2828 W Devon, and *Tel-Aviv Kosher Bakery* (☎ 773-764-8877), 2944 W Devon, have smoked fish, baked goods and other items ready to eat.

WICKER PARK/BUCKTOWN

Ground zero for trendy and vibrant Bucktown is the six-way intersection of Damen, North and Milwaukee. The Blue Line El stop at Damen will put you right there. Farther north along Damen, public transportation is more problematic. A cab ride from River North will run about $6.

Organic mushrooms and chemical-free brie are among the items offered at *Sun/Moon* (☎ 773-276-6525), 1467 N Milwaukee (Map 9). Don't even ask if the carrot juice at this simple deli is organic – they'd be insulted.

The $1.15 tacos at *El Chino* (☎ 773-772-1905), 1505 N Milwaukee (Map 9), are one of the best bargains in this part of town. There are eight kinds to choose from, and you can eat them in the Formica-clad

RICK GERHARTER

The heart of Bucktown: The convergence of Damen, North and Milwaukee dining area while listening to Bruce Springsteen blare from the speakers.

Two interesting Italian places are side by side: *Buona Fortuna Cafe* (☎ 773-278-7797), 1540 N Milwaukee (Map 9), is a big, open storefront with gold pillars. The small menu features delicately seasoned items such as basil-crusted chicken for $14. Just north, *Luna Blue* (☎ 773-862-2600), 1552 N Milwaukee (Map 9), is funkier and has a more intimate dining room. The menu veers toward the heavily spiced foods of Sicily. Anchovies, garlic and tomato sauces are the rule at this equally moderately priced place.

PaPa Jin (☎ 773-384-9600), 1551 N Milwaukee (Map 9), is low-key in its decor and menu. Everything is casual and not very expensive, such as the hot Mongolian shrimp for $8.

The *Deluxe Diner* (☎ 773-342-6667), 1575 N Milwaukee (Map 9), is a high-concept new addition to the street. Right near the corner of North and Damen, it relies on a 1930s diner motif replete with lots of glass and stainless steel. The kitchen isn't staffed with greasy guys named Gus, but with a team of talented chefs. You'll know you're not in some retro throwback when you note that the mashed potatoes come flavored with bacon and jalapeño peppers and the spaghetti comes with wild mushrooms and other gourmet touches. There's a full bar, and the place is open really early and really late. If it's your birthday, your entrée is free.

The tangerine and olive walls and leopard-skin motif set the mood at *Soul Kitchen* (☎ 773-342-9742), 1576 N Milwaukee (Map 9). Big, bright dishes drawn from the South but with eclectic accents come aggressively spiced. The Jamaican jerk chicken skewers are fiery and a relative bargain at $5.75. Sweet and crunchy pecan-coated catfish is $11.50. Other interesting touches include the collard greens seasoned with cilantro and barbecued lamb with mango sauce. Wrap everything up with cinnamon-spiced coffee. This highly recommended corner spot is an excellent example of the kinds of innovative restau-

rants found not just in this neighborhood but throughout the city.

You can watch all the action of the neighborhood from the appropriately named *Cafe Cafina* (☎ 773-227-8400), 1588 N Milwaukee (Map 9). The cheerful staff serves from a long list of coffees. Best of all, the prices are distinctly non-Starbucks: a large (not a 'grande') is only $1.45.

Named after the Victorian era's liquid version of LSD, *Cafe Absinthe* (☎ 773-278-4488), 1954 W North, at the corner of Damen (enter off the alley; Map 9), is a bustling, hip place that exemplifies the neighborhood. Although it isn't hallucinogenic, it is high in style. Lots of beautiful bistro dishes are here, at prices that will clear your head: think $25 to $30 per person before drinks. If it seems noisy in the dining room, try the Red Dog Supreme Funk Parlor nightclub, upstairs. Curious what's cooking? (It changes constantly.) The kitchen has a big window overlooking North Ave.

Damen Ave

Another street away from the center that emerged as a hip spot in the early 1990s, Damen is home to some of the city's hottest and most innovative restaurants and clubs. *Pontia Cafe* (☎ 773-252-7767), 1531 N Damen (Map 9), is the perfect slacker diner for the neighborhood, residing in an old gas station that has sort of been converted. Its mismatched booths are in the old garage section, where the management hasn't really had time yet to cart away all the mechanic's stuff. The very young and pierced crowd is sort of served by an equally young and pierced staff. Sample conversation between a dazed and confused female customer and a dazed and confused employee: 'Hey, like, are we gonna get our food someday?' 'Oh wow, sorry. What did you order?' Long pause. 'Hmmm . . . Like, I don't know.' If you do get your food, expect interesting sandwiches, such as artichokes and orange zest on olive panini.

Busy Bee (☎ 773-772-4433), at 1550 N Damen (Map 9), has weathered the massive changes in the neighborhood without showing any signs of joining in. The ageless and thereby efficient wait staff serves up Polish classics for just a few – very few – dollars. Pierogis (Eastern European versions of ravioli) come with a variety of fillings, such as cheese, bacon and sauerkraut. Look for the seasonal fresh mushroom soup and the roasted duck. The fennel-laden sausage is better than you're likely to find in the old country. Adding to the classic Chicago atmosphere, the rumble from the El tracks directly above will stir your coffee for you.

Con Fusion (☎ 773-772-7100), at 1616 N Damen (Map 9), is a witty takeoff on the fad of fusion cooking. The menu changes with the seasons and moods of the chefs. Asia may contribute a salad with tofu dressing one night, America a spicy sausage creole another. Entrées such as salmon with soba noodles cost in the high teens. Everything is black and white, from the menu to the walls. The large dining area is matched by a large garden.

Forgot to get cash? Possibly the world's most convenient ATM is built right into the wall at the *Northside* (☎ 773-384-3555), 1635 N Damen (Map 9). The food is also convenient at this bar, which has a large adjoining dining room, the front of which is an atrium. The menu favors grazers with finger-food classics such as nachos and dipables such as hummus. Beware of rich guys on Harleys trying to act cool, however.

The many bottles of hot sauce on the tables at *Mama's Paradise Cafe* (☎ 773-772-6770), 1646 N Damen (Map 9), are a sign that maybe they got the 'paradise' part right. A mural of Eve in her garden is a backdrop for meals of eggs Benedict or one of a long list of omelets that average about $6.

Silver Cloud (☎ 773-489-6212), at 1700 N Damen (Map 9), takes itself seriously, perhaps too much so. The sloppy joes cost $6.75. They're good, but the price seems a bit steep for a trip back in time to your grade school cafeteria. Still, the corner location has a good view for people-watching, and the sidewalk tables are usually jammed.

Completely hidden behind bags of Oreos and other dubious convenience foods is *Lydia's Cafe* (☎ 773-235-7252), at 1704 N Damen (Map 9). Lydia's dishes up some excellent Latino food from the back room of a neighborhood grocery. The usual tacos, tostadas and the like are here, plus some unusual items made with plantains and other tropical items. Pasteles ($7) is a delicious green banana and pork concoction from Puerto Rico – it's definitely worth fighting your way past the Ho-Ho's and Twinkies.

Pause on a hot day for some cool homemade Italian ice at *Miko's* (☎ 773-645-9665), 1846 N Damen (Map 9). You can sit under the large oak tree in front and enjoy fruit flavors such as lemon, raspberry and peach for $1.50.

Classic French food at nonclassic prices (read: cheap) is the winning combination at *Le Bouchon* (☎ 773-862-6600), 1958 N Damen (Map 9). This quaint little spot that flies the tricolore over the street is often packed with neighborhood types who know a bargain when they bite it. All the standards from France are here. The pepper steak and frittes are très bon. The Lyonnaise salade is a winner at $5. Other faves, from escargot to chocolate mousse, are listed on the short menu. Want to see the tiny kitchen? Head to the bathroom – it's on the way.

More than 100 kinds of potatoes are grown in Peru. You won't find that many at *Rinconcito Sudamericano* (☎ 773-489-3126), 1954 W Armitage, at the corner of Damen (Map 9), but you will find some wonderful mashed potatoes with ground meat. Other moderately priced Peruvian treats include ceviche (a very popular fresh fish appetizer) and grilled beef heart (eek!) with spicy salsa. There's enough art and artifacts filling the place to keep your eyes wandering for hours.

The furniture and the food are right out of a Chilean farmhouse at *Empanadas Unlimited* (☎ 773-772-1335), 2046 N Damen (Map 9). The namesake stars of the menu are filled with various ingredients, including the traditional mixture of beef, onions,

RICK GERHARTER

Wicker Park grocery

raisins, olives and eggs for $4.10. On nice nights you can eat under the trees on the long porch.

Snooty young people are at home at *Meritage Cafe & Wine Bar* (☎ 773-235-6434), 2118 N Damen (Map 9). The wine list is almost as long as the gaze down the nose you get from the haughty help. But if you're ready for this kind of scene, you'll be rewarded with some really good food, such as a terrine of Oregon blue cheese and wild mushrooms for $6 and scallops with a ragout of black beans for $17. The former corner bar has been renovated just enough to let the light in but still preserves the Victorian character of the building.

The attitude is cocky at *Merlot Joe* (☎ 773-252-5141), 2119 N Damen (Map 9) – sort of like Bordeaux meets the Bronx. One read of the clever menu and you'll say to the waiter, 'Are you talkin' to me? *Are you talkin' to me?!?*' The affordable choices feature that staple of budget menus in Paris, the ubiquitous couscous, for $9. Country pâté goes for $5.50. Merlot Joe has one of the many tree-shaded porches on this part of Damen, open all summer long.

Mexican artist Frida Kahlo is the inspiration for *Frida's* (☎ 773-489-3463), 2143 N Damen (Map 9). Happily, the murals in the stylish dining room are inspired more by the sweeping works of Diego Rivera than by Kahlo's organ-covered efforts. The food is equally appealing and is cooked with ingredients, such as epazote, not usually found this side of the border. Beautiful $3.50 tamales are authentically cooked and served in fresh cornhusks. Roasted vegetables give the salsas a smooth and smoky flavor. The menu changes often to reflect the seasonal availability of the ingredients imported from Mexico.

WEST SIDE

Good restaurants both veteran and new are scattered throughout the West Side. The best way to reach any of the choices listed here is by cab. Note that you'll want to call one from the restaurant when you're ready to go, or you'll be waiting a long time on the sidewalk for one to happen along.

The best burrito in the world is at *Tecalitlan* (☎ 312-384-4285), 1814 W Chicago Ave (Map 10). Weighing more than a pound and costing $4, the carne asada burrito with cheese is not just one of the city's best food values, it's one of the city's best foods. Add the optional avocado and you'll have a full day's worth of food groups wrapped in a huge flour tortilla. For a tasty, greasy change, have them mix the carne asada with pork. The many other Mexican staples on the menu are all cheap and good. I've been known to stop here on my way into town from the airport.

Where vendors once hawked zucchinis and cucumbers, one of the most innovative Chinese restaurants in town has set up shop. It's a spot guaranteed to catch people heading west to Bulls games. *Red Light* (☎ 312-733-8880), 820 W Randolph (Map 10), serves up fare that isn't anything like the fortune-cookie standard. In fact, mention 'sweet and sour pork' to the waiters and their already inscrutable attitudes might just freeze you right out the door. Roasted duck and rock shrimp are a few of the stars amid the fresh ingredients. The lo mein noodles are fantastic, but like everything else on the menu, only for those of high means.

Southern cooking makes good – very good – at *Wishbone* (☎ 312-850-2663), 1001 W Washington (Map 10). The perfect corn muffins set the tone for a menu featuring spicy classics such as blackened catfish, fried chicken and baked ham. A big choice of sides includes sweet potatoes that should be a lesson to all the cooks who kill them every Thanksgiving. This is the place to find out just what hoppin' John is. Breakfasts come with hot, fresh buttermilk rolls. At lunch you can opt for the speedy cafeteria line. Prices are cheap: $6 to $8 will get you loads of chow. Oprah's studios are just down the street, and she has been known to stop by.

Great outside in the garden when it's nice, fine inside the other nine months of the year, *Jaks Tap* (☎ 312-666-1700), 901 W Jackson, two blocks west of Halsted (Map 10), is run by the same smart people who run the Village Tap, on the North Side. Among the 40 beers on tap here are 30 from Midwestern microbreweries. If they have Solsun from Michigan, clear your day's agenda and start ordering. Can't decide? They'll give you samples. The menu is a clever extrapolation of the usual bar food. Burgers ($7) might come with guacamole or hummus; quesadillas come with a smoky salsa.

Immediately west of the Loop and close to Union Station, where some Metra and all Amtrak trains depart, *Lou Mitchell's* (☎ 312-939-3111), 565 W Jackson (Map 10), draws hordes who line up to eat elbow to elbow. The draw is breakfast dishes that are tops in town. Whether it's omelets

hanging off the plates, fluffy flapjacks, crisp waffles or anything else on the long menu (most items are $4 to $6), you can expect perfect preparation with premium ingredients. Cups of coffee, at $1.25 each, are bottomless, just like the charm of the owners, who hand out free treats to young and old alike.

Greek Town

The immigrants moving in are now yuppies in search of lofts, rather than Greeks in search of a new life, but a string of authentic restaurants keeps Greek Town true to its name. Prices are uniformly cheap and the crowds uniformly lively, preserving elements that have kept this neighborhood, centered on Halsted St right across the expressway from the Loop, popular for generations. There are several choices beyond the three listed here that are good, such as *Rodity's* (☎ 312-454-0800), 222 S Halsted (Map 10). Why not wander the street and pick the one where the saganaki (flaming cheese) is burning the brightest and the ouzo (a Greek liqueur) is the coldest?

The culinary pick of the strip is *Santorini* (☎ 312-829-8820), 800 W Adams (Map 10), at the corner of Halsted. Fish, both shelled and finned, honor the legacies of

Greek fishermen. The room is boisterous yet cozy, thanks in part to the large Aegean fireplace. Everything, from the bread to the baklava, goes down swimmingly. Portions are huge, which encourages convivial sharing. Fresh whole fish is prepared and served in a tableside display.

Seemingly bigger than any one island, the *Greek Islands* (☎ 312-782-9855), 200 S Halsted (Map 10), is a stalwart of the strip that can accommodate groups of up to a few hundred. The blue-checked tablecloths are perhaps the best part of the noisy place, which always seems to be hosting a table full of accountants in the corner. The beady-eyed waiters are less fun here than waiters elsewhere. There are definitely places on Halsted that do the same standards – moussaka, gyros and company – both better and friendlier.

The *Parthenon* (☎ 312-726-2407), at 314 S Halsted (Map 10), has anchored Greek Town for three decades. The amount of saganaki set ablaze here may be a principal factor in global warming. All the usuals are present, and the lamb comes in many forms. This place is a favorite with Greeks returning to the city from their suburban refuges. The yelps of 'Opaa!' as the cheese ignites reverberate off the walls of the small dining area.

Little Italy

Taylor Street is the focus of this still vibrant neighborhood just southwest of the Loop. The University of Illinois at Chicago has helped stabilize the area, but a public housing project plopped down right in the middle makes safety a bit problematic. Take a cab to any of these places to play it safe. They all offer valet parking.

Still family run after several generations, *Tufano's Vernon Park Tap* (☎ 312-733-3393), 1073 W Vernon Park, just south of the expressway and near the university (Map 10), serves up the kind of old-fashioned Italian food that has become trendy again. Spaghetti and meatballs and other rib-sticking classics are good, filling and cheap. The blackboards carry a long list of daily specials, which can include

such wonderful items as pasta with garlic-crusted broccoli. Entrées average $12. Amid the usual celebrity photos on the wall are some really nice ones showing Joey DiBuono and his family and their patrons through the years. The surrounding neighborhood is leafy and has changed little over the years. Oddly, nearby Vernon Park has been renamed Arrigo Park.

Osteria del Vecchio (☎ 312-666-7333), 1321 W Taylor (Map 10), is a prime spot for chicken Vesuvio, a Chicago creation in which potato wedges, olive oil, herbs and garlic are placed inside a chicken and roasted. The results are worth the effort, especially here.

At 1500 W Taylor (Map 10), *Rosebud* (☎ 312-942-1117) is not only the beginning of a movie but also the beginning of an empire of Italian restaurants in the city. Massive piles of prime pasta, such as lip-shaped cavatelli, come with one of the finest red sauces in town. Even those with reservations can wait an hour or more. So what's the problem? Have some good red wine and settle in for some people-watching – you're bound to see several people who regularly turn up in bold type in the local gossip pages.

PILSEN

During the months when the weather is not miserably cold, Pilsen could be a side street in Mexico City. Blaring signs in Spanish all but obscure the architecture of this neighborhood, which derives its name from the Czechs who originally lived here 100 years ago. Vendors sell ice cream and especially good rice-pudding pops from carts. Others sell corn on the cob that, once bought, is dipped in melted butter and then rolled in spices. Mariachi music bursts out of stores and apartments. The whole scene makes for good strolling, and the innumerable restaurants make for good eating. The 18th St stop on the CTA Blue Line puts you at the west end of the strip.

Pilsen's Bohemian roots merge with its contemporary reality at *Cafe Jumping Bean* (☎ 312-455-0019), 1439 W 18th St (Map 10). Neighborhood artists lounge around on the cast-off furniture, awaiting the inspiration for their next creation. A long list of coffees – many with a Mexican flavor – leads an eclectic menu of snacks, baked goods and other treats, all priced cheap. There's usually a chess game going on at one of the tables. Dominoes are big too.

Look for the blond mermaid on the sign at *Playa Azul* (☎ 312-421-2552), 1514 W 18th St (Map 10). She's the leading symbol for this seafood restaurant, which serves various choices of whole fish, such as red snapper, as well as classic Mexican coastal appetizers, such as ceviche. Get the broiled shrimp with extra garlic for an extra-good and tasty meal. The generously portioned dishes average $7.

Nuevo Leon (☎ 312-421-1517), 1515 W 18th St (Map 10), is right out of Mexico City. Behind the wrought iron on the windows is a brightly lit gem that has superlative versions of all the usual suspects – tacos, tamales, enchiladas, etc. In addition, you can enjoy the menudo (tripe soup), chicken mole and steaks grilled up with onions, tomatoes and jalapeño peppers. Prices are peso-size. The soft corn tortillas are hot and just as fresh as everything else.

There's no shortage of Mexican bakeries both here and elsewhere in Chicago, but *Panadería Laredo* (☎ 312-733-9293), 1540 W 18th St (Map 10), is one of the best. As is usual at these places, you grab a pair of tongs and a tray as you enter and pick and choose from the cases to your stomach's content. Your selections, which should definitely include some of the cinnamon-encrusted buns, are tallied up at the cash register – and they won't cost much. Panadería Laredo specializes in whipped-cream cakes, such as the lavish first communion models on display, complete with little statues of devout children.

CHINATOWN

Chinatown is easily reached by the El – ride the Red Line to the Cermak stop and you're one block east of Wentworth Ave,

the traditional heart of the neighborhood. There are scores more restaurants in Chinatown than the ones listed here. Wanderers will be rewarded by discovering little noodle shops seemingly transplanted from China. New places crop up weekly in the new Chinatown Square development, southwest of Wentworth along Archer Ave.

Phoenix (☎ 312-328-0848), 2131 S Archer (Map 4), rises above the old veterans of Chinatown with excellent, fresh food prepared by chefs direct from Hong Kong. Midday sees an endless parade of dim sum issuing forth on trolleys from the kitchen. On Sunday the parade is lengthier yet. Dinner entrées, including a sizzling shrimp that lives up to its name, range from $9 to $16.

Bring your reading glasses to *Hong Min* (☎ 312-842-5026), 221 W Cermak (Map 4): the menu is an encyclopedia of Cantonese cooking. Tired standbys such as chow mein and sweet and sour dishes come back to life here. If it crawled, swam, quacked or mooed, you can probably order its culinary incarnation. The moody decor makes you think skullduggery is afoot – Hong Min would make a good movie set.

Sit back from 10 am to 3 pm at *Three Happiness* (☎ 312-791-1228), 2130 S Wentworth (Map 4), as cart after cart bursts from the kitchen carrying steaming arrays of little treats. The staff may or may not be ready to help you choose, so plunge in and pick a plate. Savvy nibblers angle for tables near the kitchen, where they can get first dibs on the emerging bounty. Everything is tallied on little cards; the meal will rarely add up to more than about $10 a head. They also do dinner here, but that's not the point. Sunday is the most popular day – be prepared to line up.

An enduring Cantonese-style restaurant, *Emperor's Choice* (☎ 312-225-8800), 2238 S Wentworth (Map 4), is known for excellent seafood and service to match. The ginger scallops are just as succulent as the name suggests. Lobster is at the center of the menu and many of the tables. Prepared several ways, it stars in several prix-fixe meals that average $25 a person. Feel like some snake? Ask for the special menu for more adventurous diners. But fear not, it doesn't list anything you'd typically call the exterminators for.

The ducks in the window at *Seven Treasures* (312-225-2668), 2312 S Wentworth (Map 4), aren't going anywhere. But the frenetic cooks at the woks in the kitchen, which overlooks the sidewalk, compensate for the ducks' inactivity. Who needs a TV food show when you can watch these Cantonese masters slicing, dicing and stir-frying up a storm? When you're tired of just looking, or you're just too hungry, step inside this steamy, bustling family restaurant. All the usual items are here – choose what looked especially good from the street.

NEAR SOUTH

The giant parking lot fills up after Sox games at the *Glass Dome Hickory Pit* (☎ 312-842-7600), 2801 S Halsted. People have been taking their parents here for 40 years. Supertender ribs in a mild sauce are the main event at the scores of tables beneath the transparent ceiling. Be sure to have some fries. Prices are moderate.

Healthy is in the stomach of the eater at *Healthy Food Lithuanian Restaurant* (☎ 312-326-2724), 3236 S Halsted. The food is homemade with fresh ingredients, but don't go looking for tofu and sprouts. The kugelis (meat-filled dumplings) are fried in good, honest bacon fat, the blinis (pancakes) are filled with sour cream, and the cakes are made with real butter. Hey – Grandma would have called it healthy. Since 1938, the prices have left the wallet feeling healthy, too.

About as good a down-home diner as you can get, *Gladys' Luncheonette* (☎ 773-548-6848), 4527 S Indiana, has been serving the notable and the common for more than 50 years. Gladys isn't in too often these days, but her hard-working husband, Kinnard Holcomb, still greets every diner as he has since the start. The white-aproned waitresses are ageless and their service timeless. The menu bursts with inexpensive soul food and other American standards.

HYDE PARK

Ride the Metra Electric Line from the Randolph St station to Hyde Park. You can exit at the 53rd, 55th-56th-57th, or 59th St stations. Alternatively, the drive south on Lake Shore Drive has nice views of the lake and the Loop. Within the environs of the University of Chicago, you'll find a true college town atmosphere. The people at the table next to yours may well be debating whether a butterfly flapping its wings in Indonesia really is responsible for global warming.

Fiery jerk chicken is the specialty at *Island Delites* (☎ 773-324-3100), 1461 E Hyde Park Blvd, just west of Blackstone Ave (Map 11). Owner Jay Martin's other Jamaican specialties include catfish and curried goat. The lines get long, the prices are Gilligan's Island-size, and you can eat in or take out.

Given Chicago's geographic obsession with 'sides,' be they North, West, South, or a combination thereof, it gladdens the heart to finally see a place apply such logic to the menu. The 'south sides' at *Dixie Kitchen & Bait Shop* (☎ 773-363-4943), 5225 S Harper (Map 11), are soulful standards such as sweet potatoes and black-eyed peas. The main events are both uptown and downtown: shrimp in garlic, blackened catfish and country fried steak. Prices are as cheap as the faux rummage-sale interior. They have good gumbo and luscious oyster po' boys. Everything is cheap, cheap, cheap, including the fried green tomatoes.

Hyde Park is also the fortunate home of a branch of *Jacob Bros Bagels* (☎ 773-493-2245), 1301 E 53rd (Map 11). See the full, rapturous details in the Gold Coast section.

Feel like you're in the midst of one of those atmospheric National Public Radio segments at *Valois* (☎ 773-667-0647), 1518 E 53rd (Map 11), where the motto is 'See your food.' A best-selling book, *Slim's Table*, by Michael Dunier, is based on the customers at this cafeteria, which has been serving up large and tasty portions for more than 70 years The standards include long-steamed vegetables, hot beef sandwiches, casseroles and good, fresh biscuits. Every-

RICK GERHARTER

South Side soul food

thing is cheap and hearty. The regulars run the gamut of Chicago denizens, from number-crunching Nobel Prize-winners to rock-crunching ditch diggers, and would make the basis for a good book . . .

The Hyde Park outlet of the local *Edwardo's* pizza chain (☎ 773-241-7960), 1321 E 57th (Map 11), is well situated right off campus. The uniformly high quality pizzas use fresh ingredients. The star of the menu is the stuffed spinach pizza, which is several inches thick with spinach and cheese and provides a week's worth of iron and calcium in one sitting. A medium that's perfect for two goes for $13.

The world's woes have been solved several times over at *Medici* (☎ 773-667-7394), 1327 E 57th (Map 11). Thin-crust pizza, sandwiches and salads are the main attractions. Burgers come in myriad choices, with optional toppings such as blue cheese and olives and an average price of $7. Vegetarians can seek refuge in the $5 veggie sandwich. For breakfast, try the 'eggs espresso,'

made by steaming eggs in an espresso machine. After your meal, check out the vast bulletin board out front. It's the perfect place to size up the character of the community and possibly find the complete works of John Maynard Keynes for sale cheap.

The motto is 'dim sum and then sum' at *Lulu's* (☎ 773-288-2988), 1333 E 57th (Map 11). This compact and fun place offers a wide range of Asian fare at cheap prices: a vast bowl of udon noodle soup is $5. Vietnamese rice and noodle salad is $6.75. On Sunday anything on the menu can be part of a $11 brunch. Desserts are large. The double-decker crispy banana split is best split.

The menu at the *Caffè Florian* (☎ 773-752-4100), 1450 E 57th (Map 11), traces its heritage back to the original, which opened in Venice in 1720 and was a meeting place for 'the intelligentsia, with patrons including the most celebrated artists, poets, dramatists, actors, musicians and philosophers of the time.' The humbler modern version serves lesser mortals, as well as such dubiously Venetian staples as black bean nachos and fish and chips. A few Italian items do make the menu, which covers much of the world and won't set you back more than about $6 a dish.

FAR SOUTH

Getting to these places can be dicey without a car.

With 40% of Chicago's population being African American, it makes sense that soul food places are common. Many are little more than storefronts serving takeout buckets of wings, rib tips and macaroni and cheese. *Army & Lou's* (☎ 773-483-3100), 422 E 75th St, near Martin Luther King Drive, is several cuts above the norm. Fried chicken, catfish, collard greens, sweet potato pie and all the other classics are here at prices that are good for your soul. If you've never had soul food, start at this warm and welcoming Chicago classic. Don't be surprised if you see a few famous black politicians, led by Jesse Jackson. And don't be surprised if some white politician shows up for a photo op.

You need a car to get to *Leon's Bar-B-Q* (☎ 773-731-1454), 1640 E 79th St, since there's no seating inside. The big slabs of ribs come with your choice of sauce, from mild to hot. I prefer hot so I can grow some hair on my chest while I fill my belly. These are some of the best ribs in town. Just watch your upholstery. The original location is at 8243 S Cottage Grove.

MARKETS

Chicago's city government has begun an aggressive program to sponsor farmers' markets throughout the city from June through October. The markets attract growers from around the region and offer excellent opportunities to try some of the wonderful Midwestern produce that seems to lose something – say, flavor – on its way to the huge supermarkets. Strawberries in June and tomatoes in August are just two of the treats.

The market schedule is rather complex, but there is an information line (☎ 312-744-9187) that will tell you when there will be one open at a convenient time for you. In the Loop there is a market on Tuesday from 7 am to 3 pm in the Federal Plaza bounded by Adams and Dearborn.

Entertainment

THEATER

After exploding locally in the early 1980s, Chicago theater had imploded by later in the decade as too many companies chased too few ticket buyers. Things have stabilized since then, and the surge in the economy has helped spark the life-giving flow of corporate dollars.

Some theater groups have their own venues; others don't. Those that have a regular home are noted in the listings in this chapter, which gives just a small idea of what's being staged. As always, check the local press – especially the *Reader* – to find out what's hot.

Buying Tickets

Ticket prices for shows range from $6 for small shows to $35 or more for main companies like Steppenwolf. Most average in the $15 to $25 range. However, there are a variety of ways to beat these costs.

Hot Tix The League of Chicago Theaters operates Hot Tix booths, where same-day tickets to participating shows are sold at half price. The lineup varies every day and is usually best early in the week. Hot Tix now sells weekend tickets beginning on Friday, and they also sell regular full-price tickets. They have three city locations: 108 N State, across from Field's (Map 3); 806 N Michigan, in the historic Water Tower (Map 5); and 2301 N Clark, in Tower Records (Map 6). You can call to see what's on offer (☎ 900-225-2225), but the calls cost a discount-nullifying $1 a minute.

Other Discounts From the number of discounts offered, buying a theater ticket can be like shopping for a bargain airfare. Students, children, senior citizens, the disabled, groups and even actors may qualify for discounts. In addition, some places have last-minute deals right before curtain and preview prices before the official pre-miere. The moral of this story is always check with the box office for any and all deals before plunking down your bucks – even at Hot Tix.

Major Companies

A classical company hosted by the University of Chicago, *Court Theatre* (☎ 773-753-4472), 5535 S Ellis (Map 11), focuses on great works from the Greeks to Shakespeare, as well as plays from certain cultures that are not often performed in the US.

The city's oldest professional theater group is also its most prestigious. *Goodman Theatre* (☎ 312-443-3800), 200 S Columbus at the rear of the Art Institute (Map 3), presents five works a year, a mixture of classics and new pieces. Their annual production of *A Christmas Carol* is a local family tradition.

Steppenwolf Theater (☎ 312-335-1650), 1650 N Halsted (Map 6), an ensemble group, helped put Chicago theater on the map when it won a Tony Award in 1985 for regional theater excellence. Among the actors here who have gone on to fame and fortune (and who regularly return to perform) are John Malkovich, Gary Sinise and John Mahoney, the crotchety old coot on *Frasier*.

The long-established *Victory Gardens Theater* (☎ 773-871-3000), 2257 N Lincoln (Map 6), is playwright-friendly and specializes in world premieres of plays by Chicago authors.

Small Companies

Across from the superb Ginger Man pub (see the Bars section), *Annoyance Theater* (☎ 773-929-6200), 3747 N Clark (Map 7), has leased its own building thanks to the enduring success of its manic romp *Coed Prison Sluts*, a goofy and generally tasteless send-up of syrupy pop culture.

Performing original works about the lives of African Americans, *Black Ensemble Theatre* (☎ 773-769-4451) is at 4520 N Beacon on the north side of the Uptown Hull House. The all-women company *Footsteps Theatre* (☎ 773-878-4840), 5230 N Clark (Map 8), performs new works and gives old classics such as *Othello* a new spin.

The comedy improv group the *Free Associates* (☎ 773-975-7171), based at the Ivanhoe Theater, 750 W Wellington (Map 7), is responsible for works such as *BS*, a much needed skewering of the TV show *ER*. When not laying waste to pop culture, they do a show skewering Shakespeare. It's about time.

Actors who hoped to lure audiences with the 'bait' of their talent founded *Live Bait Theater* (☎ 773-871-1212), 3914 N Clark (Map 7), in 1987. They've been reeling them in ever since. Many of the productions are the works of founders Sharon Evans, Catherine Evans and John Ragir. They also have a casual restaurant and bar in the same building.

True marionette magic is staged by the experts at the *Puppet Parlor* (☎ 773-774-2919), 1922 W Montrose, who have spent years perfecting their art. The shows are usually based on classic fairy tales such as 'Beauty and the Beast.'

Shattered Globe Theater (☎ 773-404-1237), 2856 N Halsted (Map 7), is a vibrant young company that concentrates on serious drama. I've seen some gripping performances here.

The creative troupe *Strawdog Theatre* (☎ 773-528-9889), 3829 N Broadway (Map 7), performs quirky works of their own writing – highly inventive and fun. *Torso Theatre* (☎ 773-549-3330), at 2827 N Broadway (Map 7), is home of the long-running late-night hit *Cannibal Cheerleaders on Crack*, a blacker-than-black farce that violates every taboo and human orifice. Bodily fluids spurt across the stage, and you'll be hugging your gut in horror or, more probably, to ease the ache of your hysterical laughter.

The people at *Touchstone Theatre* (☎ 312-404-4700), 2851 N Halsted (Map 7), took over Steppenwolf's old space and share its spirit and devotion to hard-edged, serious work.

Venues

The productions at the *Apollo Theater* (☎ 773-935-6100), 2540 N Lincoln (Map 6), seem to be one high-energy tribute after another to the music of the 1950s. The enormous, 4300-seat *Arie Crown Theater* (☎ 312-791-6190), in the East Building at McCormick Place, 23rd St and Lake Shore Drive (Map 4), is almost lost in the far more enormous convention center. It books more concerts than stage productions, though it does put on the *Nutcracker* every year.

A huge and beautiful old theater, the *Auditorium Theater* (☎ 312-902-1500), at 50 E Congress (Map 3), is worth the price of admission even if the performance stinks. It usually books short runs of traveling companies. The *Briar St Theatre* (☎ 773-348-4000), 3133 N Halsted (Map 7), presents major theatrical works that often later end up as movies, as *Six Degrees of Separation* did.

The grandest of the grand old movie palaces, the *Chicago Theater* (☎ 312-443-1130), 175 N State (Map 3), was restored in 1986. Now run by the Disney organization, it will feature a rotating lineup of stage versions of Disney classics.

The *Ivanhoe Theater* (☎ 773-975-7171), 750 W Wellington (Map 7), presents long-running shows such as *Hellcab*, which features an uncomfortably accurate portrayal of a crazed taxi driver, by the Famous Door Theatre Company. In the Blackstone Hotel, the *Mayfair Theatre* (☎ 312-786-9120), 636 S Michigan (Map 4), is the home of *Shear Madness*, an endlessly running murder-mystery farce that will probably charge right into the new millennium.

A community-based African American theater, the *New Regal Theatre* (☎ 773-721-9230), 1645 E 79th St, on the South Side, books touring national acts. Built in 1927, its ceiling in the grand lobby replicates an Oriental rug in tile. The *Organic Theater* (☎ 773-327-5588), 3319 N Clark (Map 7), is a large community theater with a history of critical and financial successes, such as *Bleacher Bums* and David Mamet's *Sexual Perversity in Chicago*. Whatever you do, don't ask about the musical version of *Gilligan's Island*.

The *Royal George Theatre* (☎ 312-988-9000), 1641 N Halsted (Map 6), is three theaters in one building: The cabaret venue presents long-running mainstream productions such as *Forever Plaid*, a send-up of all-male singing groups. The main stage presents works with big-name stars, and the gallery hosts various improv and minor works performed by small troupes. The place to go for traveling Broadway productions is the *Shubert Theater* (☎ 312-977-1700), 22 W Monroe (Map 3).

At *Tommy Gun's Garage* (☎ 312-728-2828), 1239 S State (Map 4), the joke starts with the phone number, which spells out 'rat-a-tat.' A dinner theater whose level of skill varies between painfully hokey and downright stupid, its performers, beginning with the guy at the door talking with lots of 'de's' and 'dems,' have an infectious energy that comes from not taking the material too seriously. Soon the large numbers of bus tour groups are singing right along.

Voltaire (☎ 773-275-2201), 3231 N Clark (Map 7) is a hip bar and club that plays host to a bunch of talented young acting groups. There can be several different shows a night at this venue.

CINEMAS

Moviegoing is enjoying a renaissance in the city. After the dismal 1970s and 1980s, which saw the grand Loop theaters close and be replaced by the sort of anonymous boxes that can be found at any suburban mall, a new generation of fancier theaters has started to emerge. The daily papers have all the listings for the first-run places. Check out the *Reader* or *New City* for the more offbeat choices.

Each October, the Chicago Film Festival brings a score of films from around the world to town for two weeks. Check with the festival (☎ 312-644-3456) for each year's schedule.

First Run

There are good and bad choices if you want to see the latest Hollywood blockbuster. Here's a guide:

The *Broadway* (☎ 773-327-4114), 3175 N Broadway (Map 7), is a good-size old neighborhood theater with a penchant for the offbeat. *Burnham Plaza* (☎ 312-922-1090), 826 S Wabash (Map 4), is a sorely needed multiplex serving the South Side. It's not a terribly great facility, however. *Chestnut*

RICK GERHARTER
The South Side's New Regal Theatre

Windy City Television

You don't have to go to Hollywood or New York to be in the audience of a national TV talk show; three are based in Chicago. If you reserve tickets in advance, you can sit in the audience and watch episodes being taped. Afterward, you may get to meet the hosts and their guests, although in the case of the latter two, you may not want to. Adhering to the currently popular trend, each show is named after its host.

The charismatic ratings leader of syndicated talk shows, Oprah Winfrey, is also a local celebrity. From her own production facility in the West Loop – Harpo Studios (wondering about the name? Spell it backward) – she tapes her wildly popular show, which features celebrities, the occasional serious news investigation and discussions of issues as diverse as racial prejudice and whom to invite to your third wedding. (Of course, let's not go overboard; you haven't lived until you've seen Oprah swoon over Ivana Trump.) Her monthly book recommendation has been credited as the single best thing to happen to serious fiction since Mark Twain.

For tickets, call ☎ 312-591-9595 at least a month in advance. Harpo Studios is at 1050 W Washington at Aberdeen (Map 10).

If Oprah is the class act of daytime TV, the following two hosts mud-wrestle for the title at the opposite end of the spectrum. They invite the kind of guests whose intimate lives could involve hedgehogs. Their programs have found ratings success, which just goes to show that you should never overestimate the intelligence of the viewers. Joining the audience can be a raucous or sickening experience.

A former stand-up comedian, Jenny Jones has become her own unintentional joke. Her monthly firings of hapless stylists unable to breathe life into her chemically damaged hair have been gleefully followed in the *Tribune*'s Inc. column.

Jones specializes in tawdry topics that involve unconventional sexual pairings. Guests for whom the chance to fly to Chicago and stay in a cheap hotel represents the high point of their lives cheerfully bare every last detail of their low-jinx. For tickets, call ☎ 312-836-9485.

The third local talk-show host, Jerry Springer, disingenuously admits that his guests are vile but that he's really trying to communicate valid moral messages. Yeah, right. Springer delivers a pious sermon at the end of each episode that's a laugh in itself. During ratings periods he heroically books neo-Nazis whom he then throws out of the studio for being Nazis. For tickets, call ☎ 312-321-5365.

The latter two shows are taped at the NBC Tower, 454 N Columbus, a block east of Michigan (Map 3). A friend who works in the building told me that security had to be increased after various 'guests' were found attempting petty crimes. ■

Station (☎ 312-337-7301), 830 N Clark (Map 5), is a former post office converted into a multiplex with smallish screens.

At 58 E Oak (Map 5), the *Esquire* (☎ 312-280-0101) is a once-grand theater that got chopped up into five small ones, with predictably unfortunate results. *Hyde Park* (☎ 773-288-4900), 5238 S Harper Ave (Map 11), is a functional multiplex in the heart of Hyde Park. It's worthwhile only if you're already in the neighborhood.

If your movie is in the main theater at *McClurg Court* (☎ 312-642-0723), 330 E Ohio (Map 3), you're in for a treat: it's one of the city's largest screens. The other two theaters were once the balcony, and they should have stayed that way. Hiding in the basement of the mall of the same name are the *900 N Michigan Theaters* (☎ 312-787-1988; Map 5). They are an oddity: a decent modern theater with two sizable screens. *Pipers Alley* (☎ 312-642-7500), in the complex of the same name at the northwest corner of North and Wells (Map 6), is a pretty decent multiplex with good sightlines.

Despite the name, the entrance to the theaters at *600 N Michigan* (☎ 312-255-9340) is off Rush St (Map 3), but the views of Michigan Ave from inside are great. A new, comfortable complex with six screens of various sizes, it has a café and concessions on each of its three floors. The *Village Theater* (☎ 312-642-2403), 1548 N Clark (Map 5), is a cool old theater broken up into several smaller ones. It shows quirky new releases and second runs at good prices.

The *Water Tower* (☎ 312-649-5790), 845 N Michigan at the mall of the same name (Map 5), is the worst of the first-run lot: It has seven smallish screens in two completely different locations in the building; check carefully to be sure you go where you need to. Some of the theaters have support columns in the sightline of some seats.

Rep Houses

Many of the following theaters have schedules that change nightly.

Even the worst film gets better when you've got a pizza in front of you and a pitcher of beer at your side. As you watch second-run Hollywood releases at the *Brew & View* (☎ 312-618-8439), in the Vic Theater at 3145 N Sheffield (Map 7), just south of Belmont, you can behave as badly as you would at home – in fact, they encourage it.

Facets Multimedia (☎ 773-281-9075), 1517 W Fullerton, at the west edge of Lincoln Park, shows interesting obscure movies that would never get booked elsewhere. This is the place to find the denizens of Chicago's film community between Hollywood contracts.

The *Film Center at the Art Institute* (☎ 312-443-3733), at the corner of Jackson and Columbus, on the east side of the Art Institute (Map 3), shows everything from dreck by students whose day jobs are unlikely to involve film to wonderful but unsung gems by Estonian directors. The monthly schedule includes theme nights of forgotten American classics.

The *Fine Arts Theaters* (☎ 312-939-3700), 418 S Michigan (Map 3), are a bit worn and the carpeting can be sticky, but what do you want from a facility that had its first performance in 1898? The main theater is an old and grand place, with a huge screen. The three smaller theaters are just that – small. This is the principal venue for 'serious' movies in the city; look for the latest Merchant-Ivory production here.

No matter what's showing, it's worth going to the *Music Box Theater* (☎ 773-871-6604), 3733 N Southport (Map 7), in the heart of the nightlife district, just to see the place. This perfectly restored theater dates from 1929 and was designed as a Moorish fantasy. Clouds float across the ceiling, which has twinkling stars. The film programs are always first rate. A second, small theater is a serviceable place for held-over films that have proved more popular than expected.

The floors creak at the *Three Penny Cinema* (☎ 773-935-5744), 2424 N Lincoln (Map 6), a ramshackle, family-run complex of tiny theaters in Lincoln Park. But what they save in maintenance, you save in admission. Tickets are cheap for out-of-prime major releases and a good selection of the better minor films.

CLASSICAL MUSIC & OPERA

You can find classical music performances throughout the year. In the summer they move outside under the stars and amid the mosquitoes.

Performances of the Chicago Symphony Orchestra and the Lyric Opera of Chicago are sold out each year to subscribers. However, even the most devout fans don't make every performance. Check with the box offices, or hang around about 30 minutes before curtain: more often than not some besuited swell will offer you a pair of tickets, and in my experience these people got class – they would sooner cough during a solo than gouge you. Check the *Reader* or *Chicago* magazine to see what's being performed.

Chicago Symphony Orchestra

The CSO enjoys lavish support locally. Their home, the former Orchestra Hall, has become the Symphony Center thanks to a major reconstruction (see Orchestra Hall Plays a New Tune). The late Sir Georg Solti was music director from 1969 to '92 and is credited with propelling the CSO to the very front ranks of world symphony orchestras. The current director, Daniel Barenboim, had the classic big pair of shoes to fill and has done so masterfully. He has molded the group with his personality, and the acclaim continues. The season runs from September to May. In the summer, when they aren't wowing some European capital, the CSO often performs at Ravinia (see Summer Venues).

Orchestra Hall Plays a New Tune

Built in 1904, Orchestra Hall has received tuba-size accolades through the years for its role in Chicago Symphony Orchestra's reaching world-class status. Its dry, clear sound gave the symphony a rich and powerful sound in its live broadcasts and recordings.

Thus, when a $110 million renovation project was announced in 1995, purists and long-time fans fretted that the hall's sound would be ruined. Skeptics could remember a botched sound-related renovation in 1966 that symphony officials spent the next two years eradicating.

Although inherent conservatism played a role in the fretting, along with a good dose of pessimism, there certainly were grounds for the concern. Engineering for sound, unlike lighting, is still a poorly understood science that relies on myriad factors, such as wall and ceiling shapes, the material used in seats and floors and many, many more details. Indeed, Carnegie Hall in New York, widely considered one of the best listening spaces in the world, is thought to get its rich sound in part from the 100-year-old varnish used on the woodwork. So a collective breath was held throughout the renovation in 1996 and '97.

The physical portion of the project was widely seen as necessary. The building is now linked to another building at 63 E Adams, giving the complex more office and rehearsal space. They are connected by a large glass rotunda that gives concertgoers new and much improved access to the hall. New construction in the rear means that the stage where the orchestra plays has been deepened, and a new acoustic crown is supposed to silence a perennial complaint by the musicians that they can't hear each other. The roof has been raised by 36 feet to allow for greater sound reverberation.

Perhaps even more important, the seating area has been expanded, though capacity has been decreased to 2500 (from about 2600) to allow for bigger seats and aisles to accommodate the fat-cat symphony patrons of today.

The whole complex reopened October 4, 1997, with a new name proclaiming its much grander form: Symphony Center. Reviews immediately indicated that the skeptics should have been wringing their hands over something else. Wynne Delacoma, the classical music critic for the *Sun-Times*, proclaimed the changes 'an impressive achievement and a major success.' The consensus is that the hall's sound is now lusher, but the clarity remains. The brass still hits heart-stirring highs, but the violins are no longer lost in the clamor. ■

The Civic Orchestra of Chicago, the training branch of the CSO, has carved out a fine reputation as well. Visiting conductors and musicians often work with them. And their tickets are free! Both groups are headquartered in the Symphony Center (☎ 312-435-8122), 220 S Michigan, across from the Art Institute (Map 3).

Lyric Opera of Chicago

One of the top opera companies in the US, the Lyric performs in the grand old Civic Opera House (☎ 312-332-2244), on the south branch of the river at 20 N Wacker. Their repertoire is a shrewd mix of old classics and much more modern and daring work. You can catch the *Mikado* one week and some totally new but emotionally stunning piece the next.

The company has had excellent luck luring top international names, such as Placido Domingo. It also has joined the international trend of projecting translations of the lyrics onto a screen above the proscenium. Purists shudder with horror; others, whose Italian or German isn't what it could be, sit back and happily read away.

Long-time artistic director Bruno Bartoletti, who is credited with propelling the Lyric to its high status, will retire in April 1999. Gregarious Andrew Davis, music director of the BBC Symphony, is set to replace him in 2000. The season runs from September to March.

Choral and Chamber Music

A vocal group founded by a group of men in 1872, the *Apollo Chorus of Chicago* (☎ 630-960-2251) is now based in suburban Downer's Grove, but they usually perform at the Symphony Center. Tickets for their Christmas performance of Handel's *Messiah* sell out every year.

The *Chicago Chamber Musicians* (☎ 773-342-5226) are dedicated to spreading the sound of chamber music. They perform the classics, as well as initiate numerous outreach programs to the community.

His Majestie's Clerkes (☎ 312-461-0723), an a cappella group named after the 'clerkes' who sang in 16th-century England, are known for their clear and haunting sound. Most of their performances are in any of the city's grand churches.

Music of the Baroque (☎ 312-551-1415), one of the largest choral and orchestra groups of its kind in the US, brings the music of the Middle Ages and Renaissance to life. Their Christmas brass and choral concerts are huge successes.

Other Opera & Orchestra

The *Chicago Opera Theater* (☎ 773-292-7521) stages contemporary and popular works during the summer. *Chicago Sinfonietta* (☎ 312-857-1062) is a multiracial group of young musicians led by the locally well known Paul Freeman; they perform classics as well as adventurous modern works by the likes of Thelonious Monk.

No Wagner here! The Evanston-based *Light Opera Works* (☎ 847-869-6300) specializes in the delightful work of composers such as Gilbert and Sullivan and Leonard Bernstein.

Summer Venues

Grant Park Classical music for the masses is performed four nights a week for most of the summer at the Petrillo Music Shell, in Grant Park at Jackson and Columbus between the Art Institute and the lake: under the auspices of the Chicago Park District, the Grant Park Symphony Orchestra gives free (read: free!) concerts, usually on Wednesday, Friday, Saturday and Sunday evenings, although events such as the jazz festival can alter the schedule. At present Chicago is the only city in the US to boast a free symphony orchestra. The performances span the classical genre, from opera to Broadway and 'pop.' The orchestra is quite good and worth far more than you pay.

The amphitheater seating in front of the stage is given on a first-come, first-served basis, although members of the Grant Park Concerts Society (☎ 312-819-0614) get reserved seats. Other seating is on the vast Grant Park grasslands. Viewing is problematic from the park – often some lout comes and puts his blanket right in front of yours.

But the sound is good. You can bring a picnic or buy food from the growing number of vendors who set up along Jackson. This is a classic Chicago experience and a great way to relax for an hour or the whole show. For information, call the society or the Park District (☎ 312-742-7638).

Ravinia Festival Ravinia (☎ 773-728-4642) is a vast open-air festival in Highland Park, on the North Shore, where the CSO and other classical, jazz, folk, ethnic and pop groups perform. The main pavilion has seating for several hundred in a bowl-like setting with a good view of the stage and the performers. But these tickets sell quickly, and most people end up sitting on the acres of lawn. Here's the catch: you can't see the performers from the lawn, nor can you hear them, except from the huge speakers hanging in the trees.

So for about $8 (pavilion seats cost much, much more), you get to sit on grass and listen to music from a speaker. Some people revel in the experience, bringing baskets of designer picnic ware, gourmet edibles and fine bubbly. They lie back, stare at the stars and let the music send their blood pressure plummeting. Others just can't see the point of all the bother (count me in this churlish lot). Bathroom lines can be long, parking can be bad and traffic after the show can negate any calming influence. You'll have to decide this one for yourself – look in the mirror and say, 'Am I type A? Or am I type B?'

If you do go, avoid the traffic and take the 45-minute Metra/Union Pacific North Line train from Northwestern station to Ravinia station ($3.20). Trains stop before and after the concerts right in front of the gates. Food and expensive drink are available at the park, which is at Green Bay and Lake Cook Rds in Highland Park.

DANCE
The city scored an unexpected coup when the world-famous *Joffrey Ballet of Chicago* (☎ 312-739-0120) relocated from New York in 1995. The large and well-funded company is noted for its energetic work,

frequently travels the world and has an impressive storehouse of pieces it regularly performs. Still, dance and ballet seem to have fallen through the cracks of the Chicago cultural scene. There are several excellent companies, and they do receive some support, but the lack of a main performing venue keeps the groups continually striving for recognition. The Chicago Dance Coalition Hotline (☎ 312-419-8383) can tell you when and where performances are being staged. Check the *Reader* also.

Ballet Chicago (☎ 312-251-8838) is a home-grown troupe that has received much acclaim for its precision and skill performing classical ballet works. The *Chicago Moving Co* (☎ 773-880-5402) was founded by Nana Shineflug, one of the pioneers of modern dance in Chicago. The works and performers are all local. Gus Giordano, of *Gus Giordano Jazz Dance Chicago* (☎ 847-866-6779), an Evanston-based group, didn't just invent jazz dance, he continues to define it after 35 years.

The preeminent dance group in the city, with an international reputation to match, is *Hubbard St Dance* (☎ 312-663-0853). They are known for energetic and technically virtuoso performances under the direction of the best choreographers in the world. Now they just need a permanent home. The racially diverse *Joel Hall Dancers* (☎ 312-587-1122) are known for their energetic performances to the work of jazz greats.

Another founder of the modern dance scene in the city, Shirley Mordine heads the dance department at Columbia College, the growing local arts school. Unlike some groups, *Mordine & Company Dance Theatre* (☎ 773-989-3310) is known for productions with elaborate costumes, lighting and sets.

The word 'muntu' means 'the essence of humanity' in Bantu, and *Muntu Dance Theater of Chicago* (☎ 773-602-1135) performs African and American dances that draw on ancient and contemporary movement. The *River North Dance Company* (☎ 312-944-2888) is a vibrant young company that brings elements of punk, house, hip-hop, mime and more to modern dance.

LIVE MUSIC

There's more music being played any night of the week in Chicago than you could ever listen to, even if you had a year. Obviously, with the city's blues and jazz roots, you can hear world-class performances in those genres. Rock is widely played as well, by everyone from garage bands to revival groups to cutting-edge names. And with the wealth of ethnic enclaves, you're sure to find about anything else you desire. More than for any other section in this book, when it comes to finding out what's happening during your visit, check the *Reader* – its listings and reviews are voluminous.

Cover charges vary widely depending on the venue, the day of the week, the musicians playing, etc. Small places presenting relative unknowns will be free on a Sunday night, while larger venues with top names on the weekend will demand $15 or more.

Jazz & Blues

In a city that has played a pivotal role not just in jazz and blues but in the genres they have engendered, such as rock, it would be foolish not to sample some of this vibrant scene. Some clubs book only jazz, some only blues and some both. Whatever your preference, there are myriad venues for each genre any night of the week. Aficionados can find well-regarded players all over town. The following listings are by neighborhood.

Near North *Andy's* (☎ 312-642-6805), 11 E Hubbard just east of State (Map 3), is a veteran jazz and blues bar and restaurant that doesn't charge a cover for its lunchtime shows. Some workers come at lunch and never quite make it back to the office.

From the pint-size balcony at the *Backroom* (☎ 312-751-2433), 1007 N Rush (Map 5), you view the jazz musicians via a mirror. Those on the equally tiny main floor enjoy the kind of intimacy you'd get if these guys were playing in your bedroom.

Look for the Pabst signs in the window to find *Blue Chicago* (☎ 312-642-6261), 736 N Clark (Map 3). The blues is mainstream and the talent lives up to the club's name. If you're staying in the neighbor-

hood and don't feel like hitting the road, you won't go wrong here. They have a second, smaller location at 536 N Clark.

You'll feel like a canned fish when a big name plays at the *Gold Star Sardine Bar* (☎ 312-664-4215), 680 N Lake Shore Drive (Map 3; the entrance off McClurg Court is more convenient). They never announce themselves in advance, but famous people regularly appear on the tiny stage of this tiny – but very tony – nightclub, a Chicago classic. Regulars can still recall the night in the mid-1980s when Pia Zadora gave her lungs, the mike and the audience a workout.

With Blues Brother Dan Aykroyd as an investor, there was no question that the *House of Blues* (☎ 312-923-2000), at 329 N Dearborn in the Marina City complex (Map 3), would make a huge impact on Chicago. The main floor is a casual eatery in a broken-down bayou setting. Video monitors show diners what's happening upstairs in the large and open music venue. You can

RICK GERHARTER
Marina City: Home to the House of Blues

RICK GERHARTER

You'll find red-hot talent at Blue Chicago.

hear excellent blues here, but the club doesn't limit itself. Some nights it's aging rockers such as Ted Nugent, other nights it's salsa. The Sunday gospel brunch features soul-stirring Chicago groups and Cajun chow. Reserve early – it's usually mobbed. Oh, and try not to notice the gift shop near the door.

At *Jazz Showcase* (☎ 312-670-2473), 59 W Grand (Map 3), owner Joe Segal presides over an elegant club that caters to jazz purists. Nobody's yelling 'Hey gimme anudda pitcha!' here.

Lincoln Park *Adagio* (☎ 312-787-0400), 923 W Weed (Map 6), west of Old Town and the North-Clybourn intersection, is a fancy and friendly jazz place that's on the radar of visiting celebrities. For a classic blues club, you can't go wrong at the appropriately named *BLUES* (☎ 773-528-1012), 2519 N Halsted (Map 6). Long, narrow and crowded, the veteran club crackles with

electric moments where the crowd shares in the music. Major names such as Carl Weathersby play here regularly.

Combine excellent and inventive cuisine with good jazz and you get *Green Dolphin St* (☎ 773-395-0066), 2200 N Ashland at Webster, a large riverside jazz venue that has scrapped the location's roots as a junk-auto dealer and replicated the look of a 1940s club.

They keep *Kingston Mines* (☎ 773-477-4646), 2548 N Halsted (Map 6), hot and sweaty so that the blues neophytes in the audience will feel like they're having a genuine experience – sort of like a gritty theme park. Two stages mean that somebody's always on. The club's popularity means they get big names.

Lilly's (☎ 773-525-2422), 2513 N Lincoln (Map 6), routinely presents excellent local blues acts. The interior has an odd Mexican air; the largely ignored balcony has good views on crowded nights.

Farther North Bigger than its sibling on Halsted, *BLUES Etcetera* (☎ 773-525-8989), 1124 W Belmont (Map 7), isn't as intimate but doesn't get as crowded either. It books top acts on a great stage with a good sound system. Heard enough? You can hit the backroom pool tables.

You can sit in Al Capone's booth at the *Green Mill* (☎ 773-878-5552), 4802 N Broadway at Lawrence (Map 8), a half block west of the Lawrence El stop. This is a true cocktail lounge, curved leather booths and all. Little has changed in 70 years – it still books top local and national jazz acts. On Sunday it has a nationally known poetry night where would-be poets try out their best work on the openly skeptical crowd.

Wicker Park/Bucktown The *Note* (☎ 312-489-0011), 1565 N Milwaukee (Map 9), is a dive, and not in an atmospheric way, either. It's rather uncomfortable, and the stage can be hard to see, but if you just want to hear great jazz, then there's no problem at all. Sunday night jam sessions with Von Freeman are very popular and cover-free.

South Loop The *Bop Shop* (☎ 312-235-3232), on S Wabash between 9th and Roosevelt (Map 4), is where you're likely to find the musicians themselves on off-nights. Its recent move from Wicker Park may prove it the forerunner of a trend. On Monday it's beat-poets night.

You're likely to find the namesake at *Buddy Guy's Legends* (☎ 312-427-0333), 754 S Wabash (Map 4), although rather than playing he's likely to be giving the crowd a circumspect gaze as he adds up a stack of receipts. Look for top national and local groups playing in this no-nonsense, cavernous space.

Tenor saxophonist Fred Anderson owns the *Velvet Lounge* (☎ 312-791-9050), 2128½ S Indiana (Map 4). Visiting jazz musicians often hang out here late at night. The tiny place rocks during frequent impromptu jam sessions.

South Side The *New Checkerboard Lounge* (☎ 773-743-3335), 423 E 43rd, is just what you would expect from one of the most well-known blues clubs in town. People from around the world and just down the street gather on the mismatched furniture to hear some of the greats. The friendly staff contrasts with the rough edges of the decor and the neighborhood. Take a cab – they'll get you one when you leave.

Talk around the oval bar centers on jazz at the *New Apartment Lounge* (☎ 773-483-7728), 504 E 75th St. The crowds are friendly at this simple storefront venue, where saxophonist Von Freeman jams on Tuesday nights.

Lounge Music
The best piano man in the city is Buddy Charles at the *Coq d'Or* (☎ 312-787-2200), on the ground level of the Drake Hotel, 140 E Walton at Michigan (Map 5). For 50 years he has entertained in Chicago with his smooth playing and mellifluous voice, which can warm even the coldest heart. Cole Porter, Frank Sinatra and others are part of his repertoire. And he

Buddy Guy

takes requests. He's on from Tuesday to Saturday, 9:30 pm to 1:30 am.

For a funky night dating back to the days before colorization, try the *Zebra Lounge* (☎ 312-642-5140), 1220 N State (Map 5), a small, smoky joint decorated entirely in black and white. The piano can get as scratchy as the voices of the crowd, older people who like to sing along. Regular ivory-stroker Tom Oman is another veteran who knows his stuff.

Rock

Lincoln Park You might think you're back in the folks' basement jamming air guitar when you're at *Lounge Ax* (☎ 773-525-6620), 2438 N Lincoln (Map 6), where the couches are old and the decor is homemade with attitude. Good local bands with names like Big Angry Fish and Red Red Meat perform most nights.

Lake View/Wrigleyville Absolutely lacking in charm when there isn't a band playing (*don't* go after a Cubs game), the sprawling *Cubby Bear* (☎ 773-327-1662), 1059 W Addison at Clark (Map 7), redeems itself through its enlightened booking policy. It's a fairly intimate place to see the likes of Johnny Cash and Seven Mary Three.

Time was when the big breweries owned their own corner bars all over town. *Shuba's* (☎ 773-525-2508), 3159 N Southport, at Belmont (Map 7), is one; look for the big Schlitz globe carved in limestone over the door. Fortunately, the beer and its brewers are long gone. Good local bands and vocalists are regularly booked into the backroom, which, when the lights are on, looks like something out of a Catholic grade school.

Acts on the verge of superstardom regularly play *Metro* (☎ 773-549-3604), 3730 N Clark (Map 7). The former classic theater draws national bands ready to give up their custom buses out front for custom jets. Fans flock in from all over the Midwest to hear the latest in rock. After the show, or even if you don't have tickets, the *Smart Bar*, in the basement, has dancing until dawn.

Wicker Park/Bucktown Two storefronts combine for one cool venue at *Double Door* (☎ 773-489-3160), 1572 N Milwaukee, near North (Map 9). It's all hard-edged, cutting-edge rock in this former liquor store, which still has its original sign out front. The bouncer will steer you less than carefully to the proper door. The night before the Rolling Stones kicked off their 1997 world tour, they showed up here and played several sets for an amazed crowd. (Obviously, the venue shed its young image when the Stones played, but who doesn't like oldies?)

The *Empty Bottle* (☎ 773-276-3600), 1035 N Western, is a creative place that seems to have hit on all cylinders from the time it opened five years ago. The music spans the styles from funk to punk. The progressive, hip bands reflect the crowd. Check out the goofy decor, which includes a door from a cop car. No word on how it was obtained.

The classic Wicker Park club, *Phyllis' Musical Inn* (☎ 773-486-9862), at 1800 W Division, features bands who want to be the next Smashing Pumpkins, or better yet, their replacements. Bored with the band? Shoot hoops in the beer garden.

Other Music

A small but elegant room across from the zoo, *Toulouse Cognac Bar* (☎ 773-665-9071), 2140 Lincoln Park West (Map 6), has smooth, tuxedoed waiters who glide among the red velvet in this **cabaret**. The singers are uniformly expert at the classics and old ballads. This place is highly recommended for a classy evening out.

You sit on folding chairs in a large old room, but the **folk music** is first-rate at the *Old Town School of Folk Music* (☎ 773-525-7793), 909 W Armitage (Map 6). Major national and local acts, such as the Lonesome River Band, play regularly. You can hear the call of the banjos from the street.

It's out of the way, but the *Abbey Pub* (☎ 773-478-4408), 3420 W Grace at Elston, on the northwest side, is the closest you can come to a major venue for **Irish music** in Chicago. The vast music area has second-level tables that let you gaze down on all the red hair below. An adjoining pub is smoky and crowded. It's about a $12 cab ride from River North.

Dreadlocks meet capitalism at the *Wild Hare and Singing Armadillo Frog Sanctuary* (☎ 773-327-4273), 3530 N Clark (Map 7), a modern **reggae** club run by guys from Jamaica but financed by local venture capitalists. It books top touring acts, but beware after Cubs games, when the baseball caps outnumber the dreadlocks by a factor of 10.

BARS

As I said in the introduction to my book the *Official Chicago Bar Guide*, this city has the best selection of bars in the US. The long winters mean that for decades, Chicagoans have pursued their social lives indoors. There are places for virtually every mood and personality. The descriptions run the gamut: neighborhood, classy, fun, loud, sports, quiet, literary, young, old, pickup, cozy, romantic, smoky – you name it. The selection here is just a smattering of the best. (Other places are listed in the Live Music section, as well as in the Places to Stay and

---

Beer Riots

Chicago has always had a taste for beer. The roots of this passion go all the way back to the beer riots of 1855. A group of xenophobes from the appropriately named Know-Nothing political party tried to stanch the flow of German and Irish immigrants into the city by banning beer sales on Sunday and raising license fees to a then-outrageous $300 a year. These rules, however, did not apply to saloons that sold the more expensive whiskey, the drink of choice for the Know-Nothings.

Riots broke out as Germans from the North Side and Irish from the South Side made their anger and beverage preferences known. Mobs roamed the city, fighting with the police and 'liberating' kegs from bars. A long-term solution to the problem was found when the two ethnic groups registered to vote and seized control of City Hall for the next 120 years. ■

Places to Eat chapters.) The best way to see if a place is for you is to wander in.

Note, too, that although the usual closing time is 2 am, many bars are open until 4 am weekdays and 5 am Saturday. Summer is also a good bar season, as many pubs now boast beer gardens and outdoor seating.

Near North

Although the following bars – with one notable exception – aren't bad, be prepared to head farther north for the best ones.

You'll feel like an extra in one of those 1930s Universal B-movie horror flicks at *Harry's Velvet Room* (☎ 312-828-0770), 534 N Clark. Heavy velvet curtains cloak the walls, and dark statues and theatrical chandeliers add character. You half expect Bela Lugosi to peek out from behind the curtains. The long drink menu emphasizes cocktails and long drinks. There's a slew of Scotches and whiskeys. The martini page lists 34 variations. Late-night Draculas can sate their hunger from the small food menu, which includes carpaccio, artichoke-heart terrine and shiitake-mushroom pizza. This place is very cigar friendly – there's one on the menu cover. Open until 4 am.

Forget the Hollywood crap, forget the thespian waiters and all the other gimmicks found in neighboring blocks, and experience the real Chicago at the *Brehon Pub* (☎ 312-642-1071), 731 N Wells (Map 3). A fine example of the corner saloons that once dotted Chicago, the Brehon purveys draft beer in frosted glasses to neighborhood crowds perched on the high stools. And there's no hideous gift shop at the entrance.

In this neighborhood where everything is faux and for sale, word of a new Irish bar sparks fears of high-concept Blarney. But fear not: *Celtic Crossing* (☎ 312-337-1005), 751 N Clark (Map 3), is owned by real Irish people and employs actual Irish bartenders. Barely a year old, it already feels like it has been here for years. Best of all, the pints of Guinness ($4, not bad) come in *imperial* pints. That's a little over three ounces more!

Older and richer gay men favor *Gentry* (☎ 312-664-1033), 712 N Rush (Map 3).

Cheezburger! Cheezburger!

Only the dimmest of rubes tries to order fries at the *Billy Goat Tavern* (☎ 312-222-1525), 430 N Michigan (Map 3), a cathedral of grease, smoke and rousing conversations that also qualifies as a tourist attraction. John Belushi brought national fame to this place with his skit on *Saturday Night Live*. Among the memorable lines: 'No fries – chips!' and 'No Coke – Pepsi!'

Local fame stems from its subterranean position between the *Sun-Times* and *Tribune*. Legions of photos of dead writers and columnists line the walls; any link between their demises and a steady diet of beer, burgers and cigarettes must be coincidental. Mike Royko was a legendary patron. On weekdays a few Cubs-logo-bedecked families

sometimes visit but are soon chased away by the after-work hordes of drunken journalists, carousing ad execs and no-nonsense laborers. It warms the heart to see a suburban family cowering next to some beer-swilling, smoke-blowing galoot. But beware: the tourists get their revenge on the weekends, when they own the place. Prices are dirt cheap, but if you like your burger to have the distinctive taste of meat, order a double. Note: When I'm in town, you can find me on Friday after work at the corner table on the far left as you enter. ■

RICK GERHARTER

Barkeep Jeff Magill

There's a good wine list, a fireplace and nightly piano music. Keep a lookout for supremely bitchy Khris Francis belting out tunes.

The best beer selection in the neighborhood is at the *Clark St Ale House* (☎ 312-642-9253), 742 N Clark (Map 3). They have a rotating selection of tap beer from some of the best Midwestern microbreweries. Work up a thirst on the free pretzels and cool off in the beer garden out back.

I include *Dick's Last Resort* (☎ 312-836-7870), 435 E Illinois in North Pier (Map 3), only to warn people off. By virtue of being a national chain with lots of advertising in in-flight magazines, Dick's has gotten itself on the map. If you're in a group and someone insists on going here, opt for a different taxi.

Old Town

One of my favorites, the *Olde Town Ale House* (☎ 312-944-7020), 219 W North (Map 6), caters to winners, losers and everyone in between. A neighborhood

staple from the days before this was a neighborhood, it has been the scene of delusionary late-night musings since the 1960s – the last time paint was applied. Grab a front-window table and settle in for a few hours, but never before 11 pm. To complete the scene, drop a quarter into the jukebox for Nat King Cole's 'Too Young.'

Marge's (☎ 312-944-9775), at 1758 N Sedgwick (Map 6), is a friendly corner pub that has survived unscathed the ravages of the neighborhood's rapid climb up the property value ladder.

The bras hanging from the ceiling set the tone at *Weed's* (☎ 312-943-7815), 1555 N Dayton, just west of Halsted and west of Old Town (Map 6). They're from patrons caught up in the spirit of a bar where beatnik meets Bohemia. The tables have candles in old wine bottles, and the bathroom walls are covered in anarchist or profane slogans. Owner Sergio Mayora – whose name has motivated him to run most unsuccessfully for mayor – keeps spirits loose with frequent shots of tequila on the house.

Why You Need to Ignore Uncle Ed

You probably know somebody like Uncle Ed: he hears where you're going and says, 'Oh yeah, Chi-town. Great place. Love it. Let me tell you where to go, that Rush St . . . ' The last time he actually hit the Windy City was for a Shriners' convention in 1973. Follow his advice and you'll want to tell him where to go. In the interest of harmony, here's what to avoid no matter how many Uncle Eds (or dubious guidebooks) tell you otherwise.

Rush St Actually, Rush St today has many fine cafés and boutiques. But the Rush St that was the dream of zillions of conventioneers is just about as dead as the '70s polyester scene that once thrived here. Few of the places from the '70s – the era when bell-bottoms, gold chains and unnatural natural fibers were in – still survive. Tread carefully along the street: cabs still disgorge loads of yahoos who keep some pretty rotten places in business.

Division St When many out-of-towners yak about 'Rush St,' they're really referring to the strip on Division west of State. A few holdovers from the block's glory days, like Mother's (☎ 312-642-7251) and Butch McGuire's (☎ 312-787-3984), survive, at 26 and 20 W Division, respectively. But they and their neighbors are mere artifacts, just like their aging patrons who have their second divorces behind them and are hoping to get lucky just one more time. ■

Lincoln Park

It's hard to find a really bad bar in this neighborhood. They all got chased away by picky residents. *Moran's* (☎ 773-549-2337), 1983 N Clybourn at Sheffield (Map 6), is a huge but mellow sports bar with a big beer garden. On Saturday in the fall they have just about every college game on the scores of TVs. But if you hate the University of Michigan, don't go. It's a Wolverine hangout.

A true singles bar for people in their 20s (although any bar can be a singles bar if you have personality), *Kincade's* (☎ 773-348-0010), 950 W Armitage (Map 6), is filled with people looking over your shoulder as they talk to you, in case somebody more appealing walks in.

DePaul students and fans gather at *Kelly's* (☎ 773-281-0656), right under the El at 949 W Webster (Map 6). The same family has been welcoming all comers since 1933. They have good burgers, but hold on to your glass when a train goes by.

Lincoln Ave Starting at Armitage, you can head north on Lincoln from pub to pub through Wrightwood Ave if your constitution holds out.

A genial older crowd of writers and would-be poets hangs out at *Sterch's* (☎ 773-281-2653), at 2238 N Lincoln (Map 6).

There's never a shortage of conversation, some of it even sensible. If you're lucky, you'll visit on 'bag night' and find out for yourself what that means.

Young drunks returning to their childhoods rule the *Big Nasty* (☎ 773-404-1535), 2242 N Lincoln (Map 6). Cans of Silly String are for sale at the bar, which also

Do Jell-O shots with the King.

does a big business in Jell-O shots (recipe: substitute grain alcohol for water in standard Jell-O recipe, and chill). Look for the huge Elvis on the facade.

Several other bars on the block are similar to one another: lots of old wood, plenty of beer and not excessively clean. They are jammed with the after-work yuppie crowd on Friday. They include *Kelsey's*, at 2265; *Waterloo*, at 2270; and *Jerry's*, at 2274 (all Map 6).

At 2446 (Map 6), *Red Lion Pub* (☎ 773-348-2695) is a British-style pub run by real Brits. Besides plenty of UK brews, this cozy spot features the best onion rings in the city ($3.95). Definitely better than Spotted Dick.

The slogan at the *Gin Mill* (☎ 773-549-3232), at 2462 (Map 6), is 'We drink our share and sell the rest.' They're very friendly about it, too, with remarkable $2-pint specials on microbrews some nights.

A rarity: the food is as good as the music (classic rock) at *Lucille's* (☎ 773-929-0660), 2470 N Lincoln Ave (Map 6). No stale pretzels or day-old popcorn here. How about munchies like bruschetta and prosciutto? They have an excellent selection of wines by the glass.

One of the liveliest 4 am bars on Lincoln is *Deja Vu* (☎ 773-871-0205), at 2624 (Map 6). The high-ceilinged old place has been buffed up with a metallic blue-and-white motif. Occasionally there's a band, and on some Wednesdays the place has turtle races. There's no sympathy if yours comes in last and you wail, 'I bet on the slow one.'

Small Brews, Big Flavor

Although it has the highest consumption of beer in the US, Chicago didn't have a single brewery in the city limits after World War II. Instead it was a thirsty target square in the cross hairs of the big brewers in Milwaukee and St Louis. That changed in the 1980s when the first of a series of microbreweries opened. Following the trend that has been hot nationwide, Chicago now boasts several excellent breweries that produce a score of tasty, unusual and daring beers.

An increasing number of bars and restaurants are serving a range of locally produced beers on tap. If you have the chance to sample any products from the microbreweries listed here, by all means do so.

Owner Ted Furman has taken his former hobby into the big time with a range of inventive **Golden Prairie** beers from his converted warehouse on the northwest side. His lagers and ales are excellent. Look for his seasonal efforts, such as stouts. If you find his rarely produced honey-ginger ale, settle back for a joyous time.

Goose Island started as a microbrewery and restaurant (☎ 312-915-0071) at 1800 N Clybourn (Map 6), and it usually has six or more widely varied brews on tap. (The food isn't bad, and the free homemade seasoned potato chips are great.) Two years ago, Goose Island opened a regular brewery near the United Center. Its product is available

RICK GERHARTER

on tap and in bottles all over town.

A bunch of accountants sick of Bud and Miller started the **Chicago Brewing Company** to produce beers they'd enjoy. Their Legacy Lager, Big Shoulders Porter and Heartland Weiss are excellent and widely available.

Baderbrau always seems to be having financial problems, but there's no problem with this excellent, hoppy pilsner.

The legendary Loop restaurant **Berghoff** operates its own brewery in Wisconsin. Widely sold, the beer is somehow best at Berghoff's own stand-up bar (☎ 312-427-3170), 17 W Adams. Try their weiss with a lemon. ■

Lake View/Wrigleyville

A refined and classy place perfect for a post-theater drink, a celebratory toast or a romantic tête-à-tête is *Pops for Champagne* (☎ 773-472-1000), 2934 N Sheffield (Map 7). They have 12 champagnes by the glass, 140 more by the bottle and scores of excellent wines as well. The snacks are suitably chichi – pâté and the like – and they have live jazz some nights.

Cody's (☎ 773-528-4050), 1658 W Barry, just west of Ashland and south of Belmont, is as laid-back as its namesake, the owner's dog. A good way to get a read on the crowd is by guessing the thickness of the dust on the Grand Marnier bottle. The bathrooms boast some of the most literate and esoteric graffiti in town. ('Soylent Green is people, but tastes like chicken.') There's a pool table, dart boards, an upright piano, a diverse selection on the jukebox and several TVs. Cody's also has an excellent beer garden with bocce.

Halsted St The following are just two of the scores of gay bars that line Halsted from Belmont north past Addison. There's everything from friendly corner pubs to hard-core leather joints.

Roscoes (☎ 773-281-3355), 3354 N Halsted (Map 7), is the kind of gay bar you could take your straight brother to. Within this very friendly corner pub is a tasty menu, a beer garden and dancing.

Scoping is the pastime at *Bucks* (☎ 773-525-1125), 3439 N Halsted (Map 7). If you feel a pair of eyes on you in this relaxed bar, it may actually be the stuffed deer looking down from the wall.

Clark St Area Going north from Belmont, Clark St is chock-a-block with bars. Many come and go with passing fancy. Start at one end of the strip and work your way to the other.

Relive college at *Yak-zies* (☎ 773-525-9200), 3710 N Clark (Map 7), with lots of young people wearing sweats and working quickly through pitchers of beer. The TVs show plenty of college sports action, while the frat crowd digs into plates of the pop-

ular Buffalo wings and unique parsley-crust pizza.

At the north end, the *Ginger Man* (☎ 773-549-2050), 3740 N Clark (Map 7), is a splendid place to finish your march. Its huge and eclectic beer selection is enjoyed by theater types and other creative folks. The G-Man, as it is often called, avoids the overamped Cubs mania of the rest of the strip by playing classical music when the Cubs play at home. There are numerous pool tables in back. This is a great place to settle in for a few hours.

Guthrie's (☎ 773-477-2900), at 1300 W Addison (Map 7), is a charming outpost on this street linking Clark with Southport. A local institution, it remains true to its mellow roots even as the neighborhood goes manic around it. The glassed-in back porch is fittingly furnished with patio chairs. Most tables sport a box of Trivial Pursuit cards. This is the perfect neighborhood bar.

Southport Lanes (☎ 773-472-6600), 3325 N Southport (Map 7), has undergone a renaissance under the thoughtful management of some upscale types. The bar actually has an annex with four hand-set bowling lanes. The main bar has an inspirational old mural of cavorting nymphs. There's a good beer selection and lots of sidewalk tables.

Andersonville

Owner Michael Roper has created one of Chicago's best bars in the name of the national beer of his ancestral Malta. *Hop Leaf* (☎ 773-334-9851), 5148 N Clark, just south of Foster (Map 8), features an intricate original tin ceiling and has a good selection of wines. The beers are artfully selected by Roper with an emphasis on American, Belgian and German brews.

Artsy folk, people who own only black clothes and creative types who have sold out to ad agencies have replaced the old Swedes at *Simon's* (☎ 773-878-0894), 5210 N Clark (Map 8). The long bar is right out of the '50s, the patrons right in their 20s. Former owner Simon Lundberg installed the portholes in the facade to remind him of the ship that carried him to America from Sweden.

Wicker Park/Bucktown

Funky and relaxed bars litter these two neighborhoods.

A former homeless man has made good at *Yo Mama's* (☎ 773-862-5293), 1466 N Milwaukee (Map 9). Jeffrey Reid runs the joint of his dreams, which has pillows on the floor, poetry readings, jam sessions and other happy, funky happenings. His philosophy is proclaimed in the front window: 'You know you really have to raise the stakes these days to be a pervert.'

There's a little bit of everything, including attitude, at *Holiday Club* (☎ 773-486-0686), 1471 N Milwaukee (Map 9): live music, sidewalk tables and enough kitschy krap from the '50s to stock a bad thrift shop. *Nick's* (☎ 312-252-1155), 1516 N Milwaukee (Map 9), is free of attitude and blessed with friendliness. The big joint has good beer and good conversation. If the roar of the El excites you, hop out to the beer garden in back.

Part club, part neighborhood hangout, *Mad Bar* (☎ 773-227-2277), at 1640 N Damen (Map 9), packs 'em in most nights. It's not enormous, but they still have lots of tables and chairs, with good drinks and even better sound. This is a relaxed place for friends to engage in the old pastimes of drinking and dancing.

An archaic Schlitz sign identifies *Lemmings* (☎ 773-862-1688), 1850 N Damen (Map 9). This mellow bar has a pool table, pinball machine, good beers on tap and a sign in the window telling local artists how they can get their work displayed in the bar.

Drink locally and think globally at the *Map Room* (☎ 773-252-7636), 1949 N Hoyne at Armitage (Map 9), a friendly corner bar where globes line the walls and a huge map of the world covers the back wall and ceiling. Gaze at the map from the overstuffed furniture and try to find some place Lonely Planet doesn't cover. The Map Room has lots of local brews and games for whiling away cold winter days.

Pet a kitty at the *Charleston* (☎ 773-489-4757), 2076 N Hoyne (Map 9), one block west of Damen. The resident cats will curl up on your lap at this thoroughly laid-back Bucktown hangout. You can't have a bad time at *Danny's* (☎ 773-489-6457), 1951 W Dickens (Map 9), just east of Damen. This old house has been converted into a funhouse. Tables, chairs and old sofas litter the many rooms on the many floors. People feel so much at home they forget where their own is.

At the north end of Bucktown, *Quenchers* (☎ 773-276-9730), at the corner of Fullerton and Western (Map 9), is one of my favorite bars. With 220 beers from more than 40 nations, there is ample opportunity to find that certain something missing from the swill peddled by the US brewery giants: flavor. Locals, artisans, laborers and visiting brew masters enjoy Earle Miller's hospitality. The prices are the cheapest in town: pints of locally brewed Golden Prairie go for $3.

South Side

A cool pub in staid old Bridgeport, *Puffer's* (☎ 773-927-6073), 3356 S Halsted, has a bright orange facade and the neighborhood's most amiable folks hanging out, talking and sampling from the excellent beer selection. A good choice after a Sox game, it's a 15-minute walk west from Comiskey Park.

Gerri's Palm Tavern (☎ 773-373-6292), 446 E 47th St, is a Kenwood-neighborhood classic that has entertained the likes of Joe Lewis, Langston Hughes and other notable African Americans during its long history. Photos of many of them are on the walls. Gerri's hosts occasional live jazz and poetry readings.

'Why?' It's a question I wrote thousands of words about on my college philosophy final, and it's a question eternally debated at *Jimmy's Woodlawn Tap* (☎ 773-643-5516), in Hyde Park at 1172 E 55th (Map 11). U of C types debate even weightier questions in this intellect-rich but bar-poor neighborhood.

DANCE CLUBS

The club scene in Chicago ranges from hip, snooty places where admittance is at the whim of some dullard at the door to casual joints where all you do is dance.

Cover charges vary widely depending on the venue or the day of the week. They can be as much as $20, or there can be no cover at all. Your best bet is to call and find out what they're charging on the night you'd like to go.

Loop

West of downtown, *Shelter* (☎ 312-648-5500), 564 W Fulton, is a cavernous club. It's as close as you can get in Chicago to a New York club with attitude, right down to the arrogant louts guarding the door. The decor changes from room to room and month to month. Once, the main dance floor was ringed with thousands of lava lamps. Shelter has regular rave nights that last three days.

Near North & Gold Coast

It's not a '70s retro bar, it's an authentic '70s bar! *America's Bar* (☎ 312-915-5986), 219 W Erie (Map 3), is part-owned by former Bears running-back great Walter Payton. The music and crowd date from his most prolific years on the field, 15 to 20 years ago. Still, it's a very lively place, with a massive happy hour buffet and another after 2:30 am.

Despite its elegant exterior (the building once housed the Chicago Historical Society), *Excalibur* (☎ 312-266-1944), 632 N Dearborn at Ontario (Map 3), is really the strip mall of clubs. On one dance floor they spin classics that would do any wedding reception proud. In a soaring space by the door called 'the Dome Room,' they book edgier rock bands more often found in Wicker Park. Other areas in this three-floor funhouse have jukeboxes, electronic games, pool and more. The touristy and suburban crowd loves every minute.

The setting and the music are timeless at the *Pump Room* (☎ 312-266-0360), 1301 N State in the Ambassador East Hotel (Map 5). Jazz and dance trios and vocalists

provide slow-dance swing every night. The black they insist you wear here would be formal, not grunge.

Lincoln Park

A two-decade veteran, *Neo* (☎ 773-528-2622), 2350 N Clark (Map 6), dates from the time that Lincoln Park was the city's hottest neighborhood. Now the streets are quiet and very upscale, and this gritty dance club just keeps going, having long since shed its trendy attitude.

Club 950 (☎ 773-929-8955), at 950 W Wrightwood (Map 6), is another veteran club that has kept its edge with a mixture of techno, British and American dance music. It's not very big, which is just as well. The enthusiasm of the tightly packed crowds aids the pounding music in drowning out the neighboring El.

Still another hit on the veterans' parade, the *Octogon* (☎ 773-549-1132), on N Clark where Wrightwood ends (Map 6), has gracefully made the jump into the late '90s with a 'mainstream' mix of techno, industrial and alternative dance music.

Even when the snow is blowing sideways, most nights it's South Beach in *Vinyl* (☎ 312-587-8469), 1615 N Clybourn (Map 6). After the dinner hour dies down, at about 10 pm, DJs spin disco, retro, house and salsa. On Sunday, brunch is served with live music from an Elvis impersonator.

The neighborhood and music are post-industrial at *Crobar* (☎ 312-413-7000), 1543 N Kingsbury, west of Old Town (Map 6). The cavernous interior is a stylish mix of materials intercepted on their way to the metal recycler. The crowd consists of yuppies gone punk for the night and punks who will never go yuppie. On many nights tattoo artists are on call for emergency skin art.

Lake View/Wrigleyville

Feeling lost, lonely, antisocial? *Berlin* (☎ 773-348-4975), 954 W Belmont (Map 7), almost under the El, caters to virtually everyone. The crowd is as mixed as the music, so you're bound to find a friend. Funky and bizarre videos alternate with MTV tracks on the scores of TV screens.

It's as hard core as you can get at *Manhole* (☎ 773-975-9244), 3458 N Halsted (Map 7), a gay club where the porn films on the TVs are mere precursors of things to come. DJs spin dance tunes with a heavy dose of disco every night but Tuesday.

The city's leading gay disco, *Vortex* (☎ 773-975-6622), 3631 N Halsted (Map 7), pounds after midnight. Donna Summer is a treasured oldie at this huge and friendly place.

Farther North

Paris Dance (☎ 773-769-0602), at 1122 W Montrose, two blocks east of Clark, is a former seafood restaurant that's little changed outside, but on the inside is now the city's main lesbian disco. The walls are a fantasy of Rubens-style oil paintings. The music shifts through various theme nights, such as grunge or country and western. Gay men are sometimes welcomed. Sometimes. They smell straight guys a mile away.

Wicker Park/Bucktown

Some of the hottest DJs in town work weekends and Monday at *Red Dog Supreme Funk Parlor* (☎ 773-278-1009), 1958 W North at Damen (Map 9). The music in this kitschy old warehouse is funk, hip-hop and house. The lively crowd is as mixed as you can get sexually and ethnically, but probably not politically.

South Side

The *Cotton Club* (☎ 312-341-9787), 1710 S Michigan (Map 4), is a swank place where dance music with a dose of funk spins five nights a week. The patrons tend to dress sharply to match the elegant surroundings. Some nights they have good live jazz at the piano bar out front.

There are three levels of dancing, comedy and jazz at the *Clique* (☎ 312-326-0274), 2347 S Michigan, near Cermak (Map 4). This is no place for half-measures in the clothing department, as the weekend bouncers can be tough. Once inside, it's a quandary where to go. The dance music is

house and the huge floor is a good default destination while you sort things out.

COMEDY CLUBS

After a burst of club openings in the 1980s, Chicago comedy has shrunk back to its roots, which are dominated by the two world-class venues listed here. Cover charges vary – call to find out.

Second City

Second City, a Chicago must-see (☎ 312-337-3992) at 1616 N Wells (Map 6), is best symbolized by John Belushi, who emerged from the suburbs in 1970 and earned a place with the improvisational troupe with his creative, manic, no-holds-barred style. Soon Belushi was on the main stage, and then it was on to *Saturday Night Live* and fame and fortune.

Since its founding in 1959, Second City has staged more than 80 revues, usually sharp and biting commentaries on life, politics, love and anything else that falls in the cross hairs of their rapid-fire, hard-hitting wit. Bill Murray is another famous alum, as are Gilda Radner, Rick Moranis, Dan Aykroyd and Elaine May. Purists point out that the quality of the performances dipped in the mid 1980s, when the stage was flooded with legions of Shelly Hack wanna-bes. Try to guess which cast members will be the next to ride the train of celebrity and success.

Second City ETC (☎ 312-642-8189), 1608 N Wells, in the Pipers Alley complex, is the troupe's second company. Their work is often more daring, as actors try to get noticed and make the main stage. Both theaters are home to the city's best comedy value most nights after the last show, when they present free improv performances to keep everybody's wit in tune and sharp.

Zanies

The city's main stand-up comedy venue was also its premier one long before a wave of closings sharply reduced competition. *Zanies* (☎ 312-337-4027), 1548 N Wells, a few doors south of North (Map 6), regularly books big-name national acts familiar to anyone with a TV. It also has a good record of perceptively booking comics you're *about* to hear about on TV. Recent performers included Tim Allen, Brett Butler, Jerry Seinfeld and Jenny Jones (before she made a joke of herself with her talk show).

The shows last less than two hours and usually include the efforts of a couple of up-and-comers before the main act. The ceiling is low and the seating is cramped, which only adds to the good cheer.

Improv & Other Places

The mere presence of Second City fuels the dreams of would-be comedians all over the city. Improvisational clubs litter the North Side like the broken dreams of funny people doomed to forever cutting up for their coworkers. The quality of the talent varies from uproarious to cute to stupid. Like on the basketball courts around housing projects, there's lots of competition to be the one in a million who hits the big time.

Other than Zanies, *All Jokes Aside* (☎ 312-922-0577), 1000 S Wabash (Map 4), is the only full-time stand-up comedy place left. It books comedians not yet ready for the big time, but often raw with talent.

Two improv teams compete with deadly seriousness to make you laugh hysterically at *ComedySportz* (☎ 773-549-8080), 3209 N Halsted (Map 7), in the TurnAround Theatre. The audience benefits from this comic capitalism.

First among the improvs, *ImprovOlympic* (☎ 773-880-0199), 3541 N Clark (Map 7), actually pays its professional performers (some shows feature Improv students who haven't quite achieved the status of 'professional' yet), and they earn every dime. Sketches hinge heavily on audience suggestions, and each turn can run 40 minutes or longer. If you're thoroughly motivated by what you see, creators Del Close and Charna Halpern offer a range of courses to suit every temp's budget. The same stage also hosts various improv groups composed of the talented alums.

I hate weddings, but if they all were as much fun as *Tony and Tina's Wedding* (☎ 312-664-8844), 230 W North, in the Pipers Alley complex, I might drag myself to more of them. The shtick is to take the worst moments of every Catholic wedding you've ever attended to high levels of parody. The audience members are the guests and get to be a part of the ceremony and reception. The results, which vary with the crowd, are usually hilarious. Needless to say, Tony's a cad and Tina's hair barely fits through the door. Admission includes the show and the Italian chow.

INTERNET CAFÉS

Places where you can access the Web and check email while having a double decaf latte or perhaps a beer and a snack are excellent ways to stay in touch while traveling and to make onward travel plans. Or you can just catch up on news from your hometown newspaper. The Internet café scene in Chicago is constantly in flux. While I was researching this book, the best outlet in the city yanked out its T1 access (geeks will weep over this) and transmogrified into an unwired Mexican restaurant. The moral of the story: call the places listed here to make certain you'll be able to browse for more than a burrito.

The *Interactive Bean* (☎ 773-528-2881), 1137 W Belmont (Map 7), is three blocks west of the El. The *Map Room* (☎ 773-252-7636), 1949 N Hoyne, at Armitage (Map 9), bills itself as 'a traveler's tavern.' See the listing for it under Bars. The *OnLine Cafe* (☎ 773-929-2777), at 2507 N Lincoln Ave (Map 6), is three blocks west of the El. *Screenz* (☎ 773-388-8300), 2717 N Clark (Map 6), is served by the No 22 Clark bus.

SPECTATOR SPORTS

Chicagoans are deeply loyal to their sports teams, despite their mixed results in competition. Attending a game is a real part of life in the city. Each of the teams, their stadiums and their fans have unique traditions that enrich the experience.

Air Jordan

Day in and day out, Chicagoans need to bless Michael Jordan not only for supplanting Al Capone as the most famous Windy City resident worldwide but also for finally giving at least one of the professional sports teams a winning tradition.

In 1984 Jordan arrived in Chicago to play for the Bulls from his home state of North Carolina, a mostly ignored draft pick. He couldn't even find the ride that had supposedly been sent for him to O'Hare, and he ended up arranging his own.

As his play perked up the previously somnolent play of the Bulls, his local reputation grew. In the 1986-87 season he lead the National Basketball Association in scoring for the first of eight times through 1996. In 1988 he was named the NBA's most valuable player for the first of four times through 1996.

His local celebrity exploded nationally in 1991, when he led the Bulls to the first of three successive championships. His affable demeanor combined with his sheer determination on the court. Advertising and movie contracts have followed, most notably his huge deal with athletic wear with Nike and his starring role opposite Bugs Bunny in *Space Jam*.

Unlike some other sports figures, the six-foot, six-inch Jordan has kept his private life private. He lives in the upscale suburb of Highland Park with his wife and three kids. He hasn't had any run-ins with the law, although there has been some carping about his love of gambling. Tragedy struck in 1993 when his father, James, was murdered. Jordan's interest in basketball waned, and he shocked the town by announcing his retirement and undertaking a professional baseball career with a minor league team connected with the Chicago White Sox.

The little white ball proved entirely different from the big orange one, however. After 18 months of lackluster performance Jordan returned to the Bulls, who had gone adrift in his absence, not even coming close to the championship in the 1993-94 season.

Near the end of the 1994-95 season an electrifying rumor swept the city: Jordan wanted to return to the Bulls. A sign of how deeply Jordan had entrenched himself in Chicago's psyche came when a crowd spontaneously blocked off the street in front of his agent's office, hoping for word of his return.

He did return, playing the remaining 17 games of the season. It was too late to lift the Bulls to the championship that year, but no one cared. The next two seasons, 1995-96 and 1996-97, Jordan led the Bulls to two more championships. All indications are that the 1997-98 season will be Jordan's last, as Bulls owner Jerry Reinsdorf has shown little interest in preserving the team and coaching staff and bearing the cost of their salaries beyond then – in fact, he told all the top talent that they'd be through at the end of the season. If Jordan is still playing and you can swing it, find a way to see a Bulls game – you'll witness possibly the best basketball player ever. ■

Basketball

Try to remember somebody who played for the Chicago Bulls before 1984. Can't? Don't worry – even die-hard fans can't. Michael Jordan has become such a part of the team, it's hard to think of the Bulls without him. It will probably take years after he leaves for the team to develop a new identity (unless they keep winning).

The Bulls play on the West Side in the huge United Center, 1901 W Madison St (Map 10), which replaced the beloved Chicago Stadium in 1995. Besides Jordan, players Scottie Pippin and the wild Dennis Rodman and New Age coach Phil Jackson are stars in their own right. Bulls games are always sold out. Always. Fans cheerfully pony up thousands of dollars for season tickets and hundreds for the chance at one of the playoff games. Bulls management, despite laboring under reviled owner Jerry Reinsdorf (for the ugly details, see the White Sox section), has done a creative job of making the United Center almost as much fun as its predecessor. There's an indoor blimp, lasers, floor games and more to keep the crowd energy up during the interminable time outs for TV commercials.

If it's early in the season or the Bulls aren't playing a good team or Jordan has retired, you can probably get tickets through a broker (look for advertisements in the sports or classifieds sections of the daily newspapers, or in the Yellow Pages) or from a concierge. Even then, you'll pay. For schedule information, call ☎ 312-455-4000.

The CTA runs special buses to the games, mostly from the Loop; call their information line – ☎ 836-7000, preceded by the area code of the area of Chicago you are in (312, 708, 847, 630, or 773) – for information. Cab rides are cheap from the Loop and Near North – $4 to $5 – and parking is plentiful. The neighborhood is improving but still not really safe enough to do much walking.

Baseball

Winning is not a tradition in Chicago baseball. The Cubs last won the World Series in 1908, the Sox in 1917. The Sox tend to have a better record, but it's still nothing that will have you reserving postseason tickets. Regardless, local baseball has a big following based on the teams' longevity in town. Traditionally, Cubs and Sox fans have a great rivalry, but in reality it tends to be rather one-sided: When the Sox lose, the mellow Cubs fans shrug their shoulders. When the Cubs lose, the grittier Sox fans, on the South Side, are jubilant.

Both teams' stadiums are easily accessible via the El, an excellent way to avoid extortionist parking fees, long traffic jams and concerns over beer consumption and driving. At both places, buy your peanuts from the vendors outside the park. They're much cheaper. The season runs from early April, when both stadiums can be very cold, to early October.

Cubs The Cubs defy logic: they are a losing team playing in an old stadium with one of the best attendance records in baseball. The Cubs have been dropping games at the corner of Addison and Clark for more than 80 years, while filling their stadium and the neighborhood with fans.

Much of the team's charm comes from intangibles such as the aesthetic of the famous ivy that covers the outfield wall. Outfielders fear running into its hard, gnarled branches, but who can argue with this gorgeous greenery? Planted in 1937 under the orders of chewing gum baron and team owner Philip K Wrigley, the ivy is but one of his legacies. The other is losing. Wrigley never made it a secret that he wanted Wrigley Field to be a nice place to watch a game. He didn't care if the team lost, a tradition its

ROB HOLMES

'The Friendly Confines'

present owner, the Tribune Company, has had little luck reversing.

With little to celebrate on the field, fans have instead celebrated the field itself. Known as 'the Friendly Confines,' Wrigley Field dates from 1916. Although often changed through the years, it retains its historic charm and is the smallest and most intimate field in Major League Baseball. Popular new stadiums in other cities, such as Baltimore and Denver, have borrowed heavily from its charm.

Few experiences in Chicago can equal an afternoon at Wrigley: the clatter of the El, the closeness of the seats, the spectators on the rooftops, the derisive return of the opposing team's home run balls, becoming friends with the folks around you and yes, the green leaves of the ivy glistening in the sun. Whether it's riding the El to the Addison stop, grabbing a pregame beer on the patio at Bernie's (see Baseball Bars) or going a little nuts in the bleachers, each Cubs fan has his or her own rituals that make a day at Wrigley not a spectator sport but an almost religious experience.

Because of the good attendance, Cubs tickets at night and on Fridays, weekends and holidays can be hard to find. Scalping is illegal and you'll feel like you're doing a drug deal if you try to buy tickets on the street.

For information, call ☎ 773-404-2827. Wrigley Field is one block west of the Addison El stop on the Red Line (Map 7). Parking stinks (it's mostly reserved for neighborhood residents with permits), so take the El or walk.

White Sox Timing is everything, and the Sox's timing sucks. By threatening to move to Florida in 1990, they extorted a new stadium out of the state. Unfortunately, that was right before the Baltimore Orioles moved into their own park, which is a re-creation and celebration of the stadiums of old (in fact, it's a lot like Wrigley Field). So the Sox now have the misfortune of playing in Comiskey Park, a 1991 big bowl that has the dubious honor of being the last of the antiseptic stadiums to be built. The old Comiskey Park was rough around the edges, but it was a memorable place to see a game.

The team itself labors under one of the least popular owners in baseball, Jerry Reinsdorf, a perplexing man who makes no effort to win any popularity contests. During the

1997 season he traded most of the team's good players away in July, saying there was no reason to keep them around since the team had no hope anyway. At the time, the Sox were only 3½ games back from first place.

As is the case with many ballparks, the best reason to go to Comiskey is the fans. They love the team despite the stadium and owner, and they direct many creatively profane slogans toward the latter. The burritos for sale on the mall-like concourse are tasty and are part of a long list of good and greasy food choices. If the Sox hit a home run at night, fireworks are shot off in celebration.

Tickets are pretty easy to come by, although it's still worth calling ahead (☎ 312-674-1000) to make certain they're available. Whatever you do, don't buy seats in the infamous 'nosebleed' upper deck, where the sharply inclined aisles are best scaled with rope and piton.

The stadium is a short walk from the Sox-35th station on the Red Line and the 35-Bronzeville-IIT station on the Green Line. The slightly suspect neighborhood is safe on game days, when it is flooded with cops. Since the city tore down several blocks for the new stadium, parking is plentiful.

Baseball Bars A great Chicago tradition is dissecting your team's latest loss at a corner tavern after the game. The following two bars are near the stadiums and boast a die-hard clientele of fans who pronounce their 'th's' like d's, as in 'da Cubs' and 'da Sox.'

At Wrigley, *Bernie's Tavern* (☎ 773-525-1898), 3664 N Clark St (Map 6), doesn't jack up its prices on game days to fleece unsuspecting fans, as the many upscale joints in the neighborhood do. The side yard filled with cheap patio furniture is one of the nicest places in Wrigleyville before, during and after a game.

At Comiskey, *Jimbo's* (☎ 312-326-3253), 3258 S Princeton Ave, is as unimpressive outside as in. But its charm lies in its crowd: people who prefer their beer out of cans, since bottles are for special occasions like weddings and funerals. For an advanced lesson in profanity, ask them what they think of the Sox's owners.

RAY HILLSTROM
Huddle at Soldier Field

Football
Bears There was a time when the Chicago Bears were one of the most revered franchises in the National Football League. Owner and coach George Halas epitomized the team's no-nonsense, take-no-prisoners approach.

The tradition continued with players such as Walter Payton, Dick Butkus and Mike Singletary and coach Mike Ditka. It even went on after the Bears were passed down to the rather patrician present CEO, Michael McCaskey. They won the Super Bowl in 1986 with a splendid collection of misfits and characters, such as Jim McMahon and William 'the Refrigerator' Perry, who enthralled and charmed the entire city.

As they say, that was then and this is now. Under coach Dave Wannstadt, the Bears have gotten worse and worse. The

1997 season was dismal. Tickets, once a hot commodity, now sell for just a little cold cash. The season runs from August to December, when you can get snowed on.

For information, call ☎ 847-615-2327. South from the Loop, Soldier Field, in Grant Park (Map 4), is a nice autumn-day walk and a really miserable winter-day forced march. Metra trains from Randolph St Station stop at nearby 12th St Station ($1.75), and the Roosevelt Road CTA El stops are a half mile away. The greatest joy for Bears fans of late has been their elaborate tailgate feasts in the parking lots before the games.

Northwestern Playing just north of the city, in Evanston, the Northwestern University Wildcats were long the doormats of the Big 10 football conference. That changed in 1995, when coach Gary Barnett took the team to the Rose Bowl. The winning ways haven't quite continued, but fan interest is much greater now, although you can usually still get tickets. For information, call ☎ 847-491-2287. The newly remodeled and renamed Ryan Stadium, 1501 Central Ave, is a short walk from the Central El stop on the appropriately shaded Purple Line.

One sure sign that the Wildcats are hot is that Barnett now has his own restaurant, just like Michael Jordan. In the Omni Orrington Hotel (☎ 847-866-8700), 1710 Orrington in downtown Evanston, Gary Barnett's is done up in the team color of purple and is filled with mementos.

Notre Dame Even though South Bend, Indiana, isn't one of the wildest places in the Midwest, home football games at the University of Notre Dame live up to their legendary reputation for tradition and spectacle. The Fighting Irish have the best overall college football record in the US, and home games are always sold out. But if you are prepared to pay, any number of people lurking about the streets in the days

and hours before a game will sell you tickets. If it's a major game, such as against USC or Michigan, be prepared to pay in the hundreds. For the unhappily ticketless, which can number in the thousands, there's an energetic tailgating scene that transforms the parking areas around the stadium into a huge party.

The games are played amid a swirl of lore that extends far beyond the field where Knute Rockne once coached. For example, from the newly expanded stadium you can see the mural on the school library nicknamed 'Touchdown Jesus.' The campus is a beautiful place to walk before, during or after the game. The bookstore will sell you anything in blue and gold you could imagine. For information, call ☎ 219-631-7356.

Hockey

Almost every year, the Chicago Blackhawks make the National Hockey League playoffs. Of course, in the NHL, almost every team can make the same boast. The Stanley Cup last came to Chicago in 1961, but the Hawks win enough games every year to keep their rabid fans frothing at the mouth.

The fans' fervor is a show in itself, though it never quite reaches the bloodletting antics of the players on the ice. Games against Detroit and the New York Rangers call for extra amounts of screaming, for which the crowd seems to have bottomless reserves. The action starts with the traditional singing of the national anthem, which here becomes a crowd performance of raw emotion.

The Blackhawks play in the United Center, 1901 W Madison (Map 10). The season runs from October to April. Tickets are often sold out, but brokers and concierges can usually obtain them for a minimal markup. Transportation and parking information is the same as for the Bulls. For other information, call ☎ 312-455-7000.

Shopping

WHERE TO SHOP

Needless to say, you can buy anything you want in Chicago, and lots more things you didn't think you wanted but have to have once you've seen them. The premier shopping street is N Michigan Ave, having surpassed the Loop for that honor in the last two decades.

The listings in this chapter include details on some of the most interesting neighborhood shopping streets, where you really can buy anything.

Loop

Shopping in the Loop was a legendary experience through the 1970s. Then the rise of suburban shopping malls and the stores on N Michigan Ave brought devastation: four of six department stores closed, and scores of smaller stores left. Recently, the area has undergone a rebirth, and although it isn't close to its former glory, numerous national retailers have moved in to serve the huge population of office workers who need to squeeze shopping into their lunch hours. Note that many of these stores are closed on Sundays.

RYAN VER BERKMOES
Outside grand old Marshall Field's

Marshall Field's The grandest old department store in the country, Field's (☎ 312-781-1000) is the best reason not to confine your shopping to N Michigan Ave. It's a full block in size, between Randolph, Wabash, Washington and State (Map 3), with 10 floors of designer clothes, furnishings, gifts, housewares, fine china and crystal and more. A recent $110 million renovation shows on every floor; it created a new central atrium as well, and escalators that show off the scope of the store. Dining under the soaring Christmas tree in the 7th-floor Walnut Room is a local family tradition, but beware – 10 million people in the region all have the same idea. The basement gourmet food court is a good place for quick snacks. The bottom level also has

a wealth of smaller-merchandise areas selling household items, gourmet food, stationery and more. Places to buy the popular minty chocolate Frango mints dot the store.

Field's has a visitor's center in the basement near the Pedway (a subterranean link between various downtown buildings); staff there make reservations at restaurants and shows and offer other services to tourists and visitors.

State St A city initiative has spruced up the State St sidewalks, installed vintage light fixtures and built elegant new subway entrances.

Carson Pirie Scott & Co (☎ 312-641-7000), 1 S State (Map 3), has lived in the shadow of Marshall Field's since it opened in 1899. Architecturally, it's a gem. Its goods are moderately priced, and the selection among its six floors is good. Carson's has a very loyal following of lunchtime shoppers.

Among the many chain stores that are transforming State St are Toys 'R' Us (☎ 312-857-0669), at 10 S State (Map 3), which is one of the busiest stores in the whole chain. TJ Maxx (☎ 312-553-0515) and Filene's Basement (☎ 312-553-1055), are among the stores at 1 N State (Map 3).

Wabash Ave Several long-time local retailers who thrive under the roar of the El have been joined by national chains, making this a vibrant shopping street.

The oldest example in existence of houseware haven Crate & Barrel (☎ 312-372-0100) is at 101 N Wabash, at Washington (Map 3). Also on this block are Eddie Bauer (☎ 312-263-6005), 123 N; the Gap (☎ 312-853-0243), 133 N; and Talbots (☎ 312-236-9515), 139 N (all Map 3).

Just south of Madison St is the 1882 Jeweler's Building, 19 S Wabash (Map 3), the center of Chicago's family jeweler trade. Hundreds of shops in this building, and those at 5 S Wabash, 21 N Wabash and 55 E Washington, sell every kind of watch, ring, ornament and gemstone imaginable. Most are quick to say 'I can get it for you wholesale!' Howard Frum (☎ 312-332-5999) runs one of the most colorful stores of the lot on the 8th floor at 5 S Wabash. A minor celebrity known locally for his nutty TV ads, Frum offers his customers free shoe shines and the chance to join running conversations that once were the focus of a feature on National Public Radio.

Get your Swiss Army knife reconditioned at Otto Pomper (☎ 312-372-0881), in the slablike Mid-America Building, at 135 S Wabash (Map 3). You also can buy a new one or pick up some travel binoculars.

Near North

Galleries, boutiques, antique malls, chain superstores and more populate the blocks north of the river.

In a classic rags-to-riches story, Morrie Mages got his start in his family's store in the old Maxwell St Jewish ghetto, where some of the city's leading retailers got their start selling clothes between the World Wars. He built the place into the world's largest sporting goods store, eventually moving it from Maxwell St into its own, renovated, eight-story warehouse at 620 N LaSalle (now across from the Rock & Roll McDonald's; Map 3). A couple of years ago the Chicago-based national chain Sportmart bought Morrie out for a fortune. Now renamed, the store continues his discounting philosophy, albeit without his inveterate promoter's spirit. Check out Mages' *Chicago Sports Hall of Fame*, on the Ontario St exterior wall.

My wife and I bought all the paper for our handmade wedding invitations from the Paper Source (☎ 312-337-0798), 232 W Chicago, at the El (Map 3). Every kind of paper capable of being produced is here, from delicate Japanese handmade creations to iridescent, neon-hued numbers. They also have a great selection of rubber stamps. Across the street, Pearl (☎ 312-915-0200), 225 W Chicago, sells discounted art supplies you can use on your paper.

Merchandise Mart Touch Camelot at the Merchandise Mart (☎ 312-527-4141), on the river and bounded by Wells, Kinzie and Orleans (Map 3). In 1945 Marshall Field sold what is still the world's largest commercial structure for a song to Joseph P Kennedy, patriarch of the noted politicians. Beautifully restored in the early 1990s, it has a modest collection of chain stores on its lower floors to service the lunchtime shopping needs of the thousands of people who work in the behemoth. But the real allure lies on the many floors devoted to distributor showrooms for home furnishings and other interior fittings. As you prowl the halls, you can find next year's hot trends on display today. Technically, only retailers and buyers are allowed on these floors, but they're simply an elevator ride away for anyone. Don't try to buy anything, though, because you're not allowed. (But think of the savings!)

RYAN VER BERKMOES

The imposing Merchandise Mart

N Michigan Ave

The Greater North Michigan Avenue Association likes to claim that the 'Magnificent Mile,' or 'Mag Mile,' as it's widely known, is one of the top five shopping streets in the world. It's hard to argue with that. Only the south end, toward the river, is a bit thin in retail, and that is expected to change over the next few years.

See the N Michigan Ave & Oak Street Shopping map to find the stores listed here and to see a full listing of the rest of the stores in the area. The crowds peak at lunchtime during the week and all day on weekends. Most of these stores are open on Sunday afternoons.

Water Tower Place In 1977 Water Tower Place (☎ 312-440-3166), 835 N Michigan, brought the concept of vertical shopping malls to Chicago, driving a stake through the heart of State St retail and forever changing the character of N Michigan Ave.

Retail business on the street has grown exponentially since then.

The mall is in many respects an anomaly. Its popularity with out-of-towners and tourists is inexplicable, since its collection of stores can be found at any mainstream mall in the nation. But as a destination it is an unbeatable draw that offers a safely familiar shopping experience within the larger urban milieu. Urban dwellers heavily patronize Water Tower for its practical assortment of useful stores. On holidays, the crowds can become unbearable.

Marshall Field's (☎ 312-335-7700) is in every respect a smaller version of the State St flagship store. Lord & Taylor (☎ 312-787-7400) has a large main floor plus six more floors that snake up through the building. The men's department is known for continual sales on excellent-quality men's wear.

Among the 100 stores on the seven levels of Water Tower Place are the WTTW Store of Knowledge (☎ 312-642-6826), level 7, a clever collection of books and other items relating to the programming of Chicago's PBS station; Michael Jordan Golf (☎ 312-944-4545), level 7, which is a misnomer, since the store features a basketball court and sells a full range of everything Michael, beyond just duffer stuff; and the Warner Bros Studio Store (☎ 312-664-9440), levels 2 and 3, which cheerfully capitalizes on that wascal wabbit and rest of the Looney Tunes gang.

Foodlife, on the Mezzanine, is a good place for a break or a meal. See Places to Eat for details.

900 N Michigan This huge mall (☎ 312-915-3916) had a rocky start in 1989. But it has found its niche as a home to an upscale collection of boutiques, which was possible because it shares management with Water Tower Place, and they simply moved all the expensive places over here.

The most visually appealing mall on the inside, 900 N Michigan suffers from an irritating escalator arrangement that forces you to traipse around each floor as you climb. But that, coupled with the exclusivity of the

RICK GERHARTER
N Michigan Ave shoe shine

shops, means that even at peak times you're not hassled by crowds.

Bloomingdale's (☎ 312-440-4460) is the mall anchor. It is unlike its New York parent in every respect, the local managers having given the store a personality more reflective of the Midwest's supposedly no-nonsense values. However, that doesn't mean it doesn't have a hip and stylish collection, which even extends to the kitchen department.

Henri Bendel (☎ 312-642-0140) has a four-level store filled with haute couture lines right out of *Vogue*.

Also on the fashion front, the following stores get the highest recommendations from the people I know who know about this stuff: Gucci (☎ 312-664-5504), on level 1; Mondi (☎ 312-943-5449), on level 4; and Max Studio (☎ 312-944-4445), on level 4.

The Oak Tree coffee shop (☎ 312-751-1988), level 6, is an old Gold Coast institution that thrived after its move to the mall.

Chicago Place This mall (☎ 312-642-4811), at 700 N Michigan, is a boondoggle. And that's too bad, because it's an attractive building inside and out, with a clever ornamentation theme derived from the wild onions for which some say Chicago is named. But as the third and last vertical mall to arrive on N Michigan Ave, it debuted in a market that was barely supporting the first two. A decreasing number of stores populate the floors, until you get to the 7th floor, which has no stores to call its own.

Saks Fifth Avenue (☎ 312-944-6500) holds its own as the mall's anchor. Customers seek out its seven floors of designer men's and women's wear. Next door, the first three levels are home to national retailers Ann Taylor (☎ 312-335-0117), the Body Shop (☎ 312-482-8301), Talbots (☎ 312-944-6059) and Williams-Sonoma (☎ 312-787-8991).

Of the remaining stores, two stand out for clever and stylish designs: Chiaroscuro (☎ 312-988-9253), level 4, which sells artistic and unusual housewares, and Tutti Italia (☎ 312-642-2808), level 5, which sells huge pasta bowls and other brightly colored items to perk up the dowdiest of kitchens.

The food court on level 8 is filled with plants and fountains and is an example of how this building could really take off if it could just get a critical mass of tenants.

Individual Stores Here are the highlights among the individual stores along N Michigan Ave:

Bigsby & Kruthers (☎ 312-397-0430), 605 N Michigan in the First Chicago bank building, is another great Chicago success story. It sells expensive casual and formal menswear of impeccable taste. The roots of this store, like so many other Chicago retailing greats, lie in the Jewish rag trade, which was a thriving one decades ago on Maxwell St.

Crate & Barrel (312-787-5900), at 646 N Michigan, is yet another local success story. Within the stunning, almost transparent, white store are modestly priced functional and stylish kitchen goods, along with sleek and comfortable furniture. It's always mobbed, and with good reason: if you bought everything in your house from here, you wouldn't go broke and people would rave about your taste. The owners deserve praise, because they could have put up any monstrosity they wished on this blue-chip site, and they opted for classy.

The prices are predictably high at the local outpost of Dallas-based Neiman Marcus (312-642-5900), 737 N Michigan, but that's part of the store's cachet. Now in its second decade, it has settled into the

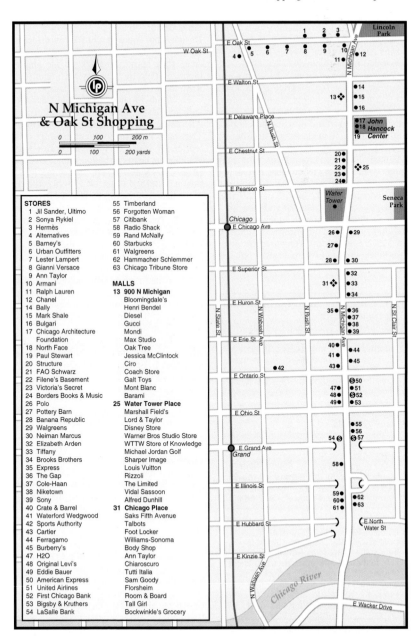

N Michigan Ave & Oak St Shopping

0   100   200 m
0   100   200 yards

STORES
1   Jil Sander, Ultimo
2   Sonya Rykiel
3   Hermès
4   Alternatives
5   Barney's
6   Urban Outfitters
7   Lester Lampert
8   Gianni Versace
9   Ann Taylor
10 Armani
11 Ralph Lauren
12 Chanel
14 Bally
15 Mark Shale
16 Bulgari
17 Chicago Architecture
    Foundation
18 North Face
19 Paul Stewart
20 Structure
21 FAO Schwarz
22 Filene's Basement
23 Victoria's Secret
24 Borders Books & Music
26 Polo
27 Pottery Barn
28 Banana Republic
29 Walgreens
30 Neiman Marcus
32 Elizabeth Arden
33 Tiffany
34 Brooks Brothers
35 Express
36 The Gap
37 Cole-Haan
38 Niketown
39 Sony
40 Crate & Barrel
41 Waterford Wedgwood
42 Sports Authority
43 Cartier
44 Ferragamo
45 Burberry's
47 H2O
48 Original Levi's
49 Eddie Bauer
50 American Express
51 United Airlines
52 First Chicago Bank
53 Bigsby & Kruthers
54 LaSalle Bank

55 Timberland
56 Forgotten Woman
57 Citibank
58 Radio Shack
59 Rand McNally
60 Starbucks
61 Walgreens
62 Hammacher Schlemmer
63 Chicago Tribune Store

MALLS
13 **900 N Michigan**
    Bloomingdale's
    Henri Bendel
    Diesel
    Gucci
    Mondi
    Max Studio
    Oak Tree
    Jessica McClintock
    Ciro
    Coach Store
    Galt Toys
    Mont Blanc
    Barami
25 **Water Tower Place**
    Marshall Field's
    Lord & Taylor
    Disney Store
    Warner Bros Studio Store
    WTTW Store of Knowledge
    Michael Jordan Golf
    Sharper Image
    Louis Vuitton
    Rizzoli
    The Limited
    Vidal Sassoon
    Alfred Dunhill
31 **Chicago Place**
    Saks Fifth Avenue
    Talbots
    Foot Locker
    Williams-Sonoma
    Body Shop
    Ann Taylor
    Chiaroscuro
    Tutti Italia
    Sam Goody
    Florsheim
    Room & Board
    Tall Girl
    Bockwinkle's Grocery

Mag Mile quite nicely, thank you, with its selection of designer clothes and accessories and gourmet foods. The café is renowned for its popovers.

Why buy your shoes at a discount when you can get them for full price at Niketown (☎ 312-642-6363), 669 N Michigan. More noise than substance, this huge, three-level place sells everything in its corporate parent's catalog. It made a splash when it opened in 1992 because it contains some Michael Jordan memorabilia (not *that* much), but by now its concept of placing merchandise in a high-concept setting has been widely copied, and it's not all that interesting anymore. Hint: if you see something you like, trek about a block south and another west to the Sports Authority (☎ 312-266-6608), 50 E Ontario; this huge sports superstore will probably have it on sale.

Merry Memories

No matter their background, people who grew up in the Chicago area are brought together by their memories of the city at Christmastime: the bustling crowds laden with bags, the tinkling of the Salvation Army bells, the holiday music playing from the stores, and red noses and cold cheeks – good excuses for a warm and sugary treat. Here are some of the seasonal highlights.

Around Thanksgiving the city puts up its huge **official Christmas Tree** on Daley Plaza.

In the Loop, Marshall Field's (Map 3) builds elaborate **Christmas windows** with a theme that changes every few years. The many windows all around the building allow for complex stories to be told. Carson Pirie Scott, one block south, also does a commendable job.

The Sunday before Thanksgiving brings the **Mag Mile lights**: zillions of little lights are strung in the trees lining N Michigan Ave, and the effect is magical. The lights stay on until Jan 31. Recently, a parade and other hoopla have been added to the tradition. ∎

Gold Coast

Designer boutiques sprout like mushrooms on the tony blocks just west of Michigan Ave. They sprout so thick on the single block of Oak St between Michigan and Rush that you'd think it was a decayed log.

The kinds of shoes that delight the eye and appall the feet are the specialty at Alternatives (☎ 312-266-1545), 942 N Rush. They have about the most cutting-edge collection of shoes in town, at prices that gladden the hearts of budding Imelda Marcoses everywhere. There's a second location at 2506½ N Clark (☎ 773-281-4801), in the heart of Lincoln Park.

Oak St The anchor at the west end of the street is Barney's (☎ 312-587-1700), 25 E Oak, at Rush. Built during the legendary New York men's store's ill-conceived over-expansion in the 1990s (debt went through the roof, and they barely avoided liquidation), the store has made barely a ripple on the local scene, but it does have a nice selection of its own designer wear and lots of trendy shoes.

Heading east, the names are like the advertiser's index in *Harper's Bazaar*. Here are a few: Jil Sander (☎ 312-335-0006) and Ultimo (☎ 312-787-0906), both at 48 E Oak; Lester Lampert (☎ 312-944-6888), 57 E Oak; Gianni Versace (☎ 312-337-1111), 101 E Oak; Sonya Rykiel (☎ 312-951-0800), 106 E Oak; and Hermès (☎ 312-787-8175), 110 E Oak.

Lincoln Park

Clark St is the main thoroughfare for shopping in Lincoln Park and has shops of every description. Halsted in the blocks north and south of Armitage has some interesting places that cater to women and children.

What the world needs is more milliners like Raymond Hudd (☎ 773-477-1159), 2545 N Clark (Map 6). Custom, creative hats have perched on stands throughout the store and on the heads of satisfied customers for almost 50 years. Given the long tradition, the store deserves special credit for its witty contemporary designs.

Native Australians drop their jaws when they see all the familiar treats from down under crammed into Kangaroo Connection (☎ 773-248-5499), 1113 W Webster (Map 6). Owner Kathy Schubert's best seller by far is Vegemite, the gooey Australian yeast concoction.

Remember the episode of the *Brady Bunch* wherein Peter built the working volcano that covered the whole clan in poop? Your own kid can get the kit for a smaller version of that at Saturday's Child (☎ 773-525-8697), 2146 N Halsted (Map 6). However, the vast majority of the toys and games concentrate on items that are a blast creatively and intellectually, rather than literally. If you're looking for some movie tie-in toy, don't come here.

Your salivary glands will be in overdrive at Sweet Memories (☎ 773-528-8200), 857 W Armitage (Map 6). The huge and detailed chocolate sculptures of subjects such as the Water Tower set the pace for the jewel-like presentations of handcrafted candy. Dieters may be able to subsist on the rich smells alone. On the other hand, they may go mad.

Lake View/Wrigleyville

Stuff that's never worn – let alone sold – on Michigan Ave is de rigueur on Halsted and Clark Sts in Lake View. Even if you're not buying, the browsing is entertainment in itself.

Halsted St North from Belmont you'll find the kind of colorful, irreverent, wild and kinky shops you'd expect in a gay neighborhood.

Gallimaufry Gallery (☎ 773-348-8090), 3345 N Halsted (Map 7), is perhaps the most staid store on the street, but that doesn't mean that their handmade artworks, toys, crafts and incense collection aren't good for extensive browsing. Besides, they do have 'essential oils.'

The naked mannequin in the window of Silver Moon (☎ 773-883-0222), 3337 N Halsted (Map 7), says it all. The weird inventory includes stuffed animal heads.

Bad Boys Chicago (☎ 773-549-7701), 3352 N Halsted (Map 7), stocks the complete line of Speedo underwear and other tight outfits for the crotch. During the store's frequent sales, the larger sizes sell quickly.

99th Floor (☎ 773-348-7781), at 3406 N Halsted (Map 7), has 'Dead Elvis Masks' for $34.50. For more formal occasions, they have black pumps with eight-inch heels in men's sizes.

The best thing about Evil Clown (☎ 773-472-4761), 3418 N Halsted (Map 7), is its name. The small store has a selection of used CDs from people liquidating their collections ahead of the creditors. The staff knows where to find the good stuff. They have a lot of fliers advertising performances by local bands.

'Smoke Crack and Worship Satan' is the felonious and heretical slogan in the window of Moon Mystique (☎ 773-665-9016), 3420 N Halsted (Map 7). Ear and nose piercings are $5 and $10, respectively. Other body parts are somewhat higher.

The 'package' underwear comes in gift packages at We're Everywhere (☎ 773-404-0590), 3434 N Halsted (Map 7). They have lots of other gift items and many T-shirts, with messages from subtle to in your face.

Cheer up with a genuine 1970s smiley face from Beatnix (☎ 773-935-1188), 3436 N Halsted (Map 7). They also have genuine vinyl furniture from the same design-challenged era. The see-through wedding dress, however, is timeless.

The Woolworth of the strip is Gay Mart (☎ 773-929-4272), 3457 N Halsted (Map 7), which sells toys, novelties, calendars, souvenirs, you name it. (Although they don't have one of those smelly parakeet sections.) One of their top sellers is Billy, the heroically endowed 'world's first out and proud gay doll.' Ken would just wilt in Billy's presence – that is, if Ken had anything to wilt.

Cupid's Treasure (☎ 773-348-3884), 3519 N Halsted (Map 7), is the place to buy all those things you wondered if your neighbors owned. Spread through three large rooms, the adult toys on display leave adult browsers giggling like children. The goods – frilly, aromatic, battery-powered, leather and more – should satisfy even the most imaginative of consenting adults. As an added bonus, the friendly sales staff is eager to help and earnest in their advice. Consider the following guidance given to one couple: 'The whip requires more skill. With the paddle, it's easy – you just spank.'

From the great logo to the clothes themselves, Flashy Trash (☎ 773-327-6900), 3524 N Halsted (Map 7), is the most stylish and hip dealer of vintage clothing in town. Such is their reputation that they've branched out into trendy new clothing.

Everything from furs to studs lines the simple pipe coat racks at Brown Elephant (☎ 773-549-5943), 3651 N Halsted (Map 7), the fund-raising resale shop supporting the Howard Brown Health Center, 945 W George (Map 7), an acclaimed clinic serving the gay, lesbian and bisexual community. Among last year's satin dresses you can find some gems, price- and style-wise.

Clark St Near Belmont are several stores serving full-on punks and teens simply interested in manifesting rebelliousness. On weekend days the sidewalks are jammed with rich teens from the North Shore, black-clad punks with blond roots and the rest of the Lake View diaspora. Adding spice to the scene are people selling socialist newspapers. ('Are you tired of working for the rich man?' begins their populist refrain.)

The Alley (☎ 773-525-3180), at 3218 N Clark (Map 7), has taken over a large chunk of the block north of the infamous Dunkin' Donuts. A vast emporium based on counterculture and pop trends, the Alley vends everything from head-shop gear to band posters to human-size dog collars. The supply of *Spinal Tap* T-shirts is, thankfully, better than the supply of puppet T-shirts. Among the labyrinth of rooms is one devoted to the Alley's 'Architectural Revolution' store, which sells plaster reproductions of gargoyles, Ionic pillars and other items that have found a mainstream market with non-dog-collar-wearing interior designers.

Around the corner at Taboo-Tabou (☎ 773-548-2266), 858 W Belmont, they sell condoms in more flavors than Baskin-Robbins sells ice cream.

A shrine to Jerry Garcia dominates the window of Smugglers Row (☎ 773-528-0885), 3238 N Clark (Map 7). Everything tie-dyed, from bandannas to undies, lines the shelves in this counterculture extravaganza.

Huge heavy boots of minimal practical value outside a steel mill (read: Doc Martens) are perennially on sale at *Air Wair* (☎ 773-244-0099), 3240 N Clark (Map 7). Celebrate your third piercing with a pair.

Comic-book collecting gets a good name at Chicago Comics (☎ 773-528-1983), 3244 N Clark (Map 7). It's big, clean, orderly, and jazz plays softly on the sound system. Besides treasured first issues of Howard the Duck, they have a huge number of alternative comics and zines from around the world.

Medusa's Circle (☎ 773-935-5950), 3268 N Clark (Map 7), has everything for raven-haired folks who like to wear heavy dark velvet clothes on hot days.

Give credit to the folks at Windward Sports (☎ 773-472-6868), 3317 N Clark (Map 7), for trying their best to bring surfing to Lake Michigan. No, they don't even try to ride the at-times 12-inch-high surf – they use the wind. Now *that* they've got, and lots of it. They're a friendly bunch, and they sell all sorts of windsurfing gear. In the summer they rent boards at Montrose Beach (see details in Things to See & Do under Offbeat Activities).

The sunny works of the artisans of Sicily are featured at Casa Campos (☎ 773-281-2272), 3326 N State (Map 7). Rustic furniture and accessories are sold with splendid pottery in bright yellows and blues.

Strange Cargo (☎ 773-327-8090), 3448 N State (Map 7), should really be called 'Retro Cargo.' Vinyl jackets from dead bowling alleys are sold side-by-side with bell-bottoms and polychromatic shades (you know: sunglasses).

Elsewhere Something Old Something New (☎ 773-271-1300), 1056 W Belmont (Map 7), looks like an explosion at a Laundromat. But amid the racks and racks of cheap clothing are some really cheap items, such as good jeans for $5.

If you need a cool little gift, try Whimsy (☎ 773-665-1760), 3234 N Southport (Map 7). The shelves are lined with stylish candle holders, little reading lamps, tiny frames and other inexpensive items that don't take up a lot of room in a bag.

Bizarre cards and wrapping paper to match them will keep you chuckling at Kate-Oh's (☎ 773-935-5240), 3440 N Southport (Map 7). The piles of retro '60s junk should help you figure out the joke behind the store's name. Hint: think Green Hornet.

Andersonville

My friend Janice praises the clothes at Studio 90 (☎ 773-878-0097), 5239 N Clark (Map 8), for being 'comfortable but not stretchy.' They have many pieces, designed by women who work in the store, that are both eclectic and cute.

Ya want some caviar in a tube? They got that and plenty more at Wikstrom's Deli (☎ 773-275-6100), 5243 N Clark (Map 8). Scandinavians from all over Illinois flock here for homemade *limpa* bread, herring and lutefisk.

The Landmark (☎ 773-728-5301), 5301 N Clark (Map 8), is a neighborhood . . . well, you get it. Anyway, it's filled with lots of little shops selling lots of neat little crafty things. I'm always enamored of the Pooh Store, which stocks all kinds of items relating to the honey-loving British bear.

Paper Trail (☎ 773-275-2191), at 5307 N Clark (Map 8), has all the cards the designers at Hallmark probably want to create, but enjoy steady employment too much to do so. They have an entire Chihuahua collection that is matched in scope only by the fat women's butt series.

Many people go to Erickson Jewelers (☎ 773-275-2010), 5304 N Clark (Map 8), not for the jewels but for the jewel-like exterior. The classic facade has been carefully maintained since its renovation in the early 1940s. Once inside, you'll find an assortment of watches, baubles and the like.

It's a throwback to the 1960s, but Alamo Shoes (☎ 773-784-8936), 5321 N Clark (Map 8), has everything from Birkenstocks to hiking boots for men and women. The

enthusiastic help hops off to the backroom and emerges with stacks of boxes until you're either too surrounded to see anymore or you find what you want. They have really good prices too.

Wicker Park/Bucktown

Milwaukee Ave is a mix of the really cheap and the really expensive. You can buy inexpensive Mexican CDs and high-priced objets d'art in adjoining stores. North on Damen, things are much more solidly gentrified.

Women in need of extra support might fancy the full-metal bra in the window at Meble (☎ 773-772-8200), 1462 N Milwaukee (Map 9). Unfortunately, it probably wouldn't be too comfortable, since it's a sculpture that costs $1100 and leads off the mix of pricey props, antiques and conceptual pieces.

You really do expect to see Arnold the pig wandering around the corner at Green Acres (☎ 312-292-1998), 1464 N Clark (Map 9). Everything you'd expect to find in a 1930s farmhouse is for sale at prices that would have fetched the whole farm back then.

An old People's Gas building is home to Collage (☎ 312-292-2993), 1520 N Milwaukee (Map 9), which sells the bright, multicolored primitive art of Mexico's Oaxaca State.

Third Eye Games (☎ 773-342-2957), 1952 W North, at Damen (Map 9), has everything for the Dungeons and Dragons set. This is the place to go if you need to get a role-playing fix.

RICK GERHARTER
Multilingual socks for sale

The sign above the door at Le Garage (☎ 773-278-2234), 1649 N Damen (Map 9), says they sell 'work clothes.' And they do if your job requires you to wear black lace and velvet tops, leather pants or pastel-colored jeans.

Lonely Planet prefers not to use the letter equivalents of phone numbers, but the one for Dandelion is just too perfect: ☎ 773-862-WEED. (That last part was 9333.) The clever owners of the store, at 2117 N Damen (Map 9), stock a creative collection of new and used clothing, jewelry and incense.

Elsewhere in the City

The New Maxwell Street Market is much changed from the original. For one thing, it has moved from Maxwell St to a stretch of South Canal between Taylor and the equiv-alent of 15th St, near the river (Map 10). That was supposedly sparked by the need for the University of Illinois to expand southward, but really it was caused by the city's desperate need to reclaim an area that had become Chicago's own wild bazaar, with drug dealers openly competing with vendors of stolen hubcaps for customers. One whole block had even seceded from the US and declared itself an anarchist state. Colorful? Yes. Orderly? Not on your life – literally.

The new location is more closely moni-tored by the city bureaucracy, but the rough edges are still there. Every Sunday morn-ing hundreds of vendors set up stalls selling everything from Michael Jordan basketball jerseys incorrectly emblazoned with his baseball number (45) to tacos for a $1. You can still buy hubcaps, but the odds that they are fresh from your own car are somewhat diminished. The market is a scenic 15-minute walk over the river from the Roosevelt El stations. From Clinton, on the Blue Line, the walk is a dud through boring blocks.

Farther Afield

If you go to Woodfield Mall (☎ 847-330-1537), in Schaumburg, at least a 30-minute drive northwest of the city on I-90, don't

tell me. Boasting that it has the largest amount of retail space in the world (the Mall of America nightmare, in suburban Minneapolis, is bigger, but much of its space is devoted to a Peanuts amusement park), it has nary a store that you can't find in Chicago. I mention it only because someone may insist on going there. Don't, unless you're doing a sociological study on the wonders of a Brobdingnagian retail monster devoid of culture or non-retail-driven life.

Marathon runners will feel at home at Gurnee Mills (☎ 847-263-7500), an end-less outlet mall in Gurnee, 40 minutes north of the city on I-94. Everything is cheap, cheap, cheap at the outlet stores run by national chains and brands such as Ann Taylor, the Gap, Panasonic, Maidenform and about 200 others. But before your bar-gain hormones go into overdrive, consider the ugly secret of many of these places: no longer do they sell their own first-quality merchandise or T-shirts that inexplicably ended up with three sleeves; instead, to protect their own retail stores and resellers, these 'outlet' stores sell second-quality merchandise produced specifically for the bargain-hunting masses. A final note: if you weary of the chase and sit down in one of the rest areas, TVs will urge you to get back up and shop.

Lighthouse Place Outlet Center (☎ 219-879-6506), about an hour and a half east of Chicago, at 601 Wabash in Michigan City, Indiana, has 135 stores, including outlets of Brooks Brothers, Eddie Bauer, Anne Klein, Nine West, Polo/Ralph Lauren and Ree-bok. There are lots of places to eat mall food there, but you're much better off at the delightful Blue Ribbon Cafe, 1407 Frank-lin (☎ 219-879-5702). Over one of their fantastic inexpensive breakfasts, lunches or dinners, try to find out what the real French chef is doing in northwest Indiana. Light-house Place is convenient to I-94 or the I-80 Indiana Toll Road. You can also ride the Metra South Shore Line from the Randolph St Station in downtown Chicago to the 11th St Station in Michigan City ($6.85 one way).

WHAT TO BUY
Antiques

Chicago is a magnet for the best antiques and collectibles between the two coasts. Serious shoppers can easily make a week of it. Casual collectors or browsers will enjoy the many antique malls that bring scores of dealers together under one roof. You will find clusters of them in the blocks around the Merchandise Mart in River North, along the stretch of Lincoln north from Diversey to Irving Park and along Belmont Ave west from Ashland Ave to Western. Cruising that last strip is like driving along a country road laced with antique stores without ever leaving the city.

The standard advice to call and check business hours before venturing out is doubly important when it comes to antique malls, whose hours can be as quirky as the dealers themselves.

The Antiquarians Building (☎ 312-527-0533), 159 W Kinzie (Map 3), has rare items from five continents in 22 shops.

The Antique Mall of Wrigleyville (☎ 773-868-0285), 3336 N Clark (Map 7), is a large place on two levels with 50 widely assorted dealers selling anything from old Americana to items you unloaded at a garage sale for peanuts just a couple of years ago. (Oops!)

The Antiques Centre at Kinzie Square (☎ 312-464-1946), 220 W Kinzie (Map 3), has 20 dealers of high-end pieces from the 18th and 19th centuries.

The Belmont Antique Mall (☎ 773-549-9270), 2039 W Belmont, is joined by its sibling, the Belmont Antique Mall West (☎ 773-871-3915), 2227 W Belmont.

At the Chicago Antique Mall (☎ 773-929-0200), 3045 N Lincoln (Map 7), 45 dealers sell more antiques than you can imagine.

Jay Robert's Antique Warehouse (☎ 312-222-0167), 149 W Kinzie (Map 3), has more than 60,000 square feet of furniture and clocks.

Rita Bucheit Ltd (☎ 312-527-4080), 449 N Wells (Map 3), is a dark and classy store specializing in Vienna Secession and Art Deco works.

Fine Art

Ten years ago Chicago's galleries were much more concentrated in the gallery district of River North. But climbing rents there have fragmented the scene. River North still has a concentration of big-name places, but you can also find scores of galleries in Wicker Park and Bucktown. The south and west Loop areas are up and coming, as artists are drawn to enormous warehouses that have been chopped up into very ungentrified lofts. There you can get 2000 square feet with 20-foot ceilings for $600 a month, if you don't mind falling plaster, no kitchen and doing your dishes in the bathroom you share way down the hall.

Openings are held on Friday evenings – usually the first Friday of the month – with the first Friday after Labor Day being the start of the season. Galleries have open receptions on these days, and you can wander around River North drinking more cheap white wine out of plastic cups than health would generally allow. Usually on the first weekend after Labor Day, the Wicker Park/Bucktown area is host to Around the Coyote, which is a festival of gallery shows, performance art, readings and other events. Although as this neighborhood, too, begins to fragment, the event's future is in doubt.

To try to make sense of the Chicago art scene, which is worth its own book, consult *Chicago* magazine, the *Reader* and the free *Chicago Gallery News*, which is usually near the door of galleries.

Michigan Ave As you'd expect, Michigan Ave is home to some of the priciest galleries in the city.

At Circle Gallery (☎ 312-670-4304), 540 N Michigan at Ohio, in the ugly Marriott (Map 3), art is in the eye of the beholder. This multilevel store appeals to a more popular – or perhaps more base – audience with shows that have included *Playboy* photography and Warner Bros cartoons.

The address of the Chicago branch of the international Wally Findly Galleries (☎ 312-649-1500) is 814 N Michigan (Map 5), but really it's situated on the small street immediately to the west of the Water

Tower. It sells pieces from a select range of contemporary American and European artists.

Richard Gray Gallery (☎ 312-642-8877), 875 N Michigan, Suite 2503, in the John Hancock Center (Map 5), exhibits works by 20th-century greats from Miró to Nancy Graves. In the same building, Alan Koppel (☎ 312-640-0730), Suite 2850, also has a contemporary focus.

Family-run RS Johnson Fine Art (☎ 312-943-1661), 645 N Michigan (the entrance is off Erie), sells the kinds of works you find in museums – old masters, recently dead masters such as Picasso, and other A-level works – at prices only a museum or a really rich person can afford. But the gallery makes an impressive effort to reach out to the masses through its educational programs.

Worthington Gallery (☎ 312-266-2424), 645 N Michigan, exhibits works by notable American and European artists alive and dead. The staff is known for its scholarly credentials.

River North Gallery District Perhaps the best way to approach this district is to just wander the blocks along Huron and Superior west from LaSalle. The number of galleries in the neighborhood hovers around 60.

Robert Henry Adams Fine Art (☎ 312-642-8700), 715 N Franklin (Map 3), shows works by pre-WWII American Impressionist, Regionalist and Modernist painters.

Akainyah (☎ 312-654-0333), 357 W Erie (Map 3), has an excellent selection of African-influenced contemporary art that is creatively displayed.

Jean Albano Gallery (☎ 312-440-0770), 215 W Superior (Map 3), features the work of artists who create three-dimensional pieces out of unusual materials. Check out Chicago artist Margaret Wharton's work with chairs.

At Ehlers Caudill Gallery (☎ 312-642-8611), in the gallery-packed building at 750 N Orleans (Map 3), vintage and contemporary works by top photographers are the focus.

In 1975, when the neighborhood was still a dump, Zolla-Lieberman Gallery (☎ 312-944-1990), 325 W Huron (Map 3), was the first gallery with acclaimed work to move here. It is noted for nurturing and enriching the careers of many young artists.

Wicker Park/Bucktown Galleries in this area open and close with a frequency dictated by the terms of one-year leases. This constantly shifting mélange defies easy categorization. However, there are a couple of good places to start.

Flat Iron (☎ 773-227-6221), on the third floor of the historic building at 1579 N Milwaukee (Map 9), exhibits themed shows by neighborhood artists. If you like something, you can go track down the creator in his or her studio. In the same building, Gallery 203 (☎ 773-252-1952) is another place to find large numbers of works by a diverse group of locals.

Gary Marks (☎ 773-342-7990), at 1528 N Milwaukee (Map 9), handles shows by local artists who have recently emerged from the pack.

Crafts
The namesake of the Douglas Dawson Gallery (☎ 312-751-1961), 222 W Huron (Map 3), is an internationally recognized expert in Asian, African and American textile art. There are always some prime examples, along with related work, on display here.

Gallery Atlantis (☎ 773-292-0889), at 2100 N Damen (Map 9), sells affordable works by Bucktown artists, including paintings, clothing and other pieces.

One of those rare government bureaucracies that makes you say 'cool' is the Illinois Artisans Shop (☎ 312-814-5321), on the second level of the James R Thompson State of Illinois Center, at Randolph and Clark, in the Loop (Map 3). The best works of artisans throughout the state are sold in this small shop run by the Illinois Department of Natural Resources, including ceramics, glass, wood, fiber, toys and more, at prices that verge on the cheap. The enthusiastic staff will tell you all about the people who created the pieces, who are chosen by a twice-yearly jury. The Illinois Art Gallery, immediately next door, sells paintings and sculptures under the same arrangement.

When told I was researching a guide-book, the proprietor of Oh Boy! (☎ 773-772-0101), at 2060 N Damen (Map 9), proclaimed, 'This is a kick-ass store for your book!' I don't know about the boot to the butt, but the works of rural artists from throughout the state are for sale here. The best stuff takes old furniture and uses it in new and unusual ways. There's lots of interesting stuff to browse here. Just watch your back.

Orca Aart (☎ 312-245-5245), at 812 N Franklin, sells unusual works in stone, seal hide and other traditional materials by Eskimo, Inuit and other northwest-coast artisans.

Portia Galleria (☎ 773-862-1700), 1702 N Damen (Map 9), sells sinuous sculptures made of colored glass. The sensual organic forms urge you to caress them.

Books

The following are just a few of the hundreds of bookstores found in the city. Check the Yellow Pages for complete listings of special-interest stores for everything from religion to socialism, and see the Hyde Park section of Things to See & Do for bookstores near the University of Chicago.

General Bookstores For serious fiction, you can't touch Barbara's Bookstores, at 1350 N Wells in Old Town (☎ 312-642-5044; Map 6) and near the entrance to Navy Pier (☎ 312-222-0890; Map 3). The staff has read what they sell, and touring authors regularly give readings.

An excellent place for browsing, with extended hours on many nights, the Lincoln Park Bookshop (☎ 773-477-7087), 2423 N Clark, is a large independent store with a wide-ranging selection. There is a good children's section in the rear, where the tykes can occupy themselves while you browse.

Tucked away in the basement of the State St store, Marshall Field's (Map 3) has an excellent all-around bookstore (☎ 312-781-4284). Besides the selection, its absolute best feature is the staff: these people have been working in the department for decades. They know their selections inside and out and are excellent for making suggestions. Also in the Loop, Brent Books & Cards (☎ 312-363-0126), 309 W Washington, has good business, art and travel sections.

Sandmeyer's Bookstore (☎ 312-922-2104), 714 S Dearborn (Map 4), in the heart of Printer's Row, holds a special place in my heart, because it's where I bought my books for my first trip to Europe many years ago. Besides a good selection on travel, the family-run store emphasizes fiction and architecture.

Special Interest In the 'Land of Lincoln,' the Abraham Lincoln Book Shop (☎ 312-944-3085), 357 W Chicago (Map 3), is a natural. New, used and antiquarian books about the 16th president, the Civil War and the presidency in general are for sale. The knowledge of the staff is authoritative; they hold regular open round-table discussions with Civil War scholars.

What would a great theater town be without a great theater bookstore? Act 1 (☎ 773-348-6757), 2632 N Lincoln, takes its bow in this category with plays, anthologies, works by local authors and a large area devoted to production and the often ignored business end of theater. I particularly like the section devoted to combating stage fright, except why are all those people looking at me?

'Seeing the world through an Afrikan point of view' is the slogan at the Afro-centric Bookstore (☎ 312-939-1956), 234 S Wabash (Map 3). Many big-name black authors give regular readings here.

The Chicago Historical Society Store (☎ 312-642-4600), 1601 N Clark St (Map 5), boasts an excellent selection of books devoted to local history, many of which are hard to find elsewhere.

The Occult Bookstore (☎ 773-292-0995), at 1561 N Milwaukee (Map 9), is redolent with incense and the gentle creak of the old wooden chairs in which browsers are scanning tomes such as *The Psychic Side of Sports* and *Blueprint for Immortality*. This old store is probably the only one in Chicago with a Druid section. If you're wondering where you'll travel next, you can arrange a reading of your future.

The leading local used-book seller, Powell's, has three large, bright, well-organized locations. 1501 E 57th (☎ 773-955-7780), 828 S Wabash (☎ 312-341-0748), and 2850 N Lincoln, a block north of Diversey (☎ 773-248-1444; Map 7).

Everything architectural can be found at the Prairie Avenue Bookshop (☎ 312-922-8311), 418 S Wabash (Map 3). This is easily the classiest and most lavishly decorated bookstore in the city. The beautiful tomes – including many hard-to-find titles – rest on hardwood shelves, and the presence of customers is muffled by the thick carpet. Soon you'll want to find a smoking jacket, take up pipe smoking and curl up in a corner leather chair.

The goal of the Savvy Traveller (☎ 312-913-9800), 310 S Michigan, near the Art Institute (Map 3), is to carry every travel-related title in print. They come close, and if they don't have a title, they'll research it and order it for you. The staffers are all travel enthusiasts between vacations. This is a good place to find obscure titles relating to your next trip tucked in between the comprehensive selection of Lonely Planet guides. They also sell gadgets such as electricity converters, luggage and atlases.

My pal Larry gets all his really obscure science fiction novels from The Stars Our Destination (☎ 773-871-2722), at 1021 W Belmont, a block west of the El (Map 7). It has thousands of titles, new and used, that you'd otherwise have a hard time finding this side of Pluto.

A T-shirt for sale in the window of Women & Children First (☎ 773-769-9299), 5233 N Clark (Map 8), in Andersonville, shows a picture of Mayor Daley with his hands at his crotch and the caption 'Vagina Envy.' Much of the selection inside this feminist and children's bookstore is actually more mainstream. The excellent selection of fiction by women authors is highlighted by the excellent selection of women authors, such as Sara Paretsky, who give readings.

Unabridged Books (☎ 773-883-9119), 3251 N Broadway, is a general-interest bookstore with a strong gay following. The travel books are in the quiet basement.

Chains The Barnes & Noble Bookseller (☎ 773-871-9004), 659 W Diversey, is jammed every day of the week and has become a prime meeting place for Lincoln Park yuppies. Listen for lines like 'Do you prefer your books hardback or soft-back?' echoing down the aisles. Another branch has opened at 1441 W Webster, at Clybourn (☎ 773-871-3610).

Archrival Borders Books and Music has a less attractive store at Clark and Broadway (☎ 773-935-3909; Map 7). Their premier store is at 830 N Michigan Ave (☎ 312-573-0564). Thousands of books are spread over four floors in a prime setting across from the Water Tower. The size of the bright and airy place means that they have room for lots of special-interest titles. They also have a good selection of magazines and newspapers by the main entrance.

Mapmaker Rand McNally & Co has a small travel book and map store at 444 N Michigan. The friendly staff is always eager to help you find what you want on the densely packed shelves.

Discount seller Super Crown has a little bit of everything at its three locations: 105 S Wabash, in the Mid-America Building (☎ 312-782-7667; Map 3); 1714 N Sheffield, near Clybourn (☎ 312-787-4370); and 801 W Diversey, at Halsted (☎ 773-327-1551).

Periodicals & Foreign Press Just outside the 24-hour Walgreens pharmacy, at the southeast corner of N Michigan Ave and E Chicago Ave, a 24-hour newsstand has selections that range from the inspirational to the perspirational. It's got about the widest selection of reading materials available anywhere at 4 am, including all the morning newspapers.

Another good place to find foreign newspapers is Europa Books (☎ 312-335-9677), at 832 N State (Map 5). As the name promises, they also carry magazines and books, primarily in European languages. A branch in Lake View called Europa Libros (☎ 773-404-7313), 3229 N Clark (Map 7), carries mostly books.

Music

For current CDs, you can't beat the prices at Best Buy. See details under Photography. The gift shop of the Chicago Symphony Orchestra is an excellent place for classical music; see Souvenirs.

Find the words to songs nobody else remembers at Carl Fischer (☎ 312-427-6652), 312 S Wabash, south of Jackson (Map 3). Sheet music for just about every song ever written, plus scores and arrangements for individual instruments, choral groups, bands and orchestras, is filed away *someplace* in this old classic, where one employee or another will be able to find even the most obscure request.

Garage-band potentates drool with utter abandon at the Chicago Music Exchange (☎ 773-477-0830), 3264 N Clark (Map 7). This is the place for vintage and classic guitars and other instruments.

Earwax (☎ 773-772-4019), 1564 N Milwaukee, near North (Map 9), has a polyglot selection of music from around the world, experimental stuff and thousands of other selections that would never make the racks of mainstream places.

Just up the street, Wax Trax (☎ 773-862-2121), at 1657 N Damen, is another excellent and funky place for offbeat stuff.

Musicians, serious jazz and blues aficionados and vintage album collectors flock to Jazz Record Mart (☎ 312-222-1467), 444 N Wabash (Map 3). Bob Koester and his dedicated staff can find just about anything, no matter how obscure. This is the place to go to complete your Bix Biederbecke collection.

A mall for music, the Music Mart (☎ 312-362-6700), at the southeast corner of State and Jackson (Map 3), is a collection of specialty shops in the first few levels of the DePaul Center, the beautifully renovated downtown campus building of DePaul University. Among the shops are ones selling obscure CDs, drums, concert pianos, stringed instruments and more.

Music giant Tower Records (☎ 773-477-5994) has a big store at 2301 N Clark. Besides all types of mainstream music, it has books, a ticket counter and an excellent selection of zines and products from the alternative press. Tower has also taken over the locally beloved Rose Records (☎ 312-663-0660), at 214 S Wabash (Map 3).

Outdoor Gear

The merchandise area at Army Navy Surplus USA (☎ 773-348-8930), 3100 N Lincoln (Map 7), would send a drill sergeant into a conniption. The place is a huge mess. But among the torn boxes and shambles of merchandise are actual military surplus items of the highest quality the taxpayer can afford. I bought some wool socks for a ludicrously low price in designer olive drab, and they still look brand new after several seasons of keeping my smelly feet warm.

Erehwon Mountain Outfitter (☎ 312-337-6400), 1800 N Clybourn, is a very serious place that sells very serious equipment for very serious trekkers. They don't have rain hats, they have 'cranial precipitation protection systems,' or something like that. Prices are high, but so is the quality.

The North Face (☎ 312-337-7200) has a very attractive store in the John Hancock Center, 875 N Michigan (Map 3), where they sell their first-rate line of backpacks, sleeping bags and other outdoor gear at full retail prices. They also have maps, books and doodads.

The smell of leather hits you in the face as you walk into Uncle Dan's (☎ 773-477-1918), 2440 N Lincoln (Map 6). A big selection of hiking boots and gear is augmented by camping supplies and many brands of backpacks, including my personal favorite, MEI. The former army surplus store is now a very relaxed place to buy outdoor equipment without lurking sales dudes who consider anything less than a frontal assault on K-2 to be for wimps.

Photography

Wolf Camera and Ritz Camera each have dozens of locations. Neither has particularly good prices on film or cameras. Walgreens and Osco drug stores are also ubiquitous and can have better sale prices on film and very good prices on overnight (as opposed to one-hour) developing. Here are the best choices for film and equipment.

Film Best Buy (☎ 312-988-4067), 1000 W North, is at the back of the huge strip mall about a 10-minute walk from the North/Clybourn El stop. This outlet of the electronics chain consistently has film for $1 to $2 less per roll than the competition. While you're there, check out the CD prices – they are usually the lowest around.

Equipment Central Camera (☎ 312-427-5580), 232 S Wabash (Map 3), sells every kind of camera and related equipment imaginable for low prices that belie its Old World appearance. The folks behind the counter know what they're talking about, and if you need a new lens for some ancient Nikon willed to you, they'll have it.

Souvenirs

The following stores sell souvenirs a few cuts above the generic T-shirt, ashtray, refrigerator magnet standard.

The Chicago Architecture Foundation (☎ 312-922-3432), 224 S Michigan Ave (Map 3), is heaven for anyone with an edifice complex. Books, posters, post cards and more celebrate local architecture. The Frank Lloyd Wright section has enough material to research a doctoral thesis. But for a good look at what literally lies under today's buildings, peruse David Lowe's *Lost Chicago*. At $16, it chronicles the many architectural gems lost to developers hell-bent on new erections.

The Symphony Store (☎ 312-435-6421), 220 S Michigan Ave, is where the Chicago Symphony Orchestra sells a large selection of CDs, tapes and albums of their performances all over the world. They even have T-shirts – highly tasteful ones, of course.

Crowds throng the Art Institute Store (☎ 312-443-3535), 111 S Michigan Ave, which has poster ($17.50) and post card ($1) versions of popular works from the Art Institute's collection. There's another branch of the store (☎ 312-482-8275) in the 900 N Michigan mall.

The *Chicago Tribune* Store (☎ 312-222-3080), 435 N Michigan Ave, sells six water glasses emblazoned with famous front pages for $19.95. Included is the memorable 'Dewey Defeats Truman' edition.

The City of Chicago Store (☎ 312-467-1111), 401 E Illinois St (Map 3), is a mecca for those wise enough not to try to steal their own 'official' souvenirs. The cheerful city workers will sell you anything from an old voting machine ($55) to a manhole cover emblazoned with the words 'Chicago Sewers' ($100). Street signs for famous local streets are $50. Bargain hunters may want to opt for the Spanish-language alley-rat warning placards ($4).

Sports World (☎ 312-472-7701), right across from Wrigley Field, at 3555 N Clark St (Map 7), is crammed with authentic Chicago sports duds. All-wool Cubs and White Sox caps just like those worn by the players are $20. Cheesy all-synthetic baseball caps just like those worn by nerds are $5.

If you want convenience and a low price, bless your lucky gift recipients with Tootsie Rolls. They're cheap, they're made in Chicago and you can get them everywhere. If you're feeling more generous, the one-pound Colonial assortment of Fanny May Candy is $11.95 The sweet-smelling white outlets blanket the city.

Excursions

The rich prairie responsible for much of Chicago's original wealth is by its very grain-growing nature not the most invigorating of destinations. In fact, one of the biggest complaints of people living in Chicago is the dearth of exciting weekend getaways.

Still, the surrounding area is not devoid of interest. The following destinations can provide a good counterpoint to your time in Chicago and are good places to stop if you are motoring off someplace else.

ILLINOIS & MICHIGAN CANAL

Dubbed a National Heritage Corridor, this linear park is administered by the National Park Service and encompasses 41 towns, 11 state parks and scores of historic sites.

The I&M Canal was the result of the desire to have a waterway for commerce that would link the Mississippi River basin with the Great Lakes, making it possible to ship goods by boat from the Eastern US to New Orleans and on to the Caribbean. In 1836 the first shovelful of dirt was turned, and during the next 12 years, thousands of immigrants, primarily Irish, were lured to Chicago to work on the 96-mile course.

After it opened in 1848, the constant flow of goods through Chicago propelled the city's economic development. In 1900 it was supplemented by the much deeper Chicago Sanitary and Ship Canal, which, besides being a much more navigable waterway, became Chicago's de facto drainpipe.

Competition from railroads and other waterways caused the I&M Canal to molder for most of the 20th century. The establishment of the park in 1984 has spurred restoration and development of the I&M Canal's remaining sites and in some of the historic towns along the route.

Orientation & Information

The Heritage Corridor driving route can be hard to follow, and the sites are greatly dispersed. It's a good idea to get some of the available free maps in advance so you can plan your itinerary – the trip can easily fill a day. One bonus: most sites are free.

The Heritage Corridor Visitors Bureau (☎ 815-727-2323, 800-926-2262), at 81 N Chicago, Joliet, IL 60431, has information on the parks, as well as food and lodging details for the region.

The Illinois & Michigan Canal Heritage Corridor Commission (☎ 815-740-2047), 15701 S Independence, Lockport, IL 60441, is the source for all the excellent National Park Service brochures and maps of the corridor. The one devoted to archaeology is especially good. They also know when various information centers along the canal are open.

Lockport

A good place to start the tour is the town of Lockport, 33 miles southwest of Chicago. The town of 10,000 is itself historic, having been bypassed by most development in favor of much larger Joliet, to its south. The center of Lockport is in the National Register of Historic Places. It is home to the **I&M Canal Museum** (☎ 815-838-5080), 803 S State Rd, housed in the original 1837 home of the canal commissioners. The museum is open daily 1 to 4:30 pm, except during Thanksgiving week and on major holidays. It has all the maps and brochures you didn't get in advance, as well as displays about life along the waterway when more passed by than just the odd fallen leaf.

The **Lockport Prairie Nature Preserve** (☎ 815-727-8700) is across the canal and the Des Plaines River from downtown Lockport, off Route 7. It is the largest untouched remnant of prairie in Northern Illinois, a riot of colorful native plants and wildflowers during the peak blooming months, May through August. It's open daily 8 am to 5 pm, from April to October 8 am to 8 pm, closed holidays.

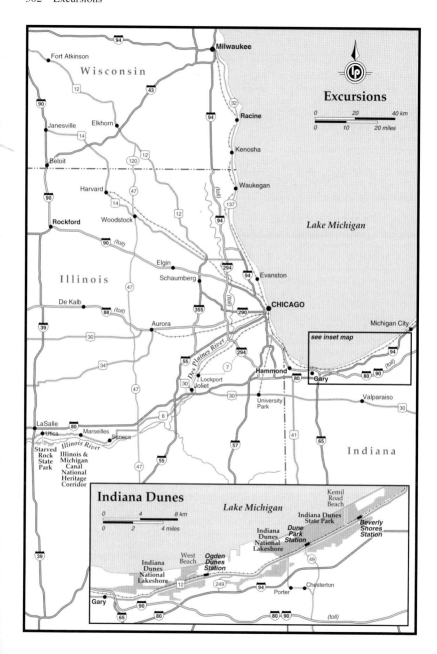

Excursions

0   20   40 km
0   10   20 miles

Lake Michigan

Wisconsin

Fort Atkinson

94

Milwaukee

12

43

32

Racine

90

Janesville   Elkhorn

14

Kenosha

Beloit

120   12

94 (toll)

Harvard   47   Waukegan

14

137

Woodstock   12   94

Rockford

Illinois

90 (toll)

Elgin

294

De Kalb   47   Schaumberg   94   Evanston

88 (toll)   355

39   Aurora   290   **CHICAGO**

30

Des Plaines River   Michigan City

see inset map

55   294   94

34   7   90 (toll)

Lockport   **Hammond**   80   80

LaSalle   80   30   Joliet   **Gary**

Utica   Marseilles   Seneca   30   Valparaiso   30

Illinois River   6   University Park   41   65   **Indiana**

Starved Rock State Park

Illinois & Michigan Canal National Heritage Corridor   47   57   55

39

Indiana Dunes

Lake Michigan

Kemil Road Beach

0   4   8 km
0   2   4 miles

Indiana Dunes State Park   **Beverly Shores Station**

Indiana Dunes National Lakeshore   *Dune Park Station*

West Beach   *Ogden Dunes Station*   49

Indiana Dunes National Lakeshore   12   94   Chesterton

Gary   249   Porter

90   80   80   90 (toll)

65   80

The surviving Lock No 1 is the highlight of the 2½-mile **Gaylord Donnelley Canal Trail**, which follows the canal through town and has several exhibits along the way.

Seneca

A small town on Route 6 off I-80, 65 miles from Chicago, Seneca is home to the **Seneca Grain Elevator**, a fascinating affair that towers over the canal, which at this point is little more than a muddy ditch. Completed in 1862, the 65-foot building is one of the oldest survivors from the early grain industry. Check with the Heritage Corridor Commission for hours and be sure to get a copy of the heavily illustrated Park Service brochure explaining the workings of the place.

Near Seneca, **Marseilles** is famous today as the site of the National Weather Service tornado warning radar and for its 'quaint' downtown, which has become home to a cluster of antique stores and cute cafés.

Utica

The **Illinois Waterway Visitors Center** (☎ 815-667-4054), is off Dee Bennett Rd and Route 178, some 88 miles from Chicago. A major lock on the waterway that replaced the I&M Canal is the focus of its several exhibits and its observation deck. The center is open daily 8 am to 5 pm, from June to September 9 am to 8 pm.

Starved Rock State Park

This park (☎ 815-667-4906), one mile south of Utica, is a popular place. More than 2000 acres of wooded bluffs feature 18 canyons carved through the limestone during the last ice age. After heavy rains there is a waterfall at the head of each canyon. Some 15 miles of hiking trails wander through the park, and there are spectacular views from the highest bluff. You can rent canoes for paddled jaunts on the Illinois River and the canyon waterways, and there are several campsites.

The park has a rustic lodge (☎ 815-667-4211) built during the 1930s, which has rooms and cabins for rent year round. Rooms in the main lodge cost $70 to $80, cabins $58 to $70.

Getting There & Away

The I&M Canal and related sights are a car-only trip. Most are easily accessible from Chicago off I-55 and I-80. Mercury Tours (☎ 312-332-1366) offers an all-day boat tour of the district that leaves from the Michigan Ave Bridge. However, departures are infrequent – only once or twice a year – so call for dates and prices.

INDIANA DUNES

From Chicago on a clear day you can see Gary, a miserable steel-making town 30 miles southeast along Lake Michigan. But beyond that are the Indiana Dunes, more than 15 miles of sandy beaches and dunes formed by the prevailing winds of Lake Michigan. The coast is dotted by development and the odd steel mill, but many long stretches of undeveloped beach and shoreland are included in state and national parks.

Information

The two agencies in charge of the parks have plenty of information about schedules, camping, special events, hiking and other details: Indiana Dunes National Lakeshore (☎ 219-926-7561), 1100 N Mineral Springs Rd, Porter, IN 46304, and Indiana Dunes State Park (☎ 219-926-1952), 1600 N 25 East, Chesterton, IN 46304.

The beaches are open daily, usually from 9 am to sunset. The schedules for the visitor centers and organized tours are much more restricted and vary widely with the seasons. Be sure to call ahead and check hours.

West Beach

Fairly uncrowded, West Beach has a fascinating nature hike around Long Lake, an inland body of water popular with birds and hikers. Another walk shows how dunes mature: vegetation slowly covers the sand, trees grow and new dunes form closer to the lake. The beach is west of the Ogden Dunes stop on the South Shore Line.

Bailly-Chellberg Visitor Center & Trail

The focus of the National Lakeshore, Bailly-Chellberg is away from the beaches; a trail winds through the forest, whose diversity continues to astound botanists. Among the plants growing here are dogwood, Arctic berries and even cactus. The 1¾-mile trail passes restored log cabins from the 1820s and a farm built by Swedes in the 1870s. The visitor center is one mile south of the Dune Park stop on the South Shore Line.

Indiana Dunes State Park

On summer days this place is jammed with people from all over the region hitting the beach. Several tall dunes are popular with people who like to climb to the top, roll all the way down and then say hello to their lunch. The park is not convenient to any of the South Shore Line stops.

Kemil Road Beach

A less-crowded beach has fewer amenities, such as the potentially troublesome hot dog stands, but makes up for it with natural beauty. Kemil Rd Beach is right in the middle of a 10-mile stretch of beach; you can escape the crowds by walking a mile or two east. The far eastern edge of the beach is dominated by Mt Baldy, a 120-foot dune with views of the lake, the beaches, the shore and the huge cooling tower of a coal-powered electric plant in Michigan City.

Camping is restricted to official areas, but people have been known to camp in the most remote stretches of the beach – sans tent, so as to not draw attention. If you do camp, dress warmly; it gets cold here. One beautiful starry night, our peaceful gazing was interrupted when my friend Rich got too close to the campfire in search of warmth and briefly caught fire.

Getting There & Away

Trains on the Metra South Shore Line (☎ 312-836-7000, 800-356-2079) depart frequently from Randolph St Station. The three key stops for the parks and beaches are Ogden Dunes ($5.75, 70 minutes), Dune Park ($5.75, 79 minutes) and Beverly Shores ($6.55, 85 minutes).

By car, I-94 puts you close to the parks. The Route 249 exit, about 40 miles from Chicago, takes you to US 12, which runs east past most of the major attractions.

MILWAUKEE

Milwaukee, Wisconsin, is easily dismissed as a small version of Chicago, but it has a different character, having been settled by large numbers of Germans, whose influence can still be strongly felt in its restaurants and breweries. The downtown is compact and has an indoor mall on Michigan St at the Milwaukee River, an area of warehouses restored as art galleries south of I-94 and the omnipresent smell of beer being brewed. The town of 600,000 was first settled by Germans in the 1840s. Later waves of Italians, Poles, Irish, African Americans and others have added to the Germanic culture.

Milwaukee shouldn't be high on your list of priorities if your visit to Chicago is short. But for longer visits, or if your travels take you this way, the town provides an interesting contrast.

Orientation & Information

Downtown Milwaukee is not too far from the lakefront, where the summer festivals occur. The Milwaukee County Transit System (☎ 414-344-6711) has a web of bus routes that serve the area. As in most US cities, the largest cab company is named Yellow Cab (☎ 414-271-1800).

The Greater Milwaukee Convention & Visitors Bureau (☎ 414-273-7222, 800-231-0903), 510 W Kilbourn Ave, Milwaukee, WI 53203, has the usual vast range of brochures and maps. *Milwaukee* magazine is a good source for city events and the latest dining and club information.

In Chicago, the State of Wisconsin operates a tourist office (☎ 312-332-7274) at 342 N Michigan, just south of the bridge. Here you can get all sorts of information on Milwaukee and the rest of the state. They offer many services, among them distributing forms to reserve camping space at the many state parks; you can file the forms there or mail them yourself.

American Geographical Society Collection

About four miles north of downtown, the American Geographical Society (☎ 414-229-6282), 2311 E Hartford, has a huge

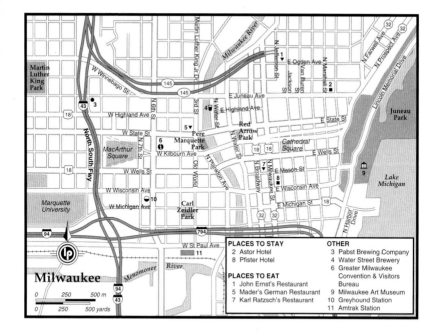

PLACES TO STAY
2 Astor Hotel
8 Pfister Hotel

PLACES TO EAT
1 John Ernst's Restaurant
5 Mader's German Restaurant
7 Karl Ratzsch's Restaurant

OTHER
3 Pabst Brewing Company
4 Water Street Brewery
6 Greater Milwaukee
   Convention & Visitors
   Bureau
9 Milwaukee Art Museum
10 Greyhound Station
11 Amtrak Station

Milwaukee

0   250   500 m
0   250   500 yards

collection of globes, maps, and other items related to geography and travel. It's open weekdays 9 am to 4 pm; admission is free.

Milwaukee Art Museum
Overlooking the lake, this museum (☎ 414-224-3200), at 750 N Lincoln Memorial Drive, has a smattering of paintings from the 15th century onward. Its location is very pretty, and you can walk quite far in the park along the lake. The museum's hours vary greatly – call to confirm them. Admission is $5, $3 for seniors and students, free for kids.

Wisconsin State Fair
An absolute treat every August (check dates with the visitor's bureau), this mammoth fair features the biggest dairy cows and the biggest hogs and the biggest bulls you've ever seen. It even has that epitome of Americana, a beauty contest. The corn dogs are fresh and the beer is cold at this major date on the social calendar for America's Dairyland. The vast fairgrounds are north of W Greenfield Ave, between 77th and 84th Streets, a little more than four miles west of downtown.

Brewery Tours
The number of huge breweries based in Milwaukee has shrunk since Schlitz immolated in the 1970s. Today there are two major plants churning out the sort of bland, watery brews America has become famous for. Happily, the tours are free.

The **Miller Brewing Company** (☎ 414-931-2337), 4251 W State, is responsible for such brands as Lite, Old Milwaukee and other beers of dubious quality. The tour features a cheery slide show, followed by visits to bottling and distribution areas that give you a good idea of how much of this stuff is swilled daily. At the tasting, see if you can get any of the Leinenkugel brands, a small brewery that Miller bought up a few years ago. Tours are offered Monday to Saturday 10 am to 3:30 pm.

The **Pabst Brewing Company** (☎ 414-223-3709), 915 W Juneau Ave, at I-43, is responsible for Pabst Blue Ribbon – or, PBR – a brand popular with buyers looking for the most ounces of beer for the fewest dollars. To its credit, Pabst boasts that they'll toss any grain into the brewing vats, whether it's corn or rice or whatever, as long as it's cheap. For your reward at the end of the tour, try the Ballantine Ale, a brand that has been popular for decades.

Places to Stay
The *Astor Hotel* (☎ 414-271-4220), at 924 E Juneau, is a delightful throwback in every way – including its architecture – to the 1950s. Doubles range from $59 to $97. The *Pfister Hotel* (☎ 414-273-8222), 424 E Wisconsin, is the grand old hotel that makes endless pfabulous wordplays on its name. Stay in the old wing; the newer, beer-can-shaped wing is no pfun at all. Singles and doubles range from $205 to $225.

Places to Eat
Mader's German Restaurant (☎ 414-271-3377), 1037 N 3rd St, has been serving mountains of German chow since 1902. The arch-competition, *Karl Ratzsch's Restaurant* (☎ 414-276-2720), 320 E Mason St, is two years younger. Both have lots of heavy wood decor and rows of beer steins. Expect to pay about $20 each for dinner.

John Ernst's Restaurant (☎ 414-273-1878), 600 E Ogden, is a classic Wisconsin supper club that serves a parade of courses featuring tasty, wholesome food and has a whitefish fry every Friday night. Prices start at $13 per person.

Entertainment
It's Milwaukee! Drink beer! But not from the huge breweries. Rather, indulge in some of the excellent microbrews from the places that have popped up around town and are putting the big boys to shame.

The *Water Street Brewery* (☎ 414-272-1195), 1101 N Water St, makes many different beers, including a weiss, a red ale and an Oktoberfest. Situated in an old warehouse, it's open until 1 am weekdays and 2 am weekends. The food is good too.

The *Lakefront Brewery* (☎ 414-372-8800), 818A E Chambers St, is not a pub, but they give tours on Friday nights and Saturday afternoons. More important, if you call them, these beer lovers will recommend bars based on what type of brew you're looking for. Of course, all will serve Lakefront's tasty and hoppy brews.

Getting There & Away
Amtrak (☎ 800-872-7245) has six trains a day from Chicago's Union Station to the station in downtown Milwaukee at 433 W St Paul Ave. The trip takes 92 minutes and costs $50 roundtrip, but various deals may be available. Greyhound (☎ 800-231-2222) has many buses each day for the two-hour trip, which costs $26 roundtrip. The station is at 606 N 7th St.

By car, take I-94 direct to downtown Milwaukee. The journey time is two hours, and Illinois will hit you up for tolls when you reach the suburbs.

Internet Resources

Web resources abound for Chicago. Many are very useful for planning your trip, and others are just fun.

GENERAL INTEREST
Digital City Chicago
www.chicago.digitalcity.com/

A vast site maintained by the *Chicago Tribune*, Digital City contains a wealth of information about Chicago and its events, attractions and more. Watch out for pages that are out of date, however.

Metro Chicago Information Center
www.mcic.org/

This nonprofit group has reams of statistical data on the city and region on its site.

Official City of Chicago Site
www.ci.chi.il.us/

Everything from airport information to public safety is contained in this sprawling site, which also has a good calendar of city events. (Note that Mayor Richard M Daley is looking more like his father all the time.)

Yahoo Chicago
www.yahoo.com/Regional/U_S_States/ Illinois/Cities/Chicago/

Yahoo has scores of links to sites in more than 20 categories relating to the city, plus its own extensive guides.

PUBLICATIONS
Chicago Reader
www.chireader.com/

The city's main entertainment weekly has pages of cultural news and schedules. It also has a very popular 'Matches' section of personal ads, if you're looking for a date.

Chicago Sun-Times
www.suntimes.com/index/

This text-based site loads quickly and has comprehensive local news, so you can find out what Chicagoans are talking about. It's also good for entertainment features and reviews.

Chicago Tribune
www.chicago.tribune.com/

The site is a bit like the newspaper itself. You can get lost in the lavish graphics and scores of links, but it has excellent cultural coverage.

TRANSPORTATION
American Airlines
www.americanair.com/

Amtrak
www.amtrak.com/

Amtrak's well-designed site has schedules, fares and special offers and will allow you to make reservations.

Greyhound
www.greyhound.com/

The national bus service has an interactive site to check fares and schedules.

Southwest Airlines
www.iflyswa.com/

The Southwest site shows fares for this discount airline, which is not listed on many reservations services.

Travelocity
www.travelocity.com/

This excellent travel-planning site is maintained by Sabre, the world's largest travel reservations system. After registering you can search for flight, hotel and car reservations worldwide using the same system available to travel agents. The interface is easy to use, and the 'Three Cheapest Flights' service consistently finds low-priced airfares.

United Airlines
www.ual.com

Loop market not online yet

CHICAGO TRANSPORTATION
Chicago Area Traffic Congestion
www.ai.eecs.uic.edu/GCM/
CongestionMap.html

This constantly updated map shows expressways color-coded for traffic congestion. Note how the routes to and from O'Hare International Airport are almost always red, indicating major congestion.

Chicago Transit Authority
www.transitchicago.com/

This site posts schedules for the multitudes of El trains and buses run by the CTA.

Metra
www.metrarail.com/

This site has schedules and fares for Chicago's regional rail transit.

ATTRACTIONS
There are scores of sites for Chicago's attractions. Most can be found through the Yahoo site listed above. Here are some special-interest sites.

Art Institute of Chicago
www.artic.edu/aic/

The Art Institute site has detailed information on major shows up to several years in advance.

Chicago Architecture Foundation
www.architecture.org/

Check this site to see the latest of the constantly changing lineup of CAF tours. It's also a good historical primer on area architecture.

International Museum of Surgical Science
www.imss.org/

An interactive feature on this site allows you to perform operations using vintage medical equipment, with predictably deadly results.

Museum of Contemporary Art
www.mcachicago.org/

The virtual reality tour here may almost save you a trip.

Museum of Science & Industry
www.msichicago.org/

A time-lapse movie shows the popular live chick-hatching display.

WEATHER
CNN Weather Chicago
cnn.com/WEATHER/html/
ChicagoIL.html

This site gives you four-day advance weather forecasts.

WGN TV
www.wgntv.com/thrlcam.html

The WGN site has several live views so you can see for yourself what conditions are around the city. It also has links to its own detailed weather forecasts.

Index

MAPS

TEXT

Sidebars

Chicago Map Section

SYMBOLS

✪ **NATIONAL CAPITAL**	✛ Airfield	🗗 Gas Station	)(Pass
◉ **State Capital**	✈ Airport	⌐ Golf Course	⌐ Picnic Area
● **City**	∴ Archaeological Site, Ruins	♨ Hindu Temple	★ Police Station
● **City, Small**	❾ Bank, ATM	○ Hospital, Clinic	▭ Pool
● Town	⌂ Baseball Diamond	❶ Information	▭ Post Office
	✕ Battlefield	点 Lighthouse	⊿ Shipwreck
	↗ Beach	☀ Lookout	❖ Shopping Mall
	✦ Border Crossing	▲ Monument	⚡ Skiing, Alpine
■ Hotel, B&B	⊥ Buddhist Temple	⦂ Mosque	⚡ Skiing, Nordic
⚠ Campground	➔ Bus Depot, Bus Stop	▲ Mountain	▥ Stately Home
⚲ Hostel	⊟ Cathedral	⋔ Museum	✿ Synagogue
⌨ RV Park	⌢ Cave	❀ Music, Live	☎ Telephone
▼ Restaurant	✝ Church	⌂ Observatory	■ Tomb, Mausoleum
❦ Bar (Place to Drink)	♀ Embassy	← One-Way Street	入 Trailhead
⚓ Cafe	⤬ Foot Bridge	♣ Park	☼ Winery
	✥ Garden	🄿 Parking	🐘 Zoo

Note: Not all symbols displayed above appear in this book.

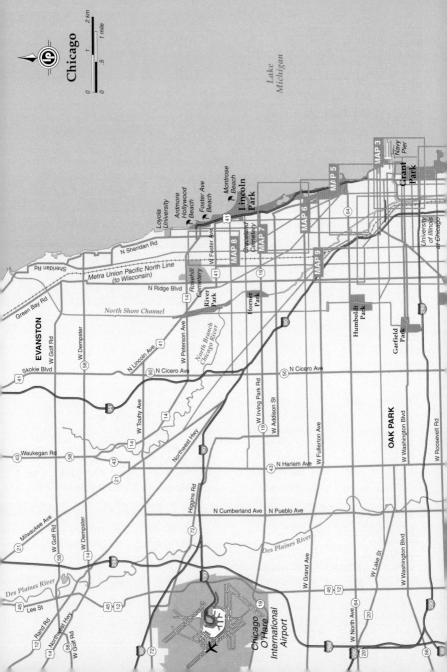

MAP 1

Wolf Lake

I-90

Calumet River

Calumet Park

41

95th St

12 20

Calumet River

Lake Calumet

I-94

Little Calumet River

130th St

S Chicago Ave

S Stony Island Ave

Rainbow Park

South Shore Country Club Park

67th St Beach

Jackson Park

MAP 11

University of Chicago

Washington Park

49th St Beach

31st St Beach

Burnham Park

S Drexel Blvd

S Martin Luther King Jr Drive

S Michigan Ave

Illinois Institute of Technology

41

MAP 4

MAP 10

Douglas Park

Garfield Blvd

McKinley Park

S Western Ave

S Archer Ave

S Cicero Ave

Archer Ave

Marquette Park

S Western Ave

Columbus Ave

Vincennes Ave

Chicago State University

Metra Electric/South Shore Line (to Hyde Park, Indiana Dunes)

S Halsted St

1

I-57

127th St

Calumet Sag Channel

50

S Cicero Ave

50

I-294

127th St

Calumet Sag Rd

Metra/BNSF Line

Sanitary and Ship Canal

W Ogden Blvd

S Harlem Ave

43

S Harlem Ave

43

34

W 79th St

171

S Archer Ave

Sanitary and Ship Canal

1st Ave

171

I-294

95th St

12 20

Southwest Hwy

7

La Grange Ave

45 12 20

34

W Ogden Blvd

45 12 20

S Archer Ave

171

Des Plaines River

I-294

I-55

45

96th Ave

45

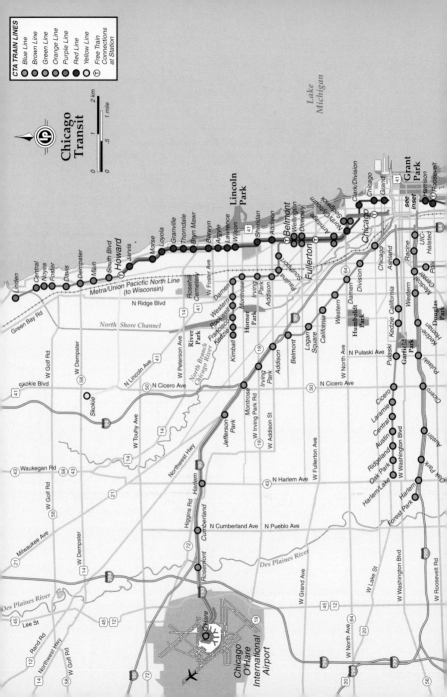

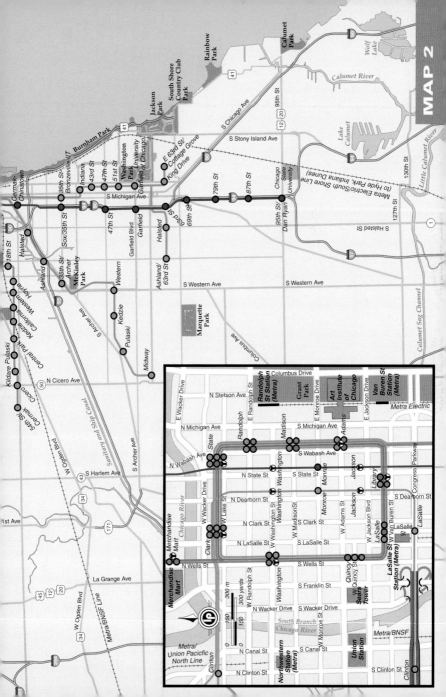

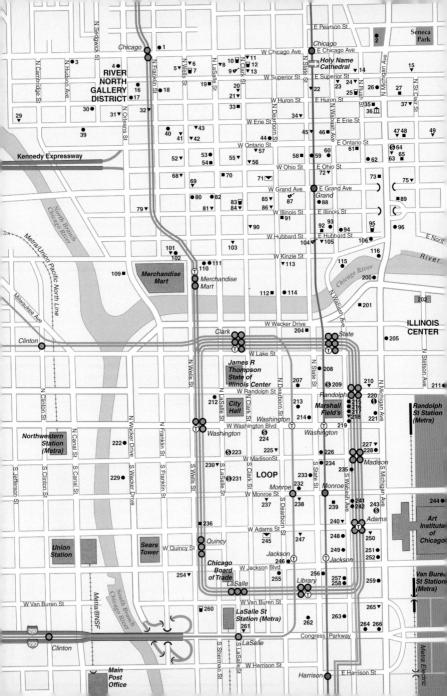

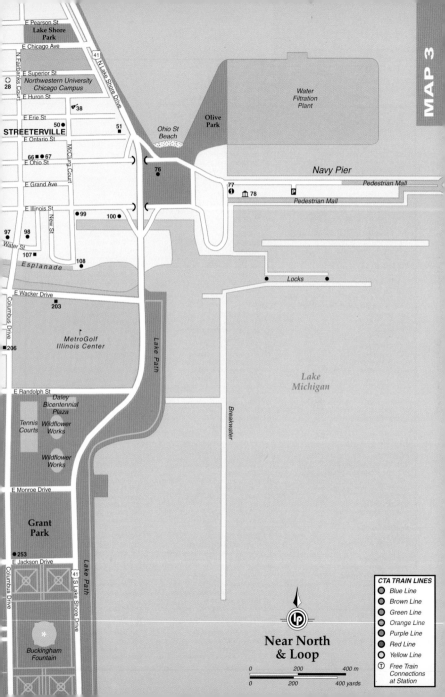

MAP 3

E Pearson St
Lake Shore Park
E Chicago Ave
E Superior St
Northwestern University Chicago Campus
E Huron St
E Erie St
STREETERVILLE
E Ontario St
E Ohio St
E Grand Ave
E Illinois St
Water St
Esplanade
E Wacker Drive
MetroGolf Illinois Center
E Randolph St
Daley Bicentennial Plaza
Tennis Courts
Wildflower Works
Wildflower Works
E Monroe Drive
Grant Park
E Jackson Drive
Columbus Drive
N Fairbanks Court
McClurg Court
New St
Columbus Drive
41
N Lake Shore Drive
S Lake Shore Drive
41

28

38
50
51
66 67
76
99 100
97 98
107
108
203
206
253
77
78
P

Ohio St Beach
Olive Park
Water Filtration Plant
Navy Pier
Pedestrian Mall
Pedestrian Mall
Locks
Lake Path
Lake Michigan
Breakwater
Buckingham Fountain

Near North & Loop

CTA TRAIN LINES
Blue Line
Brown Line
Green Line
Orange Line
Purple Line
Red Line
Yellow Line
Free Train Connections at Station

0   200   400 m
0   200   400 yards

MAP 3 KEY

NEAR NORTH

PLACES TO STAY
19 HoJo Inn
27 Radisson Hotel & Suites
33 Hotel Wacker
35 Omni Chicago Hotel
46 Cass Hotel
48 Motel 6
51 Days Inn Lake Shore Drive
54 Ohio House Motel
58 Embassy Suites Chicago
61 Lenox Suites
65 Best Western Inn of Chicago
66 Holiday Inn–Chicago City Centre
70 Best Western River North Hotel
73 Chicago Marriott Hotel
89 Hotel Inter-Continental Chicago
91 Hampton Inn & Suites
92 Courtyard by Marriott Chicago Downtown
107 Sheraton Chicago Hotel and Towers
109 Holiday Inn Mart Plaza
112 Westin River North

PLACES TO EAT
5 Earth
6 Crab House
8 Cafe Iberico
11 Pockets
13 Paradigm Kafeteria
14 Giordano's
15 Gino's East
20 Mango
21 Mike's Rainbow Restaurant
22 Della Robbia
23 Blackhawk Lodge
24 Rosebud on Rush
26 Pita Pavilion, Chicago Place
29 Erie Cafe
31 Mr Beef
32 Tuttaposto
34 Thai Star
37 Avanzare
41 Ed Debevic's
42 Planet Hollywood
43 Wildfire, Big Bowl
45 Bijan
47 Bice, Howard's Bar & Grill
49 Hatsuhana
52 Carson's – The Place for Ribs
55 Rock & Roll McDonald's
56 Rainforest Cafe
57 Hard Rock Cafe
58 Papagus
62 Heaven on Seven
63 Bandera
68 Cornerstone Cafe
69 Brown Dog Tavern
72 Pizzeria Uno
75 Boston Blackies
79 Gene and Georgetti
81 Michael Jordan's Restaurant
84 Gordon
85 Spago
86 Ben Pao
90 Frontera Grill, Topolobampo
101 Havana Cafe Cubano, Club Creole
103 Brasserie Jo
105 Shaw's Crab House, Blue Crab Lounge
107 Spectators
113 Harry Caray's

OTHER
1 Paper Source
2 Water Tower
3 Abraham Lincoln Book Shop
4 Ehlers Caudill Gallery
16 Jean Albano Gallery
17 Douglas Dawson Gallery
18 Robert Henry Adams Fine Art
28 Northwestern Hospital
30 Zolla-Lieberman Gallery
36 Terra Museum of American Art
39 Akainyah
50 CBS
53 Sportmart
59 Tree Studios
60 Medinah Temple
62 600 N Michigan Theaters
64 American Express
67 McClurg Court Theaters
71 Post Office
73 Circle Gallery
76 Lake Point Tower
77 Information
78 Chicago Children's Museum
80 Rita Bucheit Ltd
82 Anti-Cruelty Society
88 American Medical Association
93 Jazz Record Mart
94 Lakeshore Athletic Club
96 Tribune Tower
97 NBC Tower
98 Floor Clock
99 City of Chicago Store
100 North Pier
102 Antiques Centre at Kinzie Square
106 Wrigley Building
108 Centennial Fountain
110 Antiquarians Building
111 Jay Robert's Antique Warehouse
114 Marina City
115 Chicago Sun-Times
116 Wendella Sightseeing Boats

BARS & CLUBS
7 Brehon Pub
9 Blue Chicago
10 Clark St Ale House
12 Celtic Crossing
25 Gentry
38 Gold Star Sardine Bar
40 America's Bar
44 Excalibur
83 Harry's Velvet Room
87 Jazz Showcase
95 Billy Goat Tavern (lower level)
100 Dick's Last Resort
104 Andy's
114 House of Blues

LOOP

PLACES TO STAY
201 Clarion Executive Plaza
202 Hyatt Regency Chicago
203 Swissôtel Chicago
204 Renaissance Chicago Hotel
206 Fairmont
236 Midland Hotel
239 Palmer House Hilton

PLACES TO EAT
203 Palm
210 Jacob Bros Bagels
218 Heaven on Seven
225 Sopraffina
227 Boudin Bakery
230 Heartwise Express
237 Italian Village
238 Voila!
240 Miller's Pub
247 Berghoff, Stand Up Bar
250 Russian Tea Time
254 European Sunny Cafe
261 Everest
265 Artist's Snack Shop

OTHER
200 Mercury Chicago Skyline Cruises
205 Lenscrafters
209 World's Money Exchange, Walgreens
211 Amoco Building
213 Skate on State, Gallery 37
214 Hot Tix
215 Talbots
216 The Gap
217 Eddie Bauer
219 Crate & Barrel
220 Visitor Information Center
221 Chicago Cultural Center, Museum of Broadcast Communications
222 Civic Opera House
223 American National Bank & Trust
224 Thomas Cook
226 TJ Maxx, Filene's Basement
228 Chicago Athenaeum
229 Chicago Mercantile Exchange
231 Northern Trust Bank
233 Toys 'R' Us
234 Carson Pirie Scott & Co
235 Jeweler's Building
241 Super Crown
242 Otto Pomper, Mid-America Building
243 American Express
245 Post Office
246 Kluczynski Building (Federal Center)
248 Tower Records
249 Central Camera
251 Orchestra Hall, Symphony Center
252 Chicago Architecture Foundation
253 Petrillo Music Shell
255 Monadnock Building
256 Music Mart
257 Afrocentric Bookstore
258 Carl Fischer
259 Savvy Traveller
260 Alcock's Inn
262 Harold Washington Library Center
263 Prairie Avenue Bookshop
266 Fine Arts Theaters

THEATERS
207 Oriental Theater
208 Chicago Theater
212 Palace Theater
232 Shubert Theater
244 Goodman Theatre
264 Auditorium Theater

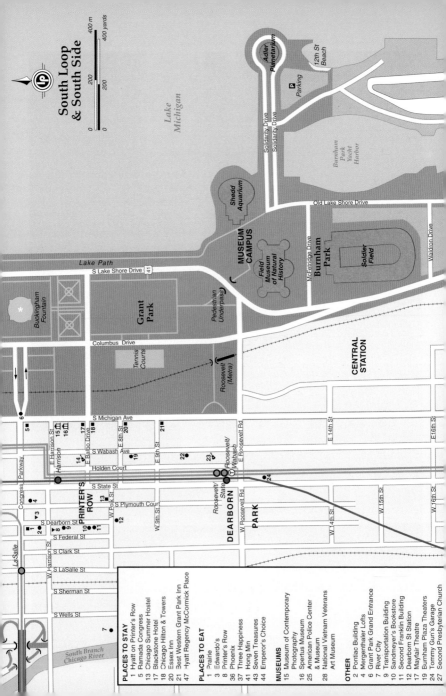

South Loop & South Side

400 m
400 yards

Lake Michigan

Grant Park

Buckingham Fountain

Tennis Courts

S Lake Shore Drive (41)
Lake Path

Columbus Drive

Pedestrian Underpass

Roosevelt (Metra)

MUSEUM CAMPUS

Field Museum of Natural History

Shedd Aquarium

Old Lake Shore Drive

McFetridge Drive

Burnham Park

Soldier Field

Waldron Drive

Solidarity Drive

Adler Planetarium

Parking

12th St Beach

Burnham Park Yacht Harbor

CENTRAL STATION

S Michigan Ave
S Wabash Ave
Holden Court
S State St
S Plymouth Court
S Dearborn St
S Federal St
S Clark St
S LaSalle St
S Sherman St
S Wells St

PRINTER'S ROW

DEARBORN PARK

E Harrison St
E Balbo Drive
E 8th St
E 9th St
E 14th St

Harrison St
Congress Parkway
S Dearborn St
W Polk St
W 9th St
Roosevelt/State
Roosevelt/Wabash
E Roosevelt Rd
W Roosevelt Rd
E 14th St
W 14th St
W 15th St
W 16th St
E 16th St

W Harrison St
W LaSalle St

South Branch Chicago River

LaSalle

PLACES TO STAY
1 Hyatt on Printer's Row
5 Ramada Congress
13 Chicago Summer Hostel
18 Blackstone Hotel
18 Chicago Hilton & Towers
20 Essex Inn
21 Best Western Grant Park Inn
47 Hyatt Regency McCormick Place

PLACES TO EAT
2 Prairie
3 Edwardo's
8 Printer's Row
36 Phoenix
37 Three Happiness
41 Hong Min
43 Seven Treasures
44 Emperor's Choice

MUSEUMS
15 Museum of Contemporary Photography
16 Spertus Museum
25 American Police Center & Museum
28 National Vietnam Veterans Art Museum

OTHER
2 Pontiac Building
4 Mergenthaler Lofts
6 Grant Park Grand Entrance
7 River City
9 Transportation Building
10 Sandmeyer's Bookstore
11 Second Franklin Building
12 Dearborn St Station
17 Mayfair Theatre
19 Burnham Plaza Theaters
24 Tommy Gun's Garage
27 Second Presbyterian Church

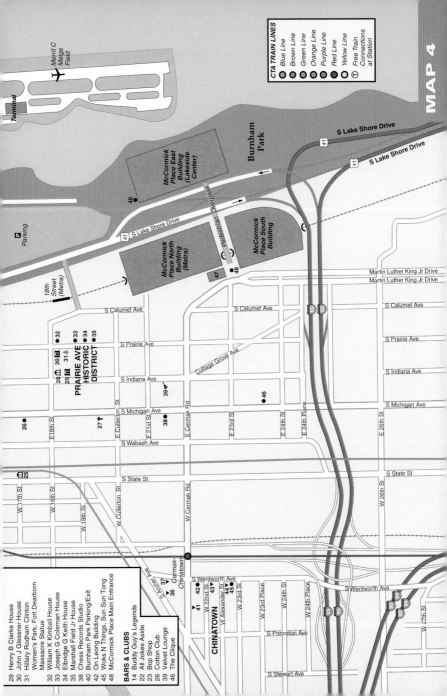

MAP 4

CTA TRAIN LINES
- ⬤ Blue Line
- ⬤ Brown Line
- ⬤ Green Line
- ⬤ Orange Line
- ⬤ Purple Line
- ⬤ Red Line
- ⬤ Yellow Line
- Ⓣ Free Train Connections at Station

Terminal

Merril C Meigs Field

P Parking

Burnham Park

S Lake Shore Drive

S Lake Shore Drive

41

41

McCormick Place East Building (Lakeside Center)

● 40

S Lake Shore Drive

41

McCormick Place North Building (Metra)

Pedestrian Overpass

McCormick Place South Building

● 47

● 48

18th Street (Metra)

Martin Luther King Jr Drive

Martin Luther King Jr Drive

S Calumet Ave

S Calumet Ave

S Calumet Ave

PRAIRIE AVE HISTORIC DISTRICT

● 32

● 33

● 34

● 35

28 ⬤ 30 🏛

29 🏛 31 🏛

S Prairie Ave

S Prairie Ave

S Prairie Ave

S Indiana Ave

S Indiana Ave

S Indiana Ave

● 39

Cottage Grove Ave

● 46

E Cermak Rd

S Michigan Ave

S Michigan Ave

● 38

● 26

● 27 †

E Cullerton St

S Michigan Ave

E 21st St

E 23rd St

E 24th

E 24th Place

E 26th St

S Wabash Ave

E 18th St

W 18th St

W 17th St

25 ⬤

55

55

55

55

90 94

90 94

S State St

S State St

W Cullerton St

W Cermak Rd

W 19th St

W 26th St

W 27th St

Cermak-Chinatown

S Archer Ave

CHINATOWN

36 ▶

37 ▶

● 42

41 ▶

W 22nd St

S Wentworth Ave

● 43 ▶

44 ▶

45 ●

W 23rd St

W 23rd Place

W 24th St

W 24th Place

S Wentworth Ave

S Alexander St

S Princeton Ave

S Stewart Ave

29 Henry B Clarke House
30 John J Glessner House
31 Hillary Rodham Clinton
    Women's Park, Fort Dearborn
    Massacre Statue
32 William K Kimball House
33 Joseph G Coleman House
34 Elbridge G Keith House
35 Marshall Field Jr House
38 Chess Records Studio
40 Burnham Park Parking/Exit
42 On Leong Building
45 Woks N Things, Sun Sun Tong
48 McCormick Place Main Entrance

BARS & CLUBS
14 Buddy Guy's Legends
22 All Jokes Aside
23 Bop Shop
26 Cotton Club
39 Velvet Lounge
46 The Clique

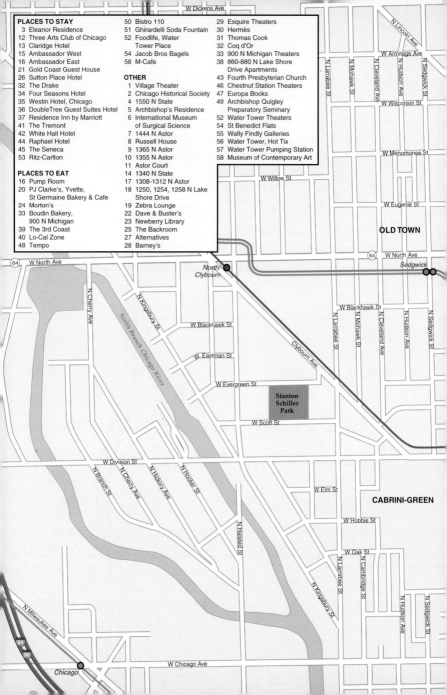

PLACES TO STAY
3 Eleanor Residence
12 Three Arts Club of Chicago
13 Claridge Hotel
15 Ambassador West
16 Ambassador East
21 Gold Coast Guest House
26 Sutton Place Hotel
32 The Drake
34 Four Seasons Hotel
35 Westin Hotel, Chicago
36 DoubleTree Guest Suites Hotel
37 Residence Inn by Marriott
41 The Tremont
42 White Hall Hotel
44 Raphael Hotel
45 The Seneca
53 Ritz-Carlton

PLACES TO EAT
16 Pump Room
20 PJ Clarke's, Yvette,
   St Germaine Bakery & Cafe
24 Morton's
33 Boudin Bakery,
   900 N Michigan
39 The 3rd Coast
40 Lo-Cal Zone
48 Tempo

50 Bistro 110
51 Ghirardelli Soda Fountain
52 Foodlife, Water
   Tower Place
54 Jacob Bros Bagels
58 M-Cafe

OTHER
1 Village Theater
2 Chicago Historical Society
4 1550 N State
5 Archbishop's Residence
6 International Museum
   of Surgical Science
7 1444 N Astor
8 Russell House
9 1365 N Astor
10 1355 N Astor
11 Astor Court
14 1340 N State
17 1308-1312 N Astor
18 1250, 1254, 1258 N Lake
   Shore Drive
19 Zebra Lounge
22 Dave & Buster's
23 Newberry Library
25 The Backroom
27 Alternatives
28 Barney's

29 Esquire Theaters
30 Hermès
31 Thomas Cook
32 Coq d'Or
33 900 N Michigan Theaters
38 860-880 N Lake Shore
   Drive Apartments
43 Fourth Presbyterian Church
46 Chestnut Station Theaters
47 Europa Books
49 Archbishop Quigley
   Preparatory Seminary
52 Water Tower Theaters
54 St Benedict Flats
55 Wally Findly Galleries
56 Water Tower, Hot Tix
57 Water Tower Pumping Station
58 Museum of Contemporary Art

OLD TOWN

CABRINI-GREEN

Stanton
Schiller
Park

MAP 5

Gold Coast

0   200   400 m
0   200   400 yards

Lincoln
Park

South
Pond

LaSalle Drive

North Avenue
Beach

Lake
Michigan

Oak St
Beach

GOLD COAST

Clark/
Division

Washington
Square

John
Hancock
Center

Seneca
Park

Lake
Shore
Park

Chicago

Northwestern
University
Chicago Campus

CTA TRAIN LINES
- Blue Line
- Brown Line
- Green Line
- Orange Line
- Purple Line
- Red Line
- Yellow Line
- Free Train Connections at Station

Old Town & Lincoln Park

CTA TRAIN LINES

- Blue Line
- Brown Line
- Green Line
- Orange Line
- Purple Line
- Red Line
- Yellow Line
- Ⓣ Free Train Connection at Station

Lake Michigan

Fullerton Beach

N Lake Shore Drive

Lake Shore Drive West

Diversey Harbor

N Cannon Drive

North Pond

N Stockton Drive

Lincoln Park

Lincoln Park Conservatory

Lincoln Park Zoo

W Fullerton Parkway

N Lakeview Ave

W Diversey Parkway

N Pine Grove Ave

Hampdon Court

Lehman Court

N Wrightwood Ave

N Deming Place

N Clark St

W Arlington Place

N Arlington Place

W Deming Place

W Schubert Ave

N Orchard St

N Burling St

N Halsted St

N Dayton St

N Mildred Ave

N Wilton Ave

Diversey

N Sheffield St

N Kenmore St

N Seminary Ave

N Lincoln Ave

N Wrightwood Ave

N Seminary Ave

W Belden Ave

N Webster Ave

N Clark St

N Sedgwick St

N Lincoln Park West

N Dickens Ave

N Cleveland Ave

N Lincoln Ave

Geneva Terrace

N Mohawk St

N Howe St

Oz Park

LINCOLN PARK

N Orchard St

N Edward Court

DePaul University

W Montana St

W Altgeld St

W Lill Ave

Fullerton

N Halsted St

N Dayton St

N Fremont St

N Bissell St

N Sheffield St

N Kenmore St

N Webster Ave

N Seminary Ave

W Webster Ave

W Clifton Ave

N Dickens Ave

N Armitage Ave

Armitage

MAP 6

North Ave Beach
North Beach
N Lake Shore Drive
South Pond
GOLD COAST
OLD TOWN
Clark/Division
Sedgwick
North/Clybourn
North Branch Chicago River

PLACES TO STAY
1 Days Inn Lincoln Park North
2 Comfort Inn of Lincoln Park
27 Arlington House
70 Days Inn Gold Coast

PLACES TO EAT
5 The Wiener Circle
6 Cohiba
7 Lindo Mexico
20 Demon Dogs
29 John Barleycorn Memorial Pub
34 Un Grand Cafe
35 Ambria
37 O'Fame
44 Asia Bowl
47 Nookies, too
50 Bruno
51 Espial
52 Jacob Bros Bagels
53 Sole Mio
56 Charlie Trotter's
57 Cafe Ba-Ba-Reebal
58 Relish
59 RJ Grunts
61 Chaplin
62 Till's
66 King Crab
73 Blue Mesa
75 Twin Anchors
83 Bub City Crabshack & Bar-B-Q
88 Fresh Choice
89 O'Briens
90 Topo Gigio
91 ¡Salpicon!

OTHER
3 Elks Veterans Memorial
4 Screenz
10 Raymond Hudd
12 Paddleboat Rental
15 OnLine Cafe
22 Uncle Dan's
24 Three Penny Cinema
25 Biograph Theater
26 St Clement's Church
28 Chicago Academy of Sciences
31 American Express
32 Reebie Storage & Moving Company
33 Tower Records, Hot Tix
36 Zoo Rookery
43 Kangaroo Connection
46 Saturday's Child
55 Sweet Memories
60 Paddleboat Rental
63 Farm in the Zoo
68 Frederick Wacker House
69 Henry Meyer House
76 Crilly Court
77 Second City
78 Pipers Alley Theaters, Tony & Tina's Wedding
79 Couch Mausoleum
80 Standing Lincoln Statue
81 Chicago Historical Society
92 Barbara's Bookstore

THEATERS
13 Apollo Theater
42 Victory Gardens Theater
72 Steppenwolf Theater
74 Royal George Theatre

BARS & CLUBS
8 Deja Vu
9 Club 950
11 The Octogon
14 Lilly's
16 Kingston Mines
17 BLUES
18 Lucille's
19 Gin Mill
21 Red Lion Pub
23 Lounge Ax
30 Neo
38 Waterloo,
39 Jerry's
39 Big Nasty
40 Sterch's
41 Kelsey's
45 Kelly's
48 Toulouse
49 Cognac Bar
54 Kincade's
54 Old Town School of Folk Music
64 Goose Island Brewery
65 Moran's
67 Marge's
71 Vinyl
82 Crobar
84 Adagio
85 Weed's
86 Olde Town Ale House

Lakeview & Wrigleyville

W Irving Park Rd (19)

Graceland Cemetery

Wunders Cemetery

Sheridan

0   200   400 m
0   200   400 yards

WRIGLEYVILLE

Wrigley Field

Southport

CTA TRAIN LINES
- Blue Line
- Brown Line
- Green Line
- Orange Line
- Purple Line
- Red Line
- Yellow Line
T Free Train Connections at Station

LINCOLN PARK

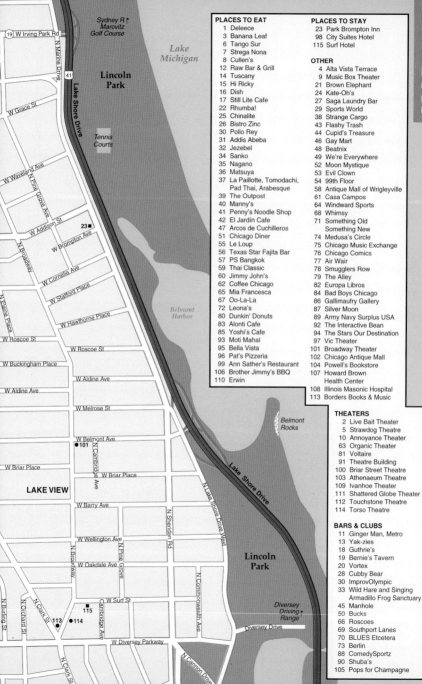

MAP 7

PLACES TO EAT

1 Deleece
2 Banana Leaf
6 Tango Sur
7 Strega Nona
8 Cullen's
12 Raw Bar & Grill
14 Tuscany
15 Hi Ricky
16 Dish
17 Still Lite Cafe
22 Rhumba!
25 Chinalite
26 Bistro Zinc
30 Pollo Rey
31 Addis Abeba
32 Jezebel
34 Sanko
35 Nagano
36 Matsuya
37 La Paillotte, Tomodachi,
   Pad Thai, Arabesque
39 The Outpost
40 Manny's
41 Penny's Noodle Shop
42 El Jardin Cafe
47 Arcos de Cuchilleros
51 Chicago Diner
55 Le Loup
56 Texas Star Fajita Bar
57 PS Bangkok
59 Thai Classic
60 Jimmy John's
62 Coffee Chicago
65 Mia Francesca
67 Oo-La-La
72 Leona's
80 Dunkin' Donuts
83 Alonti Cafe
85 Yoshi's Cafe
93 Moti Mahal
95 Bella Vista
96 Pat's Pizzeria
99 Ann Sather's Restaurant
106 Brother Jimmy's BBQ
110 Erwin

PLACES TO STAY

23 Park Brompton Inn
98 City Suites Hotel
115 Surf Hotel

OTHER

4 Alta Vista Terrace
9 Music Box Theater
21 Brown Elephant
24 Kate-Oh's
27 Saga Laundry Bar
29 Sports World
38 Strange Cargo
43 Flashy Trash
44 Cupid's Treasure
46 Gay Mart
48 Beatnix
49 We're Everywhere
52 Moon Mystique
53 Evil Clown
54 99th Floor
58 Antique Mall of Wrigleyville
61 Casa Campos
64 Windward Sports
68 Whimsy
71 Something Old
   Something New
74 Medusa's Circle
75 Chicago Music Exchange
76 Chicago Comics
77 Air Wair
78 Smugglers Row
79 The Alley
82 Europa Libros
84 Bad Boys Chicago
86 Gallimaufry Gallery
87 Silver Moon
89 Army Navy Surplus USA
92 The Interactive Bean
94 The Stars Our Destination
97 Vic Theater
101 Broadway Theater
102 Chicago Antique Mall
104 Powell's Bookstore
107 Howard Brown
   Health Center
108 Illinois Masonic Hospital
113 Borders Books & Music

THEATERS

2 Live Bait Theater
5 Strawdog Theatre
10 Annoyance Theater
63 Organic Theater
81 Voltaire
91 Theatre Building
100 Briar Street Theater
103 Athenaeum Theatre
109 Ivanhoe Theater
111 Shattered Globe Theater
112 Touchstone Theatre
114 Torso Theatre

BARS & CLUBS

11 Ginger Man, Metro
13 Yak-zies
18 Guthrie's
19 Bernie's Tavern
20 Vortex
28 Cubby Bear
30 ImprovOlympic
33 Wild Hare and Singing
   Armadillo Frog Sanctuary
45 Manhole
50 Bucks
66 Roscoes
69 Southport Lanes
70 BLUES Etcetera
73 Berlin
88 ComedySportz
90 Shuba's
105 Pops for Champagne

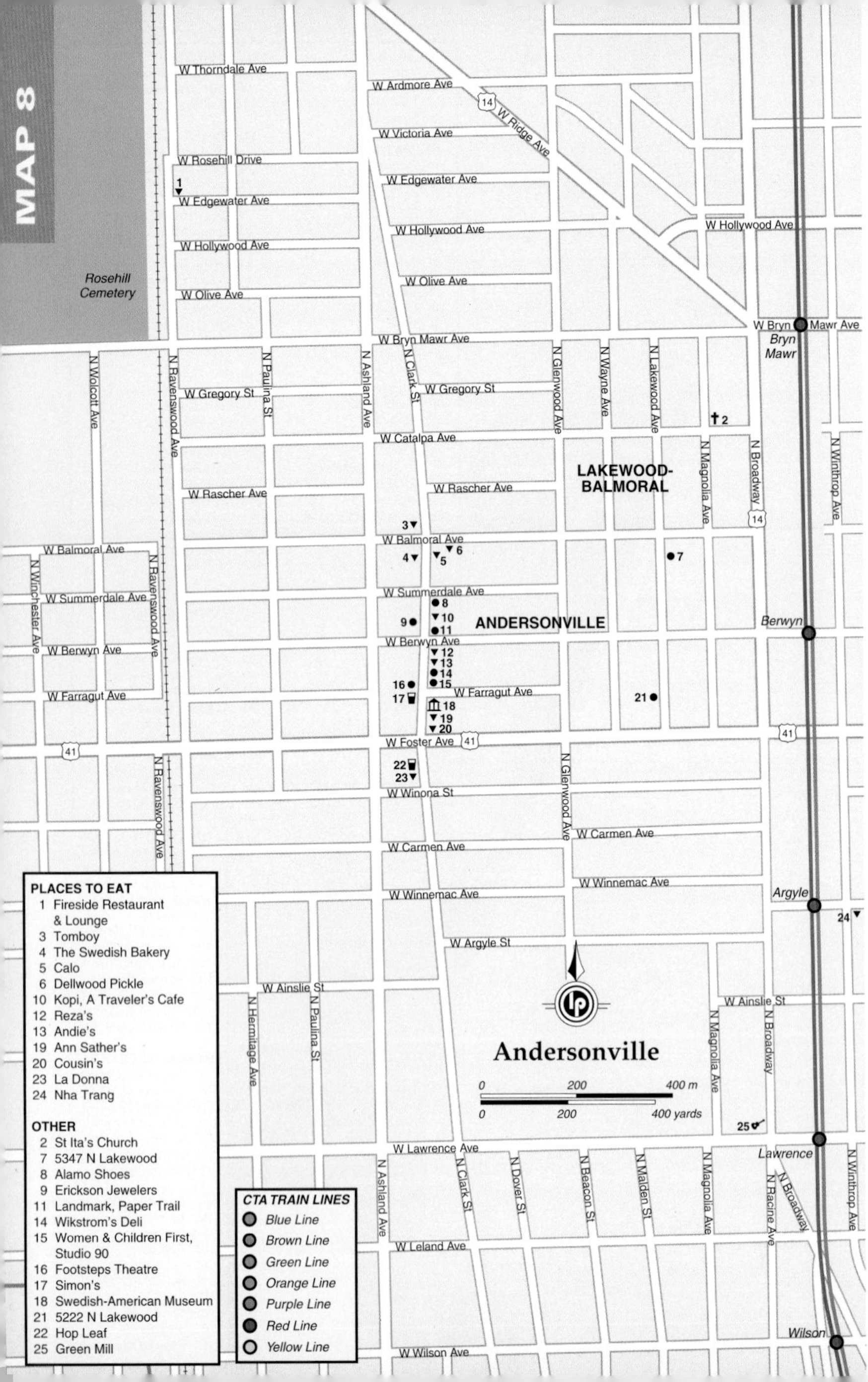

MAP 8

W Thorndale Ave

W Ardmore Ave

14 W Ridge Ave

W Victoria Ave

W Rosehill Drive

W Edgewater Ave

W Edgewater Ave

W Hollywood Ave

W Hollywood Ave

W Hollywood Ave

Rosehill
Cemetery

W Olive Ave

W Olive Ave

W Olive Ave

W Bryn Mawr Ave

W Bryn Mawr Ave

Bryn
Mawr

N Wolcott Ave

N Ravenswood Ave

N Paulina St

N Ashland Ave

N Clark Ave

W Gregory St

W Gregory St

N Glenwood Ave

N Wayne Ave

N Lakewood Ave

†2

N Magnolia Ave

N Broadway

N Winthrop Ave

W Catalpa Ave

LAKEWOOD-
BALMORAL

W Rascher Ave

W Rascher Ave

14

3▼

W Balmoral Ave

W Balmoral Ave

W Winchester Ave

4▼   ▼6
     ▼5

●7

W Summerdale Ave

W Summerdale Ave

●8

Berwyn

W Berwyn Ave

9●   ▼10
     ●11

ANDERSONVILLE

W Berwyn Ave

▼12
▼13
●14
●15

W Farragut Ave

16●
17▼

W Farragut Ave

21●

🏛18
▼19
▼20

N Ravenswood Ave

41

W Foster Ave   41

41

22▼
23▼

W Winona St

W Carmen Ave

N Hermitage Ave

N Paulina St

W Carmen Ave

N Glenwood Ave

W Winnemac Ave

W Winnemac Ave

Argyle

W Argyle St

24▼

N Ashland Ave

N Clark St

N Dover St

N Beacon St

N Malden St

W Ainslie St

W Ainslie St

N Magnolia Ave

N Broadway

N Racine Ave

N Winthrop Ave

Andersonville

0   200   400 m
0   200   400 yards

25▼

Lawrence

W Lawrence Ave

Wilson

W Leland Ave

W Wilson Ave

PLACES TO EAT
1 Fireside Restaurant
   & Lounge
3 Tomboy
4 The Swedish Bakery
5 Calo
6 Dellwood Pickle
10 Kopi, A Traveler's Cafe
12 Reza's
13 Andie's
19 Ann Sather's
20 Cousin's
23 La Donna
24 Nha Trang

OTHER
2 St Ita's Church
7 5347 N Lakewood
8 Alamo Shoes
9 Erickson Jewelers
11 Landmark, Paper Trail
14 Wikstrom's Deli
15 Women & Children First,
   Studio 90
16 Footsteps Theatre
17 Simon's
18 Swedish-American Museum
21 5222 N Lakewood
22 Hop Leaf
25 Green Mill

CTA TRAIN LINES
● Blue Line
● Brown Line
● Green Line
● Orange Line
● Purple Line
● Red Line
○ Yellow Line

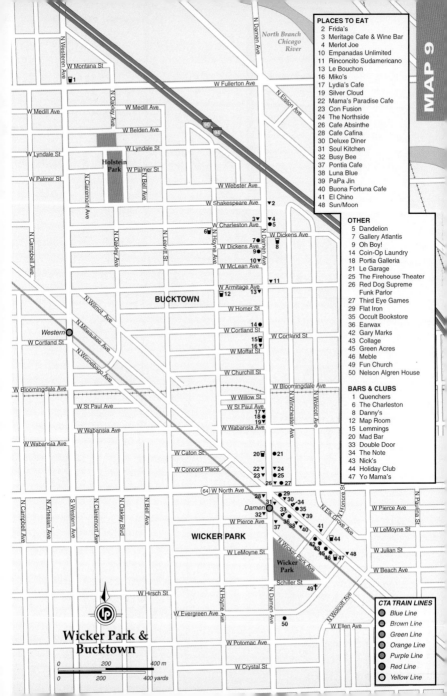

N Damen Ave
North Branch Chicago River

MAP 9

PLACES TO EAT
2 Frida's
3 Meritage Cafe & Wine Bar
4 Merlot Joe
10 Empanadas Unlimited
11 Rinconcito Sudamericano
13 Le Bouchon
16 Miko's
17 Lydia's Cafe
19 Silver Cloud
22 Mama's Paradise Cafe
23 Con Fusion
24 The Northside
26 Cafe Absinthe
28 Cafe Cafina
30 Deluxe Diner
31 Soul Kitchen
32 Busy Bee
37 Pontia Cafe
38 Luna Blue
39 PaPa Jin
40 Buona Fortuna Cafe
41 El Chino
48 Sun/Moon

OTHER
5 Dandelion
7 Gallery Atlantis
9 Oh Boy!
14 Coin-Op Laundry
18 Portia Galleria
21 Le Garage
25 The Firehouse Theater
26 Red Dog Supreme
   Funk Parlor
27 Third Eye Games
29 Flat Iron
35 Occult Bookstore
36 Earwax
42 Gary Marks
43 Collage
45 Green Acres
46 Meble
49 Fun Church
50 Nelson Algren House

BARS & CLUBS
1 Quenchers
6 The Charleston
8 Danny's
12 Map Room
15 Lemmings
20 Mad Bar
33 Double Door
34 The Note
43 Nick's
44 Holiday Club
47 Yo Mama's

BUCKTOWN

WICKER PARK

Wicker Park

Western

Damen

Wicker Park & Bucktown

0   200   400 m
0   200   400 yards

CTA TRAIN LINES
● Blue Line
● Brown Line
● Green Line
● Orange Line
● Purple Line
● Red Line
○ Yellow Line

N Orleans St
N Sedgwick St
N Hudson Ave
N Cambridge St
W Oak St
W Ontario St
N Larrabee St
W Illinois St
N Elm St
N Kingsbury St
N Halsted St
GOOSE ISLAND
North Branch Chicago River
N Hooker St
N Hickory Ave
N Cherry Ave
N Branch St
W Fry St
May St
Chicago
N Elston Ave
W Ogden Ave
Milwaukee Ave
N Noble St
Milwaukee Ave
N Bishop St
W Chicago Ave
W Fry St
N Armour St
N Ashland Ave
W Pearson St
W Walton St
W Chestnut St
N Marshfield St
N Paulina St
N Hermitage Ave
N Wood St
W Rice St
N Honore St
N Wolcott St
N Winchester Ave
N Damen Ave
N Hoyne Ave
UKRAINIAN VILLAGE
N Hoyne Ave
W Division St
W Thomas St
N Leavitt St
W Walton St
W Iowa St
W Rice St
N Oakley Ave
W Chicago Ave
N Western Ave
W Superior St
W Huron St
W Erie St
W Ohio St
W Race Ave
W Grand Ave
W Hubbard St
W Kinzie St
N Oakley Ave
W Grand Ave
N Campbell Ave

W Grand Ave
N Kinzie St
W Wayman St
Milwaukee Ave

W Carroll Ave
Lake St
Randolph St
N Ada St
N Loomis St
W Fulton St
Ashland
N Ashland Ave
Union Park
N Paulina St
N Wood St
W Wolcott St
W Monroe St
W Damen Ave
W Hoyne Ave
W Carroll Ave
W Fulton St
W Leavitt St
W Walnut St
Lake St
N Walnut St
W Lake St
Washington Blvd
Warren Blvd
W Madison St
N Oakley Ave
N Western Ave

N Wacker Drive   S Wacker Drive
N Canal St   S Canal St
N Clinton St   W Washington Blvd   S Canal St
W Madison St   W Monroe St
Clinton   N Jefferson St   Northwestern Station ◼11   S Jefferson St   Adams St   † 18   Union Station 19
N Desplaines St   S Desplaines St   Jackson Blvd
◼10
N Halsted St   S Halsted St   12 ▶   13 ▶   14 ▶   17 ▶
◻9   N Green St   S Green St   GREEK TOWN
N Peoria St   S Peoria St
N Sangamon St   S Sangamon St   16 ▶
N Morgan St   S Morgan St
N Carpenter St   8 ▶
7 ●   S Aberdeen St
N Aberdeen St
N May St   6 ⊞   15 ▲   W Gladys Ave
N Racine Ave   S Racine Ave
N Elizabeth St   S Ada St
S Loomis St
S Laflin St
S Ashland Ave
S Paulina St
S Wood St
United Center   S Honore St
Damen Ave
S Steeley Ave
S Hoyne Ave
S Leavitt St
Washington Blvd   S Madison St   S Oakley Ave   S Adams   S Jackson Blvd
S Western Ave

5 ⬆
3 ⬆
† 3
2 ⬆

CTA TRAIN LINES
Blue Line
Brown Line
Green Line
Orange Line
Purple Line
Red Line
Yellow Line

MAP 10

West Side

Main Post Office

New Maxwell St Market

PLACES TO STAY
10 Quality Inn-Downtown
22 Hyatt at University Village

PLACES TO EAT
4 Tecalitlan
8 Wishbone
9 Red Light
12 Santorini
13 Greek Islands
14 Rodity's
16 Jaks Tap
17 The Parthenon
19 Lou Mitchell's
23 Rosebud
25 Osteria del Vecchio
26 Tufano's Vernon Park Tap
27 Mario's
33 Panaderia Laredo
34 Playa Azul
35 Nuevo Leon
36 Cafe Jumping Bean

OTHER
1 St Nicholas Ukrainian
   Catholic Cathedral
2 Ukrainian Institute of Modern Art
3 Saints Volodymyr & Olha Church
5 Polish Museum of America
6 Museum of Holography
7 Harpo Studios
11 Bat Column
15 Haymarket Riot Monument
18 Old St Patrick's Church
20 Main Bus Station
21 Cook County Hospital
24 Thalia Hall
28 Jane Addams Hull House Museum
29 Chicago Fire Academy
30 Holy Family Church
31 Maxwell St Station
32 St Adalbert Roman Catholic Church
37 Lozano Public Library
38 José Clemente Orozco Academy
39 Mexican Fine Arts Center Museum
40 St Pius Church

LITTLE ITALY

PILSEN

University of Illinois at Chicago

University of Illinois at Chicago Medical Center

Arrigo Park

Harrison Park

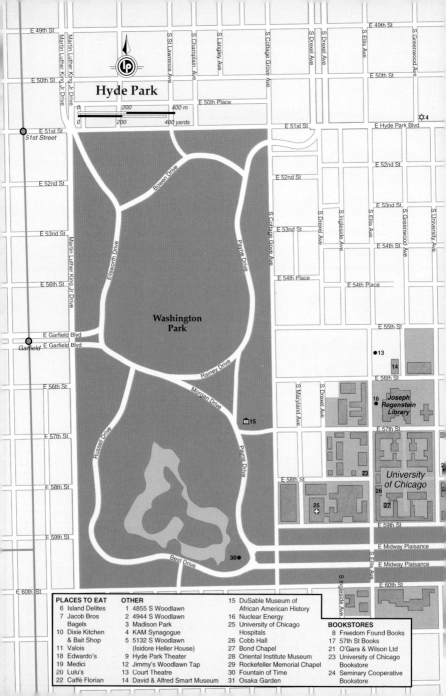

Hyde Park

PLACES TO EAT
6 Island Delites
7 Jacob Bros Bagels
10 Dixie Kitchen & Bait Shop
11 Valois
18 Edwardo's
19 Medici
20 Lulu's
22 Caffè Florian

OTHER
1 4855 S Woodlawn
2 4944 S Woodlawn
3 Madison Park
4 KAM Synagogue
5 5132 S Woodlawn (Isidore Heller House)
9 Hyde Park Theater
12 Jimmy's Woodlawn Tap
13 Court Theatre
14 David & Alfred Smart Museum
15 DuSable Museum of African American History
16 Nuclear Energy
25 University of Chicago Hospitals
26 Cobb Hall
27 Bond Chapel
28 Oriental Institute Museum
29 Rockefeller Memorial Chapel
30 Fountain of Time
31 Osaka Garden

BOOKSTORES
8 Freedom Found Books
17 57th St Books
21 O'Gara & Wilson Ltd
23 University of Chicago Bookstore
24 Seminary Cooperative Bookstore

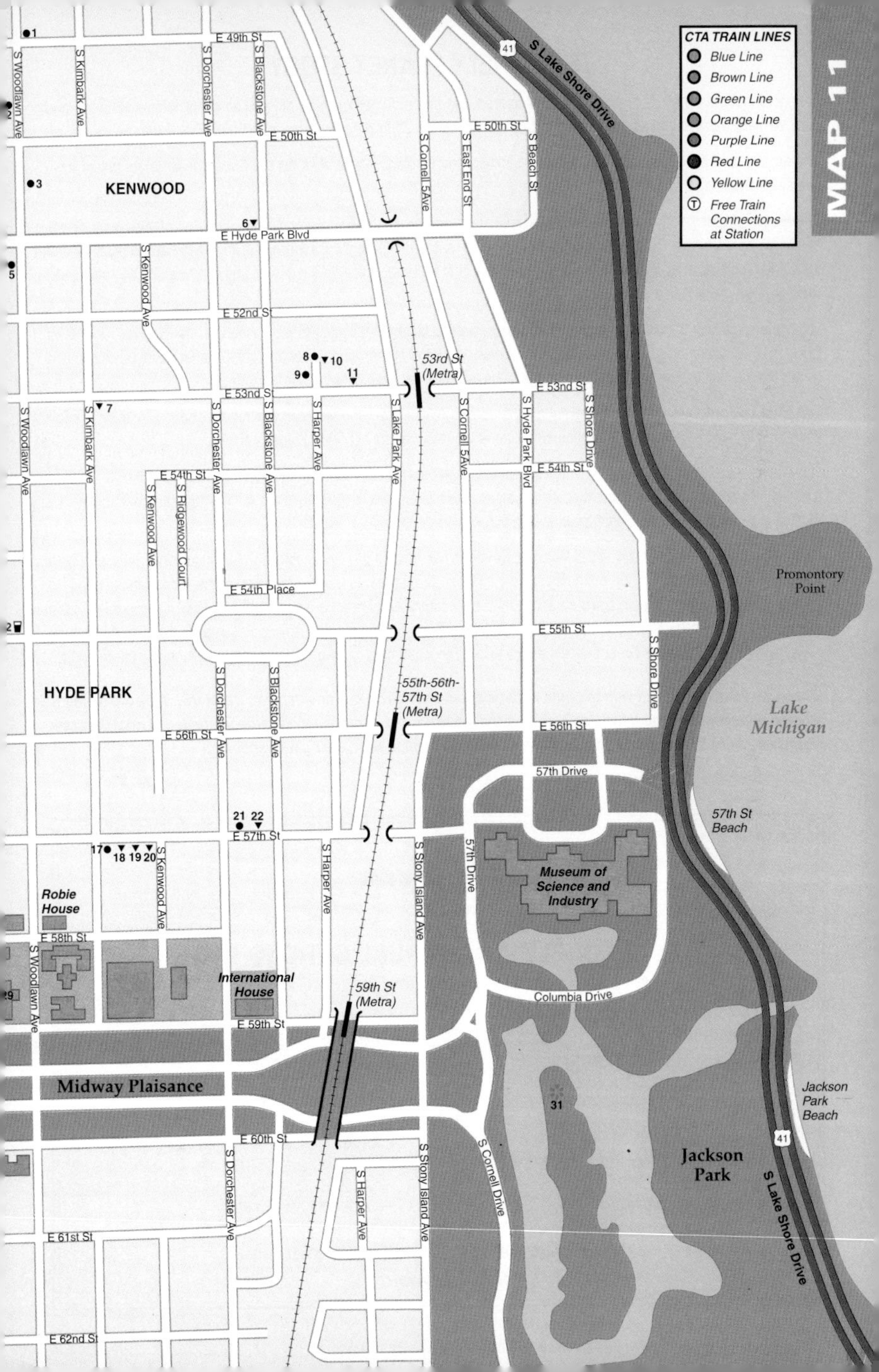

MAP 11

CTA TRAIN LINES
- Blue Line
- Brown Line
- Green Line
- Orange Line
- Purple Line
- Red Line
- Yellow Line
- ⊤ Free Train Connections at Station

S Lake Shore Drive

41

E 49th St

S Woodlawn Ave
S Kimbark Ave
S Dorchester Ave
S Blackstone Ave

E 50th St

S Cornell Ave
S East End Ave
S Beach St

E 50th St

KENWOOD

E Hyde Park Blvd

S Kenwood Ave

E 52nd St

53rd St (Metra)

E 53rd St

E 53rd St

S Hyde Park Blvd
S Shore Dr

E 54th St

S Woodlawn Ave
S Kimbark Ave
S Dorchester Ave
S Ridgewood Court
S Kenwood Ave

E 54th St

S Blackstone Ave
S Harper Ave
S Lake Park Ave
S Cornell Ave

E 54th Place

Promontory Point

HYDE PARK

E 55th St

55th-56th-57th St (Metra)

E 55th St

S Shore Drive

Lake Michigan

E 56th St

E 56th St

E 56th St

57th Drive

57th St Beach

Robie House

E 57th St

S Harper Ave
S Stony Island Ave
57th Drive

Museum of Science and Industry

E 58th St

S Woodlawn Ave

International House

Columbia Drive

59th St (Metra)

E 59th St

Midway Plaisance

Jackson Park Beach

E 60th St

Jackson Park

S Dorchester Ave
S Harper Ave
S Stony Island Ave
S Cornell Drive
S Shore Drive

E 61st St

S Lake Shore Drive

41

E 62nd St

31

THE LONELY PLANET STORY

Lonely Planet published its first book in 1973 in response to the numerous 'How did you do it?' questions Maureen and Tony Wheeler were asked after driving, busing, hitching, sailing and railing their way from England to Australia.

Written at a kitchen table and hand collated, trimmed and stapled, *Across Asia on the Cheap* became an instant local bestseller, inspiring thoughts of another book.

Eighteen months in South-East Asia resulted in their second guide, *South-East Asia on a shoestring*, which they put together in a backstreet Chinese hotel in Singapore in 1975. The 'yellow bible', as it quickly became known to backpackers around the world, soon became *the* guide to the region. It has sold well over half a million copies and is now in its 9th edition, still retaining its familiar yellow cover.

Today there are over 350 titles, including travel guides, walking guides, language kits & phrasebooks, travel atlases and travel literature. The company is the largest independent travel publisher in the world. Although Lonely Planet initially specialised in guides to Asia, today there are few corners of the globe that have not been covered.

The emphasis continues to be on travel for independent travellers. Tony and Maureen still travel for several months of each year and play an active part in the writing, updating and quality control of Lonely Planet's guides.

They have been joined by over 80 authors and 200 staff at our offices in Melbourne (Australia), Oakland (USA), London (UK) and Paris (France). Travellers themselves also make a valuable contribution to the guides through the feedback we receive in thousands of letters each year and on our web site.

The people at Lonely Planet strongly believe that travellers can make a positive contribution to the countries they visit, both through their appreciation of the countries' culture, wildlife and natural features, and through the money they spend. In addition, the company makes a direct contribution to the countries and regions it covers. Since 1986 a percentage of the income from each book has been donated to ventures such as famine relief in Africa; aid projects in India; agricultural projects in Central America; Greenpeace's efforts to halt French nuclear testing in the Pacific; and Amnesty International.

'I hope we send people out with the right attitude about travel. You realise when you travel that there are so many different perspectives about the world, so we hope these books will make people more interested in what they see. Guidebooks can't really guide people. All you can do is point them in the right direction.'

– Tony Wheeler

LONELY PLANET PUBLICATIONS

Australia
PO Box 617, Hawthorn 3122, Victoria
tel: (03) 9819 1877 fax: (03) 9819 6459
e-mail: talk2us@lonelyplanet.com.au

USA
150 Linden St
Oakland, CA 94607
tel: (510) 893 8555 TOLL FREE: 800 275-8555
fax: (510) 893 8572
e-mail: info@lonelyplanet.com

UK
10a Spring Place,
London NW5 3BH
tel: (0171) 428 4800 fax: (0171) 428 4828
e-mail: go@lonelyplanet.co.uk

France:
1 rue du Dahomey, 75011 Paris
tel: 01 55 25 33 00 fax: 01 55 25 33 01
e-mail: bip@lonelyplanet.fr

World Wide Web: http://www.lonelyplanet.com
or *AOL keyword: lp*